A LAND
OF DISCORD
ALWAYS

A LAND OF DISCORD ALWAYS

Acadia from Its Beginning to the Expulsion of Its People 1604–1755

CHARLES D. MAHAFFIE JR.

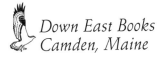 *Down East Books*
Camden, Maine

Copyright © 1995 by Charles Delahunt Mahaffie Jr.
ISBN 0-89272-362-9
Cover Illustration by Chris Van Dusen
Color Separation by High Resolution
Printed and bound at Bookcrafters, Fredericksburg, Va.

2   4   5   3   1

Down East Books
P.O. Box 679, Camden, Maine 04843

LIBRARY OF CONGRESS CATALOGING-IN-PUBLICATION DATA

Mahaffie, Charles D.
    A Land of discord always : Acadia from its beginning to the
expulsion of its people 1604–1755 / Charles D. Mahaffie, Jr.
        p.   cm.
    Includes bibliographical references and index.
    ISBN 0-89272-362-9
    1. Acadia—History.   I. Title.
F1038.M24   1995
971.6'01—dc20   95-8904
                                                                    CIP

CONTENTS

PREFACE

ACADIA HAD ITS BEGINNING in 1604, when Frenchmen fortified a little island that lies in the St. Croix River halfway between the state of Maine and the province of New Brunswick. It lasted a century and a half—until 1755—when its people were torn from homes and homeland and its farms and villages were destroyed. It lives on in the language and legends of more than a million Canadians and Americans whose ancestors were the Acadians.

It rose and fell in the shadow of a mighty neighbor, the Puritan powerhouse on Massachusetts Bay. Sometimes it was a threat; more often Acadia was seen as an opportunity by the full-time merchants and part-time soldiers who built New England. Its story is one of economic and military interplay between mismatched antagonists, one strong and aggressive and nearly always the winner, the other weak and halting and usually the loser.

Acadia was a battleground, an important arena in the struggle that cost France her North American empire and ensured that the United States and Canada were molded in the image of Britain. But it was also a place where men and women worked and played and raised their children. In its forests, Indians lived the waning days of an ancient culture. Beside its marshes were the homes and farms of the Acadians, emigrants from France who turned out to be colonial America's most unusual people.

They came from the Old World, but the lifestyle they built in Acadia had no Old World parallel. They were peasants who would not be peasants, Europeans who fit no European mold. They intended to fight no wars, pay no taxes, bend to no one's authority. They wanted nothing to do with the struggle for North America. They wanted only to be let alone, and for a time their perversity served them well. In the end, it brought them disaster.

A sympathetic British statesman later complained that "we did upon pretenses not worth a farthing, root out this poor, innocent, deserving people, whom our utter inability to govern or to reconcile gave us no sort of right to extirpate."[1] And surely, from hindsight, there seems little to excuse what the British did in Acadia in 1755. Yet in many ways the Acadians brought it on themselves. They would not adapt. They would not even make a show of accepting the rule that began in 1710, when Britain took Acadia away from France. Governor after British governor, trying to bring them under control, could only sputter in frustration and send home reports of "perfidious subjects," "a very rebellious crew," "ungovernable people."

They lived in a world apart. They paid little attention to the Frenchmen who tried to govern them before the British conquest, and they paid less attention to the English-speaking officials who came afterward. Thus, in 1755, when the Seven Years' War for empire was upon them, nervous British and American soldiers did to the Acadians what a fearful United States government did to its Japanese-American citizens after Pearl Harbor: They drove them from their homes.

This book tells the story of Acadia and the Acadians up to the time of their expulsion. It tells how Europeans first came to live in an obscure corner of North America, how a unique society grew and prospered, and how all was lost in the cataclysm the Acadians called *le grand dérangement.* It tells the story of Acadia's Indians, how their land and lifestyle slipped away in the face of foreign ways and foreign guns. And it describes the contest of the great nations as they fought it out in Acadia—how Frenchmen and Indians confronted Britons and their increasingly self-reliant colonials, and how Britons and Americans blundered and battled their way to victory.

It is a story with few present-day traces. Like Atlantis, old Acadia seems gone beneath the waves. Today's Nova Scotia and New Brunswick have different, newer roots; in Maine, little recalls Acadia save archaeological finds, roadside historical markers, and a namesake national park. The Acadians themselves were peaceable folk who troubled no neighbors, caused no wars, and left no great mark on modern history, but because of their terrible fate, their story is extraordinary. What were they doing there in the first place? How did such tragedy come to them? What went wrong?

Curious, then fascinated, I have tried to find out, and this book is the result. It is an attempt to put in one volume, and in a form that will appeal to all readers, a synthesis from many accounts of the bravery and cowardice, the foresight and foolishness, and the design and happenstance that determined Acadia's turbulent history.

As to form: I have used both contemporary and current place names, in a way that I hope will prevent confusion. If they were different from those used now, the old names are shown parenthetically in the map on pages 12 and 13. For the names of Indians and Indian tribes, I have followed the Smithsonian Institution's *Handbook of North American Indians*. Except for references in the notes to British and American documents, which I have dated as I found them, dates are New Style—that is, they are in the style of the Gregorian calendar that governs most of the world today and was in effect in France and her colonies while Acadia existed. Until 1752, Britain and her colonies used the Julian calendar. During the seventeenth century, the British were ten days behind the French; in the first half of the eighteenth century, the difference was eleven days. To illustrate: Americans celebrate George Washington's birthday on February 22. That is New Style. By his mother's reckoning, General Washington was born on February 11.

I am grateful to Elise Mahaffie, who drew the modern-day map. And I am particularly indebted to my wife for cheerful encouragement and good-natured acceptance of years spent puzzling over an obscure colony and its people: For those, and countless other reasons, this book is dedicated to Judy.

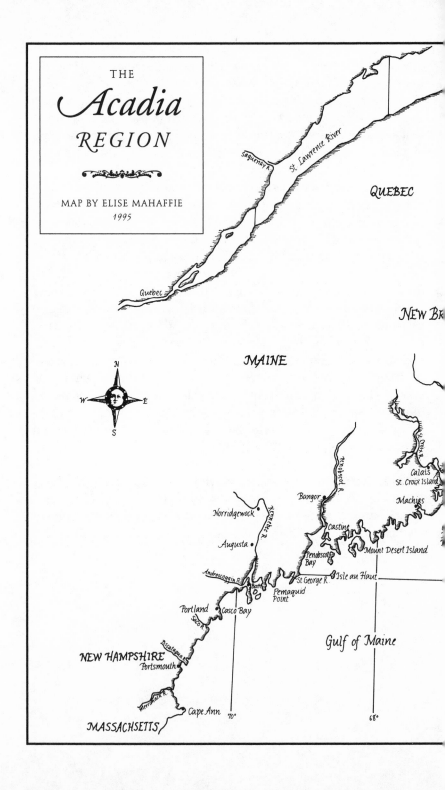

THE

Acadia

REGION

MAP BY ELISE MAHAFFIE
1995

QUEBEC

St. Lawrence River

Saguenay R.

Quebec

NEW BR

MAINE

N
W E
S

Norridgewock

Augusta

Kennebec R.

Bangor

Penobscot R.

Castine

Penobscot
Bay

St. Croix R.

Calais
St. Croix Island

Machias

Mount Desert Island

And003coggin R.

Bath

St George R.

Isle au Haut

Pemaquid
Point

Portland

Casco Bay

Saco R.

NEW HAMPSHIRE

Piscataqua R.

Portsmouth

Gulf of Maine

Merrimack R.

Cape Ann

70°

68°

MASSACHSETTS

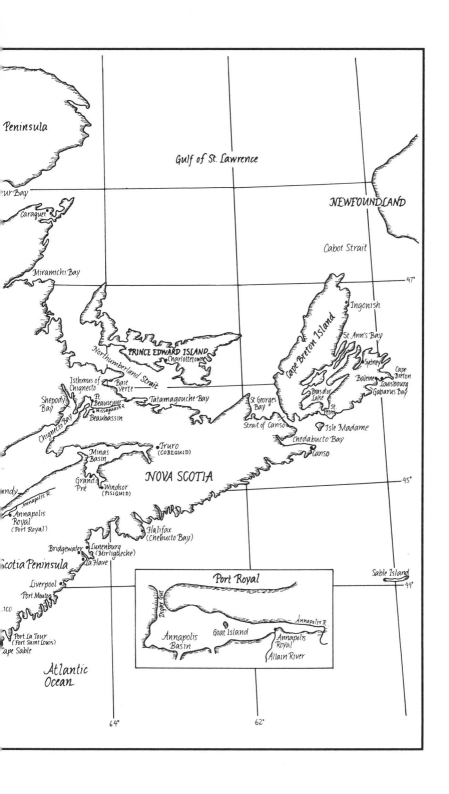

Peninsula

Gulf of St. Lawrence

ur Bay

Caraquet

NEWFOUNDLAND

Cabot Strait

Miramichi Bay

47°

Ingonish

Cape Breton Island

St Ann's Bay

Northumberland Strait

PRINCE EDWARD ISLAND

Charlottetown

Sydney

Isthmus of Chignecto

Baie Verte

Cape Breton

Baleine

Louisbourg

Shepody Bay

Ft. Beausejour

Missaguash R.

Beaubassin

Tatamagouche Bay

Bras d'or Lake

Gabarus Bay

Chignecto Bay

St Georges Bay

St. Peters

Strait of Canso

Isle Madame

Chedabucto Bay

Truro
(COBEQUID)

Canso

Minas Basin

NOVA SCOTIA

45°

Grand Pré

Windsor
(PISIGUIT)

undy

Annapolis R.

Annapolis Royal
(Port Royal)

Halifax
(Chebucto Bay)

Bridgewater

Lunenburg
(Mirligueche)

Scotia Peninsula

La Have

Sable Island

Port Royal

Liverpool

44°

Port Mouton

Digby Gut

Annapolis R

.ico

Annapolis Basin

Goat Island

Annapolis Royal

Port La Tour
(Fort Saint Louis)

Allain River

Cape Sable

Atlantic Ocean

64°

62°

1 | INDIANS AND FISHERMEN

Native Americans Meet Strange People

1500–1604

MEN AND WOMEN CAME TO ACADIA long before it had that name—millennia before, when the Ice Age was ending and the glaciers were receding. They were native Americans, Indians, descendants of hardy Asians who trekked across the land bridge from Siberia. By the turn of the sixteenth century, when their clash with Europeans was about to begin, they were loosely organized in tribes, each with its own variant of the Algonquian language and each with its own territory. Micmacs lived around the Gulf of St. Lawrence and on the long peninsula that, with Cape Breton Island, is today the province of Nova Scotia. Maliseets and Passamaquoddies were across the Bay of Fundy on what is now the New Brunswick shore. Abenakis made their camps in the mountains and woods that stretch west and south through the state of Maine.

They lived on the bounty of the land and the sea. In fall and winter, the men hunted moose, deer, bear, caribou, and beaver. In spring and summer, they fished. Unlike those farther south, the Indians of Acadia did little farming. Their lives were tied to the woods and the streams, where they could hunt and trap, and to the rivers and the bays and the ocean, where there were fish—teeming millions of fish.

It was the fish that brought Europeans. In the Gulf of St. Lawrence and in the ocean off Maine, Nova Scotia, and Newfoundland are the great North Atlantic banks, shallow places where plant and animal plankton thrive and nourish the big codfish that have for centuries been hunted there by the fleets of seagoing nations. Until overfishing wasted them, the banks were a protein factory, one of the world's most important natural resources, and for the fishermen who sailed to America in the wake of Christopher Columbus and John Cabot, they were a bonanza.[1]

They were on the banks as soon as word about the New World began to spread in Europe. There were Normans, Bretons, West-Country Englishmen, Basques, Spaniards, and Portuguese. The first were there by 1504, and as the century neared its end, the fleet became a throng: three hundred ships, for example, in 1586.[2] Some, particularly the Basques, hunted whales. Others were after seals and walrus. Most, though, came to catch the Atlantic cod. When it is salted and dried, codfish is an imperishable, nutritious, cheap food, and codfishing was very big business. In 1607, a traveler on Acadia's Atlantic shore came upon an old captain who had counted forty-two transatlantic voyages.[3] For him and men like him, transatlantic commuting was nothing unusual. It was a way of life. They knew the bays and beaches of Acadia and Newfoundland as well as they knew the quays and taverns of home.

In their casual way, the fishermen explored the coast, and they gave names to what they found. Spanish ships must have made their rendezvous at the spacious harbor that adjoins present-day Sydney, Nova Scotia. The fishermen called it Spanish Bay, La Baye des Espagnols. For two centuries, Louisbourg on the Atlantic coast of Cape Breton Island was Havre à l'Anglois, English Harbor. Cape Breton itself likely was named by Basques for their port town Cap-Breton, on the Bay of Biscay.[4] And the best known of all the fishermen's lairs, a clump of islands at the mouth of Nova Scotia's Chedabucto Bay, was called Canso, probably from a Micmac word. It still has the name the old fishermen gave it, and it still is a center of the fishing industry.

At first the fishermen had no reason to go ashore, except out of curiosity or to repair their ships and find water and firewood. They salted fish aboard ship and sailed home as fast as they could with as much as they could carry. But then their ways began to change. They found that by curing their catch on the beaches, they could accumulate a bigger cash cargo. That meant working ashore and coming in contact with native people; thus arose the trade in furs that would in time dominate the lives of the Indians as well as the foreigners who intruded on their world.

Well-dressed Europeans demanded fur coats and muffs, and fur trim for fancy clothes. Fashion also dictated high-topped hats made of felt from beaver fur. Northeastern North America was full of beaver and other furry mammals, and it was not long before the fishermen realized that Indians were eager to trade skins for knives, axes, kettles, and other manufactured goods that could be had cheaply and in large quantities at home. The French explorer Jacques Cartier was offered furs when he probed the Gulf of St. Lawrence in 1534.[5] European fishermen had been there first, making deals.

Fur came to equal and then to surpass fish as the chief attraction of North America. Wealth flowed to Europe, and the Indians benefited too, mostly in terms of new tools and technologies. Iron kettles, for example, made a big difference to people who cooked by dropping fire-heated stones in hollow tree trunks. European goods eased their lives, but in the long run the native people were heavy losers.

European fishermen and traders brought European diseases to people who had no immunities to smallpox, measles, typhus, diphtheria, and influenza. The Indians died by the thousands. By the end of the sixteenth century, there were only about three thousand Micmacs, a thousand Maliseets and Passamaquoddies, and ten to twelve thousand Abenakis.[6] Before the Europeans arrived, there may have been four or five, perhaps even ten times as many Indians.[7]

Europeans also brought alcohol. It was new, appealing, and addictive. Demoralization thus accompanied depopulation, and as European influence grew stronger, Indian life and culture came close to falling apart entirely.[8]

In Acadia, before the strangers came, Indians had lives that were sometimes hard but were reasonably tranquil—lives for the most part unaffected by the kinds of ecclesiastic, economic, and political conflicts that tormented Europeans. Social structures were simple. Friends and relatives casually allied themselves in bands, which joined to form the larger tribes. Easygoing leadership was provided by sagamores, chiefs who ruled by consent. Spiritual matters and illnesses were looked after by shamans, mystics who combined the duties of clergyman and physician. Sometimes the sagamore and the shaman were the same man, sometimes a woman.

There were deities. Indian lives were regulated and Indian fates were decided by spirits, good and bad.

There was also conflict. Wars were fought between bands and tribes. They were not, however, religious wars, wars of acquisition, or wars to ensure or deny dynastic succession. An insult, real or fancied, could spark a war. Indian wars were sporadic, and by European standards, they were not very bloody.

Usually there was food enough for everyone. Hoarding and greed had little place in Indian life. The people lived wherever they found what they liked to eat. Their villages might be pitched where the fishing was good, or near hunting grounds they and their ancestors had always known. The land they used was not owned by men and women but was held in a communal relationship with the spirits of the forest. The Indian did not share the European's theory of property, or his ideas of economic reward and exploitation. A man earned prestige if he was skillful at the hunt, brave in war; a woman earned it if she was good at making camp, gathering food, caring for children. Status was not in possessions but rather in the esteem of family and friends.

It all began to change when Indians became involved with Europeans—with their politics, their religions, their wars, and their market economy. People began to think about exclusive hunting territories. Communal relationships began to disappear. And relations with the environment began to change, too. The subsistence hunter became a commercial hunter. The rules by which the people lived had always commanded reverence for the animals, even the plants and fish that supported life. The hunter took from nature what he needed to feed his family and share with his band, carefully preserving the rest. But with European contact, the old taboos faded. If the shaman who had enforced them could not stop the awful new diseases, why pay attention to him at all? And the traders paid in goods for all the furs they could lay their hands on. Since they seemed particularly keen for beaver, why not kill all the beaver? Soon there were fewer and fewer beaver, and the Indians began to depend on Europeans not just for trade goods but for food itself.

The coming of Europeans thus produced a lessened, weakened, and dispirited native people. Indians, who suffered from many things, but never from a lack of courage, fought back nonetheless. In Acadia, where they confronted both the British and the French, they fought the British. When Britain and France made war on each other, Indians took the side of France. That tells something about the rival colonizers. The French were not always models of enlightenment, but in the eyes of Acadia's Indians, they were far better than the British.[9]

French colonists had more tolerance for the strange cultures they found in North America. They were willing to meet Indians on their own ground, regarding them as partners in the fur trade and as souls ripe for salvation. In both ways, Indians were important as individuals, and most of the French treated them accordingly, with courtesy and respect. They wanted to change them but at least gave them credit as fellow human beings. The British, however, shared the urge to change but not the respect. The British settlers who filled New England saw Indians as heathens who might conceivably be brought to God and the benefits of right-thinking society, but who, if they did not quickly see the light, were simply in the way. They were willing to treat Indians justly, but it was justice by British legal standards, with British concepts of property and contract. Those concepts meant nothing at all to an Indian.

The French were just as eager that Indians be made to see the light—in their case, the light of the Roman Catholic church—but if converts backslid, if they would not shake off ancestral beliefs, the French were ready to humor them and try and try again. The priests they sent into the wilderness learned the Indian languages and adapted their thinking and preaching to Indian culture, and they were everywhere liked and respected. To the Indians they represented France, and they were superb ambassadors.

Most significant was the Briton's hunger for land, his craving to explore it, own it, cultivate it. What to an Indian was the hunting ground of his ancestors was to a New England settler a potential farm, fenced and tidy, where there was no room for a wandering, shiftless savage. As the population of New England grew, the need for land grew with it, and Indians were pushed farther and farther back. They were no fools. They knew what was happening. It was something they had to fight.

The French never presented that threat. There were, for a start, many fewer of them. There was plenty of room for Frenchmen and Indians in North America, and in Acadia the land the French settlers took for their farms was reclaimed by diking tidal marshes to keep out the sea. Marshes were not much use to Indians. Micmacs must have watched and wondered as shouting, sweating Acadians hustled to pile up dirt before the next tide rolled in. No doubt the Indians thought it a waste of time and trouble, but it was the crazy Frenchmen's problem, nothing to worry about.

There were other influences. British colonists came in family groups, whereas most of the early French settlers were unattached young men. They romanced Indian women, creating lasting kinship ties. Toward the end of the seventeenth century, one of the French leaders, a nobleman, married the daughter of an Abenaki sagamore. Their children grew up to hold prominent positions in French society. Nothing like that happened in New England, and it made a difference.

So did religion. Under the influence of missionaries, Indians trooped enthusiastically into backwoods chapels to embrace the faith of the French. Their conversions were not always as total as the priests had hoped: The ancestral religion had room for new gods and new rituals. The Indians figured they could supplement the old ones; they did not have to replace them. Yet even if the Indian's faith might not be quite the same as the Frenchman's, they were still fellow Catholics. Other things being equal, Catholics ought to fight on the same side.

For the French, the effect of all this was Indian friendship in peace and alliance in war. The Abenakis, particularly, fought Britons hard and often. Their territory, on the frontier of New England, was the scene of almost constant bloodshed. The others, farther away and less afflicted by New Englanders' land grabbing, were not so quick to join the fight. Ancient enmities were slow to die, and in the early days Micmacs, Maliseets, and Passamaquoddies were more interested in making war on each other and on Abenakis than in fighting the British. As time passed, however, and New England's pressure built, all the native people joined the French in the partnership that kept the struggle for Acadia alive through a century and a half.

2 | ST. CROIX

Frenchmen Make a Start

1604–1605

IN THE SUMMER OF 1604, a band of adventurers from France landed on an island eight miles downstream from what is now Calais, Maine. Before the snow began to fall that autumn, they hammered together fortifications and buildings and settled down to spend what turned out to be six terrible months of winter. Nearly half of them died, but a colony was born. After the Spanish in Mexico and Florida, it was the first of the enduring European settlements in North America.

Frenchmen had already tried and failed at the hard business of colonizing. In 1541, and again in 1542, King Francis I sent settlers to the valley of the St. Lawrence, the land Cartier had discovered and given the Indian name *Canada*. Disease killed some; intractable terrain drove the rest away. During the 1550s and 1560s, French Protestants—Huguenots—crossed the ocean to escape persecution at home. One group was forced out of Brazil by the Portuguese; another was defeated by hunger and quarreling in what is now South Carolina; still another fell to Spanish massacre in Florida. Finally, in 1598, in an enterprise driven more by hope than by reason, sixty men and women were taken from the jails and sent to establish a settlement on Sable Island, a desolate bit of storm-swept land in the North Atlantic a hundred miles east of the Nova Scotia Peninsula. Eleven survived, to be brought home a few years later and displayed as long-haired curiosities at the court of King Henry IV.

Colonization had miscarried, but commerce was flourishing. French fortunes were being made from the fur and fish of North America. A permanent presence was needed, and policymakers in Paris thought they knew how to rouse the entrepreneurs who would bring it about. Offers were made for exclusive rights to the trade in furs, and at the turn of the new century, the appeal of monopoly profit brought forth capital and men who were willing to try again. False starts in 1600 and 1603 by traders named Chauvin and de Chaste were followed in 1604 by the venture that finally gave France her American colony.

Its founder was a onetime member of Chauvin's expedition named Pierre Du Gua de Monts, a Huguenot who, despite his adherence to a disfavored religion, was a man of rank and influence.[1] During the sixteenth-century Religious Wars, which had set French Catholics against their Protestant countrymen, he had fought beside Henry of Navarre, the champion of the Protestants. His side had lost, but de Monts had received his rewards—a pension and governorship of his hometown in Saintonge Province—after the dashing prince of Navarre became Henry IV of France. To gain the crown, Navarre had been forced to renounce Protestantism. He had not, however, renounced his Protestant friends, and on November 8, 1603, he handed de Monts a patent that made him proprietor and sole developer of all of North America between the fortieth and forty-sixth parallels—or from present-day Philadelphia to Cape Breton.[2]

The king called it *La Cadie,* soon to change to *Acadie* in French, *Acadia* in English. The name may have derived from a fanciful description by the Florentine explorer Giovanni da Verrazano of a shore, probably North Carolina's Outer Banks, that he had sailed past in 1524 and imagined as a Grecian paradise, an American Arcadia.[3] More prosaically, the root may have been the Micmac word for a tract of land, *quoddy,* or *cady,* scrawled on a chart by some unknown navigator from the fishing fleet.[4] In any case, de Monts's grant put Acadia in the history books.

Its inhabitants were labeled "barbarous, atheists, without faith or religion, to be converted to Christianity, and to the belief and profession of our faith and religion."[5] So much for native Americans! De Monts was to bring them to obedience, and he was given a king's power to distribute land, appoint officials, make laws, and if necessary make war. In the words of the American historian Francis Parkman, who had a gift for imagery, "withered Feudalism, with her antique forms and tinselled follies, was again to seek a new home among the rocks and pine trees of Nova Scotia."[6]

Feudalism it was, and not surprisingly. Feudalism was the only system the French knew. Their farms were allocated by a seigneur from the lands of his fiefdom. Justice was dispensed and protection was given by the seigneur, who in return was owed feudal dues, deference, labor, and armed service. That was social order, and it was inevitable that it would be exported to Acadia and later to Canada. It would not work well in places where, unlike Europe, there was much land, few men and women to tenant it, and consequently little seigneurial clout. In the years to come, the seigneurs of New France were seldom taken very seriously.[7] Feudal relationships never disappeared entirely, however; they underlay society.

De Monts was seigneur of Acadia. More important, he was given a ten-year fur-trade monopoly that covered not only Acadia but also the vast region above and beyond it, past the Gaspé Peninsula and the mouth of the St. Lawrence and up the valley of the great river itself.[8] That meant all the furs from Acadia as well as Canada. In theory, this locked up every pelt north of the Chesapeake. To quiet the screams of the other traders, it was provided that de Monts's monopoly might be shared by any of them who would help pay the costs of colonization.

Those costs would be considerable. De Monts was obliged to transport and support sixty colonists a year.[9] He was authorized to conscript convicts and vagabonds, as previous colonizers had, but he meant to do better than sweep the jails of France. He would hire men with skills, men who would make something of Acadia. To be their employer and buy their supplies, he organized a trading company. Some of his competitors joined it; others, balking at the cost, refused. They preferred to rely on the enterprising seamen who crowded every port and would cheerfully encroach on anyone's monopoly, king's orders or no king's orders, if money could be made. They expected, too, that their protests would quickly wear down the king and his ministers. Even in an absolute monarchy, the voice of commerce is heard.

Militant Catholics added their own complaints. They objected to any grant of favor to a Protestant, and particularly to the idea that a heretic like de Monts was charged with converting the savages. But the king persisted. Henry IV had no worries about Protestants—he had been one himself most of his life. And he believed in colonization and trusted his old comrade-in-arms to bring it about. With royal support, his monopoly proclaimed in the ports of France, de Monts was able to charter the ships he needed and enlist the men who would be his colonists.

Among them, the best known—second in position and prestige only to de Monts himself—was a Catholic nobleman with a martial past, a burning ambition, and a formidable name: Jean de Biencourt de Poutrincourt et de Saint-Just.[10] He had been Navarre's enemy in the Religious Wars, but they reconciled when peace came, and by 1604 he had become, like de Monts, a royal favorite. The king himself, it was said, had "testified with his own lips that he [Poutrincourt] was one of the most honorable and valiant men in his kingdom."[11]

And the king was right. Poutrincourt was honorable and valiant to a fault. He was also stiff-necked, quixotic, and impossibly proud. He had estates in Picardy and Champagne; he was governor of Méry, a town near Paris; he had won glory in battle after battle. Yet it was not enough. With the Religious Wars ended, there were no more battles to fight, and, if the truth be known, the Poutrincourt fortunes were beginning to run down just a bit. Acadia offered land that would ensure forever the wealth of his heirs and the glitter of his name, and with visions of a huge new seigneurie dancing before him, the vainglorious patrician signed the roll.[12] His energy and enthusiasm equipped him superbly to lead the colony he would take over from de Monts a few years later. His stubbornness and naiveté meant trouble.

There was also a younger man, as aspiring as Poutrincourt but more pragmatic. He was Samuel de Champlain, a ship captain's son from de Monts's own Saintonge.[13] De Monts hired him as his geographer, and he could not have made a better choice. Although Frenchmen still knew little of Champlain in 1604, he was already a confident and experienced soldier, sailor, explorer, and cartographer, having honed his skills in the army and on Spanish ships in the Caribbean. He had sailed with de Chaste and seen the valley of the St. Lawrence, where he would later earn the title "Father of New France." Now he would tie his fortunes and his considerable talents to de Monts and Acadia.

From the captain of one of de Chaste's ships, Champlain had brought back a report that somewhere on the Bay of Fundy there was a mine of pure copper.[14] The captain, in fact, had never been to the Bay of Fundy, and the mine did not exist, but the lure of the red metal put the nearly unknown bay on de Monts's chart and in his sights when he and his men set out from Le Havre in early March 1604. If copper might indeed be found, something more than codfish and beaver could be sent home to build profits.[15]

De Monts had recruited laborers, artisans, a miner, a minister, two priests, and a few nonworking aristocrats like Poutrincourt—120 men in all. They filled two ships, one commanded by de Monts himself, the other by a veteran of the Chauvin and de Chaste expeditions named François Gravé Du Pont. The ships' decks were piled high with building materials and small boats for probing strange coasts, and their holds were crammed with weapons and gear; in any but the calmest sea, the men who crowded aboard must have been uncommonly miserable. An ocean voyage in the seventeenth century was no fun, and it could be particularly fearsome if the crew had to fight, as de Monts's crew did, the westerly winds of the North Atlantic and the icebergs and storms of early spring.

They made it, nonetheless, in two months—not bad for an east-west crossing in the days of sail. De Monts and Gravé had planned to rendezvous at Canso, but de Monts sailed too far south and made his landfall at Cape La Have, on the Atlantic coast of the Nova Scotia Peninsula some forty miles below modern Halifax. His first port of call was Liverpool Bay, twenty miles away. Then he sailed down the coast to a harbor that still has the whimsical name he gave it, Port Mouton, because a sheep, a *mouton,* fell overboard there.

There was fresh game at Port Mouton, a welcome relief from the dull rations of the long voyage, and de Monts decided to stay a while. He sent men in one of the small boats in search of Gravé. At the same time, he sent Champlain to find the Bay of Fundy and a safe harbor on its shore.

Now Champlain was in his element. He was on his own, exploring strange places, making discoveries. He and his crew steered for Cape Sable, then worked their way around it and up the coast, carefully noting everything they saw. Past the site of modern Yarmouth, they came upon St. Mary's Bay, the long, narrow inlet that stretches behind Long Island on the Nova Scotia side of the mouth of the Bay of Fundy, and it seemed an appropriate place. They sailed back to Port Mouton, where Champlain reported he had found at least a temporary haven, so as soon as Gravé was located and dispatched to the St. Lawrence to spend the summer trading, de Monts reembarked his men and sailed on to St. Mary's.

He might have planted his colony there, but after spending a few days tramping around and finding no place that he thought could be easily fortified he announced that it would not do. There was plenty of summertime left, so with Poutrincourt and Champlain and a few sailors, he set out to probe the Fundy coasts, sailing first to the northeast, as far as the capes that guard the Bassin des Mines, or Minas Basin (so called because of the copper that everyone knew had to be somewhere nearby), then across Chignecto Bay and down the north-western shore to Passamaquoddy Bay and what is now the state of Maine. Along the way, on June 24, he and his men discovered the great river of New Brunswick. It being St. John's Day, they gave it the saint's name.

Somehow the Saint John and the fine harbor at its mouth were not what de Monts was looking for. Perhaps he was put off by the reversing falls, the deep gorge where white water surges upriver when the tide floods and downriver when it ebbs; boats can pass only at the slack. In any case, he found what he wanted at the top of Passama-quoddy Bay—an island in the river that now separates the United States and Canada. Because the nearby waters seemed to form a cross, de Monts named his island St. Croix. Later, the river took the name.

Champlain explained that "vessels could pass up the river only at the mercy of the cannon on this island, and we deemed the location the most advantageous, not only on account of its situation and good soil, but also on account of the intercourse which we proposed with the savages of these coasts and of the interior, as we should be in the midst of them."[16] And St. Croix Island was indeed well located, both as a gun emplacement and as a fair-weather post for trading with the Indians, who had already begun to greet the French explorers with demonstrations of friendship and eagerness to bargain. The island, however, was not livable in winter. It was, Champlain said later, a place by which "we were greatly deceived."[17]

Much better sites had been in the Frenchmen's grasp. Saint John Harbor was one, and even better was a place they had stumbled upon early in their circuit of the Bay of Fundy, when they sailed through a narrow gap and found behind the cliff-lined Nova Scotia shore a hidden estuary some ten miles long and four miles wide—today's Annapolis Basin. Champlain called it "one of the finest harbors I had seen along all these coasts, in which two thousand vessels might lie in security."[18] Another colonist, an enthusiast named Marc Lescarbot, was even more rhapsodic a few years later, after the French had made the Annapolis Basin their home:

> This port is environed with mountains on the North side: towards the South be small hills, which (with the said moun-tains) do pour out a thousand brooks, which make that place pleasanter than any other place in the world: there are very fair falls of waters, fit to make mills of all sorts. At the East is

a river between the said mountains and hills, in the which ships may sail fifteen leagues and more, and in all this distance is nothing of both sides the river but fair meadows.[19]

Lescarbot was given to hyperbole, but the picture he paints is not far off the mark. "For the beauty thereof," de Monts and Champlain named their discovery Port Royal.[20]

It was there that Acadia would have its capital, and Poutrincourt knew immediately that Port Royal was where his dreams lay. Like Verrazano, he had found his American Arcadia. In an inward eye, he saw the shimmering basin surrounded by fields of grain, fat cattle, brimming barns, cozy homes, and contented peasants, all at the beck and call of a mighty lord, who was, of course, Poutrincourt himself. He asked for it, de Monts gave it to him, and Poutrincourt had his New World seigneurie.

De Monts should have shared his friend's vision. Men could survive and prosper at Port Royal. At St. Croix they could not, but it is easy to see how he made the mistake that came near snuffing out his colony before it was even a year old. In summer, Passamaquoddy Bay and its islands are enchanting, irresistible if one has no experience with a Maine winter. Too, St. Croix is in the latitude of Bordeaux. Perhaps de Monts suspected that its climate might be different. He had no idea how different it would be.

The men who had been left at St. Mary's were summoned to St. Croix, and while warm weather was still with them, they built a fort, living quarters, a storehouse, and an oven for baking the bread that all Frenchmen crave. They had to endure one of Maine's summer disenchantments: "The mosquitoes," Champlain wrote, "annoyed us excessively in our work."[21] Nevertheless, the work was done, and the French thought they were ready for the months ahead. Poutrincourt sailed home with Gravé and the oceangoing vessels, taking the first shipment of fish and pelts. De Monts would stay to see what winter brought. So would Champlain, but first he would find out what lay farther south and west.

He is remembered as the founder of Canada, but Champlain deserves nearly equal fame for his explorations of the rivers and harbors of the land that became New England. The observations and soundings he made during voyages in 1604, 1605, and 1606 produced charts that are still admired by men and women who sail the Gulf of Maine and Massachusetts Bay.[22] Had his government taken better advantage of his talents, the history of the United States might have followed a much different course.

In September 1604, he sailed with twelve Frenchmen and two Indians to Penobscot Bay, then up the Penobscot River as far as present-day Bangor. Between Passamaquoddy Bay and Penobscot Bay, he skirted Mount Desert Island and Isle au Haut, naming the first for its bare mountaintops, the second for its height. Today they are Maine's magnificent oceanside preserve, Acadia National Park. They still bear the names Champlain gave them.

Along the Penobscot, he met and made friends with an Abenaki band and their leader, an important sagamore named Bashabes. Then he sailed on toward the mouth of the Kennebec, but his guides had enemies there, so he had to postpone exploring it until the next year. By the beginning of October, he was back at St. Croix—in time to spend a grim winter with de Monts and seventy-seven of his men.

It was harsh, even for that part of Maine. The trees had hardly turned color when the first snow fell. Three and four feet covered the ground until the end of April. And the Frenchmen were plagued by their location. De Monts had chosen an island because it could be defended easily, but it turned out to be a trap. St. Croix Island has no freshwater springs, and too little timber to keep fires roaring through a long winter. By early December, ice floes jammed the river, surging downstream with the current and making it impossible to reach mainland fuel and water sources. A well yielded only brine, so they had to drink melted snow. The north wind swept their shelters, whistling through cracks in the storehouse walls and freezing their provisions, even some of the wine.

Winter gales tortured them. Scurvy killed them. Like other seamen and explorers who tried to live on salt meat, ship's biscuit, and little else, de Monts and his men did not realize that humans cannot survive long without ascorbic acid, Vitamin C. They had heard of a cure Indians had shown Cartier seventy years earlier, a potion made from a tree they called the *annedda*.[23] But none of Acadia's Indians seemed to know anything about an *annedda* tree, and without the Indian remedy—or fresh meat, fruit, and vegetables—legs and arms swelled, gums bled, and teeth fell out. Weakened by the cold, hammered by the wind, disillusioned by the endless winter, thirty-five of the settlers died.

Then, on June 15, 1605, Gravé returned from France. He brought food, sixty new colonists, and reason to hope that Acadia had a future.

3 | PORT ROYAL

Southerners Prove Hostile
And Explorers Choose a Home

1605–1607

IT WAS PLAIN THAT IF THE FRENCH were to stay in Acadia, they would have to move to a warmer climate, if they could find one. While supplies were still being carried ashore at St. Croix, and the new arrivals were still shuddering at tales of the winter just past, de Monts and Champlain and twenty of their men shoved off to look for a new home. They had plenty of options. Their king had given them a big piece of North America, and no other Europeans were lodged anywhere north of Spanish Florida.[1]

They laid their course for what the Indians called the land of the Armouchiquois, which meant, in present-day terms, the coast of New England between Maine's Saco River and Rhode Island's Narragansett Bay. It was farther south and thus would be warmer than St. Croix Island. It turned out, however, to be nearly as unwelcoming.

First they explored the islands and channels that crowd the mouth of the Kennebec, the watery maze Champlain had passed up in 1604. Their guide, a Micmac named Panounias, was a better diplomat than the Indians who had gone along the year before, and with the help of the local Abenakis, they made their way upstream as far as Merrymeeting Bay, just above modern Bath. After a few days, they headed back to the ocean and southwest across Casco Bay. Once offshore, they could see, far off in the west, the snow-capped peaks of New Hampshire's White Mountains.

When they reached the Saco River, they found men and women raising corn, beans, squash, and tobacco. Unlike the Indians of Acadia, these people were settled, staying near their fields year-round. Their language was different, too. Panounias could understand only a few words. Probably they were Pawtuckets, northernmost of the southern New England tribes that de Monts and Champlain lumped together as Armouchiquois. Down the coast to Plymouth Bay were the Massachusetts. Then came Pokanokets, who lived around Cape Cod Bay and Narragansett Bay. It was a subtribe of the Pokanokets, the Nausets, who drove the intruders away.

From the Saco, they had followed the shore to Cape Ann, where Champlain—who had an extraordinary ability to communicate across cultural and language barriers—persuaded a group of Indians to draw a chart of Massachusetts Bay. Thus armed, he probed Boston Harbor, and he and his comrades stayed long enough to give the Charles River a variation of their leader's name: For a little while, it was the River du Guast. But even with that honorific, the place that would become New England's metropolitan hub failed to appeal, and they sailed on. First they went to Plymouth Bay, then across Cape Cod Bay and around the tip of the cape to the first opening they found on the Atlantic side, a marshy cove they called Mallebarre, near what is now Eastham, Massachusetts.

There a sailor fetching fresh water was accosted by a band of Nausets. They wanted the kettle he was carrying, not his life, but there was a scuffle, and when it was over, one of the Frenchmen was dead. His shipmates, panicking, unlimbered their weapons and blazed away. The Nausets, watching from a safe distance, probably enjoyed the show, and they must have found it particularly entertaining when Champlain's musket exploded in his hands, "near killing me," he said.[2]

It was not a major battle, but it was a major embarrassment—enough to sour de Monts on the land of the Armouchiquois. Prudence called for retreat and reassessment of the sterner climate but friendlier natives of the Northeast. Thus, the French retraced their route, stopping again at the Saco, where they exchanged gifts with a sagamore named Marchin, and again at the Kennebec, where angry Indians told them about a big ship and marauding Europeans. Frenchmen were not the only strangers on the coast of Maine that summer. The big ship was British, Captain George Waymouth's *Archangel*.[3] He had kidnapped five of the Abenakis' young men—a bad start for British relations with a tribe whose friendship could have meant so much.

Back at St. Croix Island, de Monts ordered a move across the Bay of Fundy. He still hoped for a more southerly home, but for the time being he would settle for the spacious harbor he had passed up in 1604—Poutrincourt's Port Royal. The group found a site on the northwest shore opposite what the French called Isle de Chevres (Goat Island) and built a new *habitation*. The complex—in the shape of a square around a courtyard—had a central well plus a forge, a storehouse, a chapel, dormitories, a common kitchen and dining hall, a trading room where Indians could come to barter their furs, and, of course, the indispensable bread oven. Archaeological digs and a drawing by Champlain have made possible a twentieth-century reconstruction at Port Royal National Historic Park, a few minutes' drive from Annapolis Royal.[4]

When the buildings were finished, de Monts sailed home to look after the affairs of his company and do what he could to preserve his monopoly. He knew that the clamor of disfavored traders must be building. Without his lobbying, the promised ten years might not outlast it. He took along most of the men who had survived the winter at St. Croix, leaving Gravé in charge of the newcomers. Champlain stayed with them, "hoping to have an opportunity to make some new explorations towards Florida."[5]

First, however, he had to endure a second winter. Luckily, it was not as bad. Scurvy was still a scourge, and twelve men died of it, but the weather was much better than the year before, and water and firewood were now close at hand. Champlain planted a garden, and his journal makes his little piece of the American wilderness sound like a park in Paris. His garden, he tells us, was surrounded by meadows and trees, "and it seemed as if the little birds round about took pleasure in it, for they gathered there in large numbers, warbling and chirping so pleasantly that I think I never heard the like."[6]

At Port Royal, the French also had the support of a helpful Micmac band and its leader, a venerable sagamore and shaman named Membertou. According to Champlain, Membertou "had the name of being the worst and most traitorous man of his tribe."[7] Nevertheless, he became a valuable friend, and he and his followers shared the tricks of living in relative comfort through an Acadian winter. It could not all be spent lounging in gardens and listening to songbirds.

By spring, Champlain was ready to continue his explorations, only to be frustrated by wind, waves, and a bungling navigator. His first try, with Gravé and a pilot named Champdoré, ended when their vessel ran up on the rocks of Grand Manan, a large island in the mouth of the Bay of Fundy just off the Maine coast. Champdoré, whose forte was damage control, not seamanship, patched it, and they limped back to Port Royal. On a second try a few weeks later, with the same hand at the helm, they failed even to clear Digby Gut, the narrow entrance to the Annapolis Basin. Their pilot, Champlain said, "was a good carpenter, skilful in building vessels . . . but in no wise adapted to sailing them."[8]

With the second grounding, Gravé had the hapless Champdoré locked up, but his skills were needed more than his failings were deplored. There were new boats to build and old ones to repair, and Gravé had to release him.

In France, de Monts was having troubles of his own. The survivors of St. Croix had told their tales, but a generous payroll finally produced enough artisans and laborers, and in April 1606 they assembled at La Rochelle to embark in the ship *Jonas*. Poutrincourt, eager to return to his seigneurie and his dream, had convinced de Monts to let him be their commander, and since by his lights it was a family venture, he had under his wing his teenage son and heir, Charles de Biencourt de Saint-Just.[9] He had also enlisted his lawyer, who welcomed the chance to get away from Paris, where, he said, an injustice had been done him.[10] Probably he had merely lost a case and was loath to face an angry client, but whatever the reason, it was lucky for historians. Observant, eager, and ebullient, Marc Lescarbot was a budding journalist who itched to write the story of the European settlement of America, the biggest story of his time. Poutrincourt gave him the chance, and Lescarbot left a sparkling account.[11]

Some of the other recruits were not models of behavior, or perhaps they were just unaccustomed to the wages de Monts paid and the delights money could buy, even in a straitlaced Huguenot town like La Rochelle. "The workmen," according to Lescarbot, "through their good cheer (for they had every one two shillings a day's hire) did play marvellous pranks in Saint Nicholas quarter, where they were lodged, which was found strange in a town so reformed as La Rochelle is, in the which no notorious riots nor dissolutions be made; and indeed one must behave himself orderly there, unless he will incur the danger either of the censure of the mayor or of the ministers of the town."[12]

Like captains everywhere, Poutrincourt had to spring his men before he could sail, and then he had more problems. Just when the *Jonas* was about to get underway, she was blown against a seawall, necessitating a month's delay for unloading, patching, and reloading.

The expedition did not put to sea until mid-May, which gave poachers the advantage in the scramble for that year's furs.

The delay also caused Port Royal to be abandoned, though only for a few days. Gravé had orders to leave if no ship had come by July 16, and when the sixteenth came and went without sight of a sail, he and all but two of his men set off to find the fishing fleet. The intrepid pair who stayed behind were to guard the settlement through a lonely winter. Gravé promised to come back for them the next year, and Membertou agreed to look after them—to treat them, indeed, as if they were his own children. But they did not, as it turned out, have to test the good faith of either. When Poutrincourt reached Canso, he sent out a boat to hug the shore and intercept Gravé. The men found him at Cape Sable, and everyone returned for a joyful reunion at Port Royal, where the *Jonas* finally anchored at the end of the month. Lescarbot tells us that Poutrincourt broke out a hogshead of wine, and everyone drank "until their caps turned round."[13]

When the celebrating was finished, Poutrincourt held a council. De Monts wanted him to make another try for a new site. The king's grant ran all the way south to the fortieth parallel. Surely on that long coast, somewhere below Mallebarre, there had to be places balmier than the Bay of Fundy and Indians friendlier than the Armouchiquois. All agreed, however, that the coming winter had to be spent at Port Royal. It was already midsummer. There might be enough good weather left to allow explorers to find a new home, but by the time they returned, it would be too late to pack up and move. It was decided that Gravé would sail home to France in the *Jonas* with most of the men who had spent the winter of 1605–06 at Port Royal. Lescarbot and the men Poutrincourt had brought would stay at Port Royal, while Poutrincourt and Champlain would lead a new exploration.

Late as it was, Poutrincourt delayed another month. Champlain must have been frantic. They did not sail until September 5—very late in the year considering all they hoped to accomplish—and their voyage at first threatened to be nothing more than a repeat of the harbor-hopping of 1605. Champlain thought it a waste of time. He would have steered straight for unexplored lands, but Poutrincourt wanted to see the country and greet the sagamores. He was viceroy of France, after all, and he was determined to act the part. If Champlain had won the argument, the French might have reached Narragansett Bay and Long Island Sound, perhaps even New York

Harbor and the Hudson River three years before Henry Hudson discovered them for Holland. As it was, they sailed only a little farther in 1606 than they had the year before.

Their diplomacy failed, too. At the Saco River they met Marchin again, and another Indian leader, Onemechin. In a try at making peace between tribal enemies, they had brought along a Micmac named Messamouet, who came with knives and hatchets and other valuable gifts. In return, Onemechin handed out corn and squash, and Messamouet took it for what it was, a deliberate insult. He left with a vow to come back and make war.

Things were no better at Cape Ann. Champlain and Poutrincourt could feel hostility, and they left in a hurry when Onemechin and his band showed up.

Then, just as in 1605, diplomacy failed entirely when they reached Cape Cod and the Nausets. It was the end of September, and Champlain had finally convinced Poutrincourt that time was running out. No more tarrying on coasts already charted. They stopped briefly and warily at Mallebarre, and this time no harm came to them. Farther south, at the cape's elbow, is Stage Harbor and what is now the pretty town of Chatham. It seemed a likely place to stop for a few days to bake a supply of bread.

Men and women appeared and then began slipping away. Sensing trouble, Poutrincourt ordered everyone to stay aboard ship after sundown, but one night five sailors disobeyed. Early the next morning, asleep on the beach, they were jumped. Knives and hatchets rose and plunged. Men screamed and fought. The Frenchmen fled across the sand, running for their lives. Two were killed outright; another made it only to the water's edge; a fourth, mortally wounded, died a few days later. It was like the previous year's experience, only much more deadly. While they buried their dead, the French also had to endure the Nausets rubbing it in. Lescarbot, relating the story secondhand, tells us that during services for the victims, the Indians "did dance and howled a-far off, rejoicing for their traitorous treachery." Later they "pulled up the Cross, digged out and unburied one of the dead corpses, took away his shirt, and put it on them, showing their spoils that they had carried away; and, besides all this, turning their backs towards the barque, did cast sand with their two hands betwixt their buttocks in derision, howling like wolves." Not surprisingly, their taunting "did marvelously vex our people."[14]

The Indians of Acadia had been uniformly welcoming. Why were these Nausets and the other southerners so hostile? No Indian tells us. Indians left no records, no explanation of their reasons for sometimes being Europeans' allies and helpful friends and sometimes their deadly, mocking enemies. Probably, though, like people of every time and place, they were driven by self-interest. Acadia's Indians had furs, and the fur trade offered desirable business relationships. With their firearms, Europeans could also be powerful allies in war. When Micmacs, Maliseets, Passamaquoddies, and Abenakis welcomed the foreigners and helped them adapt to a strange country, they were looking to their own welfare, to profitable trade and military hardware.

Not so in southern New England, where the economic situation was different. The southerners had the same interest as the northerners in European goods, but because their rivers did not reach as far inland, they did not have the same ability to find furs. Perhaps they could gain by violence what they could not gain by trade. Too, they probably knew that the French were already allied with tribes that were their ancient foes. Their enemies' friends must be enemies too.

And plain dislike played a role. Lescarbot revealed the attitude his countrymen brought to the land of the Armouchiquois. They were, he wrote, "traitors and thieves, and one had need to take heed of them. . . . They are subtle, thievish, and traitorous, and though they be naked . . . if one turn never so little his eyes aside, and that they spy the opportunity to steal any knife, hatchet, or anything else, they will not miss nor fail of it."[15] French antipathy guaranteed Indian hostility.

Poutrincourt was ready to give up exploring anyway. He had not been so eager to find a new home. Port Royal was good enough for him. It was his seigneurie, and it was there he wanted the colony to stay. First, though, because a gentleman's code did not permit unanswered insults, he would get even. His plan was to entice a few of the offending Nausets with trade goods. Then his sailors would force them aboard ship and transport them into slavery at Port Royal.

Fortunately for the Indians and the enduring reputations of Poutrincourt and Champlain, the shameless scheme failed. The Nausets were too quick to be snared, no slaves were taken, and the French left Cape Cod for good at the end of October.

Two weeks later, they were back at Port Royal, where Lescarbot had been left in charge of preparations for winter. The golden days of late summer and early fall had not, however, been much devoted to hard work. Instead, the Frenchmen had spent the time feasting and drinking the wine that was a big part of every cargo from home. Although Lescarbot was no taskmaster, he *was* a part-time dramatist, and to welcome Poutrincourt he had produced a seaborne pageant called *The Theatre of Neptune in New France.*[16] Costumed and rehearsed, and probably a little drunk, its players awaited the arrival of their chief. When his ship appeared, the show began.

First a boat pulls out from shore. It is rowed by Tritons, mermen from Greek mythology. Amidships stands the god of the sea, Neptune himself—long-bearded, booted, robed in blue, trident in hand. He greets Poutrincourt in verse, recalling history's fabled explorers and promising equal glory for their worthy successor, the great Poutrincourt. The Tritons add their voices, echoing the compliments. One, the show's comic relief, gets a laugh by warning of old Neptune's wandering eye and fancy for pretty Indian girls.

Then a canoe comes up, carrying make-believe Micmacs. They have gifts, pledges of everlasting devotion, and more verses of praise for the mighty sagamore of the French. Lescarbot knew how to flatter a client.

Getting into the spirit, Poutrincourt thanks everyone, and, as the boats are rowed to the *habitation,* all join in song. Trumpets sound, cannon roar, and a merry companion, most likely Lescarbot himself, invites his leader to come ashore and drain his cup.

The pageant presaged the winter of 1606–07, when there were good times at Port Royal. Once again the weather was mild, and there was plenty to eat and drink. One Sunday in January, Lescarbot and his friends enjoyed a boating party, entertaining themselves with wine and song. Another day, they picnicked "merrily in the sunshine."[17] Champlain, who knew that boredom could be a problem, organized an *Ordre de Bon Temps* to while away winter afternoons. The rustic society—probably North America's first men's club—sponsored banquets catered in turn by each officer and gentleman, who on his appointed day served as grand master, dutifully marching into the smoky dining hall, staff in hand, followed by a parade of his friends with heaping platters and overflowing flagons. Lescarbot thought the fare the equal of a fancy Paris restaurant, "and at far lesser charges."[18] The ranking Indians enjoyed it, too. Lescarbot recalled that Membertou particularly liked the wine, "because (saith he) that, when he hath drunk of it, he sleepeth well, and hath no more fear nor care."[19]

It was a winter-long party, but it ended on May 24, when a ship arrived with orders from de Monts. Hurt by Poutrincourt's delayed sailing in 1606 and the loss of furs to poachers, the third year of his venture was a failure. Worse, the hatmakers of Paris, distressed by the rising price of beaver, had joined the excluded traders and put enough pressure on the king and his ministers to cause cancellation of the monopoly. For a time anyway, Port Royal had to be left to the Indians, and it may have been just as well.

An Indian war was heating up, one that might have embroiled the French had they stayed. The cause was the killing of Panounias, Champlain's guide in 1605, by men from the Saco, followers of Onemechin and Marchin. The Abenaki sagamore Bashabes became involved and sent Panounias's body back to the Micmacs with apologies and hopes for peace, but Messamouet was still smarting from Onemechin's insult the previous year, and Membertou would have none of any peacemaker's apology. He whipped up his people with a fiery speech, and everyone agreed to seek revenge. In June, right after Poutrincourt began to mothball Port Royal, a flotilla of canoes and several hundred Micmacs left for the Saco.[20]

In August, they were back, celebrating the demise of twenty of their enemies—by Indian standards, a big victory. They had started the Tarrantine War, so called in later years by New Englanders for the name they gave the tribes of Acadia. Pitting the Micmacs against the people of the Saco and some of the Abenakis, including Bashabes and his followers, the war lasted off and on until 1615, when Micmac raiders penetrated Bashabes's lair on the Penobscot River and killed him. Frenchmen never became involved. If they had, they likely would have taken the side of their particular friends the Micmacs, with ruinous consequences for their relations with the Abenakis. Instead, France was able to retain the loyalty of both tribes, and to profit handsomely from their support.

4 | BRITONS
AND JESUITS

New Venturers Appear

1607–1611

WHILE THE FRENCH WERE LEAVING Port Royal in the summer of 1607, Britons were splashing ashore along the Kennebec River. Others were building a fort and planting a crop on the north shore of the James River in Virginia. The sailors of Elizabeth I had fought off Spain's Armada, and the great queen had died, her nation secure. Under her successor, King James I, the British were starting an empire.

The Kennebec venture was abandoned the next year, defeated by its leaders' incompetence and its settlers' inability to get along with Abenakis. The Jamestown settlement, however, survived a shaky start to become the first of Britain's successful colonies in North America, the foundation of the United States. And the promoters of the two British colonies had broad ambitions. Their charter called for plantations in

> that part of *America,* commonly called Virginia, and other parts and Territories in *America,* either appertaining unto us, or which are not now actually possessed by any *Christian* Prince or People, situate, lying, and being all along the Sea Coasts, between four and thirty Degrees of *Northerly* Latitude . . . and five and forty Degrees of the same Latitude, and in the main Land between the same four and thirty and five and forty Degrees, and the islands thereunto adjacent, or within one hundred Miles of the Coast thereof.[1]

That took in a big piece of France's Acadia: The forty-fifth parallel cuts across Nova Scotia and the Bay of Fundy about thirty miles above the Annapolis Basin. Too, Britons never paid much attention to the part about possession by another prince or people—and thus were sown the seeds of the century-and-a-half-long struggle that would begin on a summer day in 1613 with the boom of British cannon across a peaceful bay on Maine's Mount Desert Island.

The hopes of France in 1607 still rested with de Monts. With little to show from the start he had made in Acadia, he shifted his sights to Canada. He persuaded the king to renew his monopoly for a year, new money was raised, and three ships were sent off in 1608. Two, commanded by Champlain and Gravé, steered for the St. Lawrence, where Champlain went on to build the city of Quebec and earn his place in history. The third ship was captained by the much-abused Champdoré, restored to favor and given the job of renewing ties with Acadia's Indians. The hope was that something might be salvaged from the money and effort de Monts and his partners had already spent.

Champdoré sailed to Port Royal, where he found Membertou and his followers asking about Poutrincourt, Lescarbot, and other old friends. The French were missed. After a few days, Champdoré headed for the Saco, where he held a solemn meeting with an emergent leader named Asticou and tried to patch things up between the Abenakis and the Micmacs.[2] He thought he had made peace, but it failed to stick. The Tarrantine War sputtered on.

Still, Champdoré's mission breathed a little life into French Acadia, and while he was on the spot, promising the Indians that Port Royal was not forgotten, Poutrincourt was working hard in France to revive the colony. The king liked him, and Poutrincourt must have delighted his fun-loving sovereign with tales of the *Theatre of Neptune* and the *Ordre de Bon Temps*. He charmed him, too, with gifts of some of the curiosities he had brought back, including Canada geese raised from the shell. Five of the big, handsome American birds were installed in the palace garden at Fontainebleau, where, according to Lescarbot, the king "delighted much in them."[3]

King Henry confirmed Poutrincourt's seigneurie, making him and his heirs forever the lords of Port Royal, but the favor carried a price. It was noted at court that although de Monts had taken priests with him in 1604, no Indians were yet converted. Pressed by his confessor, a Jesuit named Pierre Coton, the king ordered Poutrincourt to include in the next group of colonists a real professional, someone who would see to it that the missionary work was done vigorously and properly. That meant a Jesuit, and Coton chose a member of his order named Pierre Biard, a teacher of theology at Lyons.

The king thought he was doing the right thing, but for Poutrincourt it was anathema. Although he was a devout Catholic, he shared with many of his countrymen a profound distaste for the militant sophisticates who soldiered in the ranks of the Jesuits—the Society of Jesus. The order's founder was a Spaniard; its members professed loyalty to an Italian pope. Surely the Jesuits were a foreign organization, not to be tolerated by patriotic Frenchmen, and Poutrincourt was a superpatriot.

He set out to evade the king's command, and at first he succeeded. Near the end of 1608, he managed to have Biard sent to Bordeaux, where a ship was said to be ready. But no one in Bordeaux knew anything about it. A frustrated Biard found "no news of any embarkation . . . no preparation, no reports, or tidings."[4]

Next Poutrincourt temporized. He told Coton that the time was not ripe, the country too raw for the savants of the religious society. He asked for a year's delay to make everything ready at Port Royal; then he would welcome anyone the king wanted to send.[5] Surprisingly, Coton agreed, and Poutrincourt was able to sign as his missionary an independent priest, one who was not a member of any order.

That problem solved—or so it seemed—he organized his expedition, and in February 1610, he sailed from Dieppe with "many worthy gentlemen and artisans."[6] They included his own son as well as another father-son team—Claude and Charles de Saint-Etienne de La Tour, who were destined for major roles in Acadia.[7] The son, Charles, was only seventeen, on his way to becoming the extraordinary man who would dominate the colony's history until midcentury. His father would be a lesser player but would add intrigues all his own.

The deeds and misdeeds of the La Tours were, however, years away when the new colonists reached Port Royal. In 1610, the future was in the hands of Poutrincourt and his son Biencourt.

There were joyful reunions with the faithful Indians, after which Poutrincourt set his men to planting. He wanted agriculture to rank with trade as the economic mainstay of his settlement. He was determined, too, to forestall the Jesuits, so he urged his secular priest, Jesse Fléché, to undertake immediate and strenuous proselytizing. A few weeks after his arrival, the missionary baptized Membertou and twenty members of his family.[8] Absolved of his sins, the wicked old shaman was transformed into a spotless communicant. If Champlain's report of Membertou's preconversion character is accurate, there must have been much to forgive.

Before he left Acadia the next year, Fléché could boast 140 conversions.[9] Their genuineness, however, is doubtful. They occurred without much communication between priest and penitent, who had no common language, and even if the Indians had a glimmer of what it was all about, they did not regard the ceremony of baptism the way the French did. For them it was a show of goodwill. They wanted their new friends to be allies in war, and they wanted them to stay and trade. Too, those converts who suffered from the new diseases may have expected that European illness would respond to European incantation. It is unlikely that many of them sincerely adopted Catholicism, or that Poutrincourt and his men really believed they had.

Nevertheless, Poutrincourt was anxious for the king to know about Fléché's success. So many conversions in so short a time were proof that Jesuits were not needed at Port Royal, and in July 1610, he sent Biencourt home with the news. He was slated to be back in four months with supplies for the winter.

But national tragedy struck—and word spread far and fast. Biencourt was at sea off Newfoundland when he learned from fishermen that King Henry was dead, stabbed by a Catholic fanatic on a street in Paris.[10] It must have brought a pang of fear that bad fortune for France would be just as bad for Acadia. The king had been a supporter of colonization and a pillar of religious tolerance. A nation deprived of strong and skillful leadership, and threatened once again by civil war, might not support a distant colony—nor might liberal Catholics like Biencourt and his father find friends at a court dominated by King Henry's conservative Italian queen, Marie de Medici, who would become the regent for nine-year-old King Louis XIII.

Biencourt's reception, however, was friendly. The regent, pleased by the list of Fléché's converts, and by an exciting young man just home from exotic lands, had him promoted to vice admiral.[11] The honor burnished a callow ego, but Biencourt was jerked back to reality when he had to confront the Jesuits, whose powerful patroness sat at the queen's side and had the royal ear.

She was Antoinette de Pons, marquise de Guercheville, a rich and religious noblewoman who, in her younger days, had sparked a special gleam in the king's eye. She had declined inclusion in her gallant monarch's list of conquests, but her beauty and virtue had so stirred him that he had given her a high position at court, and in 1610 she was a wealthy grande dame, an intimate of the queen, and a champion of the Society of Jesus.[12] She was in a position to ensure that this time no ruses and no dissembling would keep Jesuits from the holy work at Port Royal.

Biard, his bags still packed, was ready. A second Jesuit, Father Enemond Massé, was assigned, and Biencourt could do nothing about it. The priests said they would meet him at Dieppe, where they would begin their sacred journey.

Then the trouble started. Although Jesuits were in favor at court, they were not so popular in other circles. Some even suspected them of complicity in the king's assassination. Two Huguenot merchants in Dieppe had advanced money and were outfitting Biencourt's ship for the return voyage, but when they learned that Biard and Massé were to embark, they stopped the work. They were, they said, willing to furnish supplies and seamen to support any other religious order. Capuchins or Recollets, for example, would be fine, but not Jesuits. If the queen wanted to send *all* the Jesuits out of France, they would gladly help. Otherwise, forget it![13]

It seemed, though, that Catholic money could overcome Protestant principle, and in the end Madame de Guercheville bought out the merchants. Biencourt was forced to sign a contract giving Biard and Massé and their order half the ship's cargo and half the profits of trade, and the Society of Jesus thus added the business of exploiting North America to its better-known task of propagating the faith.[14] Biard and Massé were able to sail for Port Royal, where they would be not only missionaries but also the seigneur's partners, entitled to share his profits.

As it turned out, there were few to share. De Monts's new monopoly had expired, and trade was wide open. Arguments with the merchants of Dieppe, the Jesuits, and Madame de Guercheville kept Biencourt in France until late January 1611, and heavy weather kept him at sea until May. Traders from St-Malo and La Rochelle arrived early and snapped up the furs.[15] From then on, French Acadia was plagued with money problems—and they were not the worst of the troubles that beset it. The coming of the Jesuits brought strife that would split the colony into separate settlements and end in the destruction of each.

5 | SAINT-SAUVEUR

French Acadia Unravels

1611–1614

THE JESUIT PRIESTS WHO TOOK UP their mission in May 1611 were different sorts. Massé was the shepherd, Biard the man of the world. Massé's concerns were with souls; Biard's were broader. Despite a scholarly past, Biard understood matters of business. He had a contract, and he wanted a say in the affairs of Acadia, a role beyond catechism and baptism.

The seigneur saw it differently. A stiff-necked soldier and proud aristocrat, Poutrincourt was not about to share his authority with a priest, let alone a Jesuit. "Show me the path to heaven," he told Biard; "I will give you good guidance on earth."[1] And when he sailed home in July to try to reverse the financial decline of his colony, leaving Biencourt in command, a bad state of affairs grew worse. An older, more seasoned leader might have made an accommodation with the aggressive Jesuit. Biencourt, a youthful vice admiral, immature and bursting with self-importance, would not. He disliked Jesuits in general and Biard in particular, and he did everything he could to make the priest wish he had never left Lyons.

Biard also had to put up with outwardly cooperative but spiritually delinquent Indians. They came to mass, but only to be sociable, not in a spirit of proper devotion. Later missionaries would have more success with them, but in 1611 their lives seemed to have no empty places that might be filled by the ethos of the French and the teaching of the Jesuits. Biard aptly described the clash of cultures that so frustrated him and Massé, and everywhere accompanied the first European settlement of America. "You will see these poor barbarians," he said, "notwithstanding their great lack of government, power, letters, art, and riches, yet holding their heads so high that they greatly underrate us, regarding themselves as our superiors."[2]

To communicate with their flock, the priests needed to speak their language. Biencourt was no help, so they tried to learn from the Indians themselves, and the results were unsettling. "They . . . ridiculed, instead of teaching us," Biard wrote, "and sometimes palmed off on us indecent words, which we went about innocently preaching for beautiful sentences from the Gospels. God knows who were the instigators of such sacrileges."[3] Perhaps it was some irreverent Micmac who devised this method of tormenting Biard and Massé. Or could it have been Biencourt?

In September, Membertou died, and despite Biencourt's promise that his father's old friend would be interred with his own people, Biard had him buried in consecrated ground.[4] In most things Biencourt's rule was absolute, but this was an ecclesiastical issue. He could not intervene. He could only seethe, and think of new ways to harry the priests.

Meanwhile, Poutrincourt was in France, trying to raise money. When he approached Madame de Guercheville, the pious marquise, keen to save souls, opened her purse. Unfortunately, however, she opened it wider than he wanted. She gave him a loan, but in exchange she became another unwelcome partner. Then she bought out de Monts, and by a deed from the boy-king Louis XIII, she had herself proclaimed proprietress of all the territory from the St. Lawrence River to Florida, excluding only Poutrincourt's Bay of Fundy seigneurie. Biard could gloat that "in this way he, who was thought to be so shrewd, found himself, against his choice, locked up and confined as in a prison within his Port Royal."[5]

The king's grant was more than a confinement of Poutrincourt. It was an outrageous flouting of the claims of Britain—a challenge made worse in British eyes by the fact that Madame de Guercheville was known to be acting for the Jesuits, who were, of course, even less popular in Protestant Britain than in Catholic France.

She entrusted administration of her empire to a Jesuit friar, Gilbert Du Thet, who sailed in late November 1611 aboard Poutrincourt's supply ship. Everyone was happy when he arrived at Port Royal with badly needed supplies, but Biencourt and Biard were soon back at each other's throats. When Biard announced that he and Massé would leave with Du Thet as soon as a return cargo of furs was loaded, Biencourt, suspecting a scheme to make off with ship and pelts and sell both for the Jesuits' account, invoked his secular authority and stopped them. Whereupon Biard, invoking a privilege of his own, pronounced Biencourt excommunicated.[6]

Lescarbot tells us that one of Membertou's sons proposed a simple solution.[7] Why not just kill the priests? Perhaps reluctantly, Biencourt declined, and a wary truce was made. It kept Biard and Massé under Biencourt's thumb at Port Royal but permitted Du Thet to sail home to report to his patroness; and it was Du Thet's report that ruined Poutrincourt.

Borrowing more money, he had put up half the cost of another voyage. The other half was to come from Madame de Guercheville, but when Du Thet reached Paris with tales of harassed and unhappy Jesuits, she changed her mind. Having seen enough of Poutrincourt, she decided to sponsor a new colony where her favorites would have temporal as well as spiritual control, and when she withdrew her support, the proud seigneur, unable to recover his deposit in time to avoid defaulting on his loan, was jailed for debt.[8] To add to his woe, his wife, seeing the family fortunes swirling down a faraway American drain, chose this particular time to ask a court for a separation of property.[9]

Thus Poutrincourt languished, and while he reflected on the perfidy of grandes dames, Jesuits, and wives, the marquise plunged ahead. To command her venture, she picked a new and more sympathetic leader, one René Le Coq de La Saussaye. A ship was chartered; twenty-seven would-be colonists, including Du Thet and a fourth Jesuit, Father Jacques Quentin, were enlisted; and on March 12, 1613, the little group set sail, bravely planning a holy enclave in the wilderness of North America.[10]

They reached Port Royal in May. La Saussaye carried a letter from the queen with an order that Biard and Massé be released, and as soon as the priests were aboard, a course was laid for the Penobscot, where they planned to settle. Storms, however, forced them into Frenchman Bay, on the eastern side of Mount Desert Island, where the ship's crew, claiming that their charter required them to sail no farther, put an end to the voyage.

The Jesuits were reconciled to Mount Desert after Indians inveigled Biard into visiting the nearby camp of Asticou, the sagamore Champdoré had met in 1608. The priest was told that Asticou was dying and in need of last rites. In fact, the death rattle in his throat was only a cough; he was suffering from nothing worse than a cold.

The idea was to sell the neighborhood, to keep the French from going away. Asticou and his band were still fighting the Tarrantine War, and they needed allies—particularly allies with muskets and cannon.

It worked. Near Asticou's camp, Biard saw

> a beautiful hill, rising gently from the sea, its sides bathed by two springs; the land is cleared for twenty or twenty-five acres, and in some places is covered with grass almost as high as a man. It faces the South and East, and is near the mouth of the [Penobscot], where several broad and pleasant rivers, which abound in fish, discharge their waters; its soil is dark, rich, and fertile; the Port and Harbor are as fine as can be seen, and are in a position favorable to command the entire coast; the Harbor especially is as safe as a pond. For, besides being strengthened by the great Island of Mount desert, it is still more protected by certain small Islands which break the currents and the winds, and fortify the entrance. There is not a fleet which it is not capable of sheltering, nor a ship so deep that could not approach within a cable's length of the shore to unload.[11]

And there they stayed. The exact site of the settlement they called Saint-Sauveur is unknown, and because it was occupied too short a time to provide archaeological traces, it never will be known, except by informed guess and deduction from Biard's description. Probably it was on the western shore of Somes Sound, near what is today the Maine resort village of Southwest Harbor.[12]

Saint-Sauveur was not destined for long life. While La Saussaye's men were busy planting their first crops, a warship from Jamestown, the *Treasurer,* was bearing down on the coast of Maine. It carried fourteen guns and sixty well-armed men under the command of a tough British sailor, Captain Samuel Argall. His mission was to expel the French.[13]

It would be a lawless act. Britain and France were at peace, and although France's pretension to all of the coast above Florida was absurd, her claim to Acadia, where Frenchmen had settled in 1604 and had by the summer of 1613 built a viable colony, was far better than any right the British could assert. Britons claimed northeastern America on the strength of John Cabot's voyages in 1497 and 1498, when he found what probably was Cape Breton Island, but even if Cabot was Acadia's first European discoverer, it was not enough.

Since the reign of Elizabeth I, Britons themselves had championed a rule of international law called the Principle of Effective Occupation. New territory belonged to the nation whose people first occupied it, not necessarily those who first discovered it.[14] Clearly the French were Acadia's first European occupants.

Legal nicety and historical precedent did not, however, stop Captain Argall. His king claimed the coast to the forty-fifth parallel, and that was all he needed to know when, in July 1613, he found the Jesuits at Saint-Sauveur. Sails billowing, colors unfurled, guns run out, the *Treasurer* closed on the unready Frenchmen. In Biard's words, "the English ship came on swifter than an arrow, driven by a propitious wind . . . the banners of England flying, and three trumpets and two drums making a horrible din."[15] As soon as they had the range, Argall's gunners fired the first volley of the battle for North America.

Biard described the futility of the French defense. "[The captain]," he wrote, "cried 'fire the cannon, fire,' but the Cannoneer was not there. Now Gilbert du Thet . . . took a match and made us speak as loudly as the enemy. Unfortunately, he did not take aim."[16] The brave but artless gunner was shot, and two other defenders drowned trying to escape Argall's boarding party, who took the Frenchmen's ship and then summarily ended their resistance.

Argall let La Saussaye and Massé and most of the others go off in small boats. They found French fishermen at Port Mouton, and by October they were in France. Biard and Quentin were taken to Jamestown, and from then until his eventual homecoming, Biard is an enigma. He may have been the peaceful man of God described in his own report of the destruction of Port Royal that fall, or he may have played a harsher part, the vengeful traitor portrayed by his enemies. But whatever his role, the outcome would have been the same. Port Royal's fate was sealed when Jamestown's governor, Sir Thomas Gates, ordered Argall and the *Treasurer* back to Acadia to drive out the rest of the French. Biard and Quentin went along, looking, according to Biard, for passage home.[17] Ironically, they found it.

With two other ships, Argall sailed directly to Saint-Sauveur and ordered his men to burn what little remained. Then he sailed up the coast, destroyed the remnants of de Monts's settlement at St. Croix Island, and crossed the Bay of Fundy to the Annapolis Basin. It was the end of October, and by the light of a harvest moon, the British threaded Digby Gut and anchored near Goat Island.

The French had no idea they might be attacked. Biencourt was visiting a Micmac camp. His men were harvesting their crops. The guns were unmanned, the *habitation* unguarded; there was no one to challenge the raiders as they landed and burned the buildings. By the time anyone realized what was happening, it was too late.

Biard tells us that on his knees he pleaded with Argall to spare Port Royal. The prayer that accompanies his account, however, seems to reveal a different wish:

> May our Lord grant that this same fire has so completely destroyed all sins, which may have been committed in this place, that they may never again arise in any other place, nor ever provoke the just and dreadful vengeance of our God.[18]

And his countrymen thought it plain enough that he was something other than their friend. They had last seen him in May, when he had abandoned them for La Saussaye and a rival colony. Finding him now at the side of foreigners laying waste their settlement, they had no trouble believing that the whole thing was Biard's revenge. In France the next year, Poutrincourt formally charged that it was the Jesuit's idea from the start, that he had "led," "driven on," and "guided" the British.[19]

Biard, of course, denied it, and to some extent he was certainly innocent. He may have been a sympathizer. He may, in fact, have been an enthusiastic cheerleader, but it was Sir Thomas Gates, not Biard, who ordered Argall's raid. Nor was Biard necessarily Argall's guide. The British captain was a skilled navigator, well able to make his way in Acadian waters. He had French charts captured from La Saussaye, and he probably had with him a 1610 British chart on which Port Royal is clearly shown.[20] Too, he must have read Lescarbot's description, which was published in English in 1609. Argall would have found Port Royal, and he would have destroyed it, with or without Father Biard.

Biard's old comrades, though, would surely have hanged him if they could have put their hands on him—and, if his story can be believed, the same fate awaited him in Jamestown. Divine intervention was required, and maybe it was granted. When Argall sailed away, Biard and Quentin were bound for Virginia and perhaps the noosed ends of British rope, but before they had gotten much beyond the Bay of Fundy the little fleet was scattered by a vicious gale. Argall made his way in the *Treasurer* to Manhattan Island, where he capped a triumphant voyage by coercing a soon-forgotten acknowledgment of British sovereignty from a band of Dutch pioneers.[21] The ship carrying Biard and Quentin, not as capably handled, was blown so far off course that its captain had to find shelter in the Azores and then on the coast of Wales, where the priests' adventures finally ended.

Biard returned to Lyons, and in 1616 he published his account. He had witnessed the opening round of the struggle for a continent, yet the events of 1613 were not, at the time, taken very seriously. The government of France officially protested the destruction of Saint-Sauveur and the taking of the ship Madame de Guercheville had chartered for the Jesuits, but French concern seemed less with an affront to national honor and territory than with "so remarkable a robbery, which costs the said dame Marquise more than a hundred thousand livres of loss."[22] The British responded by sending back the ship. They refused any other compensation, "seeing that her ship entered by force the territory of [Virginia] to settle there, and to trade without their permission."[23]

The French left matters there. The king's ministers did little for Madame de Guercheville, and they did nothing at all for Poutrincourt, whose remaining months were tragic indeed.

Having finally repaid the borrowed funds lost in 1612, he had emerged from debtors' prison to find new partners, merchants of La Rochelle named Georges and Macain. With their backing, he obtained a ship and supplies, and in December 1613, he embarked on a last voyage to Port Royal. Arriving in March, he suffered the final blow to a star-crossed dream. The vision he had seen when he sailed into the Annapolis Basin with de Monts and Champlain in 1604 lay around him in the ashes of the British fires. Heartbroken, he gave up, taking most of his men home with him.

He died the next year—proud, brave, and to the end incredibly stubborn and tragically foolish. France was embroiled in one of her periodic rebellions, this one led by the Prince de Condé. Condé's forces occupied Méry, and Poutrincourt, who had returned to his old military profession, set out to retake it for the king. Royal troops reached it first and accepted the surrender of Condé's commander, but Poutrincourt thought that as the town's governor, the honor should have been his. Accordingly, with a few followers he charged into his own allies, waving his sword and shouting, "Long live the king and Poutrincourt!" The king's incredulous soldiers killed him on the spot.[24]

6 | NOVA SCOTIAE IN AMERICA

Scots Have a Try

1614–1632

THE BRITISH LEFT A WRECKED *habitation* and ruined hopes, but French Acadia was not abandoned. With the death of Poutrincourt, his son Biencourt became seigneur and leader of a handful of men who stayed to fly the Fleur-de-Lis and trade for the account of Georges and Macain.

Among them were Claude and Charles La Tour. Soon after Argall's raid, Claude went off to trade on his own at Penobscot Bay.[1] His son Charles stayed on at Port Royal, where he became second-in-command and helped Biencourt build the fur business that kept the little colony alive. Charles and Biencourt hoped, too, that the mother country might stir itself to help them make more of their piece of America. A letter has survived, sent in Biencourt's name to excite interest at home.[2] It describes resources crying out for development; it invokes the glory of France; and, in a more practical vein, it hints at boundless profit, there for the taking. If settled by Europeans, Biencourt wrote, Acadia would be the equal of Peru, the brightest star in the Spanish empire.

The comparison was strained, but it hardly mattered. France's neglect was profound, and it would not end until the ascendancy in 1624 of Armand-Jean Du Plessis de Richelieu as chief minister of King Louis XIII. With the great cardinal to guide them, Frenchmen rediscovered a national interest in faraway places, but Biencourt did not live to see it. He died in 1623, a year before Richelieu took office. He and La Tour had by then moved from Port Royal to a site near Cape Sable, where they built a new post called Fort Saint Louis. It is now a pretty park at the edge of Port La Tour, the little Nova Scotia town that has the name of the man who took Biencourt's place.

La Tour managed it without authority from home. Unlike Biencourt, who had a hereditary seigneurie and a commission as vice admiral, he had no right to occupy land or command men in Acadia. He was not given a commission of his own until 1631, but Charles La Tour was the sort who seized opportunity where he found it, and when Biencourt died, he made a winning grab. Acadia might not, after all, be the equal of Peru, but after 1623 it was La Tour's, and it was lucrative. With an Indian wife and three daughters, and a booming fur trade at his command, he could look forward to prosperity and perhaps repose at Fort Saint Louis.

He would not, however, have wanted a quiet life—nor was it his destiny to have one. A bid for Acadia was underway, led by a Scot who yearned to build a New Scotland next to the land Captain John Smith had explored in 1615 and proclaimed "New England." He was Sir William Alexander, laird of Menstrie near Stirling, on Scotland's River Forth.[3] Later he became earl of Stirling. He is known to history as a colonizer and to literature as a poet. Although his poetry would hold few readers today, it was popular among seventeenth-century literati, and it helped make the Scottish bard an intimate of King James I, himself a poet of sorts.

Alexander's interest was roused by a promoter named Sir Ferdinando Gorges, leader of a group called the Council for New England, which held the right to parcel out North America between the fortieth and forty-eighth parallels. That was much more land than needed for the New England that Gorges and his associates had in mind. Furthermore, a big piece of it was claimed by France, and there were headaches enough in settling foreign lands without fighting the ambitions of another powerful nation. Why not put the storm-washed northeastern part in Scottish hands? Let the Scots worry about the French!

The idea appealed to Alexander. "My Countrimen," he said, "would never adventure in such an Enterprise, unles it were as there was a *New France,* a *New Spaine,* and a *New England,* that they might likewise have a *New Scotland* . . . which they might hold of their owne Crowne and where they might bee governed by their owne Lawes."[4] And sure enough, the Council for New England knew just the place. On October 9, 1621, the king signed papers giving Alexander all the territory between the St. Croix River and the Gaspé Peninsula, including the Nova Scotia Peninsula, Cape Breton Island, and the empty and still mostly unknown Prince Edward Island. Like all important documents in those days, the grant was in Latin. It provided that Alexander's domain should have and enjoy forever the name *Nova Scotiae in America.*[5]

In 1622, Alexander sent a ship with men he had hired to start the process. They got only as far as Newfoundland, where they took shelter for the winter, and by spring, when a second ship arrived, all but a few were dead or scattered to the fishing fleet. Those who remained spent the summer coasting Cape Breton Island and the Nova Scotia Peninsula, then sailed home, bringing their sponsor descriptions of a beckoning land, but nothing else to show for two expensive voyages.

Undiscouraged, Alexander next tried his hand at salesmanship, writing a tract called *An Encouragement to Colonies.* Published in 1624, it shows the enthusiastic Scot at his best, full of confidence and patriotism. His prose is much better than his poetry. He begins with the history of emigration—indeed, with Moses leading the Jews out of Egypt—then goes on to describe Spain's Latin empire and the first settlement of North America. Next he focuses on Port Royal, where he says he will put the capital of New Scotland. He paints an entrancing picture of brooks, rivers, and meadows—none of which, of course, he had ever seen—and he gives his readers a colorful account of the recent, sad history of European settlement, blaming its failure on ill-disposed, quarrelsome Frenchmen.

When Poutrincourt sailed to France in 1611, Alexander tells us, he left "his Sonne *Biencourt* in his place, who being a youth at that time of more courage than circumspectnesse, disdayning to be controlled by them whom he had invited thither, and scorning their insupportable presumption, and imperious kinde of carriage, using Spirituall armes for Temporall ends, whose spleene had excommunicated and branded him with a Spirituall censure, hee threatened them by his Temporall power with a more palpable punishment." The threat, according to Alexander, sent Biard and Massé off to Saint-Sauveur and their encounter with Captain Argall, after which "father Biard . . . comming backe from Virginia, with Sir Samuel Argall, out of the indigestable malice that he had conceived against Biencourt, did inform him where he had planted himselfe offering (as hee did) to conduct him thither." Not to be outdone, Biencourt then turned traitor himself, making Argall an offer "(if hee might have a protection) to depend upon our king, and to draw the whole Furres of that Countrey to one Port, where he would divide them with him."[6]

Obviously such people were no fit tenants for a virgin land. Upright Scots, particularly when led by the well born, would be another matter entirely. Alexander's tract was written for the gentry, who were exhorted to bring commoners to work the fields of New Scotland. They would find their pleasure in the splendid hunting the country afforded, and everyone would feel right at home. Alexander renamed a few rivers to guarantee it. Thus the St. Croix, which would mark the border between New Scotland and New England, became the Tweed, after the river that separates the old entities. The Saint John was rechristened the Clyde.

When *An Encouragement to Colonies* failed to stir Scotland, the king tried a different stimulus, an order of hereditary nobility called the Knight Baronets of Nova Scotia, which he created for worthy Scots who would take allotments of land and lend financial support. It sounded good, but not good enough, and by March 1625, when King James died, the knighthood had not a single member.

The new king, Charles I, was also an ardent supporter of New Scotland, and he pushed the lairds harder. He was moved by affection for his father's friend, and also by the prospect that New Scotland might siphon off some of his more fractious subjects. A scheme for transporting Highlanders was, he thought, a fine thing for New Scotland, "and for debordening that our kingdome of that race of people which in former times hade bred soe many trubles ther."[7]

Charles brooked no obstructionism. When the lesser barons objected to an order of nobility ranking above them, and the royal secretary for Scotland had the temerity to forward their petition, Charles fired him and named as his new secretary none other than Sir William Alexander. The lairds, it seemed, had better get in line. And the king made it easy for them. Under feudal law, a lord was required to take *seisin*—formal possession of his fief—on the spot. Finding that it was far away and "altogether destitute of public scriveners and notaries, requisite for taking seisins," Charles decreed a legal fiction by which Nova Scotia became physically a part of the old country.[8] Seisin might then be taken at Edinburgh Castle amid an appropriate legal assemblage. It was imaginative, and, helped by royal arm-twisting, it worked. By the end of 1628, Scotland could boast sixty-four knight baronets of Nova Scotia. Their descendants can, if they choose, still sport the title.

With the knights' support, Alexander was able, for a while, to make his dream a reality. In the summer of 1629, two settlements were started, and they might have succeeded had a particularly frivolous war not interfered.

It stemmed from the marriage in 1625 of King Charles to King Louis XIII's sister Henriette-Marie. Difficulties had begun when Charles's confidant, the duke of Buckingham, journeyed to France to escort the princess to Britain and took the opportunity to make a pass at Louis's wife, Anne of Austria. Then, after the wedding, Louis accused Charles of disrespecting Henriette-Marie's Catholic religion, and he delivered a financial blow by refusing to pay the full amount of her dowry. It all boiled over in 1627, when Buckingham led an army to relieve Huguenots who were besieged by Louis and Richelieu at La Rochelle. On the Isle de Ré, just off the city, French and British soldiers fought it out, and in the end Buckingham was beaten. When another expedition failed, Charles sued for peace.

It was a fiasco for Britain, but it had a bright spot. In an unintended sidelight, a private war across the Atlantic, three daring young adventurers challenged the French in the Gulf of St. Lawrence and came away with a brilliant victory. They were David, Lewis, and Thomas Kirke, sons of a merchant of London and Dieppe.[9] Seeing a chance to grab the fur trade, their father and a few associates had obtained letters of marque—commissions to arm ships and capture enemy vessels—and in 1628 they sent the brothers to the St. Lawrence, each commanding a privateer. Thirty-one-year-old David was their admiral. Their aim was to take Canada from France.

At the same time, the French sent a fleet of their own, gathered and equipped by a powerful new organization called the Company of New France, which had been created by Richelieu to exploit Canada and Acadia. The company had taken over Madame de Guercheville's rights, and the king had made it seigneur of the St. Lawrence Valley with a fifteen-year monopoly of the fur trade. In exchange, the company was obliged to transport and support three hundred colonists a year, and its first expedition was a big one, with men and supplies for Champlain at Quebec and Charles La Tour at Fort Saint Louis.[10] One of the ships carried Claude La Tour, who had left Penobscot Bay and sailed home to find financial backing for himself and his son. He was returning, well pleased with the connection he had made with the affluent Company of New France, when he fell victim to the Kirkes and their family navy.

The Kirkes had entered the Gulf of St. Lawrence early that summer, seized a French post at Chaleur Bay, and then sailed upriver as far as the Saguenay River, where they stopped to send a demand that Champlain surrender Quebec. They could boast that they had already captured one of the ships coming to his relief, the ship carrying Claude La Tour.[11]

Champlain refused to give up, and rather than attack his stronghold, the Kirkes decided to starve him out by turning back the rest of the French fleet. They found them near the Gaspé, and the company's transports, filled with passengers and freight, were no match for the nimble privateers. The Kirkes sailed home with their booty and their prisoners, leaving Champlain to wither away through a long winter.[12]

Contemplating the shambles that had been made of the first venture of the Company of New France, prisoner Claude La Tour concluded that the wind was shifting. He was an adaptable man. It was time to change sides. He had not been a captive long before he became his captors' friend, and when they reached London, David Kirke introduced him at the court of King Charles. There he met one of Queen Henriette-Marie's attendants, who became his wife, probably his third. Another of the courtiers he met was Sir William Alexander, and the Frenchman and the Scot made a deal. Claude would lend his knowledge and his influence in Acadia to Alexander and his New Scotland, and he would prevail on his son Charles to hand over Fort Saint Louis. In exchange, father and son would have a piece of New Scotland, and what could be more fitting, if they took the Scottish side, than that each La Tour should become a knight baronet of Nova Scotia.

Claude had no scruples about changing his allegiance. He thought he recognized a winner, so he climbed aboard. That was one mistake. Another was his promise that Charles would go along.

Claude sailed to Acadia in 1629 with Alexander's oldest son— another Sir William Alexander—who had led an expedition the previous year and left "seventy men and tua weemen" somewhere in North America.[13] Beyond those words, taken from a contemporary letter, we know nothing of the Scottish pioneers of 1628. They had no Lescarbot or Champlain to write their story. Probably, like the men Alexander sent in 1622, they wintered in Newfoundland, then scattered, died, or somehow made their way home.

Those who arrived in 1629 did a little better. One group, led by Claude La Tour and young Alexander, landed at Port Royal and chose a site on what was later called the Allain River, a stream that flows into the Annapolis Basin at the edge of present-day Annapolis Royal. Their settlement, which they named Charlesfort, lasted three years. A second, less fortunate group settled on Cape Breton Island at a place called Baleine, near the Havre à l'Anglois, where in the eighteenth century the French would build their magnificent fortress of Louisbourg. They had time to do no more than watch their leader, Lord Ochiltree, strut his credentials at the expense of a few passing French fishermen.

The Company of New France was not as dead as Claude La Tour thought. In August, one of its officers, Captain Charles Daniel, sailed to St. Ann's Bay on the northeast coast of Cape Breton Island, where he built a fort and left a garrison. Then he went gunning for the settlers at Baleine. The war had ended four months earlier, and Daniel knew it, but he had no more compunction about destroying a settlement during peacetime than Argall had had at Saint-Sauveur and Port Royal in 1613. On September 18, his men overran Ochiltree's garrison and captured everyone.

The nature of the action differs between the French and Scottish accounts. According to his own narrative, Daniel found Ochiltree in a place that belonged to France, busily extorting payments from law-abiding fishermen. "To prevent the said Lord from usurping the country belonging to the King my master, and from exacting tributes from his subjects," he had no choice but to order an assault. The fort was fiercely defended, but the French conquered it by "attack on several sides with hand and pot grenades and other combustibles."[14]

Ochiltree's version is that Daniel's men entered the fort by trickery, disarmed an unsuspecting garrison, then tore down and stamped on King Charles's colors "with so much disdayne that the lyke hes nether beein seine nor red off in the tym of ane standing peace betwix two kings." His people were so cruelly mistreated that Ochiltree was moved to ask "whatt greatter barbaryty could the Turke have used to Christians?" To crown it all, Daniel "did call the King of Britain ane usurpater."[15]

It was an important victory for France, however achieved, but in the meantime Alexander's other settlers were digging in at Port Royal. Daniel's success at Baleine and his fort at St. Ann's would not count for so much if the Scots could hold their ground in the Annapolis Basin area, and if Claude La Tour could hand them Fort Saint Louis.

Claude had proven his worth. In recognition, an agreement was signed in October 1629 at Charlesfort in which young Sir William Alexander bound his father to give the two La Tours a share of the fur trade and a strip of Nova Scotia's Atlantic coast beginning near present-day Yarmouth and stretching around Cape Sable as far as Mirligueche, today's Lunenburg.[16] When Claude arrived back in Britain early the next year, he found the senior Sir William ready to do his part; Claude had already been dubbed a knight baronet of Nova Scotia. The land grant was formally awarded on May 10, 1630, "upon condition that the said knight de la Tour, and his said sonne, as he hath promised, and for his said sonne by these presents doth promise to be good and faithful vassals of the Sovereign lord the king of *Scotland* . . . and to give unto him all obedience and assistance to the reducing of the people of the country."[17] Charles's baronetcy was conferred at about the same time.

With his new title, and his new wife, Claude made a last voyage to Acadia the next spring, sailing with men sent to reinforce Charlesfort. They stopped first at Cape Sable, where Claude went ashore to tell Charles of the honors accorded father and son and to arrange the surrender of Fort Saint Louis. But the meeting did not go the way Claude had planned it.

The career of Charles La Tour makes it plain that, like his father, he was not a man to let such abstractions as loyalty and patriotism interfere with gain. His failure in 1631 to follow Claude's choice of land and knighthood over king and country cannot be explained on moral grounds. Rather, it was the result of a different guess as to who would wind up in control of Acadia—and, as it turned out, Charles picked the winner.

There are two reports of the father-son reunion. Both are hearsay, and both cast the younger La Tour in a light much better than he deserved. In his version, published in 1632, Champlain says that Charles "had not allowed himself to yield to the persuasions of his father, who was with the English; for he would rather have died than to consent to such baseness as to betray his king."[18] The other account is by a friend of Charles's named Nicholas Denys, who years later wrote a history of Acadia in which he relates Charles's response "that he was under great obligation to the King of England for so much good-will towards him, but that he had a master able to appreciate the loyalty which he owed to him, and that he could not deliver the place into their hands, nor accept any commission other than that which he held; that he thanked the King of England for the honor which was done him, but that he could not accept any rewards except from the King his master."[19]

According to Denys, the Scots tried force.[20] Charles and his garrison defended themselves, and there were casualties. Unwilling to fight it out, they weighed anchor and sailed on to Charlesfort, taking Claude and his wife with them.

She must by then have lost her illusions about life in New Scotland and family prospects. Given his failure to deliver Fort Saint Louis, her husband's position in the Scottish camp was precarious. She declared, though, that she would stand by him, and later that year Claude and Charles reconciled. The duplicitous old baronet and his wife moved to Cape Sable, where Charles built a home for them and they lived out their lives. Denys visited them in 1635 and found them "very amply provided."[21]

7 | ACADIANS AND PURITANS

A Community and a People Are Born in Acadia, and New England Fills

1632–1636

THE WAR ENDED IN A TREATY signed in April 1629 at Susa, a fortress town on the border of Savoy.[1] In Europe, the British had gained nothing but humiliation. In America, however, they had won Quebec, which Champlain finally surrendered to the Kirke brothers in July 1629. That was a major triumph, but it came three months after the Treaty of Susa was signed, and the treaty required that places taken after its date be given up. Britain's rule of Canada would have to await the next century.

Port Royal was another matter. The British conceded that Sir William Alexander's Scots had settled there after April 1629, but was it a prize of war or was it an empty place long abandoned by France and thus not subject to the treaty at all?[2] Three years of ponderous negotiations were required before that and the other questions left unanswered at Susa were resolved, and while the diplomats argued in Europe, no one gave anything away in Acadia. In 1630, the Company of New France sent reinforcements for Charles La Tour, and he built a second fort, this one at Saint John Harbor. Bearing his name, it would be his stronghold. The Scots were reinforced too, and to add to the confusion, traders were infiltrating from a new British colony at Plymouth Bay. In 1628, they built a post upstream on the Kennebec River at the site of present-day Augusta, Maine's capital; at about the same time, they moved into Penobscot Bay, near what is now the campus of the Maine Maritime Academy at Castine. By 1631, they had pushed even farther east to Machias, just below Passamaquoddy Bay.

The British had a good case for keeping Port Royal, and they probably would have prevailed in the wrangling over it had King Charles not decided in the end that he needed money more than he needed a colony. In 1629, he had dissolved the unruly Parliament, resolving to govern without it. This seemed a solution to his political problems, but it left him in financial straits. Although Parliament was a hotbed of awkward democratic ideas, it was also the source of funds. Louis XIII still owed the unpaid part of Henriette-Marie's dowry. Perhaps the French would make a deal. Port Royal would be abandoned when the dowry was paid in full.

Cardinal Richelieu jumped at the bargain, and Charles thus sacrificed New Scotland to the demands of his wallet. He tried to make amends to Sir William Alexander by conferring an earldom and a monopoly of coinage in Scotland, and by promising to pay £10,000. But the money was never paid, and the monopoly was not enough to restore Alexander's ruined finances. When the earl of Stirling finally breathed his last, his creditors were gathered round.

The king paid his respects to the national interest by declaring that nothing really was forfeited. His surrender of Port Royal was, he said, a way of putting Britain and France on an equal footing, nothing more. The order he sent the settlers preserved his position but was nonetheless plain abandonment:

> . . . Forasmuch as a final agreement hath been passed between us and our good Brother the Most christian King, And that for the conclusion thereof we have consented that port Royal shall be restored to the same condition wherein it was prior to the beginning of the last wars, To the end that there may be no advantage on one side or the other . . . and Without prejudice to any previous right or title . . . Our pleasure and will is, and we command you by these presents, that with all diligence you cause to be demolished the Fort which was built at the sd. place by our well-beloved William Alexander knt, and to remove yourselves thence with your goods . . . Leaving the limits thereof wholly deserted, and depeopled.[3]

Later he said the same to the knight baronets. All that had happened was "the Colonie [was] forced of late to remove for a tyme by meanes of a treatie we have had with the French."[4] It could be reborn at an empty Port Royal, or wherever else Alexander and the baronets might choose.

Acadia was, however, duly and formally returned to France by the

Treaty of St.-Germain-en-Laye in March 1632.[5] King Charles's protestations were as phony as his declaration a few years earlier that Edinburgh Castle was in Nova Scotia.

To make sure, Richelieu sent an expedition almost as soon as the ink was dry, and to lead it he picked a man whose stature guaranteed success. He was Isaac de Razilly, a famous naval hero and the man who more than anyone, except Richelieu himself, had fathered the Company of New France.[6] Financing came from that company and later from a second firm, the Razilly-Condonnier Company, formed by Razilly, his brother Claude de Launay-Razilly, and an investor named Jean Condonnier. Ships were chartered and colonists were recruited. They were mostly *engagés:* laborers, artisans, and farmers hired for a prescribed period, after which they were free to go home. But some meant to stay, and everyone expected that once buildings were up and land was cleared, there would be wives and children and permanent homes.

On September 8, 1632, Razilly planted his banner on the western shore of the La Have River, near Cape La Have. The site is marked today by a monument, a museum, and a few cannon. Land was allotted and men started building and planting. Razilly's cousin, a young naval officer named Charles de Menou d'Aulnay, began regular voyages to sell fish and fur in Europe.[7] The future historian Nicholas Denys established a lumber mill and a fishery.[8] D'Aulnay brought back supplies and settlers, and by 1635 there were a hundred permanent colonists, both men and women. They grew crops and raised cattle, pigs, goats, and chickens. Their spiritual needs were served by Capuchin friars. They had a mill, a chapel, perhaps even a school. Theirs was a community, something very different from the fortified trading posts of Biencourt and La Tour.

Razilly had been given another task in 1632, one that sounded harder even than building a colony—to dislodge the disappointed Scots at Port Royal. King Charles had ordered them to go in peace, but to Razilly and his men, it must have seemed more likely that they would stay and fight. In September, a few days after the French landed at La Have, a band from Charlesfort had attacked La Tour's post at the Saint John River, surprising and subduing the garrison and making off with all the furs and trade goods—hardly a sign of complaisance. But the Scots were docile when Razilly sailed into the Annapolis Basin three months later. Perhaps their foray was just a way of squeezing a last-minute profit out of New Scotland. Booty from Fort La Tour may have been among the goods they sold the unsuspecting French when, in December 1632, they surrendered without firing a shot.[9]

Fort La Tour's proprietor had missed the Scottish raid. Charles La Tour was in France that summer, making a deal with the Company of New France. In 1631, he had finally received a commission as governor and lieutenant general, but then Razilly appeared. Not to worry; La Tour was interested in beaver, not farms and chapels and schools. As long as Razilly did not try for a disproportionate share of the trade, why fuss? La Tour got along with Razilly, and he made an alliance with Denys as well. They were men of affairs; they understood each other. D'Aulnay was a different type—a starchy aristocrat, easily disliked—but while Razilly was in charge at La Have, La Tour had no difficulties in Acadia, nor did he have much trouble arranging matters in Paris. In exchange for agreeing to maintain his forts at the Saint John and Cape Sable, he was assigned a quarter of the furs.[10] The profit potential was huge, and he returned well satisfied.

His concern, and Razilly's, then became defense of trade and territory against pressure from the southwest. New Scotland was dead, but New England was fast filling with able and aggressive people.

The first had come to Plymouth Bay in 1620. They were the Pilgrims, precursors of a wave of men and women called Puritans who left home because they could not abide the Anglican church that Elizabeth I had made their state religion. Puritans looked to the Old and New Testaments, word for word, as their guide in all things, and they found nothing in Scripture about the bishops, priests, vestments, and liturgy that Anglicanism retained from the Church of Rome. They demanded a simple church, a pure church, free from any doctrine or ritual not taken directly from the Bible. Most of them stayed to fight their battles at home, but some, concluding that Britain was irredeemable, left to find their Zion in America.

The heart of their venture was the Massachusetts Bay Company, the Puritan founder of the city of Boston and the Commonwealth of Massachusetts.[11] A predecessor company had a grant from the Council for New England to occupy land from three miles south of the Charles River to three miles north of the Merrimack River. The Bay Company, which took over in 1629, had the same territory, but it was an altogether different organization, not a tenant of the Council for New England. The council had been circumvented, and between the

Charles and the Merrimack it was dispossessed. The new company had its own royal charter, it had no landlord, it had all the powers of government, and it held them and its piece of America directly from the king. Men with extraordinary political and legal skills had been at work. King Charles was no friend of Puritans, but these Puritans were wealthy men, artful men, men of influence, and they had their way.

Puritan luck was at work too, or was it Puritan guile? There was a peculiarity in the charter. Routinely it provided for a management group consisting of a governor, deputy governor, and eighteen assistants, and for a general court to elect them. Remarkably, it said nothing about a meeting place. An oversight perhaps, but it meant that the General Court might sit anywhere. It might, for example, sit in America, and without king and ministers looking on, it would be nearly sovereign.

Here was a vehicle for men and women who disdained a state religion tainted by popery, a Catholic queen, a king ruling without a parliament, and a homeland surely headed for perdition. Among them was John Winthrop, the squire of Groton Manor in Suffolk. "I am veryly perswaded," he told his wife, "God will bringe some heavye Affliction upon this lande, and that speedylye."[12] The solution was America, and with the charter of the Massachusetts Bay Company in their baggage and self-government in their future, the Puritans were determined to create an example so all the world would know how true servants of God order themselves and live their lives. In Winthrop's famous words, "Wee shall be as a Citty upon a Hill."[13]

Winthrop was elected governor. His deputy was Thomas Dudley of Northampton. Company members who would not leave were bought out, and in 1630, the governor, deputy governor, assistants, General Court, and charter of the Massachusetts Bay Company removed en masse from old to New England. Seven hundred emigrants went with them; four hundred had gone the previous year. Some twenty thousand would follow.

Not all were Puritans. New England got its share of idlers, drunks, whores, and thieves. Yet the Great Migration brought mostly earnest, hard-working men and women who left home for reasons of conscience, not out of economic necessity or to escape the law. They were helped by the work ethic they brought with them, and also by the fact that they occupied land already emptied by Indian epidemics.[14] Few of those Armouchiquois who had so harried de Monts and Poutrincourt were left to resist the settlers of Massachusetts Bay. The Puritans thought it an auspicious sign, surely the hand of God, and their enterprise was a success from the start. By midcentury, New England would hold nearly twenty-three thousand Britons.[15] They would face on their northeastern frontier about four hundred Acadians.[16]

Those Frenchmen were nevertheless scary. Their religion alone confounded the Puritans. In January 1633, Winthrop learned that Razilly and his settlers had landed at La Have, with "divers priests and Jesuits among them." He summoned the assistants, "in regard the French were like to prove ill neighbors (being Papists)." They fortified Boston Harbor and sent men to hold the ground north of Cape Ann, lest "an enemy, finding it void, should posess and take it from us."[17]

They should have spent their money on other activities. The French would never seriously claim that Acadia reached past the Kennebec, or perhaps Pemaquid Point, a few miles east of the Kennebec's mouth. That was enough, even so, to put them in conflict with the Puritans, who were sure that if the French colony existed at all, it ended at Passamaquoddy Bay and the St. Croix.

At first the French had the better of it. What they lacked in numbers was made up in the bravado of their leaders. In 1632, raiders attacked the Plymouth Colony's post on Penobscot Bay. According to Plymouth's governor, William Bradford, they lulled the traders by pretending to be lost and by "many French compliments they used," then robbed them. They left with a taunting reminder of Buckingham's defeat, "bidding them tell their master when he came that some of the Ile of Rey [Isle de Ré] gentlemen had been there."[18]

The next year, men led by La Tour pillaged Machias. Plymouth's protests were met by La Tour's threat to take prisoner any Briton he found east of Pemaquid. When he was asked to show his commission, "he answered, that his sword was commission sufficient, where he had the strength to overcome; where that wanted, he would show his commission."[19]

In August 1635, Razilly sent d'Aulnay to formally enforce the French claim on the Penobscot. Subtler than La Tour, he accomplished his mission without bloodshed and indeed with some courtesy, promising to pay for the goods he took, though not for the post itself, "saying that they which built on another man's ground do forfeit the same." He sent the Plymouth men home with "a great deal of compliment and many fine words," and assurances that his orders were to dislodge New Englanders only as far as Pemaquid.[20]

The fine words failed somehow to mollify the thrice-abused Pilgrims. Ready for war, they sent their redoubtable soldier of fortune Captain Miles Standish to Penobscot Bay to thrash the upstart French, but d'Aulnay was dug in, and Standish's gunners wasted their ammunition in a fruitless bombardment. Powder and shot used up, they sought more in Boston, but there they found that the Bay Colony would join Plymouth's war only if Plymouth paid all the cost.[21] With that they gave up, and Penobscot Bay became French.

It was, however, the high point. French fortunes began to decline at the end of 1635, when Razilly died at La Have.

He had done wonders. Under his leadership, French Acadia had been reborn. Its resources were exploited, its borders were expanded, and, most important, Razilly's recruiters had found men and women to come and establish a homeland. A passenger list has survived to tell us about some of them. In April 1636, the ship *Saint-Jehan* left La Rochelle with seventy-eight emigrants from Paris, Dijon, La Rochelle, and villages named Bourgueil and Chinon in the Loire Valley. Among them were five saltmakers, three sailors, a woodchopper, a toolsmith, a cooper, four tailors, a shoemaker, a vinegrower, a miller, a gardener, a gunsmith, and nineteen farmers. Seven men brought their wives; six brought children. One of the passengers was an enterprising widow named Périgault with two sturdy sons at her side. Another was twenty-one-year-old *demoiselle* Jeanne Motin, daughter of a stockholder in the Razilly-Condonnier Company and the intended bride of Charles d'Aulnay.[22]

Not all the *Saint-Jehan*'s passengers would stay. Some sought only fortune and excitement, but others came with minds made up to begin new lives in a new land. Such were Pierre Martin and his wife, from Bourgueil. They became the parents of Mathieu Martin, reportedly the first child born in Acadia of a European father and mother.[23] Others whose surnames reappear in generation after Acadian generation were Isaac Pesseley from Champagne and Guillaume Trahan from Bourgueil. One twentieth-century Acadian has traced her ancestry to Rose Bayols, a *Saint-Jehan* emigrant from Dijon who married one of Razilly's first contingent, Pierre de Comeau.[24]

With other men and women brought by Razilly and the leader who followed him, Charles d'Aulnay, plus a few more who came in the last half of the century, the *habitants* and *habitantes* who endured the voyage of the *Saint-Jehan* engendered a people. Today they are more than a million. They live in Maine, Massachusetts, Louisiana, Quebec, New Brunswick, Nova Scotia, and Prince Edward Island. Those in Canada and New England still call themselves Acadians. Those in Louisiana are Cajuns. In one way or another, all have their roots in the tiny settlement that grew and prospered so long ago on Nova Scotia's La Have River.

8 | WARLORDS

*Massachusetts Takes Sides
In a French Fight*

1636–1645

CHARLES D'AULNAY WAS AN INTELLIGENT and able man, but he was also a haughty man who wore his Old World nobility too proudly and made enemies too easily. Notably, they included Charles La Tour and Nicholas Denys; d'Aulnay also alienated the men who controlled the purse strings and policies of the Company of New France. Throughout the struggle for supremacy that followed Razilly's death, the company favored La Tour, while d'Aulnay found his own support in well-placed friends and relatives and in the well-endowed Razilly-Condonnier Company. When he married Jeanne Motin, he probably collected a dowry of her father's shares.

He began his campaign by getting rid of Denys—an easy task. Unlike La Tour, who had forts and armed men, Denys had only his fishery and his mill. D'Aulnay merely cut off his ocean transport, forcing him out of business and out of Acadia.[1]

At about the same time, he moved his headquarters to Port Royal, where he could more readily deal with La Tour. D'Aulnay brought most of the families from La Have and settled them at the head of the Annapolis Basin. They built a fort, the Capuchins joined them, and the town that is now Annapolis Royal was born.

Half a day's sail away—in Saint John Harbor on a piece of land now called Portland Point—stood its counterpart. Today the site is half-hidden beside a freeway in New Brunswick's busy metropolis. In 1636 it commanded the harbor and access to the Saint John River, second only to the St. Lawrence as a lode of fur and fortune. La Tour still had his commission, and his own soldiers, and to match the Capuchins at Port Royal there were Recollet friars who had come to

Fort Saint Louis and followed him to Fort La Tour. As the contest for Acadia began, La Tour seemed to hold most of the cards.

D'Aulnay gained equal status in 1638, when he was sent a commission of his own, but his backers in Paris could not win him the absolute power he sought. He was told to cooperate with La Tour, and La Tour was allotted the same share of the fur trade he had enjoyed under Razilly. The king's ministers also tried to reconcile La Tour's and d'Aulnay's overlapping jurisdictions, but knowing little about Acadia's geography, they got it backward. They preserved La Tour's rule of the Saint John and d'Aulnay's of Port Royal and La Have, but they gave the rest of the Nova Scotia Peninsula to La Tour and the rest of the mainland to d'Aulnay.[2] That put each warlord in the other's backyard, and the fighting started two years later.

First La Tour, like d'Aulnay, took a wife. Little is known of his Indian wife, the mother of his daughters. Their marriage, blessed by the Recollets, was not a casual liaison that he could have abandoned readily, so probably she had died. Her place was taken by a Frenchwoman, and for a man accustomed to an easygoing Indian spouse, the adjustment must have been awkward. The new Madame La Tour was a woman of style. Her marriage contract required that she be equipped with rings and jewelry, and that she be conducted from France "in a manner in accordance with her quality, together with her suite, which shall be two waiting women and one manservant."[3]

Her name was Françoise-Marie Jacqueline. La Tour must have met her when he was in Paris in 1632 and 1633 making his deal with the Company of New France. The romance matured at a distance, and they were married in 1640. It was said that she was an actress, that she had led a disreputable life. We know only that she was a doctor's daughter from a small town southwest of Paris.[4] We know too that she was *une femme très formidable,* her husband's match in guile and courage. La Tour had chosen a worthy second for his duel with d'Aulnay.

When the marriage was only a few months old, La Tour took Françoise-Marie Jacqueline to Port Royal, perhaps announcing it as a protocol visit to introduce d'Aulnay and Jeanne Motin. More likely, his purpose was to examine d'Aulnay's accounts and find out whether he was cheating in the division of revenue decreed by the king. Or was a feisty new husband just looking for a chance to pick a fight and show off?

D'Aulnay was off with two of his ships on a voyage to Penobscot Bay, where he had rebuilt the old Plymouth Colony trading post and made it his own Fort Pentagoet, so called after the Indian name for the Penobscot River. He had left orders that La Tour was not to be allowed ashore while he was gone, so when the newlyweds sailed into the Annapolis Basin, they were turned away. Then d'Aulnay himself appeared, and La Tour, smarting from the insult, ordered his men to open fire. One of d'Aulnay's ships was dismasted, but La Tour lost the battle. Fighting at sea, after all, was d'Aulnay's profession, and La Tour and Françoise-Marie Jacqueline were his prisoners.[5]

They were released when La Tour agreed to the Capuchins' proposal that the king make peace. Thus, the ministers were given a second chance to straighten things out, and this time they did better. Instead of trying to split the difference, as they had in 1638, they took account of La Tour's aggression and came down on d'Aulnay's side. The Company of New France could not smooth over the fracas its man had started at Port Royal, and by edicts issued in February 1641, his commission was canceled and he was ordered to report to the king to explain his conduct. D'Aulnay was ordered to arrest him if he refused.[6]

La Tour ignored the order, but he needed help, and he sought it in an improbable place. In November 1641, there appeared at Boston one Monsieur Rochett, sent from Fort La Tour to propose trade and an alliance.

The idea must have greatly discomfited the Puritans. Here was someone who would have them take sides among the "ill-neighbors" who so worried them. But La Tour had been artful enough to find a Huguenot to send as his first ambassador, and Rochett's proposals held a powerful allure—trade at the Saint John, where the beaver were. Although the Puritans were wary of foreign entanglement, the stimulus of profit could overwhelm their caution.

After a few days' deliberation, they temporized. Rochett was told that trade was no problem, but for the time being, at least, there would be nothing more.[7] He sailed back to Fort La Tour with not much to report except a friendly reception. Still, the bait was laid.

D'Aulnay had in the meantime gone to France, where in January 1642 he bought out Claude de Launay-Razilly and took control of the Razilly-Condonnier Company. In February, he obtained a second decree against La Tour, and in May he established an alliance with a rich

La Rochelle merchant named Emmanuel Le Borgne. With a big loan from Le Borgne, he hired more ships and men and returned to Port Royal with what he thought was force enough.[8]

La Tour, however, had also been reinforced. Official disfavor or no, the Company of New France had sent arms and soldiers, and he was strong enough to respond with characteristic swagger when d'Aulnay sent the new order for his arrest. He tore up the order and imprisoned the men who brought it.[9] Prudently, d'Aulnay decided against an assault. Instead, he organized a blockade of Saint John Harbor.

Blockading is one of the more difficult military arts, and, given the limitations of their ships and their navigation systems, it was particularly hard for sailors who tried it in the seventeenth century. D'Aulnay's blockade was sometimes effective, sometimes not, and it did not stop La Tour from sending another of his lieutenants to Boston in October to try again to draw the Puritans into the fight. This time it was Jacques de Murat, an officer who brought a new lure—the whiff of a chance at converting the papists at Fort La Tour. Murat was a Catholic, but he was flexible, and he and his men knew how to warm Boston hearts. "They staid here about a week," Winthrop wrote, "and were kindly entertained, and though they were papists, yet they came to our church meeting; and the lieutenant seemed to be much affected to find things as he did, and professed he never saw so good order in any place."[10]

Puritans liked good order more than almost anything else, and they liked being told that they had achieved it in their "Citty upon a Hill." And Murat did more than listen to their sermons and lay compliments on their autocratic way of governing. He accepted a testament, which he promised to read. Indeed, he made himself so popular that he was followed home by traders sent to start commercial relations.

It was the germ of the alliance that potentially could put La Tour back on top, and perhaps matters could be turned around in France as well. With orders out for his arrest, he could not risk going there himself, so he sent his wife, and in the spring of 1643, Françoise-Marie Jacqueline found just the man she needed.

The era of Richelieu was over. He had died in December, and was succeeded as the king's chief minister by another political cardinal, Jules Mazarin. A second of Richelieu's posts, vice admiral of France and head of commerce and navigation, had become a sinecure held by his nephew, the duc de Fronsac. Perhaps it was Françoise-Marie

Jacqueline's charm, perhaps a bribe from the Company of New France. In any case, Fronsac overrode the outstanding decrees and issued an order restoring La Tour's old title. At the same time, he directed the Company of New France to send a warship to help him, and Françoise-Marie Jacqueline had everything she could have wanted. She sailed home aboard the 120-ton *Saint-Clement,* with soldiers and sailors and official papers embossed and inscribed by the vice admiral of France proclaiming her husband's ascendancy.[11]

At the Saint John she found d'Aulnay's blockade in one of its effective periods. The best she could do was get a message to the fort with her good news, then wait while La Tour and Murat made their way to the *Saint-Clement.* Once aboard, they set a course for Boston, where La Tour brought off the most extraordinary coup of an extraordinary career.[12]

They arrived on June 22. It was an event the city would not soon forget. The day was fine, the wind was fair, and the townspeople expected neither visitors nor trouble. No one noticed the French man-of-war as it slipped past the outer islands and into Boston Harbor, where Mrs. Edward Gibbons was making her way to an outing at the family farm. She was spotted by Murat, who had met her the previous year, and he and La Tour shoved off in a ship's boat to pay their respects. Frightened by their shouts, she had her boatman land at an island where Winthrop had a country house. The governor and his family were there, taking their leisure in the fine summer weather.

La Tour and Murat followed her ashore, introduced themselves, and soon put things right. La Tour seized the opportunity to state his case, and in the relaxed setting of a whitecapped harbor and a sunny day in June, the Puritan and the papist hit it off. Winthrop would promise nothing without consulting the other leaders of the colony, but he formed an immediate good impression of his eloquent visitor.

After supper, Winthrop escorted La Tour to the Gibbonses', where he would lodge. Mrs. Gibbons was over her scare, and in her household all was forgiven. Her neighbors, however, had finally realized that foreigners were in town, and there was consternation over the unannounced and unopposed arrival of a French warship. But La Tour showed great goodwill, and everyone was comforted that the captain and some of the crew of the *Saint-Clement* were Huguenots, who, along with La Tour and Françoise-Marie Jacqueline, dutifully attended church meetings. The citizens settled down—warily, to be sure—to find entertainment in their exotic guests. The French musketeers put on a show for them on the Common the next week, complete with drills, volleys, and a pretended charge that duly alarmed the ladies.

On the day after his arrival, La Tour's plea was considered by Winthrop and as many members of the General Court as he could round up. La Tour showed them the orders signed by the vice admiral of France describing him as the French king's lieutenant general and directing the captain of the *Saint-Clement* to help him put down d'Aulnay's rebellion. The documents convinced Winthrop and his advisers that La Tour was in the right. They would not give him direct military assistance, but they would let him hire the ships and men of Massachusetts to take his side in war.

Their decision, made in haste and without touching the appropriate political bases, raised a storm. The elders, the clergymen of the colony, had not been consulted, and they were outraged. To placate them, Winthrop called another meeting, this time to debate whether Scripture allows Christians to aid idolaters. Books of the Old and New Testaments were consulted, and in the end the decision was affirmed. The Bay Colony would help its neighbor, just as the Samaritan helped the traveler in Luke, chapter 10.

Thus La Tour's preparations could proceed, but controversy raged on. Ministers trembled at the thought of alliance with a papist. Sermons were preached on the danger even of letting La Tour stay in town. The blood of Boston, it was said, would surely spill. John Endecott of Salem, soon to replace Winthrop as governor, voiced the fears of many when he said, "We shall have little comfort in having anything to doe with these Idolatrous French."[13]

Seven civil and religious leaders of Essex County sent a letter on the day La Tour and his new allies set sail. It was a plainspoken and perceptive protest, probably drafted by the Ipswich minister and humorist Nathaniel Ward.[14] Had they arrived in time, words like these might have changed minds:

> We have littel hope to revoke resolutions so farre transacted and ripned, but we presume it shall not be taken amisse, if we labour to wash our hands wholly of this dissigne. . . .
>
> The grounds of warre ought to be just, and necessary. For the justice of this Warre by la Tore agaynst Daulnay, we conceive that all the light and information, New England hath, or may probably receive, cannot be sufficient for us to determine

it positively; we understand it hath beene variously judged in the Courts of France, one while for Daulnay, another while for la Tore, and it is not impossible that la Tore hath now rather outfreinded than outpleaded Daulnay. . . . For our owne interest, if it be cleare that Daulnay hath offered us such great wrong, as invites us to a warre, (which we much question . . .) we suppose it would stand more with the honor of our Religion and Plantation, to proceed professedly and orderly agaynst him, then for us English to become but margent notes upon a French text. . . .

The ends of warre ought to be religious, what glory is intended hereby to God we see not, and how our peace shall hereby be setled we forsee not, but suspect it will rather be a beginning than an end of our troubles and feares. . . .

We feare our sheepe have hastned to their slaughter.[15]

They were right. D'Aulnay had indeed been "outfriended," not "outpleaded." The Puritans were indeed "to become but margent notes upon a French text."

Why did Winthrop and his advisers permit armed intervention in a colony of France? Why did they take sides in a fight that had nothing to do with them? Why did they bless a venture their friends knew to be, and called, plain folly? In a long and tedious answer to the Essex letter, Winthrop tried to explain. Beneath interminable rhetoric, it comes down to the Puritan leaders seizing an "opportunity to save a distressed neighbor, to weaken a dangerous enemy without our chardge or engagement." D'Aulnay and whatever rights he might have in Acadia are brushed aside with this inspired if irrelevant recollection of all the things that were bad in the world of John Winthrop:

The Lord hath brought us hither through the swelling seas, through perills of Pyrats, tempests, leakes, fyres, Rocks, sands, diseases, starvings: and hath here preserved us these many yeares from the displeasure of Princes, the envy and Rage of Prelats, the malignant Plotts of Jesuits, the mutinous contentions of discontented persons, the open and secret Attempts of barbarous Indians, the seditious and undermineing practises of hereticall false bretheren, and is our Confidence and Courage all swallowed up in the fear of one D'Aulnay?[16]

The real reasons for Massachusetts's mistake were two. The first was religious and political. The men La Tour brought with him included Protestants, and La Tour and Françoise-Marie Jacqueline probably implied and may have promised that they themselves were ready to see the light. Moreover, they might be able to bring to the Protestant fold and to the bosom of the Bay Colony the rest of the Catholics on the Bay of Fundy. The Puritans were intrigued by the idea of converting papists—particularly such interesting ones as La Tour and his glamorous wife—and they must have found even more appealing the prospect of others abandoning not only their faith but with it their loyalty, and adding their territory to Massachusetts. It was not the last time that New England ambitions would run to annexation of Acadia.

Too, there was an economic motive. Britain's Civil War had just begun, and the old country's Puritans expected to win it. They no longer needed to seek freedom of conscience in America; they would have it at home. The Great Migration had ended, and the merchants of Boston were suffering through a recession. Opportunities for trade to the south were blocked by the Dutch and the New Netherland they had built on the Hudson. If a friendly and indebted La Tour could be established as lord of the northeast, it seemed that gratifying profits might follow.

One of the merchants, La Tour's host Edward Gibbons, led the financing. La Tour hired seventy soldiers and five ships with their crews. It cost him a mortgage of Fort La Tour, but in a contract drawn up in Boston in July 1643, Gibbons and his partner Thomas Hawkins agreed that their ships

> shall directly saile In Company with the shipp clement appertaining to the said mounseir de la Tour . . . as neer unto the fort of the said mounseir La Tour In the River of St Johns as the above named shipp may Conveniently ride at Anchor; And further wee promise to Joyne with the said shipp clement In the defence of ourselves, and the said mounseir La Tour; against mounseir dony (his) forces or any that shall unjustly assault; or oppose Mounseir Latour In his way to his forte as above saijd, and for any further Assistance we the said Edward Gibbons and Thomas Hawkins promise no further then by a mutuall Consent of the said mounseir La Tour with the Age(nt) and his Counsell by us Appointed or the major parte of them.[17]

Hawkins, the agent who would commit the men of Massachusetts, would go along.

They sailed on July 24, arriving at Fort La Tour a few days later and easily lifting the blockade.[18] D'Aulnay's ships fled to Port Royal, La Tour persuaded Hawkins to follow, and on August 6, the *Saint-Clement* and its Massachusetts consorts entered the Annapolis Basin.

La Tour and Hawkins sent messages ashore demanding that d'Aulnay make peace. When they received in return another copy of the official order for La Tour's arrest, Hawkins began to have second thoughts. He would not order his men to attack d'Aulnay's fort. He did, however, allow La Tour to recruit volunteers, and a promise of booty induced about thirty of the New Englanders to land at the Allain River and join an assault on a mill a little way upstream.

It was taken and burned. Three of its defenders were killed, seven were wounded, and one was captured. Nearby crops were destroyed and a few cattle were killed, but that was all. La Tour had to be satisfied with the mill, and it was not in the end a decisive or even a particularly destructive battle that was fought that August day at Port Royal. The invaders made a cautious retreat to their ships, and while d'Aulnay's gunners lobbed a few rounds after them, they sailed out of the basin and back to the Saint John. En route, they captured a cargo of skins from Fort Pentagoet, thus producing a small return on Gibbons's and Hawkins's investment. Otherwise nothing was achieved except the compromise of La Tour's friends at Boston and the loss of whatever support his cause might still have found in Paris.

When Winthrop learned what had happened, he called it "offensive and grievous," and tried to dissociate himself.[19] He could argue that he had authorized nothing more than relief of Fort La Tour, that Hawkins had overstepped his mandate. Yet few sympathized. The fiasco at Port Royal had much to do with Endecott's victory in the next election.[20]

Worse was the damage to La Tour, who was guilty now of open alliance with Protestants in an attack on his flag and his countrymen. The Capuchins wrote a scathing denunciation, and d'Aulnay had all the mileage he needed when he sailed to France that autumn and reversed everything Fronsac had done for Françoise-Marie Jacqueline. He came back with a sixteen-gun warship, reinforcements for his blockaders, and still another order for La Tour's arrest.[21]

Françoise-Marie Jacqueline had also gone to France after the attack on Port Royal, but this time she found no official sympathy and no exploitable duke. The Company of New France could do nothing for her. Indeed, the cause of La Tour was in such disfavor that to make her way home, she first had to sneak across the English Channel to London, where a captain named John Bayley agreed to take her to Fort La Tour.[22]

Bayley, however, had other matters and other ports of call in mind. Nearly six months passed before he finally delivered her, and even then it was to Boston, not to Fort La Tour. Arriving on September 27, 1644, she learned that her husband, who had been there since July trying to pull off another Puritan intervention, had sailed only eight days earlier.[23] She was stuck. Low on funds, with no way home, she had not much left but grit and wile.

They would do. She sued Bayley and the ship's owner for breach of contract. A Frenchwoman against Britons in a Massachusetts court might have been given very long odds, but she won her case; to satisfy the judgment, she was allowed to seize and sell Bayley's cargo.[24] With the proceeds, she bought supplies for Fort La Tour and hired the ships that finally, at the end of the year, took her home.

La Tour had returned three months earlier. His visit to Massachusetts, unavailing in the end, had come startlingly near success. He had gone to Salem to meet Endecott, then to Boston to plead his case to the elders and the General Court. He talked of his baronetcy and of his grant from Sir William Alexander, and he convinced many of his hosts that a proper Scottish title was about to be trampled. Winthrop tells us that even some of the elders wanted to help him, and that Endecott—who just a year earlier had fretted so about "having anything to doe with these Idolatrous French"—was "moved with compassion towards him."[25]

When he left, La Tour had an honor guard and salutes. They liked La Tour in Boston, but his eloquence this time had gained him no allies. The Puritans had come to their senses. Endecott may have been moved with compassion, but he would not make the mistake Winthrop had made. Instead of hostile men and hired guns, he and his council sent d'Aulnay a pledge that "in this way of the tender of love and peace, and removal of whatsoever may hinder it, we shall readily first walk in." They said they had refused La Tour's new plea for help and had "expressly prohibited all our people to exercise any act of hostility either by Sea or Land against you, unless it be in their own defense," and they declared that the raiders who had come from Massachusetts the previous year "did not act either by command, counsel or permission of the Government here established, they went volunteers without any commission from it . . . and for any unlawful action, which any amongst them might possibly commit, (if there be any) we do not approve of."[26]

They were relieved when a conciliatory letter came back from d'Aulnay.[27] It seemed to forgive the affair at Port Royal, and it was followed by an emissary, a Capuchin traveling as "Monsieur Marie," who turned out to be an extraordinary diplomat. In a treaty signed at Boston on October 18, 1644, Massachusetts officially recognized Acadia as a province of France and d'Aulnay as its governor. Just as though each were a sovereign nation, the two colonies agreed as follows:

> The Governor and Magistrates doe promise to Mons. Marie aforesaid, that they and all the English within the jurisdiction of the Massachusets in New England, shall observe and keep firme peace with Mo'r De Aulney, Governor etc. and all the French under his government in Accady; and alsoe Mor. Marie promiseth for Mor de Aulney that he and all his people shall keep firme peace allsoe with the Governor and Magistrates aforesaid, and all the inhabitants of the sayd jurisdiction of the Massachusets; that it shall be lawfull for all their people as well French as English to trade with each other, so as if any occasion of offence should happen neither of them shall attempt anything against the other in a hostile way, except complaynt and manifestation of the injury be first made, and satisfaction according to equity be not given. Provided allwayes that the Governor and Magistrates aforesayd be not bound to restraine their merchants from tradeing with their ships with what people soever, whether French or others, in what place soever inhabiting.[28]

By a side agreement, not included in the official treaty, it was understood that d'Aulnay might continue his blockade of Fort La Tour, but he would pay for any Massachusetts cargoes he intercepted.[29]

Thus, the Bay Colony was out of the mess Winthrop had led it into the previous year, and its merchants were free to trade with both sides. D'Aulnay could maintain his blockade, and he could mount an assault without worrying about Puritan interference. It was a good solution for everyone except La Tour, his garrison, and his creditors.

Françoise-Marie Jacqueline knew about Monsieur Marie's treaty, and she had an idea how it might be circumvented. If Fort La Tour could be made to seem a Huguenot haven—the La Rochelle of America—Massachusetts might be tempted back into the fight, treaty or no treaty. The Puritans might follow the example of King Charles I and the duke of Buckingham in 1627 and send a Protestant army to lift a Catholic siege. She had not been home long before she began talking like a Protestant, and she and La Tour may have gone so far as to announce their conversion. In any case, they said enough to cause the defection of the Recollets and a handful of La Tour's soldiers, who were welcomed across the bay at Port Royal.[30] Learning from them that La Tour was about to go off on another mission to Boston, d'Aulnay realized that the time was ripe.

Fort La Tour fell on Easter Sunday in 1645. There is an eyewitness account by one of d'Aulnay's officers. Denys and Winthrop also wrote about the siege and its aftermath, and all three describe a furious battle, a bloody dénouement of Acadia's civil war.

The defenders were led by Françoise-Marie Jacqueline. Denys says that through three days and three nights of bombardment, the "Lady Commandant" fought at the head of her men, surrendering only after d'Aulnay promised quarter to all and after one of her soldiers, a Swiss, accepted a bribe and let d'Aulnay's men through a breach in the wall.[31] D'Aulnay's officer, however, says nothing about a traitorous Swiss or a promise of quarter. According to him, a last call for surrender was answered by "a volley of cannon balls, hoisting the red flag on their bastions with a thousand insults and blasphemies," whereupon d'Aulnay's men overran the fort.[32] Winthrop reports that the defenders' accurate fire killed twelve of the besiegers and almost sank their ship.[33]

Casualties were heavy, and if quarter was promised, it was not given. Denys tells us that all but one of La Tour's men were hanged, and that Françoise-Marie Jacqueline was made to watch, "with a cord around her neck."[34] She was imprisoned at Fort La Tour, where she died on June 15. If d'Aulnay's officer is credible, the cause of death was "spite and rage."[35]

9 | PROGRESS AND CHAOS

Puritans Pay Tribute, Acadians Build,
And Claimants Scramble

1645–1654

CHARLES LA TOUR, WHO WAS IN BOSTON when he learned that his fort was taken, lost little time in regret and recrimination. Instead, he sailed in a fishing boat to Newfoundland, where his father's old friend David Kirke was governor, to look for new allies and plan a comeback. Probably he produced his baronetcy and his grant from Sir William Alexander, as he had in Massachusetts, but Kirke remembered what had happened at Fort Saint Louis in 1631. He would furnish nothing more than a ship to take his visitor back to Boston.[1]

There La Tour convinced his merchant friends to finance him in a trading venture, using Kirke's ship. The supposedly shrewd Yankees knew what might happen to funds lent the beguiling Frenchman. Winthrop tells us that Edward Gibbons, whose money was secured by a mortgage on the fallen Fort La Tour, "by this loss was now quite undone."[2] But Gibbons and his associates could not resist La Tour, and good money was thrown after bad. He repaid them by hijacking the ship and its cargo, whereupon a chagrined Winthrop lamented, "(as the scripture saith) that there is no confidence in an unfaithful or carnal man. Though tied with many strong bonds of courtesy, etc., he turned pirate."[3]

And so ended the romance between La Tour and the Puritans. The "distressed neighbor" who had charmed them, sat through their endless sermons, pried open their purses, and enticed them into dangerous foreign adventure had, in the end, robbed them. He sailed his stolen ship to Quebec, where he found old friends and spent the next four years as an honored guest.

During those years, d'Aulnay was master of Acadia, with no more worries about internal opposition. Nor need he concern himself about his nervous neighbors on Massachusetts Bay. They had made peace, but they were fearful nonetheless. Would the peace stick? Would d'Aulnay and France retaliate for Massachusetts' taking the losing side in Acadia's civil war?

D'Aulnay had begun to flex his muscles even before his victory at the Saint John. In March 1645, he sent a letter to the Puritans complaining that the Bay Colony had violated its treaty obligations when Françoise-Marie Jacqueline was permitted to hire ships and buy supplies for Fort La Tour. "I know not how you will name such kind of dealing," he said. "As for me, I should rather perish than to promise that, which I would not perform." He disdained the excuse that had been concocted in Boston:

> To say . . . that they were Merchants of London, whom you cannot hinder from trading with whom they please, this were good, if we did not well know, that La Tour, being worth nothing, and altogether unknown to your said Merchants, they would never trust such persons,—if you (or) other Gentlemen were not his security. Moreover, that persons who desire peace with their Neighbors, as you say you do, would have hindered such proceedings if they had pleased,—it being easily done in such places, as we are in.

And he had even more scorn for the Puritans' disavowal of the Hawkins expedition: "To say that your English, who have done such acts of hostility, were not sent by you; pardon me, Sir, if you please, if I tell you this is the mocking of a Gentleman to render such answers."[4]

There was truth in what he said, and the truth hurt. D'Aulnay was unrelenting. In a November letter, he plainly threatened war if Massachusetts did not "give satisfaction."[5]

The next spring, Winthrop reclaimed his job as governor, and high on his agenda was Acadia and its own, menacing governor. Reflecting everyone's wish, if not quite the true facts, the General Court resolved that the government of Massachusetts "hath not had any hand in the said expedition against the said Mounsr D'Aulney, or any act of hostility comitted, either by LaTore, or Capt Hawkins, or any other French or English else, in the warr."[6] It decided that a high-level delegation, including Thomas Dudley, the seventy-year-old deputy governor, should be sent to pacify d'Aulnay at Port Royal. "Some thought," Winthrop wrote, "it would be dishonorable for us to go to him, and therefore would have had the place to have been Pemaquid. But others were of a different judgment, 1. for that he was lieutenant general to a great prince; 2. being a man of generous disposition, and valuing his reputation above his profit, it was considered that it would be much to our advantage to treat with him in his own house."[7] In other words, a little groveling might save having to pay the damages they knew they owed.

D'Aulnay declined to put them to the trouble. Perhaps he wanted to avoid the expense and bother of entertaining foreigners, especially a crotchety old Puritan like Dudley. Instead, he sent to Boston his trusty Capuchin, the remarkable Monsieur Marie.

Marie demanded money, but it became clear after a few days of haggling that he would settle for an admission of guilt and a token payment, and Winthrop and his colleagues, who knew they were in the wrong, were ready to oblige. In spite of the General Court's declaration of innocence, they agreed among themselves that "we could not free Capt Hawkins and the other voluntaries of what they had done."[8] They had an idea. They owned an ornate Mexican sedan chair. It had been on a ship captured in the Caribbean by a British privateer, whose captain had brought it to Boston and presented it to the governor. It was no use in Massachusetts, where there was little chance of anyone's letting himself be carried about like a Spanish grandee. It might, though, serve as a peace offering.

It did. Marie accepted it, and both sides renewed their promises of peace. D'Aulnay had no more use for a sedan chair in frontier Port Royal than Winthrop had in Puritan Boston, but he must have relished the symbolism. He had forced the New Englanders to pay tribute.

He could also enjoy the high favor of his government. To the victor at the Saint John belonged the spoils dispensed from Paris. In 1647, he received a new commission as governor and lieutenant general, and he was thanked in the name of the king for having "by our express commandment taken again by force of Arms and put again under our power the Fort of the River St. John, which Charles of St. Etienne, Lord De la Tour, was possessed of, and, by open rebellion, endeavoured to keep against our will . . . by the help and countenance of Foreign Protestants." His seigneurial rights were confirmed, and he and his heirs were given a monopoly over all the furs of Acadia—which was defined this time as beginning at the mouth of the St. Lawrence and reaching "as far as the Virginias."[9]

D'Aulnay was building an empire. He had forts at Port Royal, Penobscot Bay, and the Saint John, each manned by members of his private army, and the fur trade, the source of important wealth, was his alone. He might have had competition from New England traders, but they remained intimidated. When he seized one of their ships, the timorous Puritans did not even protest, thinking it "not safe nor expedient for us to begin a war with the French."[10] When Nicholas Denys returned and built a post at Chaleur Bay, d'Aulnay put him out of business, just as he had in 1636.[11] His revenues began to build. If his luck held, it would not be long before he could repay the money he had borrowed from Le Borgne and keep for himself all the profits of trade.

Early in 1650, however, his luck ran out. A canoe carrying d'Aulnay and a servant overturned near Port Royal. The servant survived, but his master perished in the frigid water. He left his widow, Jeanne Motin, and eight young children.

He left, as well, a colony that was starting to bloom. It held between three and four hundred people, most of them permanent settlers.[12] Some had been in the groups brought by Razilly, more had been brought by d'Aulnay himself, and now there was a generation of young men and women born in Acadia. The people, according to Denys, had "multiplied much."[13]

A few still lived at La Have, but most were at Port Royal, where d'Aulnay had built his manor house and his fort. The Allain River once again turned a millstone, and the Capuchins had a chapel and a school for the sons of the colonists and some of the Indian boys. Madame de Brice, a widow who had come from France to be governess for the d'Aulnay children, schooled the girls.[14] And to support it all, there were the beginnings of an agricultural economy.

The key to their success—and indeed the key to understanding the way of life that evolved in Acadia in the last half of the seventeenth century—is in one of nature's most remarkable phenomena, the tides of the Bay of Fundy. The bay is so formed and so located that it has the world's highest tidal range—twenty to thirty feet near its mouth, forty to fifty feet in the narrow bays and basins at its head. Where the shore is low and flat—as it is in the lower Annapolis Valley and the Minas Basin and at the ends of Chignecto Bay—the tides of thousands of years have brought and taken away sediment, tons of it every day. More has been brought than taken, and some seventy-six thousand acres of tidal marshland are the result.[15]

Using a simple system borrowed from the Netherlands and other low-lying parts of Europe, the Acadians turned it into cropland and pasture. Earthen dikes held back the tides and ditches drained the marshes. The ditches led to wooden sluices under the dikes and gates hinged at the top, called *aboiteaux,* which opened automatically at low tide with the flow of water out of the marsh. As the tide rose, the reverse flow pushed them shut, keeping out the sea. Fresh water from springs and streams flushed the salt, and the marshes dried, leaving meadowland so rich that even today it produces fine stands of hay without fertilizer.[16]

The Acadian way of farming began in the Annapolis Valley. It spread in later years, as Acadians built new communities. It was unique in America, and it fostered a lifestyle that was nearly as unique. Unlike the settlers of New England and the colonies farther south, and unlike their countrymen in the valley of the St. Lawrence, Acadians did not have to fell trees, pull stumps, and pry boulders before they could plant a crop. Their marshes had no trees, no stumps, and no boulders, and their lives were not totally given over to hard work. Once their dikes and *aboiteaux* were in place, there was time for other things, time for fun.

It was no utopia, however. Keeping up the dikes was hard work, and frontier life was nowhere very easy. Still, the Acadians' lot was different from the grinding peasant existence of men and women who tilled the soil of other places. Their land was plenteous, they enjoyed a healthy climate and an agreeable country, and the Indians who shared it were their friends. As long as the rest of the world let them alone, they would prosper. But the rest of the world, of course, would not. New Englanders, once over their fright, were attracted anew by ideas of annexation, and troubles came in torrents from the Acadians' home government. D'Aulnay's death and the disappearance of authority at Port Royal could not have happened at a worse time in terms of France's ability to oversee a distant colony.

King Louis XIV had inherited the throne in 1643, when he was five. In 1650, when d'Aulnay died, the Sun King was still a little boy. Affairs of state were in the hands of Richelieu's successor, Cardinal Mazarin, and the queen mother, Anne of Austria. She was said to be in love with the cardinal. The bourgeoisie and nobility were not, and between 1648 and 1653 they launched successive, unsuccessful rebellions, collectively called the Fronde. The name came from the slings, *les frondes,* used by the rioters, *les frondeurs,* who swarmed the streets of Paris.

During the Fronde, colonial administration drifted. Men with friends at court or money to bribe a minister arranged for decree after decree to be issued in disregard of logic, justice, and what had gone before. In the case of Acadia, everyone rushed to grab what he could, and amid confusion and corruption, the claims to d'Aulnay's empire became hopelessly scrambled.

D'Aulnay's creditor Le Borgne made the first move. In the spring of 1651, he sent a gang of mercenaries to Port Royal, and Jeanne Motin was efficiently looted. Then his men went after Denys, who was back again, this time on Cape Breton Island at a post called St. Peters, just above the Strait of Canso.[17] They forced him into exile in Quebec, and Le Borgne could think himself lord of Acadia.

He had, however, reckoned without Charles La Tour, who, as soon as he learned of d'Aulnay's icy demise, did what came naturally. Seizing the chance, as was his way, he sailed to France, where he was immediately and astoundingly successful. In February 1651, new decrees were issued dismissing all the old charges against him and making him Acadia's governor, with the same monopoly over the fur trade d'Aulnay had held. At the same time, he was given official thanks for his tireless labors to convert the savages and uphold the authority of the king—labors that were appreciated in Paris even if they might not have been so apparent to those who knew La Tour in Acadia. It was noted, too, that his pious and patriotic work would have continued, "if he had not been hindered by Charles de Menou, sieur d'Aulnay Charnisay."[18]

The honors and fatuous compliments came despite the fact that only four years earlier, La Tour had been guilty of plain treason, and everyone knew it. His turn of fortune was doubtless the doing of the Company of New France, which was determined to regain the Acadian trade at the expense of d'Aulnay's heirs and Le Borgne.

Armed with his new commission, La Tour arrived at Port Royal in September 1651 and forced Jeanne Motin to turn over a new fort d'Aulnay had built at Saint John Harbor, across from the old, ruined Fort La Tour. With that as his base, he set out to reap the patrimony of the d'Aulnay children, which had in fact been affirmed in yet another royal decree issued in May.[19] Never mind the king's grant of the same rights to La Tour a bare three months earlier.

Denys, reincarnated as well, was back at St. Peters, and Jeanne Motin was in a bind. Needing powerful help, she sent one of Madame de Brice's sons to France to find a benefactor in a high place, and since there was plunder to be had, a benefactor was available. He was the king's great-uncle, the duc de Vendôme, an illegitimate son of Henry IV, who agreed to use his influence in exchange for half the profits from the fur trade and control of the posts held by La Tour at the Saint John and Denys at St. Peters.[20] Such were the ways of government and justice in France in the years of the Fronde.

Le Borgne responded by sending another party to Port Royal to make off with more goods before it was too late. La Tour's reaction was altogether different, characteristically dramatic, and, even for him, particularly deft. During the winter of 1652–53, after Le Borgne's latest raiders had come and gone, he sailed across the Bay of Fundy and proposed marriage to Jeanne Motin.

What should she do? She was a widow and a mother sorely beset. Her alliance with Vendôme had not saved her from being plundered a second time by Le Borgne, and she must anyway have been unsure of the duke, who moved in high, corrupt circles, far away. Here at hand was the champion she and her children so badly needed, a man to be reckoned with, a man like her late husband. Perhaps, too, there was something else. Perhaps she was not immune to the charm that had served her aging suitor so well since the days of Poutrincourt. In any case, she agreed, and in July 1653 they were wed.[21] La Tour was then about sixty, his bride in her thirties. She would have five children by the rival her first husband had so cordially hated.

Soon after the ceremony, Le Borgne himself showed up. La Tour, who had an uncanny ability to be elsewhere when misfortune came to his wives, was at the Saint John. Jeanne Motin was defenseless, and Le Borgne put her in prison. Then his men raided the settlement at La Have and, once again, Denys's post at St. Peters. This time the hapless proprietor of St. Peters was not given an easy sentence to the comforts of Quebec. He was "placed in a dungeon, with irons on my feet."[22]

Indomitable, he got free and made his way to France, where at the end of 1653, the Company of New France awarded him the coast and islands of the Gulf of St. Lawrence from Canso to the Gaspé.[23] In January, the king confirmed the grant, making Denys governor and proprietor of all the territory in and around the gulf, including Cape Breton Island and Prince Edward Island.[24] He returned to St. Peters, flourished his papers, and convinced Le Borgne's commander that he had no choice but to hand over the post.[25]

Mercifully, Denys's grant was the last of the inconsistent and ill-considered French concessions of property and government in Acadia. With Le Borgne at Port Royal facing down d'Aulnay's rightful heirs, with Denys at St. Peters claiming ownership of everything above the Strait of Canso, and with La Tour thumbing his nose at everyone from the Saint John, the situation by 1654 was so muddled as to seem beyond repair. Suddenly, however, the Puritans intervened, and the French imbroglio was moot.

10 | NEW ENGLAND ASCENDANT

Boston Is the Capital

1654–1670

IN BRITAIN, JUST AS IN New England, Puritans were dominant. King Charles had tried to suppress them. Thousands had fled, and a flourishing Massachusetts was born. Those who stayed behind had found their chance in 1640, when the king finally summoned a parliament. He could not control it, both sides resorted to arms, and from 1642 until 1648, king and Parliament fought Britain's Civil War. Because of the military genius of an obscure Puritan member named Oliver Cromwell, Parliament and its army won. The king was beheaded, Puritans took control, and they ruled until 1660. A parliament sat until 1653, when the army took power directly and Cromwell became lord protector, king in all but name.

In 1651, the Puritan Parliament tried its hand at international economics. In the process, it provoked a war with Holland that would, in a complicated and unintended way, subject Acadia and the Acadians to fourteen years of rule from Boston.

The Navigation Act of that year banned imports in any except British ships or the ships of a British colony. It applied to world trade the principles of mercantilism that had dominated British economic thinking since the time of King Henry VIII, and it was aimed at the free-trading Dutch. After nearly a century of rebellion, the people of the northern Dutch provinces had thrown off the rule of Spain and created a nation. They had at the same time built a big and efficient merchant marine, and they were piling up wealth in their little country from the world's ocean commerce. British mercantilism did not sit well with the burghers of Amsterdam.

The war began in 1652, and the Dutch discovered, to their sorrow, that Cromwell's generals could fight as well at sea as ashore. After two years and four lost naval battles, they made peace. Cromwell let them out at a cost of mostly commercial concessions. He was not enthusiastic about fighting fellow Protestants, nor was he keen on territorial expansion at Dutch expense.

He had, however, while the war was still alive, agreed to a scheme cooked up in New Haven for an invasion of Manhattan. It had little support in Boston, but the members of the General Court had finally agreed that their men might be enlisted. Probably they were swayed by Cromwell's choice of a leader. He was one of their own, Robert Sedgwick, a Charlestown merchant and major general of the Massachusetts militia.[1] Second in command would be Sedgwick's son-in-law, John Leverett, a future governor.

Sedgwick and Leverett were in Boston in the summer of 1654, ready to sail to the Hudson, when frustrating news came. The war was over. What then might be done with the men they had trained? What better than to use them to conquer French Acadia? As Leverett put it in a letter to Cromwell,

> Whereupon wee see the Lord ishewing the work committed to us by your highnes, in reference to the Dutch, haveing prepared and fitted the shipp, and entertayned men; so that there was a fittness for some material service . . . it was conseived, that to spend a little tyme upon your coast in lookeing after the French might turne to some accompt, and be of some use to the English in these parts.[2]

In his own report, written a few days before his fleet sailed, Sedgwick explained that the destruction of the French would be carried out "according to our commission."[3]

He had orders to make war on Holland, not France, but he had authority to take French ships. Although Britain and France were at peace, British ships were being seized by French privateers sailing under commissions issued by the dead king's oldest son, who was recognized by the French as Charles II, legitimate king of Britain. In reprisal, Sedgwick and others had commissions to seize the ships of France, and it was that commission, a corollary of the so-called War of Reprisals, that he used to justify his conquest of Acadia.

It was a stretch, but Sedgwick was equal to it. Like Virginia's Samuel Argall in 1613 and France's Charles Daniel in 1629, he was not a man to worry about fine points of international law. It has been said that he had Cromwell's secret orders.[4] More likely is that he was acting without authorization from London, but with the enthusiastic support of his friends in Boston. Surely they knew what their major general was doing when he and several hundred of the Bay Colony's young men left in mid-July, their sails billowing in "a fair wind to the French coast."[5]

After three days at Saint John Harbor, probably devoted more to parley than to gunfire, Sedgwick accepted La Tour's surrender.[6] Then he sailed across the Bay of Fundy and disembarked his men at Port Royal, where Le Borgne had a strong fort but not much will to fight. The businessman of La Rochelle was good at sending men to plunder and intimidate, not at leading them in battle, and he gave up after a single skirmish—compelled, according to Denys, by "lack of courage [rather] than of all kinds of munitions of war and provisions, of which he had ample to hold out well rather than to capitulate."[7]

Terms were signed on August 16, 1654.[8] They permitted the people to stay or go as they chose, and most of them chose to stay. It may indeed have occurred to them that new rulers might not be so bad. In the years since d'Aulnay's death, they had known no effective government, only a tangle of competing claims and quarreling claimants to their lands and loyalties. Their king had done nothing to protect Port Royal from annual plunder. They probably figured that Sedgwick and whoever came after him could not be much worse, so they stayed, hoping to adapt as best they could and wanting more than anything else to be let alone. For the most part, they got their wish.

Sedgwick followed up his victories at the Saint John and Port Royal by planting his flag at La Have and at d'Aulnay's old Fort Pentagoet on Penobscot Bay. He left Denys alone at St. Peters, no doubt thinking him too far away to bother. Le Borgne was sent to France with his men, La Tour to Britain. Sedgwick left garrisons behind, then sailed home to Boston and everyone's applause. The General Court uttered a perfunctory protest that he had exceeded his authority, but in truth his exploit was welcome.[9] Massachusetts had turned full circle from the day only eight years earlier when a fancy sedan chair had been its peace offering to d'Aulnay. In 1654, the Puritans were annexation minded, and they were looking northeast.

The land between Massachusetts and the Kennebec River had been taken over in 1622 by Sir Ferdinando Gorges and a partner named John Mason. In 1629, they divided it. Mason's share is modern New Hampshire. Gorges's is southwestern Maine. Neither proprietor ever governed effectively, and by the 1650s, men from Massachusetts were filling the vacuum. Annexing Acadia would be a much more audacious leap but a logical next step. It would stretch the Bay Colony to the St. Lawrence, and it would guarantee its merchants the furs of the Saint John and the fish of the Acadian banks. Thus, the General Court sent Leverett to London in 1655 to ask that Cromwell let Massachusetts absorb its big neighbor.[10]

The lord protector, however, had other ideas. He saw Acadia not as an extension of Massachusetts, but rather as a pawn in a game of diplomacy he was playing with Cardinal Mazarin.

The relationship of Britain and France had become unusually complex. Revolution had swept each country. In Britain, the Puritans had won the Civil War, but the axman had transformed Charles I from despot into martyr, and Cromwell faced resurgent royalists at home and abroad. In France, Mazarin and Anne of Austria had survived the Fronde, but it was a close call. Their hold was shaky, and they also had to worry about the turmoil in Britain. Would the tide of revolution spread to the Continent? Mazarin's concern for the monarchy explains his acquiescence in Sedgwick's theft of Acadia. Afraid that war with Britain might awaken the Fronde, the nervous chieftain of the French would bear almost any affront.[11]

For his part, Cromwell was concerned lest France come to the aid of the royalists, but he need not have worried. Although the French recognized Charles II, they were not about to help him to the throne. Mazarin's was a policy of appeasement, and it paid off when his emissaries and Cromwell's signed the Treaty of Westminster, promising that neither country would aid rebels and enemies of the other. The treaty left to arbitration the question of whether or not the British would keep the "three forts, namely Pentagoët, St. John, and Port Royal, very recently captured in America."[12]

But the arbitrators were never appointed. Because Mazarin put Europe first, Cromwell never had to restore Acadia to France. Instead, in 1656 he gave it to two of his own subjects and a handy Frenchman. The Britons were Thomas Temple, an ambitious aristocrat, and William Crowne, a wealthy member of the Puritan Parliament. The Frenchman, of all people, was Charles La Tour.

He had, it seemed, done it again. Sent to London a prisoner like his father a quarter century earlier, he had reached one last time into his ample baggage to find his Nova Scotia estate and his rank as knight baronet. He cheerfully asserted his old rights, and this time he had no problem about the allegiance that went with them.

Cromwell's price, however, was more than a shift of fealty. La Tour was required to pay the debts he had run up in Boston and the costs of the garrisons Sedgwick had left in Acadia; to make good those obligations, he had to accept Temple and Crowne as partners. The three were named joint owners of "the country and territory called Acadie, and part of the country called New France," which agglomeration was defined as extending from Mirligueche around Cape Sable and the Bay of Fundy and down the coast to Maine's St. George River, which lies just below Penobscot Bay.[13]

La Tour had, in fact, been used.[14] His documents gave a gloss of legality to Cromwell's land grab, and shortly afterward he was bought out by Temple and Crowne, who had no intention of sharing their prize with a renegade Frenchman. Probably he threw in his cards without an argument. A half century of battles and intrigues must have taken a toll. The old warlord, who had held center stage for so long, let himself be pensioned off to familiar ground at Cape Sable, where he lived another ten years in comfortable retirement with Jeanne Motin.[15]

His place, though hardly his role, was taken by Temple, a man with a need to find his fortune outside Britain. The nephew of an influential member of Cromwell's council, he might have enjoyed a lucrative position in the protector's government had he not been suspected of royalist leanings. He later claimed, after the Restoration, that he had plotted to free King Charles and that the martyr, on his way to execution, had passed the word that when his son regained the throne for the House of Stuart, he should "have a care of honest Tom Temple."[16] If the story was true, Honest Tom needed an ocean between himself and Cromwell. Acadia gave him the chance, and his well-connected uncle paved the way. He was made governor, and he and Crowne moved to Boston.

At first they divided their property, Temple taking the east and Crowne the west. Then Temple obtained financing from a merchant named Thomas Breedon and leased Crowne's half. Finding the budding capital of Massachusetts more appealing than frontier Port Royal, he made it his headquarters, and until 1670, Boston was the seat of what little government Acadia had.

Temple did not rule it all, however. Nicholas Denys was still lord of Cape Breton Island, and Sedgwick had done better by Denys than just leaving him alone. He had rid him of Le Borgne. It was typical of Denys, though, that his ventures failed. What profit he managed to squeeze from the fishery and the fur trade was eaten up by interest on his debts, and his luck, never good, ran all the way out in the winter of 1668–69, when his post at St. Peters burned to the ground.[17]

The Micmacs called him Greatbeard, and the nickname tells us something of Acadia's most appealing pioneer. Always energetic, always optimistic, always trying, nearly always failing, Denys worked hard all his life, but he left behind only one accomplishment. After the fire at St. Peters, he wrote his *Description and Natural History of the Coasts of North America (Acadia),* which takes up the story almost where Lescarbot, Champlain, and Biard left it. He published it in France in 1672, hoping to recoup in literature his losses from commerce, but he was probably just as disappointed in that as he was in all his other projects. A modern editor gives his opus this one-sentence pan: "As to literary merit, the book has none; nor has it, properly speaking, any style."[18]

What it does have, though, is descriptions of the trading and fishing that gave Acadia life, of its Indians, of events. Denys knew everyone and traveled everywhere. Because of him and his book, we have a glimpse of the years of colony building.

Denys and his Gulf of St. Lawrence barony never menaced Temple. Le Borgne, however, tried a comeback. In 1658, he sent his son, Alexandre Le Borgne de Belle-Isle, to raise the family standard at La Have. It was the only attempt anyone made to regain Sedgwick's conquest for France, and it was a flop. Temple would tolerate Frenchmen on Cape Breton Island, which was actually outside his grant, but La Have was another matter. He sent men to retake it, and when they appeared, Belle-Isle surrendered as fast as he could.[19] Like his father, Belle-Isle was no soldier.

A more serious threat came in 1660, when the monarchy was restored in Britain. Cromwell had died two years earlier. His son Richard inherited the title, not the genes, and the people were in any case fed up with republicanism. They wanted a king. A new parliament met in April and invited Charles II home from exile. The Merry Monarch landed at Dover in May, went in joyous procession to London, and ascended the throne amid nationwide jubilation.

With him came a scramble for spoils, and Acadia was one of the plums. Needing a champion in London, Temple picked his backer Breedon, but Breedon double-crossed him, and the new king seemed to know nothing about a royal obligation to Honest Tom Temple. Acadia was awarded to a courtier named Thomas Elliott, whose only qualification was friendship with the king's adviser, the earl of Clarendon, and whose only interest in Acadia was in sponging from it a passable living. Breedon bought him off with a promise to pay £600 a year, then had himself made governor, and Temple suddenly was shorn of office and empire.[20]

By 1662, however, he had it all back. Hurrying to London, and showing a remarkable ability to maneuver in the corridors of power, he recovered his province and took, in addition, a place on the roll of knight baronets.[21] He had to assume the pension Breedon had promised Elliott, but for eight more years, the newly dubbed Sir Thomas and his merchant-backers in Boston were able to milk the commerce of Acadia, even as they troubled little over its governance or development.

They never tried to make anything of it except a wellspring of revenue, but the Acadians profited nonetheless. A pattern of trade was established. As a source of goods and a market for produce, New England became the mother country France never was, and its role long outlasted Temple, whose rule ended as it began, the unforeseen and incidental consequence of a war between Britain and Holland.

The Second Dutch War was a result again of commercial friction. An added cause was King Charles II's grant in 1664 of a huge slice of North America to his brother James, the duke of York. The gift of New York included weakly governed New Netherland, and the duke's men easily forced the Dutch proprietors' surrender. When Dutch protests were ignored, war began, and this time Holland's navy fought Britain's to a standoff. Worn down by ignominious defeats at sea and by the Great Plague and the Great Fire—back-to-back calamities that befell London in 1665 and 1666—Charles made peace, agreeing to modify the Navigation Act and to exchange his South American jungle colony, Surinam, for clear title to New York.[22]

He also had to settle with France. The wounds of the Fronde were healed, and Louis XIV, at last an adult, was secure on his throne and beginning the labors that would obsess his reign: pursuit of *la gloire* and expansion of his rule to the Rhine, the Alps, the Pyrenees, and the sea. He brought France into the Second Dutch War because Holland was his ally of the moment and had a part to play in his designs on the Spanish Netherlands, modern Belgium. Probably he gave little thought to America, but his sailors made conquests there, notably the Caribbean islands of Antigua and Montserrat and the British half of St. Christopher. When time came for peacemaking, the British needed a bargaining chip to get the islands back, and someone thought of Acadia.

By the 1667 Treaty of Breda, France agreed to restore Britain's Caribbean possessions. In exchange, Britain would surrender "the country which is called Acadia, situated in North America."[23] Unfortunately, there was no definition. That left Temple free to dream up an argument that Acadia was just a small part of the territory Cromwell had given him and Crowne and La Tour in 1656, consisting only of the old grant from Sir William Alexander to the La Tours and thus limited to a narrow piece of the Atlantic coast. It did not include—and he was, he said, not obliged to surrender—Port Royal, the Saint John, or Fort Pentagoet.

The French would adopt almost the same theory in the next century, after France herself had agreed to a treaty requiring surrender of an undefined Acadia, but things were different after the Treaty of Breda. King Louis's diplomats expected more than a strip of rockbound seashore, and the French ambassador in London saw to it that the order for Acadia's surrender contained a specification: "as namely, The Forts and Habitations of Pentagoet, St. John, Port-Royal, la Have and Cape de Sable."[24]

But when a French commissioner brought the order to Boston, Temple sent him home. A mistake, he said, must have been made: Fort Pentagoet, the Saint John, and Port Royal are in Nova Scotia, not Acadia. The Treaty of Breda said nothing about a surrender of Nova Scotia.[25]

His dodge, plus French delay in restoring British territory on St. Christopher, bought him two more years. He finally gave in after King Charles sent him a peremptory order to hand over Acadia, including Fort Pentagoet, the Saint John, and Port Royal, "forthwith and without all manner of doubts, difficulties, scruples, or delays."[26] That was difficult language to evade, and Temple complied in a treaty he signed on July 7, 1670, with Hector d'Andigné de Grandfontaine, the man who would be French Acadia's first royal governor.[27]

11 | CONFUSION RENEWED

Frenchmen Try to Govern, Dutchmen Invade, and Indians Fight Back

1670–1678

THE COLONY GRANDFONTAINE RECLAIMED was changed from the one France had lost sixteen years earlier. Time and Sir Thomas Temple's rule had done away with feuding French claimants. Acadia was a better place because of that, and Acadians were also better off because of the ties they had made with New England. Boston had sellers of tools, firearms, and textiles and buyers of Acadian grain and livestock. New England had become a window on the world beyond the North Atlantic waves and the Fundy tides.

There was, though, another consequence. Although Acadians had found a surrogate mother country, they had missed the chance for a real one. In the 1660s, King Louis XIV was not yet engrossed in European war and diplomacy. He had time and attention to spare for New France. He sent soldiers to garrison Canada, hardworking men and women to people it, able men to govern it. It would not be long before Europe took precedence, not long before the king decided that he needed fodder for his armies more than he needed settlers for his colonies, but Canada had a running start, and the years of her endowment could have been a time of building for Acadia as well, had it not been a British domain. While Canada grew strong, Acadia grew apart.

By 1670, there were about five hundred Acadians.[1] They had never stopped being French. In terms of language, religion, and *joie de vivre,* they are French today. Yet as recollections of France dimmed, and as trade with New England became more and more important, and in the absence for almost twenty years of any sort of French authority, they had begun to slip their national ties. They meant to give no sovereign their full allegiance. They were adopting the mind-set that in later years would give them the name "French neutrals."

They probably did not notice that a new style of government arrived with Grandfontaine. Before 1654, they had been ruled by seigneurs, lords who theoretically held the powers of dictators. With the restoration of French rule, Acadia became a royal province, directly under the king. Feudalism survived in a limited way. Seigneuries were still granted, but they made their holders little more than landlords.[2] One of the new seigneurs was Le Borgne's son, Belle-Isle. His misadventure in 1658 had not soured him on Acadia, and he was ensconced at Port Royal, where he had married a daughter of Charles La Tour and Jeanne Motin and where, by inheritance and marriage, he ought to have been a leader. No one, however, paid him much attention. It was said that he ignored his seigneurial obligations—indeed, that he was so fond of wine that often he could not even sort out his tenants.[3]

As a formal matter, Acadia was governed from Quebec, where a supreme royal governor presided over all of New France. Beginning in 1672, it was the formidable compte de Frontenac. There was also an intendant, who was responsible for social and economic administration, and both the governor and the intendant of New France had nominal jurisdiction over Acadia as well as Canada. But for purposes of government, Acadia might have been on a different planet. It could be reached from Quebec only by portage and canoe via the Saint John, the Penobscot, or the Kennebec—or, in the ice-free months, down the St. Lawrence and across the stormy gulf. The journey was long, uncomfortable, and rarely made, so there was very little supervision of Acadian affairs.[4]

Had the king's senior officials shown more interest, Acadia's governors might have done better, for they needed all the help they could get. They never came close to accomplishing their mission—to secure their borders and end the economic dominance of New England.

Under the principles of mercantilism, a colony was expected to supply raw materials to its mother country and buy the mother country's finished goods. Acadians supplied their raw materials to New England and bought New England's goods. The profits of the fishery also flowed southwest to New England, not home to France, and it was all anathema in Paris, but no one was ever able to change Acadia. It was a colony of France but an economic appendage of New England. France was far away, her goods expensive. New England was close by, its goods cheap.

And if France did little to exploit Acadia, she did less to defend it. Soldiers, guns, and ships enough to enforce French claims to territory were never sent. Since the 1630s, the French had insisted that their boundary was the Kennebec River, and although the Treaty of Breda had no definition, it should have been clear to everyone that the province Britain gave up in 1670 reached, if not to the Kennebec, at least as far as the Penobscot. Temple had surrendered Fort Pentagoet, and there was no denying that Fort Pentagoet guarded Penobscot Bay. Nevertheless, the British insisted that the border was the St. Croix River. The assertions of Britons, and Frenchmen too, about the limits of Acadia were never much constrained by fact.

The disputed area—Maine east of the Kennebec—had been given to the duke of York in 1664 as part of his New York. That was one thing in 1664, when Britain controlled Acadia. It was another in 1670, when Acadia belonged to France; to attest to the French view of where the boundary lay, Grandfontaine made his headquarters at Fort Pentagoet, right in the middle of the duke's claim.

His ploy did not impress Edmund Andros, the duke's governor of New York, who was sure of his territory and later built a fort at Pemaquid to prove it. Nor did it stop Massachusetts, which had already completed its annexation of southwestern Maine and was now pushing its authority into the settlements beyond the Kennebec. Each of the big British colonies encroached, and the French were too feeble to resist either one.

Indeed, the French were too feeble even to resist the captain and crew of a lone Dutch frigate whose bizarre invasion in 1674 made Acadia, for a little while, a presumed colony of Holland.

It was yet another of those improbable American consequences of a Dutch War. This one had been started in 1672 by Louis XIV, who was aiming for the Rhine and found Holland in his way. Because King Charles had taken a payoff, Britain took the side of France. The Dutch, hard pressed, opened their dikes to stop the French, then turned for leadership to their young Prince William III of Orange. In 1674, William bought off the British for cash and a second surrender of New York, which a Dutch fleet had recaptured early in the war. Four years later, he made peace with France, on terms similarly bearable, and Holland was saved. Portentously, in the peacemaking with Britain, William won the hand of Mary, oldest daughter of the duke of York and next behind her father in the line of succession.

Acadia became a footnote to the Third Dutch War after Captain

Jurriaen Aernoutsz, who had planned to engage Britons and French-men in the North Atlantic, anchored in New York Harbor in July 1674 and learned that his nation was at peace with Britain, though still at war with France. At the same time, he met a hustling trader named John Rhoades, who was familiar with the northeast coast and the instability of the French. Rhoades convinced him that he could conquer Acadia, and in August, with Rhoades sworn to allegiance and serving as his pilot, Aernoutsz sailed to Penobscot Bay and challenged Fort Pentagoet.[5]

Grandfontaine had been replaced the previous year by Jacques de Chambly, an experienced officer who should have been capable of defending his fort against a single warship. He had, however, only thirty soldiers, and the Dutch overpowered him. One of the French officers was sent to Frontenac with a demand for Chambly's ransom, and Aernoutsz buried bottles with messages proclaiming his con-quest. Then he sailed to the Saint John, where he captured a fort the French had built upriver and buried more bottles. He went nowhere near Port Royal, but he claimed all of Acadia for William of Orange, giving it a new name. Thenceforth it would be New Holland.

Frontenac was sure the Puritans were behind the whole affair, and in an angry letter he accused them of it. He was wrong. The plot was laid in New York, not Boston. The leaders of Massachusetts knew nothing about it. Still, a Dutch Acadia might not be so bad, particu-larly if no one interfered with New England's traders and fishermen, so when Aernoutsz sailed to Boston in September, his triumph was accepted for what it was—a legitimate act of war. Massachusetts merchants were pleased to buy the cannon he had captured at Fort Pentagoet and to negotiate the bills of exchange Frontenac sent to ransom Chambly. At the same time, they sent men to fish and trade, glad to be rid of the annoying French authorities, who had begun un-der Grandfontaine to sell fishing permits and talk about excluding foreigners altogether. An unhappy French trader complained the next year that "the English are . . . trading on our lands, fishing and set-tling along the coast from Cape Sable to Cape Breton. If I had the authority, I would make them pay what Colonel Temple used to col-lect when he owned this land, that is, fifty livres per boat or ketch."[6]

Aernoutsz believed that the authority was now in Dutch hands, and before he sailed home, he detailed two of his officers to go back with Rhoades and hold New Holland until someone in Amsterdam could organize a formal government. With ships and men hired in

Boston, they carried out their orders, and the first vessels they found became Dutch prizes. Unfortunately, however, the ships were from New England, and the Puritan attitude hardened. When the Dutch conquered a French province, it was an act of war. When they interfered with New Englanders trading and fishing, it was piracy. Governor John Leverett organized a fleet, and in a short battle in the Bay of Fundy—a one-day undeclared war between Massachusetts and Holland—the Dutch and their mercenaries were routed. Aernoutsz's officers and Rhoades were taken to Boston for trial.

They were ably defended. Their lawyer argued that Massachusetts had no business prosecuting the agents of a foreign sovereign for acts committed outside Massachusetts. If you have a problem, he told Leverett and the judges, take it up with the Prince of Orange. He compared Aernoutsz's campaign with Sedgwick's in 1654. If these defendants are pirates, he said, so were Sedgwick and his men, who did not even have the cloak of a declared war. That gave Leverett something to think about, and in the end the defendants got off. Puritan bloodlust was satisfied by sentences of hanging, which were never carried out.

The Dutch got around to taking official notice in 1676, when they named New Yorker Cornelis Steenwyck governor of the "Coasts and countries of Nova Scotia and Acadie."[7] But Steenwyck had no army or navy to go with his title, and Aernoutsz's conquest went for nothing. Few outside Amsterdam took it seriously, and no one profited except New Englanders, who were able for a few years to swarm the coasts unhampered. Acadia is not even mentioned in the Treaty of Nijmwegen, which in 1678 ended the war between France and Holland.[8]

Most Acadians never saw a Dutchman, and they would not have cared if they had. Their concerns were to live their lives and raise their children with as little interference as possible from the princes of Europe and the violent men they sent to do their bidding in America. And those were not unlike the concerns of the men and women who shared their land. The Indians' lot, though, was different. After a century and a half of exposure to European civilization, they were in deepening trouble. Their lives were changing. Their lands were being nibbled away. Their culture was disappearing.

Denys reported it.[9] When he first came to Acadia, the Indian way of life was already into its decline. By the time he wrote his book, disintegration was well along. Everyone had firearms. They made Indian warfare a damaging business, and they led hunters to overkill the game on which their families depended for food. European disease, too, had continued its deadly work. Bands were dying out, tribes thinning. And old customs were disappearing. Deaths, for example, were no longer followed by a material send-off, the deceased taking to another world the treasured possessions of family and friends. The missionaries accomplished that change, and perhaps it was an improvement. Surely the old tradition was wasteful. Still, it had meaning. With such changes came loss of the pride and morale fostered by ancestral ways.

Worst was abuse of the Europeans' alcohol. Denys tells us about it:

Since they have taken to drinking wine and brandy they are subject to fighting. Their quarrelling comes ordinarily from their condition; for, being drunk, they say they are all great chiefs, which engenders quarrels between them. At first it needed little wine or brandy to make them drunk.

But at present, and since they have frequented the fishing vessels, they drink in quite another fashion. They no longer have any regard for wine, and wish nothing but brandy. They do not call it drinking unless they become drunk, and do not think they have been drinking unless they fight and are hurt. However, when they set about drinking, their wives remove from their wigwams the guns, axes, the mounted swords (spears), the bows, the arrows, and (every weapon) even their knives. . . . After that they have a fine time, beating, injuring, and killing one another. . . .

If it is found that any one among them is hurt, he who will have done it asks his pardon, saying that he was drunk; and he is pardoned for that. But if some one has been killed, it is necessary that the murderer . . . should make to the widow some present. . . . And to make the peace complete, he must pay for another drinking bout. . . . To buy the brandy it was then necessary that he sell his gun, his blanket, or other thing in order to get it. This will cost them five to six skins; they will give this to the fishermen for a bottle or two of brandy. . . . If the brandy they have is not sufficient to make them drunk they will give everything they possess to obtain more.

"Thus the fishermen," he wrote, "are ruining them entirely."[10]

Ruined they might be, but there was still fight in the Indians of northeastern America, and pressure on their land brought them finally to resist. The battle for survival began in southern New England in 1675, when Pokanokets started the bloody war that has the name of their leader, King Philip. In King Philip's War, the Plymouth Colony and settlements up and down the Connecticut Valley were terrorized. A toll was taken of New England lives, but the Pokanokets lost. Their leader's head became a trophy for the New England militiamen who finally trapped and killed him.[11]

The Pokanoket rebellion had no direct effect in Acadia, except perhaps to prompt the Abenakis' own first war of resistance. The causes were land grabbing and the simple inability of New Englanders to understand Indians or treat them as people. Settlers had moved onto Abenaki land. Protesting Indians were met with outrage at their effrontery and demands that they give up their arms. Then a band of sailors playfully drowned a baby—trying, they said, to find out whether Indian children knew instinctively how to swim. The baby was the child of a sagamore, and the First Abenaki War was underway.[12]

It was fought on the frontier, where Indian raids met not very effective resistance from Massachusetts militiamen preoccupied with King Philip. When it was over, the Abenakis, unlike the Pokanokets, had survived. Indeed, in some ways they had won. The treaty they made at Casco Bay in 1678 required the settlers to pay for the land they took. The payment was not much—a peck of corn a year.[13] It was enough, though, to give the Indians a little of the recognition they were due as owners of the land, and a measure of the respect they were owed as human beings.

12 | BEFORE THE STORM

*Acadians Spread Out
As Tensions Mount*

1678–1688

BY 1678, FRANCE HAD REGAINED CONTROL. Chambly, the governor who had lost his colony to the Dutch, was enjoying a palmier assignment in the Caribbean, and when no replacement was forthcoming from Paris, Frontenac named his own. He was Michel Leneuf de La Vallière de Beaubassin, a Canadian well connected in Acadia. His first wife was a daughter of Nicholas Denys; his second was a niece.[1]

He was governor until 1684, during a time of modest burgeoning. The trickle of immigration, stopped by Sedgwick's conquest, had resumed with the restoration of French rule in 1670. To start things off, sixty men and women had been sent from the mother country. More came later, and there were a few from Canada. In addition, soldiers and *engagés* were encouraged to stay and settle when their service was over, and some did, wooing Acadian women away from home-grown suitors and bringing new names and bloodlines to a community already endangered by inbreeding.[2]

Most of the population increase, however, was from within, just as it always had been and always would be in Acadia. And the new settlements were founded not by outsiders but by Acadians themselves.

A pioneer spirit moved them, though never very far. They were careful to limit their migrations to places washed by the familiar tides of the Bay of Fundy, and they began at the Isthmus of Chignecto, which ties the Nova Scotia Peninsula to the mainland at the top of the bay. The trailblazer was Jacques Bourgeois, a venturesome surgeon and farmer who had come from France in 1642 and prospered at Port Royal, marrying one of the *Saint-Jehan* immigrants, Jeanne

Trahan, and siring ten children.[3] In 1672, he had seen a new opportunity and with his own and five other families established himself at Chignecto, where dikes and *aboiteaux* soon tamed the tides. Four years later, La Vallière became seigneur, and by 1686, a census could count 127 Acadians growing grain and tending livestock, reaping the bounty of the greatest ocean of tidal marshland in eastern North America.[4] The Trans Canada Highway between Sackville, New Brunswick, and Amherst, Nova Scotia, today runs atop the remnants of the village they called Beaubassin.

The other new settlements were on the Minas Basin, where two of Port Royal's leaders, Pierre Melanson and Pierre Terriot, moved in 1682.[5] The first farms were at Grand Pré, which means great meadow. Made famous by the expulsion of the Acadians and Henry Wadsworth Longfellow's *Evangeline,* it is now a national historic park a few miles from the town of Wolfville and the campus of Acadia University. A memorial church, gardens, and a notional statue of the heroine recall the tragedy.

From Grand Pré, Acadians spread up the nearby Avon River to a place they called Pisiquid, now Windsor, and then to Cobequid, now Truro, at the end of the Minas Basin. In 1689, Mathieu Martin, the first native-born Acadian, was made seigneur of Cobequid.[6] Young couples, the women just entering their childbearing years, came to find new farms, and the Minas communities boomed. By the turn of the century, they would be the center of Acadia's population.[7]

It was not just the ample marshland that lured Acadians to Chignecto and Minas. In those relatively obscure places, they were less likely to attract attention. They preferred shadows to the glare of official light on their trade with the New Englanders who sailed their sloops and ketches every year to the far nooks and crannies of the Bay of Fundy. They probably hoped, too, that isolation would spare them the curse of war. The wars that were coming to Acadia would, however, engulf them all.

Those wars pitted Britons and New Englanders against Frenchmen and Indians, and the French could not have fought them without the Indian alliance and the men who nurtured it. Foremost were the missionaries. They taught the religion that helped tie the Indians to France, and they served as friendly intermediaries with French officialdom, the source of arms and ammunition.[8] To New Englanders, they seemed to fill the woods with their preaching and proselytizing, and in many ways they were indeed the most effective of the French *capitains des sauvages.* But the best known, the most storied, was not a priest. He was a soldier—Jean-Vincent d'Abbadie de Saint-Castin.[9]

Second son of a nobleman of the old province of Béarn on the slopes of the Pyrenees, he had come to America as a teenager to seek a fortune blocked at home by the iron law of primogeniture. Serving at Fort Pentagoet in 1674, he was the officer who carried the news of Chambly's defeat, and Frontenac had sent him back to Penobscot Bay with orders to stay and win the Indians to France's side. In the same year that his brother died childless and he became, after all, the third baron Saint-Castin, young Jean-Vincent began a new life as leader and counselor of the Abenakis. The rivers and forests of Maine, it seemed, had more allure than a chateau and estate in Béarn.

Too, there was a woman. She was the daughter of an important sagamore named Madockawando, and his marriage may have earned Saint-Castin sagamore status. He did, in any event, acquire an influence far beyond what might have been expected of the ex-officer— ostensibly just a fur buyer—who in 1677 built a post near the ruin of Fort Pentagoet.[10] The town that now occupies the site of the old French fort has his name, anglicized to Castine.

His story is sung in epic poetry. Longfellow tells of letters home:

> Full of a young man's joy to be
> Abroad in the world, alone and free
> Full of adventures and wonderful scenes
> Of hunting the deer through forests vast
> In the royal grant of Pierre du Gast;
> Of nights in the tents of the Tarrantines;
> Of Madocawando the Indian chief,
> And his daughters, glorious as queens,
> And beautiful beyond belief;
> And soft are the tones of their native tongue,
> The words are not spoken, they are sung![11]

John Greenleaf Whittier paints an older Saint-Castin:

> . . . one whose bearded cheek,
> And white and wrinkled brow, bespeak
> A wanderer from the shores of France.
> A few long locks of scattering snow
> Beneath a battered morion flow,
> And from the rivets of the vest

Which girds in steel his ample breast,
   The slanted sunbeams glance.
In the harsh outlines of his face
Passion and sin have left their trace;
Yet, save worn brow and thin grey hair,
No signs of weary age are there.
   His step is firm, his eye is keen,
Nor years in broil and battle spent,
Nor toil, nor wounds, nor pain have bent
The lordly frame of old Castine.[12]

The baron made good copy, but there was more to him than the wilderness-wanderer, the nobleman-among-savages of the poets. He was a soldier, carrying out Frontenac's orders. At the same time, he was a hardheaded trader, busily lining his purse. The roles were not inconsistent in colonial America, and it was not just Madocka-wando's beautiful daughter and a chance to serve his king that kept Saint-Castin in Acadia. A contemporary tells us that he made a fortune, "two or three hundred thousand Crowns, which he has now in his Pocket in good dry Gold."[13]

His business partners were from Boston, chief among them a remarkable merchant named John Nelson, the nephew and heir of Sir Thomas Temple.[14] Nelson's ventures were well known, and under both French and British law, they were illegal, but no one ever stopped him. He even kept a warehouse at Port Royal. To him, Acadia was a personal fief, "my property."[15]

Nelson was no Puritan. He was described as "an Episcopalian in principle, and of a gay, free temper."[16] And perhaps that was why he got along so well with the French. He knew them better than anyone else in Boston, and despite his aberrant personality, he was chosen in 1682 as Massachusetts's ambassador to put commercial relations on a basis more respectable than smuggling and poaching.[17]

Trade was not really a problem. Although they would not admit it, the French needed New England's goods and they would go on tolerating its traders. Indeed, La Vallière was quietly told to allow their coming and going, that Acadia could not survive without it.[18] New Englanders were also interested in Acadia's coal deposits, and in that case too, French officials could protest, but they did not really care. There was not much use for Acadian coal locally, and few captains would risk its catching fire on the long voyage to Europe. The French were, however, increasingly upset about their failure to share the wealth of the ocean. The fishery dispute reached a crescendo in the 1680s, beginning a conflict that has occupied diplomats ever since. Nations still squabble over the fish of the Atlantic banks.

Newfoundland's Grand Bank is bigger, but for New England's seventeenth-century fishermen, the Acadian banks were where money could be made quickly and conveniently. Codfish ran there ten months of the year, and the ice-free coves and harbors of the Maine and Nova Scotia coasts are close by Boston, Salem, Marblehead, and Gloucester. Year after year, men of those and other ports made the short voyage and dried their catches on French territory, treating Acadia as an extension of New England. Both Frontenac and La Vallière protested, and although the Puritans had no thought of making major changes, they wanted to make a conciliatory response.

They were nearing the climax of a bitter dispute with the king and his Lords of Trade, a dispute that threatened their cherished independence. The lords were a committee of the Privy Council created in 1675 to oversee the colonies. They had an agent in Boston, one Edward Randolph, whose job was to snoop. Trade with French Acadia was one of the items Randolph ferreted out to discomfort king and lords. Another was the Puritans' attitude. In their view, the Navigation Acts applied in Massachusetts only insofar as they, the Puritans, might consent to them. Perturbed by their independence and dismayed at their arrogance, King Charles was threatening to send his attorney general to court to revoke their charter. In 1682, they did not need a quarrel in their own front yard.

They sent Nelson to Quebec to quiet things down, and he came back with a compromise. The French would permit use of Acadian beaches by fee-paying licensees, and they would put licensing in Boston hands. For its part, Massachusetts would condemn violations of French law, although it would do nothing that would actually inconvenience the traders. In October 1682, the General Court announced its displeasure, in terms less than draconian:

> This Court, being informed by the Right Honorable the Earle of Fronteneac, governor of Canada, and Mounseier De la Valier, governor of Accadie, that severall of the inhabitants of this colony have committed irregularities in their trading, making of fish, and fetching of coales within the territories belonging to the French . . . it is hereby declared, that this

Court doth not allow and approove of any such irregularities, and that all persons so offending are liable to the poenalties and forfeitures provided against them by the lawes of those governments where such offences shall be comitted.[19]

At about the same time, La Vallière made Nelson his agent for the sale of licenses.[20]

It was an artful deal, and it might have taken the pressure off, except that La Vallière's home government had already decided on a more straightforward remedy. In Paris, a new company was formed and given the task of ensuring that Frenchmen, not New Englanders, harvested the offshore treasure.[21] In 1683, its men built a base at Chedabucto Bay, and right away they found themselves competing with New Englanders licensed by Nelson on La Vallière's authority. Ships were seized, angry protests flew back and forth, and Nelson's compromise was shattered.

La Vallière was in trouble anyway. His patron, Frontenac, had stepped on too many Canadian toes and had been recalled, and without Frontenac's backing, La Vallière was vulnerable. He was replaced by one François-Marie Perrot, who took office in 1685 and demonstrated that if the fortunes of France were to be saved, he was not the man to do it.[22] Possessed of vast influence but little ethic, he had been governor of Montreal under Frontenac and had been demoted for illegal trading. His connections brought him Acadia in consolation, and once in office, he went his accustomed way. New Englanders were logical business partners, so Perrot did business with New Englanders and France remained shut out of its fishery.

In 1686, another try was made for a resolution—this time by diplomats in London. With the death of King Charles II the previous year, and the accession of the duke of York as King James II, Britain and France had tilted very near each other. The new king openly avowed the faith of his mother, and he was even more eager than his brother had been to appease Louis XIV. He knew he might need French help to restrain his restive subjects, who, for the first time since the sixteenth century and "Bloody" Mary I, confronted a Catholic sovereign.

But hard issues divided the great powers, and many of them involved America. The Treaty of Whitehall was limited to those American questions. Its purpose was to carve the New World off, to keep disputes peculiar to it from causing war in Europe, and, conversely, to provide for neutrality in America, "if ever any rupture shall occur in Europe between the said crowns (which God forbid)."[23] It expressed a theory then current in international law and diplomacy, the Doctrine of Two Spheres, which held that hostile acts on one side of the ocean need not commit nations to war on the other.[24]

The overlapping territories claimed by Britain and France were too much for the diplomats at Whitehall. They left the resolution of that problem to commissioners. They did, however, address New England's usurpation of Acadia's fishery, agreeing that the French should have exclusive rights to the beaches and leaving the deep-sea fish to the fleets of both countries. That was the right solution, recognizing both the sovereignty of France in Acadia and the freedom of the seas off its shores. If commissioners could have compromised the border disputes, and if New England's fishermen could have been persuaded or compelled to stay where they belonged, the Treaty of Whitehall might have worked. War, however, came too soon.

13 | KING WILLIAM'S WAR

Puritans Battle Their Demons

1688–1697

IN EUROPE, IT WAS THE War of the League of Augsburg, named for an alliance built by William of Orange to check the surging ambitions of Louis XIV.

As the seventeenth century neared its end, *le grand monarque* was resplendent in his new palace at Versailles and plotting hegemony. With Spain in decline and a Francophile on Britain's throne, little except William stood in the way, and when Louis revoked Henry IV's Edict of Nantes and France resumed its official persecution of Protestants, he had his chance. Europe's Protestant states allied themselves with Holland. They were joined by Spain, Austria, and Bavaria, and the League of Augsburg was born.

It was not, however, enough. William needed Britain, and in 1689 he got her.

He did it by becoming her king, and he had the support of almost everyone who mattered. Britain's Glorious Revolution was no foreign conquest. The ruling classes had no use for James II, but neither were they in a mood for a reprise of the experiment of 1649–60. The Civil War had loosed dangerous thoughts of egalitarianism; the infrastructure of rank and wealth had been in danger of crumbling with the monarchy. The Prince of Orange was the answer, a king to the bone, and his wife Mary was reassuringly a Stuart, possessed of the divine right. The aristocracy called, William heard, and he landed in Devon in November 1688. James's commanders went over to his side and the king fled to France. Early the next year, Parliament offered the crown to Mary and a regency to William. When William rejected the regency, Parliament thought again, and in February 1689, William and Mary were proclaimed king and queen.

James tried a comeback, and there was bloody fighting in Scotland and Ireland until, on July 1, 1690, William won his great victory at Ireland's River Boyne. He had in the meantime brought Britain into his alliance, and the duel of the superpowers began. It would not finally end until the summer day 125 years later when Wellington's veterans met Napoleon's Old Guard at Waterloo.

In America, the War of the League of Augsburg bore King William's name. It gave New Englanders a chance to retake Acadia, and perhaps at the same time to exorcise their French and Catholic demons. For starters, their frontier was aflame. Surely the French were to blame.

There may indeed have been a French hand in the Indian raids that began in 1688, a year before the start of the mother countries' war. Early that year, men from Massachusetts had plundered Saint-Castin's post on Penobscot Bay, goading the Abenakis and their mentor to revenge. But that was not the real cause of the Second Abenaki War. All over the frontier, New Englanders were trampling Indian rights—interfering with river fisheries, grazing cattle in Indian fields, taking land without paying even the pittance agreed in the Treaty of Casco Bay. The last straw came when Indians who had killed a few trespassing cattle were rounded up and carried off to prison in Boston.[1]

The Puritans did not, of course, understand that their troubles were self-induced. They blamed the French missionaries, and in their worst nightmares there lurked something even deeper and darker—a plot hatched by their own royal governor, the first they ever had.

King Charles had made good his threat. In 1684, the Court of Chancery had declared the old charter vacated, and Massachusetts was no longer the effectively independent commonwealth John Winthrop and his colleagues had founded a half century earlier. In 1686, the former governor of New York, now Sir Edmund Andros, was sent to rule it as part of something altogether different, the Dominion of New England, a short-lived potpourri that was to include not only Massachusetts, Plymouth, Connecticut, Rhode Island, and New Hampshire, but also New York and New Jersey. It was a concept way ahead of its time. The person of the governor, the idea of royal government, and the prospect of being part of a supercolony had absolutely no appeal in Boston.

Indeed, the Puritans detested Andros, and in their fantasies he took the lead in a grotesque conspiracy to deliver them to the "great

Scarlet Whore." The Second Abenaki War was a device to exhaust the militia, a part of the scheme. A tract published in April 1689 told it all:

We are again Briar'd in the Perplexities of another *Indian War;* how, or why, is a mystery too deep for us to unfold. And tho' 'tis judged that our *Indian* Enemies are not above 100. in number, yet an army of *One thousand* English hath been raised for the Conquering of them; which army of our poor Friends and Brethren now under *Popish Commanders* (for in the Army as well as in the Council, Papists are in Commission) has been under such a conduct, that not one *Indian* hath been kill'd, but more English are supposed to have died through sickness and hardship, than we have adversaries there alive; and the whole War hath been so managed, that we cannot but suspect in it a branch of the Plot *to bring us low;* which we leave to be further enquir'd into in due time.[2]

And, absurd as it was, it was believed. Fear of the Catholic plot prompted rebellions that swept not only Massachusetts but also New York and Maryland in the spring and summer of 1689, when Britain's Glorious Revolution had its American twin.

Andros had spent the winter in Maine building frontier forts and trying to quiet the Abenakis. Word of Prince William's landing brought Andros back to Boston and the people into the streets. On April 28, citizens usurped the city. The Acadian trader John Nelson was at the head of the group that forced Andros's surrender.[3] With his council, he was sent to London to answer charges, and the temporary Council of Safety, representing the Puritan elite, took over. Its members wanted most of all to restore the old commonwealth, but first they had to fight King William's War.

It began badly for them, and it never much improved. In the summer of 1689, Abenakis sacked Dover, New Hampshire. Then they leveled the fort Andros had built at Pemaquid. Worse, at the beginning of 1690, Frontenac, reappointed to his post in Quebec, loosed a blitzkrieg that devastated Schenectady in New York, Salmon Falls in New Hampshire, and Falmouth, modern Portland, on Casco Bay. No one had supposed that the French and Indians could strike so far and with such terrible effect. Something had to be done.

Perhaps an invasion of Acadia would turn the trick. In fact, the Puritans had already decided to try it. News of the carnage at Salmon Falls had just arrived when, on May 8, a fleet with seven hundred men set out for Port Royal.[4] Their commander was one of Boston's most popular figures, a bootstrap Brahmin named Sir William Phips.

In a day when inherited wealth and class distinction still had meaning, Phips was a marvel, a totally self-made man.[5] At eighteen, he had left a hardscrabble farm for the metropolis, where he married and promised his wife that someday he would own a brick house. In fact, he did much better, sailing to the Caribbean and dredging up a fortune from a Spanish wreck and returning with wealth, knighthood, and everyone's admiration and acclaim. His popular esteem was such that he was a natural choice to command the men who were sent to conquer Acadia—and that, Phips's first campaign, was a pushover.

Acadia did not amount to much in 1690. Phips brought nearly as many soldiers as there were men, women, and children in the whole French colony. A census two years earlier had counted 175 men, 161 women, 290 boys, 220 girls, 4 priests, 2 monks, a nun, and 28 soldiers —in all, 881 people.[6] And the only fortified place, Port Royal, was nothing to give an invader pause. "No more than a little paultry town," one visitor called it.[7] A British officer, Captain Francis Nicholson, who had been sent by Andros to scout it out in 1687, reported that the Acadian capital "stands upon a Small neck of Land about a mile round, there is the ruine of an old Earthen Fortification (formerly distroyed by the English)[;] there is about 40 Soldiers whereof tenn were old ones. . . . It being Sunday when I was there I observed what Number of Inhabitants they had, and I do not think there were 80 familyes belonging to the place. On the Neck there is about 15 houses and all very mean ones, as are those both above the River and below."[8]

At the water's edge was the fort d'Aulnay had built a half century earlier. Nicholson noted its rotting timbers and overgrown earthworks. Under a new governor, Louis-Alexandre des Friches de Meneval, rebuilding had begun, but emplacements were yet to be built for the cannon, and Meneval had only eighty-six soldiers to man his weedy ramparts.[9] Louis XIV had built the finest army Europe had ever seen. He had spared very little of it to defend Acadia.

The fleet sailed into the Annapolis Basin late in the afternoon on May 19. Phips sent ashore a demand for surrender, and Meneval, contemplating his men, his fort, and his chances, found the logic of survival more compelling than *la gloire*. He handed over his sword, then watched an orgy of pillage and desecration. Despite promises that private property and the church would be respected, Phips's men "cut down the cross, rifled the Church, Pu'lld down the High-Altar, breaking their Images: and brought our Plunder . . . into Mr. *Nelson's* storehouse."[10] John Nelson still did business at Port Royal. In peace and war, the wheels of commerce turn.

Phips had the inhabitants choose a council to govern in place of Meneval, and from the roster we can glean Port Royal's upper crust. One member was the bibulous seigneur Belle-Isle, a logical if ineffectual choice. An officer of the garrison called Chevalier was made president. Another member was Mathieu de Goutin, a wily *fonctionnaire* who had taken office two years earlier and would serve twenty more years as Acadia's chief clerk and judge. The others were settlers named Pierre du Breuil, René Landry, and Daniel Le Blanc.

Phips gave the council a heavy charge. The members were to "prevent all prophaneness, Sabbath-breaking, Cursing, Swearing, Drunkenness, or Thieving, and all other Wickedness." He promised that the people might continue to practice their religion, adding the pious hope that "you will all ere long learn better than hitherto you have been Taught."[11] But even if they remained Catholics, he expected everyone to pledge loyalty to the king and queen. He rounded up as many men as he could find at Port Royal, sent for more from the Minas settlements, and administered an oath of allegiance, the first of many that would be proffered in the years to come. The refusal of a later generation would cost the Acadians their homeland, but in 1690, according to Phips's journal, they swore unqualifiedly, amid "great Acclamations and Rejoicings," to "bear true Faith and Allegiance to Their most Excellent Majesties *William and Mary* of *England, Scotland, France and Ireland* King and Queen: *so help you God in our Lord, Jesus Christ!*"[12]

The acclamations and rejoicings are doubtful, given the treatment Phips and his men had accorded their church and property. Still, some Acadians took the oath that their children and grandchildren would refuse unless they were promised that they would never have to bear arms against France. Apparently no one thought of that consequence of allegiance to the British crown. They swore as Phips asked because it seemed a way to be rid of him and his men, and it worked. They went away.

In Boston, Phips was acclaimed a military genius. Enthusiasm was such that the conqueror of Acadia was sent off again that summer with a much larger army, this time to take Quebec and end the war at a stroke.

Quebec, however, was no Port Royal, and Frontenac was too skillful. Phips's fleet managed the St. Lawrence, but his siege was a disaster, and after a few days of floundering about and trying to fight in a cold rain under the guns of the fortress of Quebec, he and his men limped home. Unlike the campaign in Acadia, there was no plunder to cover costs; to pay them, Massachusetts had to issue paper money, the first ever in the colonies. The badly burned Puritans would mount no more invasions until the war was nearly over.

Nor would they do much to take advantage of Phips's triumph at Port Royal. The fiasco in Quebec, along with aggressive French and Indian campaigning on the frontier, allowed France to preserve a semblance of sovereignty.

The man who accomplished this was one of Meneval's officers, Joseph Robineau de Villebon. In France when Port Royal fell, he had returned to find Phips just gone, Meneval a prisoner, and himself the resident senior officer. It was luck that put this capable captain in a critical place at a critical time, and he was made governor. From a fort far up the Saint John, where it meets the Nashwaak River across from what is now downtown Fredericton, he directed Frenchmen and Indians in a brilliant campaign of hit-and-run attacks that kept New Englanders on edge and Acadia in French hands all through King William's War.

Preoccupied with war, Villebon did little governing. He left whole the arrangement Phips had made at Port Royal, and he made it clear in his reports home that although Chevalier as council president might salute British colors, he was still a French officer, acting with his commander's approval. "Without these compromises," he wrote, "it would be impossible to exist in this country."[13]

As it turned out, Chevalier did not have to salute any colors except his own. The Puritans abandoned the authority they had grabbed by conquest, even though it was confirmed the next year by their king and queen. They were distressed that their new charter did not restore self-government, but they were greatly pleased to find that it fulfilled long-held territorial ambitions, enlarging their borders to include the Plymouth Colony to the south, and to the northeast, "all lands and hereditaments lying and being in the country and territory commonly called Accadia or Nova Scotia, and all those lands and hereditaments lying and extending between the said country or territory of Nova Scotia and [the Kennebec]."[14] That was what they had wanted since 1643 and Winthrop's misguided alliance with La Tour, what they had requested and been denied after Robert Sedgwick conquered Acadia for them in 1654, and what they had sent Phips to achieve in 1690. They had already formalized their annexation of Maine below the Kennebec by buying it from the heirs of Sir Ferdinando Gorges. Except for the few miles of coast that belonged to New Hampshire, the Bay Colony now spread from Cape Cod to the St. Lawrence.

Yet all they did was choose a governor, and he never served. He was a landholder from Maine named Edward Tyng, who sailed to Port Royal in the fall of 1691 with the ubiquitous John Nelson and did not like what he found. When the people assured him that the Indians would attack him, and insisted they would stand by and watch, he decided that Port Royal was not for him. Like Temple, he would govern from the safety of Boston. His plans, however, went far awry when he and Nelson, on their way home, were captured by French sailors. Nelson was sent to internment in Quebec. Tyng wound up in a prison in France, where he languished and died.[15]

That ended the only Puritan attempt to govern Acadia. Phips, who had become the new royal governor of Massachusetts, sent a ship the next summer, but the Acadians' attitude was the same. They would give the New Englanders no comfort at all.[16] So much for fidelity to King William and Queen Mary! And Phips made no effort to bring them to heel. He had other problems.

Villebon's campaign had begun early that year, when an Abenaki band destroyed the village of York in Maine. Then a bigger attack—this one including French soldiers, Micmac and Maliseet warriors, and Abenakis from the Penobscot—was launched in Wells. A desperate defense saved the day, but a single victory would not win the war, and the frontier became unlivable. Garrisoned towns like Wells might survive; the isolated farmer could not. His life and the lives of his wife and children were at risk every day he spent trying to scratch a living from the rocky soil.

To confound the raiders, Phips ordered the fort at Pemaquid rebuilt, and when a first attack on it failed, the Abenakis thought the tide might be shifting. In the summer of 1693, thirteen of their sagamores signed a treaty of peace, but Abenaki and Puritan were not made for each other, and by the next year, the Indians were back in the French camp. In July 1694, one of Villebon's officers led them in a devastating attack on Durham, New Hampshire. He reported 104 settlers killed, 27 prisoners taken, and 60 houses burned.[17] The tide had turned back toward France, and it reached its flood in the summer of 1696, when French soldiers and Abenaki and Micmac warriors returned to Pemaquid and forced its garrison into an ignominious surrender.

Massachusetts launched a campaign of its own that same summer, its first since Phips's invasion of Canada in 1691. The commander was Colonel Benjamin Church, a famous Indian-fighter, the leader of the militiamen who had killed King Philip in 1676. This time, there would be no tempting fate below the cliffs of Quebec. The target was a sure thing—the undefended Acadian settlement at Beaubassin, where Church and his men devoted themselves to burning buildings and mutilating livestock.[18] The inhabitants, Church reported, "were much troubled to see their Cattel, Sheep, Hogs and Dogs lying dead about their houses, chop'd and hacke'd with Hatches."[19]

Heading home, Church stopped at the Saint John and pondered an attack on Villebon's stronghold. He rejected the idea—wisely, as things turned out—but as he was sailing away, he was stopped by a ship from Boston with positive orders to root the French commander out of his lair, and he turned back to try.[20]

As a matter of strategy, it made sense, certainly more sense than destroying homes and animals at Beaubassin. As a matter of tactics, however, the impromptu attack was doomed. Secure in his fort and well supplied with intelligence, Villebon knew the New Englanders were coming, and when they reached the Nashwaak, he greeted them with a fusillade of musket and cannon fire. Forced to douse their fires, they could not even cook their rations, let alone mount a siege, and they gave up after a day and a night and made their way downriver.[21]

It was Phips's failure all over again, albeit on a lesser scale, and it lent more discouragement to the ambitions of the Puritans—ambitions dampened nearly to extinction anyway by the loss of Pemaquid. Few were sorry to learn the next year that the war in Europe had ground to an inconclusive halt, and that Britain and France were at peace.

14 | RESPITE

A Lifestyle Blooms

1697–1702

BY THE TREATY OF RYSWICK in September 1697, Louis XIV regained the "Countries, Islands, Forts, and Colonies" that were French before the war.[1] Thus Acadia was restored to France, although it had never really belonged to Britain. The reins of government, such as they were, had been held all through the war by Joseph Robineau de Villebon at his fort on the Saint John.

Arguments over fish, trade, and borders resumed almost immediately. In October 1698, Villebon sent a letter to Boston complaining, "that several of your fishermen are off our coast and that you also permit trade between your people and the French settlements. You must expect . . . that I shall arrest all English found fishing or trading." He added that he was "expressly ordered by His Majesty to maintain the boundary of New England from the source of the Kennebec to its mouth, leaving the river itself free to both nations."[2]

He was within his rights, at least as far as trade and inshore fishing were concerned, but New Englanders were not going to abandon their business interests or tell their fishermen to forgo the Acadian coves and beaches, nor would they accept a border at the Kennebec. Acadia might have been handed back to France, but Acadia had never reached so far. The General Court sent King William a copy of Villebon's letter with a protest that the French governor was threatening "the ancient and hitherto uncontroverted limits and extent of this Your Majesty's Dominion and the undoubted right and privilege of Your Majesty's subjects to fish in those Seas, as they have been used time out of mind." It was suggested that the king "give speedy Check unto the bold Insolencies of the French!"[3]

Nothing had changed. Acadia belonged to France. Massachusetts claimed a big piece of it and meant to dominate all of it. French protests were "bold Insolencies." And as always, Acadians were uninvolved and uninterested. Rights of outsiders to trade, rights to fish, quarrels over borders: None of those things meant much to them. They wanted only to be let alone to enjoy the uncommonly agreeable lifestyle they had built from the bounty of the marshes.[4]

Their secret was simple: They did not work as hard as other people. Their land must have seemed a gift from a particularly beneficent God, a reward for upholding true religion in the wilderness. After diking and draining, the marshes grazed cattle and sheep and produced plentiful crops, seemingly unaided by human hands. Fruit trees blossomed and bore. The Annapolis Valley is still famous for its orchards. Pigs and chickens cluttered every farmyard, and fish begged to be caught. Acadians used weirs—simple devices made of branches—to trap the fish as the tide went out. Not much labor is involved in catching fish in a weir.

Their relaxed ways both vexed and intrigued the men who tried to govern them. They did not find in Acadia groveling peasants like those they were used to ordering around at home. One of the king's clerks complained that young Acadians "do nothing but hunt or negotiate with the natives." Their fathers, he said, refused to farm the uplands because they would not "undertake new labors."[5] Villebon reported that the people "work only when it is absolutely necessary for the maintenance of their families."[6] Once, because of Acadian indolence, he proposed using New England crews in the offshore fishery. "This," he said, "the settlers will not do because they are not sufficiently industrious, and because the work is arduous."[7] Another governor, resigned to his fate, described the Acadians as "really the most happy inhabitants of the earth."[8]

A literary Parisian named Dièreville, who spent a year in Port Royal at the turn of the eighteenth century and wrote a book of prose and poetry about it, described a people who "love their ease," "only work that they may live," and "take things as they come." In verse he regaled his readers with tales of Arcadian delight:

> Yet ever is the Habitant content
> With his abode; he only for
> His living works, and no one speaks
> To him of Taxes or of Tithes, nor are
> There any payments to be made at all.

Each one in peace beneath a rustic roof,
Empties his Bread-box and his Cask;
And, in the Winter, keeps himself quite warm
Without a farthing spent on Wood; where else
Could such advantages be found?

He was impressed, too, by the Acadians' fruitfulness, and he saw a connection between it and their distaste for hard work:

Men cause themselves no great fatigue
By labor in this Land; and as they have
No other intrigues, they beget
Abundant offspring by their Wives.

When young Acadians marry, he said,

. . . they are free
To populate the World; which is,
Moreover, that which they do best.

In every family there were five or six children, sometimes more. He found "the swarming of Brats . . . a sight to behold."[9]

Surely Dièreville overstated. A modern student of Acadian life and culture blames "the blinkered vision of his life as a privileged and cultured bachelor" that kept him from "understanding . . . the lives of those who worked the land and drew food from the seas and the forests."[10] Still, there must have been a bit of truth in the unvarying reports of officials and visitors alike. If not the place of indolence, ease, and bucolic bliss that Dièreville and others described, neither was Acadia a place of deprivation and suffering. Acadian numbers attest to that. By the turn of the century, the population had grown to nearly fifteen hundred.[11] Immigration had brought some, but for the most part, the new Acadians were homebred, the fruit of early marriage, ample food, a healthy climate, and the way of life Dièreville found so conducive to fertility.

A few made their livings fishing and trading at isolated little posts scattered along the Atlantic, Fundy, and gulf shores. Most of them, however, were at or near Port Royal, the three Minas settlements, and Beaubassin. There was also an enclave near Cape Sable, which is notable not because it was a population center but because in all Acadia it was the only true seigneurie. Its lord was Philippe Mius d'Entrement, a Norman who had served La Tour in the early 1650s and been rewarded by a grant at Pubnico Harbor, where he built and bossed a farming and fishing community and sired a dynasty with ties to nearly all the Acadian elite.[12] A daughter married Pierre Melanson of Grand Pré; two sons married daughters of Charles La Tour and Jeanne Motin; a grandson married a daughter of Saint-Castin. Descendants of Mius d'Entrement can still be found at Pubnico.

The other Acadians got along without a functioning seigneur. Indeed, they did without much government at all. They were a glaring exception among the men and women of their time, most of whom were tyrannized by mighty feudal lords, corrupt bureaucrats, and voracious tax collectors. There were good things to match the bad in France's failure to become the mother country for Acadia that she was for Canada. Like everyone who was French, Acadians were subjects of a powerful and despotic king, but Acadians were few and far off, and as the years went by, they gained a de facto independence. When Villebon died and a new governor, Jacques-François de Brouillan, arrived in 1701, he lodged the capital once again at Port Royal, where he no doubt expected to find properly submissive peasants, ready to pay his taxes and do his bidding. He found instead "true republicans, not acknowledging royal or judicial authority."[13]

To the people, the long-lasting Mathieu de Goutin was probably more important than their governors. Resolution of disputes is a governmental function that few societies can do without, and for twenty-two years de Goutin was their chief clerk and judge. His decisions could be overruled in Quebec, but Quebec was far away, and de Goutin's judgment was usually final. Too, he had married Jeanne Thibodeau, daughter of an unusually prolific Acadian family, and in one way or another, he was probably related to a significant number of the litigants who appeared before him.[14] Who, after all, would quarrel with Uncle Mathieu?

There were less formal systems of justice as well. During Villebon's time, the Minas and Chignecto settlers elected panels to settle arguments over farm boundaries, stray cows, and the like.[15] And parish priests served as arbiters, often with the last word on any subject. Indeed they could, if they chose, brandish the ultimate sanction. It was a brave man who would chance having the Sacrament withheld.

Acadians lived simply, but for their time they lived well. Their diet was more than adequate. Pork was a favorite, usually cooked with cabbage and turnips to make soup or stew. There was ample grain for breadmaking. Fruit, vegetables, and milk were abundant. And there were even a few luxuries. Maple sugar was one; another was a beer brewed from fir and spruce branches boiled with molasses. One visitor found it "very appetizing and refreshing and a protection against scurvy."[16] Dièreville, who eased the rigors of his stay by bringing along a good Bordeaux, sampled the local product anyway and pronounced it "not unpleasant."[17]

Spinning, weaving, sewing, cobbling, and tanning furnished life's accoutrements. According to Dièreville:

> There's nothing which they cannot do;
> And by a hundred different needs inspired,
> They make the things they lack; their wool
> Is fashioned into Clothing, Caps, and Socks,
> They are no way distinguished by new styles,
> And still wear hooded Capes; their Shoes
> Of Elk and Seal skin are flat-soled
> And made for comfort. From their flax
> Linen is also woven, and thus by
> Their industry, their nakedness is veiled.[18]

There were, though, things the Acadians needed and wanted and could not produce for themselves, including firearms, fancy textiles, and the more sophisticated tools and farm implements. Some also might have wanted to supplement their homebrew with harder or finer stuff. Such things were supposed to come from France. Instead, they came from New England. Dièreville complained that the French "do not understand Trade. . . . We know better than [other nations] how to take Towns, as all Europe bears witness, but we do not understand so well the settlement of a Country."[19] Another observer put it in terms of simplest economics. "The *French*," he said, "they will prize their Goods too high, though they are not so good as those of the *English* . . . yet the *English* sell their Commodities cheaper."[20]

And the men in charge always winked. Once, while King William's War raged, Villebon made a point of interrupting a visit to the settlers at Beaubassin, "that I might not be a witness to their trading."[21] As he himself said, "Without these compromises[,] it would be impossible to exist in this country."[22]

15 | QUEEN ANNE'S WAR

*New Englanders Squabble
And the French Survive*

1702–1707

THE WAR OF THE SPANISH SUCCESSION, Queen Anne's War in America, was a watershed. It and the Peace of Utrecht, which ended the fighting in 1713, mark the beginning of France's decline and Britain's rise to the pinnacle of world power.

The war was fought to decide which of Europe's dynasties would have the throne of Spain on the death of unhappy, unhealthy, childless King Charles II, Carlos the Sufferer, the last of the Spanish Hapsburgs. One contender was the French House of Bourbon. Another was the Austrian branch of the Hapsburg family, headed by Leopold I, the Holy Roman Emperor. Louis XIV proposed his second grandson, Philip of Anjou. Leopold's candidate was his son, Archduke Charles. But neither was acceptable to the nations of Europe. The emperor already ruled Austria and Hungary and had nominal sovereignty over the states of Germany. France, driven by the Sun King, was an expansionist threat to everyone. And Spain, though in decline and nearly bankrupt, still held an empire unequaled in history, reaching from the Philippines in Asia to Central and South America, Florida, Mexico, Naples, Sicily, and Belgium. No one wanted to risk Spain's affiliation with France or the Holy Roman Empire, and treaties providing for her partition had been made in anticipation of Charles's death. The sickly king, however, as the end neared, found a strength he had never known in a life of futility and pain. He would not give up the unity of his empire, and by a will made a month before he died in 1700, he named Philip of Anjou successor to his throne and all his lands.

Thus, Spain was in Louis's pocket, but he pushed his luck too far and too fast. His troops marched into Spanish Belgium, and he grabbed the lucrative *asiento,* the contract to supply slaves to Spanish America. Britain's Parliament, reluctant to fund an expensive war so soon after the last one, was swayed by the double coup, and its members came all the way around when the exiled James II died and Louis noisily proclaimed James's son James Edward legitimate king of Britain. Given all that, it seemed that the Austrian archduke might not be such a bad Spanish king after all, and in May 1702, two months after the death of King William, Britain joined Holland and the emperor in a long and bloody war to put him on the throne. Queen Mary's sister Anne had the task of seeing it to a conclusion.

New England's leader in the war was Joseph Dudley, named royal governor of Massachusetts and New Hampshire in 1702.[1] He was native born, a child of the late years of the sturdy old Puritan Thomas Dudley, and he should have been a favorite of the Establishment. Unfortunately, he was not.

He was a more modern man than his father, too modern for the men who had made Massachusetts's Glorious Revolution. Their disaffection had begun during their disputes with Edward Randolph and the Lords of Trade, when Dudley's was a voice of moderation and compromise. The Puritan oligarchs, sure that their own opinions reflected the word of God, had no time for moderation and compromise, and when Dudley took office in the dominion government of Sir Edmund Andros, they knew he had turned his coat. They thought they were rid of Dudley after the heady days of April 1689, when they bundled him off to London with Andros to answer charges of misgovernment, but the charges got the attention they deserved, and the victims of the Massachusetts rebellion were freed to go about their business.

Dudley's brought him to New York, where as chief justice he presided at the trial and execution of the leaders of that colony's own Glorious Revolution. Then he went off again to Britain to lobby for governorship of the people who had thrown him out. It took a while, but twelve years after his fall, the Puritans' nemesis was back in town.

He took office just as Queen Anne's War was getting underway. Sensibly, he tried first of all to placate the Abenakis, meeting their sagamores at Pemaquid in the fall of 1702 and again at Casco Bay the next summer. They exchanged gifts and pledged everlasting friendship, but the peace Dudley concluded had even less life than the one

Phips had negotiated ten years earlier. The Indians' fear and loathing of Britons was too strong, and on a cold February morning in 1704, at Deerfield in the Connecticut Valley, they showed whose side they were on. Homes and barns were burned, some 50 settlers were killed, and 111 men, women, and children were marched off through the snow to Canada.[2]

All New England cried out for vengeance, and it was had that summer on the Acadians—who, of course, had nothing at all to do with the Deerfield raid. Dudley gathered 550 militiamen and sent them to the Bay of Fundy. Their commander, just as in 1696, was the celebrated Colonel Benjamin Church, now grown so old and fat that when tracking Indians in the woods, he kept a brawny sergeant at his side to boost him over fallen trees.[3]

His instructions suggest the scorched-earth policies of later wars. He was to "use all possible methods for the burning and destroying of the Enemies Housing, and breaking the dams of their Corn grounds . . . and make what other spoils you can upon them."[4] Church and his men did just that. At the Minas Basin, they burned crops, houses, and barns, and to the more lasting damage of the settlers, they broke the dikes. They did the same at Beaubassin, but on Dudley's orders they spared Port Royal.[5]

That decision, when it became known, brought howls of protest. Dudley justified it by explaining that the question of an attack on the French capital was before the queen and her advisers—implying that a force would come from Britain the next year. His enemies claimed that the real reason was his tie to the Acadian trade. The Puritan preacher Cotton Mather led the charge. "The story," he wrote, "grows now too black a story for me to meddle with.—The expedition baffled—The fort never so much as demanded—An eternal grave stone laid on our buried captives—A nest of hornets provoked to fly out upon us—A shame cast upon us that will never be forgotten."[6]

Mather and his friends believed that Dudley wanted Port Royal taken only if it was intact. Scorched earth and broken dikes would do for the Minas Basin and Chignecto—not Port Royal, where the governor had commercial interests. But was it true? Was Dudley really guilty of arranging Queen Anne's War to line his own pocket?

Probably not. If there were grounds to expect an expeditionary force from Britain, why risk New England lives in an assault on Acadia's only stronghold? The Minas settlements and Beaubassin were easy targets. Port Royal had soldiers and cannon best left to the regulars. Despite the efforts of his many enemies, no one ever proved that Dudley rigged the campaign of 1704, or even that he profited at all from the wartime trade.

Everyone knew, though, that the trade went on, and angry New Englanders wanted someone to punish. Try as they might, they could not pin it on Dudley, but they found evidence against some of his friends, among them a Scot named Samuel Vetch, lately arrived in Boston from New York.[7]

Vetch was one of the unfortunates who had joined a venture to build a New Edinburgh on the Isthmus of Darien, modern Panama, where the Atlantic and the Pacific almost come together and whence it was hoped the treasures of the Orient might flow to Scotland.[8] It was a huge undertaking, riding a wave of Scottish patriotism and financed by nearly half the capital north of the Tweed. But the English, whose East India Company's monopoly was threatened, did all they could short of actually joining Spain to see it squelched, and New Edinburgh was a disaster. In 1699, some of the survivors turned up in New York. One of them was Samuel Vetch.

He was not a man to be held down long. If fortune eluded him in the tropics, he would find it in North America, and just off the boat from Darien, he became a trader and a quick success, helped no little by his marriage to Margaret Livingston, daughter of one of New York's richest merchants, and by friendships he made with Dudley of Massachusetts and Fitz-John Winthrop, governor of Connecticut and grandson of the patriarch John. In 1705, Vetch moved to Boston, and a few months later, Dudley tapped him for a mission to Quebec, with his own son William, to negotiate an exchange of prisoners. They were to talk, as well, of other things.

It was a year of relative quiet, an opportunity for New England and New France to think back to the Treaty of Whitehall and the Doctrine of Two Spheres. Let the old countries batter each other in Europe. Americans had better things to do. Which side first proposed a truce in 1705 is not known. Clearly the French were willing. Brouillan had suggested a pact between Acadia and Massachusetts in 1701, a year before the war started.[9] The Massachusetts council had temporized, and when Joseph Dudley took office, he turned down Brouillan.[10] By 1705, however, he had changed his mind. His negotiators, Vetch and William Dudley, carried a gift of wine for the marquis de Vaudreuil, the governor of New France, and they had Dudley's authority to negotiate an end to the hostilities.[11]

Vaudreuil was already enjoying informal peace on his New York frontier. French treaties with the Iroquois tribes had held, and without Indian help, New Yorkers preferred trade to war. Hoping to accomplish the same thing in the northeast, Vaudreuil sent back with Vetch and William Dudley a written proposal.[12] Interestingly, his draft purported to bind the Indians along with the French. He professed an ability to control his allies, an ability he may not have had.

The sticking points in Boston were prohibitions on New Englanders trading and fishing. The old arguments would not go away, and in the end there was no separate peace. Vetch's venture into diplomacy had failed.

He had, however, taken the opportunity to do business, and Dudley's enemies, pursuing the governor through his friends, found out. They hauled Vetch and five of his associates before the General Court, where all six were tried and found guilty of trading with the enemy. In Vetch's case, an act was passed levying a fine of £200.[13] The legislators, it was said, were "in a rage about it and say that it put knives into the hands of those barbarous infidels to cut the throats of our wifes and children . . . most of them were so furious as to have him confined in the stone cage, for fear he should get away."[14]

Later the queen's attorney general upset the convictions, holding that the General Court had no jurisdiction.[15] Dudley probably knew that was how it would come out. He may even have orchestrated the whole thing. Mather accused him of it. "Yet you permitted it," the preacher thundered. "Yet you promoted it, yet you *managed* it when a personal advantage might come out of it. The people were ensnared, the country endangered."[16] But if Dudley managed it, he managed it well. His friends got off, and scandal was kept from the governor's office.

Still, the point was made. Sensitive to the denunciations of Mather and others, Dudley had to do something to prove he was no friend of the French. His answer was another invasion of Acadia, and this time Port Royal would not escape. "I shall direct," he wrote Fitz-John Winthrop, "what I hope will be in their power, to leave no home standing in the French part, to destroy their stock and cut their banks, which will leave them no tillage; but the attack of the fort I shall leave to a Council of War upon the place, not doubting their courage to do what is in their power."[17] Thus, he left his commanders an out. His enemies, later on, would make much of that.

In May 1707, more than a thousand men set sail from Boston.[18]

In terms of numbers and guns, they were a mighty army. Their problem was that they did not know what they were doing. They were laborers, fishermen, and mechanics, led by officers as unprepared as their men. The generalissimo was Colonel John March, a militia officer who had seen frontier service and whose courage was undoubted, but who knew little about warfare of cannonade and siege and nothing about commanding big forces. His counterpart on the French side, in contrast, was a capable professional, an experienced soldier named Daniel d'Auger de Subercase.[19]

Forty-six years old, he had learned his trade in Europe, then served in Canada against hostile Iroquois and in Frontenac's defense of Quebec against Phips in 1690. He had been promoted to Acadia from a command in Newfoundland, where he had held together the tiny French settlement on Placentia Bay and had waged a successful if remote little war on Britons across the Avon Peninsula in St. John's. Made governor of Acadia in April 1706, and arriving to find the defenses of Port Royal in their usual sorry state, he had quickly put things right. Behind the ramparts of a rebuilt fort, some three hundred ably led French soldiers, Indian warriors, and armed Acadians awaited March and his men when, on June 6, 1707, they sailed into the Annapolis Basin.

They split their force, some landing on the south shore and some on the north, out of range of the fort. March's plan was to close by land and squeeze the French. To do it, each of his detachments had to advance four or five miles into the teeth of Subercase's sorties. Then they were to bring up their big guns and mount a siege. It was a job they came nowhere near accomplishing.

They did, however, show courage under fire. Indeed, they once chased the French back to the fort, even shooting Subercase's horse out from under him, but when they had fought their way to bombardment range, their organization, their morale, and their campaign fell apart. The engineers balked at bringing up the big guns, saying it was too dangerous. March lacked the will to overrule them, and his men were worn out and discouraged by their hard push and losses suffered along the way. Discipline broke down. Indecision ruled. They spent eight days before the fort while enlisted men grumbled and officers argued. Confronted by a real fortification and determined opponents who knew the craft of war, the plowboys and tradesmen of New England had no idea what to do. Finally, they simply gave up, boarded their ships, and sailed back to Casco Bay to await orders—defeated as much by their own incompetence as by Subercase's aggressive defense.

To the citizens of Boston, it was a matter of cowardice, pure and simple. Four of March's officers went there to report to Dudley. Here is an account of their reception, sent by an observer to Fitz-John Winthrop in Connecticut:

> The last Tuesday morning Coll: Appleton, Redknap . . . Sutton . . . and Holmes . . . arrived here, having left some of the army and fleet at Casco Bay. They were sent by March to inform the Governor of their proceedings and actions at Port Royal. They landed at Scarlet's wharfe, where they were met by severall women, who saluted them after this manner: "Welcome, souldiers!" and presented them a great wooden sword, and said withall "Fie, for shame! pull off those iron spitts which hang by your sides; for wooden ones is all ye fashion now." At which one of the officers said, "Peace, sille woman, etc," which irritated the female tribe so much the more, that they called out to one another as they past along the streets, "Is your piss-pot charg'd, neighbor? Is your piss-pot charged, neighbor? So-ho, souse the cowards. Salute Port Royal. Holloo, neighbor, holloo"; with a drove of children and servants with wooden swords in their hands, following them with the repeated salutations "Port Royal! Port Royal!" . . . I think by the afternoon there was some hundreds of boys gathered together into a company, and the people about had furnisht allmost all of them with wooden swords or old stocks of guns, a drum, and a red peice of cloth fastned upon a stick for an ensign, and in this equipage they marcht through the towne, hollowing "Port Royal! Port Royal!"

"Never," Winthrop's correspondent wrote, "did poor men receive so many affronts from an insulting rabble. . . . They had better have been whipt than ever have come to towne to be so greeted."[20]

Dudley's response was to send reinforcements with orders to try again. He sent along advisers—two more militia officers and a minister. Presumably, rule by committee would cure the failures of command that had dogged the first attempt. March was not recalled, as he should have been, but he was too despondent to lead anyone anywhere, and eventually the advisers got around to relieving him. Probably he had suffered what today might be diagnosed as a nervous

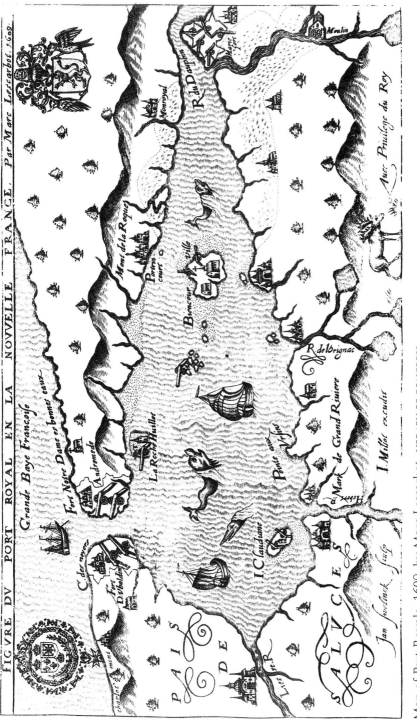

Map of Port Royale, 1609, by Marc Lescarbot. LIBRARY OF CONGRESS.

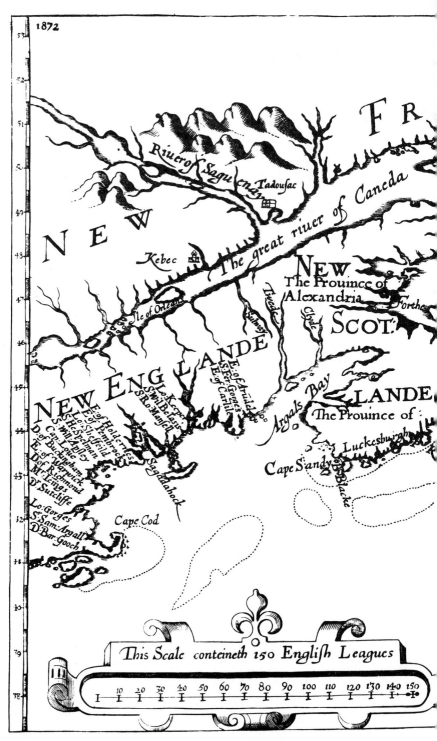

1872

FR

Riuer of Saguenay   Tadousac

The great riuer of Caneda

N E W

Kebec

Ile of Orleans

NEW
The Prouince of
Alexandria

Forthe

Iweede

Clyde

SCOT.

NEW ENGLANDE

E. of Arundell
S. Fer. Gorges
E. of Castill

Argals Bay

LANDE

The Prouince of

Lo. Ker.
E. of Holdernes
E. of Pembrock
Lo. Sheffeild
S. He. Spelman
S. Will. Alley
Ca. Lowe
D. of Buckingham
E. of Warwick
D. of Richmond
Mr. Lings
D. Sutcliffe
Lo. Gorges
S. Sam. Argall
D. Bar. Gooch

S. Will. Betaps
S. Ro. Manseu

Sagadahock

Cape Cod

Luckesburgh

Cape Sandy

Blake

This Scale conteineth 150 English Leagues

10 20 30 40 50 60 70 80 90 100 110 120 130 140 150

English map c. 1624, with place names adopted by Sir William Alexander.

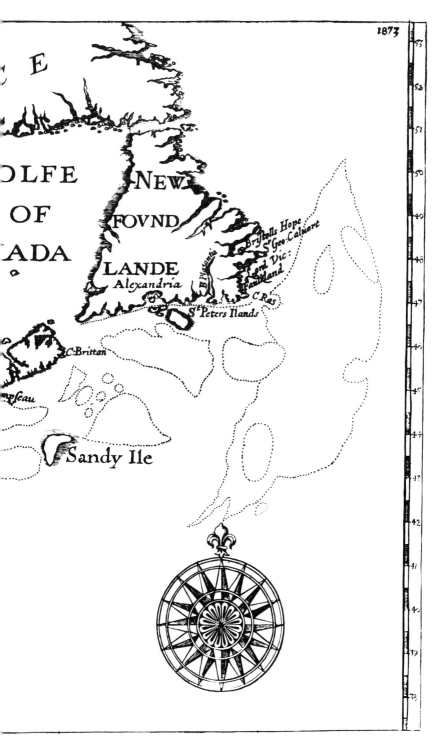

1873

E

OLFE

OF

ADA

NEW

FOVND

LANDE
Alexandria

B. Placantia

Bryftolls Hope
S. Geo: Caluert
Lord Vic:
Faulkland

C. Ras

S. Peters Ilands

C. Brittan

mpfeau

Sandy Ile

53

52

51

50

49

48

47

46

45

44

43

42

41

40

39

38

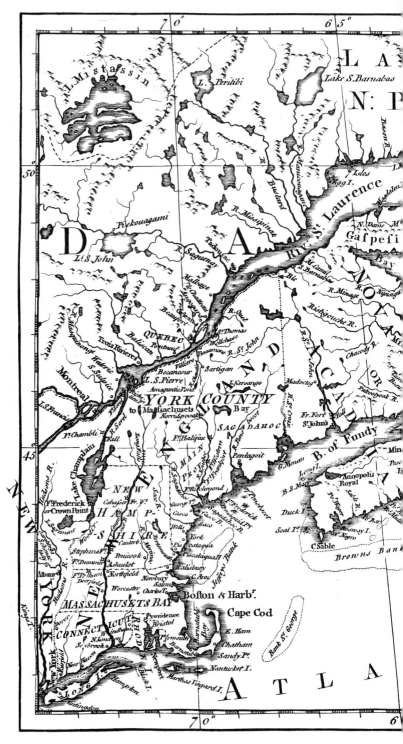

Map from *London Magazine,* August 1755. AUTHOR'S COLLECTION.

A MAP of the BRITISH & FRENCH PLANTATIONS in NORTH AMERICA

The Port Royal National Historic Site is a reconstruction of the original Port Royal Habitation, 1605. The dwellings, workshops, and stockade flank a rectangular courtyard. CANADIAN HERITAGE (PARKS CANADA).

The Fortress of Louisbourg National Historic Site is a reconstruction of a portion of the prosperous town as it appeared in the 1740s. CANADIAN HERITAGE (PARKS CANADA).

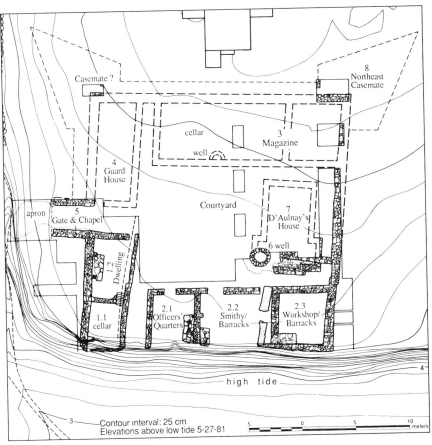

University of Maine excavations at Fort Pentagoet have revealed nearly half of the original foundation walls. Dotted lines indicate features known from documents and confirmed by ground-penetrating radar or test excavation. ALARIC FAULKNER AND CATHERINE T. BRANN.

The oldest surviving blockhouse in Canada was erected at Fort Edward in 1750. Fort Edward was one of the main assembly points during the expulsion of the Acadians. CANADIAN HERITAGE (PARKS CANADA).

Excavated walls at Fort Beauséjour National Historic Park. This French stronghold was built in 1750 to counter the British presence at Fort Lawrence. CANADIAN HERITAGE (PARKS CANADA).

breakdown. Given the medical science of 1707, no one could have known. His chaplain, John Barnard, said of the unhappy colonel: "Though he was himself a valiant man, yet, I think his capacity was below the post he sustained."[21]

He was replaced by Colonel Francis Wainwright, who on August 20 led 743 reluctant New Englanders back to the Annapolis Basin. Even with the reinforcements Dudley had sent, they were as many men as could be found. Desertion had been heavy while the army lay at Casco Bay.

Warned of another attempt, Subercase was ready. Wainwright put his men ashore on the north side of the basin, much nearer the fort this time, then marched them to the mouth of the Annapolis River. From there, he intended to bombard the French and launch an encircling movement upriver behind the town. But the defenders kept up a steady fire and drove the New Englanders back. Snipers filled the woods, and neither the bombardment nor the maneuver Wainwright had in mind was ever organized. In a message to the advisers, he described his own and his army's despair:

> It is truly astonishing, to behold the miserable posture and temper that most of the army are in, besides the smallness of our number, to be attacked by the enemy which we expect every moment.
>
> I am much disordered in my health by a great cold. . . . In fine, most of the forces are in a distressed state, some in body and some in mind, and the longer they are kept here on the cold ground the longer it will grow upon them, and, I fear, the further we proceed the worse the event. God help us.[22]

Given their colonel's state of mind, God help them indeed!

After ten days, Wainwright tried to force the issue. His men had been driven back down the north shore by Subercase's fire. When they were out of range, he had them ferried across the basin to try their luck on the opposite side, but on August 31, the French and Indians charged out and chased them to their ships. According to Reverend Barnard, whose wig was shot off, "we all embarked, and returned for Boston as fast as we could."[23]

16 | TAKEOVER

Acadia Receives a New Sovereign

1707–1710

VIEWED FROM VERSAILLES, Daniel Subercase's triumph was a skirmish, a praiseworthy but piddling success in a faraway corner of the world. In Europe, where it mattered, France was losing the war. Britain's greatest soldier, the duke of Marlborough, had won at Blenheim in Bavaria and again at Ramillies in Belgium. Gibraltar and Barcelona had fallen, and the emperor's champion, Eugene of Savoy, had driven the French from Italy. Louis XIV had to think of peace.

Across the English Channel, his antagonists flourished. Queen Anne led a government and a people confidently making their way into modern times. On the right were the Tories, representing the landowners and the clergy. On the left were the Whigs, the party of the newly powerful middle class, the party of commerce and trade. No one represented or even thought much about the men and women who kept the farms, made the goods, manned the ships, and fought the wars. Still, the push and shove of Tory and Whig sparked a tinge of democracy, and democracy meant a nation better ruled and a war better fought. The reign of Anne was a time of greatness.

It was, too, the time of Marlborough. On the Continent, he handed the French defeat after defeat. It seemed he could not lose. At home, his wife, Sarah, was the queen's confidante. Between them, the duke and duchess seemed to hold all the strings.

Powerful as they were, though, they could not dominate, and as the war ground on, the duke lost the support of the Tories. It was they, the gentry, who paid the taxes that supported his expensive campaigns. Then Sarah lost her place as royal favorite. Her successor, Abigail Masham, leaned the Tory way, and Marlborough's days were numbered.

A Tory government in London might be just what the French needed. After each defeat, new taxes had been imposed and shattered armies revived, but even a country as resilient as France and a king as masterful as Louis XIV could not keep it up forever. When the allies won another big victory, this one in 1708 at Oudenarde in Belgium, he offered to concede to most of their demands. They insisted, however, that Louis drive his grandson from the throne of Spain. That he would not do, a new army was raised, and in 1709 it fought Marlborough and Eugene almost to a draw at Malplaquet on France's northern border. It was the bloodiest battle of the War of the Spanish Succession, the bloodiest Europe had ever seen. It stopped the allies' advance on Paris and gave Louis time to wait for Britons to tire of carnage and turn against the Whigs.

War and diplomacy engrossed Europe, and not much attention was paid to America. France particularly, her back to the wall, had little time or treasure for overseas adventure. At Port Royal, Subercase had official commendations, but that was it, and he watched in frustration as his funds dried up and his command deteriorated. In 1707, he was warned that his expenses must "never exceed the appropriations."[1] In 1710, on the eve of his severest test, he was told to find the specie that everyone thought was hoarded by the Acadians and pay his bills with it, since nothing more would come from Versailles.[2]

His regular soldiers were conscripts rejected from the armies fighting Marlborough, and boys banished to the colonies for misbehavior at home. "I have," he complained, "been in as much need of mad houses as of barracks."[3] Nor could he rely on his militia. Failure of support sapped the zeal that had animated a few Acadians to feats of arms against March and Wainwright. They were all reverting to the neutrality they had professed in the previous war. Why fight for a king who ignored them?

And bickering and petty sensationalism—preoccupations of French officialdom in peace and war—never let up. La Vallière had fought with the men who tried to develop the fishery in the 1680s, Perrot had quarreled with Saint-Castin, and neither Meneval nor Villebon could get along with the well-entrenched Mathieu de Goutin. In 1702, a messy love affair rocked Port Royal. One of the officers wooed and won, without the intercession of clergy, a charming widow, Madame Freneuse; the liaison was reported to Versailles almost as though it were a British invasion.[4] Another time, the saga of damage done by cows in an unfenced garden made its way into an official dispatch.[5] As the French regime neared its end, even Subercase, as fine an officer as France had ever sent, was squabbling with de Goutin. Brouillan, who fought with everyone and was himself accused by de Goutin of scandalous behavior with Madame Freneuse, called Acadia "a land of discord always."[6]

It did not make for a cohesive government or a garrison that could take on a professional army, and that was just what Samuel Vetch had in mind when, late in 1706, he stepped ashore in Britain and into the cauldron of her complex politics. First he had to upset his Massachusetts conviction. That done, he aimed to bring the mother country and her troops into the war in America, conquer Canada and Acadia, and have himself named governor of it all.

He had well-connected friends, his father-in-law Robert Livingston and his patron Joseph Dudley had more, and Vetch himself was no rustic provincial pleading an obscure colonial cause. He was good at pulling the levers of authority. He knew whom to see and how to convince. By March 1707, he had in hand the attorney general's opinion overruling the General Court, and he was ready for greater things. Much depended, though, on Dudley, and Vetch must have wondered whether Dudley could last.

The guns of the implacable Puritans boomed their invective across three thousand miles of ocean. Wanting evidence, they conjured up "dark designs," including this from a pamphlet printed in London in 1708:

> When the War first broke out. . . . Governour *Dudley* was earnestly Sollicited, and his Leave Intreated by some, to go and Destroy that Nest of *Hornets,* which was like to be so Grievous a growing Plague to the Country. . . . But the Proposal was Rejected, which made People Suspect some *Dark Designs,* and that *Port Royal* was reserved for some special Advantages not Obvious to the Vulgar.
>
> Afterwards, when the Governour could no longer withstand the Cry of the Country, Colonel *Church* was allowed to go. . . . Yet the said *Church* had not only the Taking of the *Fort* left out of his Orders, but was positively *Forbidden* to Meddle with it. . . .
>
> The Reason Pretended by the Governour . . . was, *That he had laid the Matter before the Queen, and had yet received no Orders about it.* Tho' the same Objection still continued, yet the

People . . . Moved for another Expedition above a Year ago. The Governour now gives a Commission for *Taking the Fort,* but whether with any *Dark Designs,* we are yet *in the Dark.* After the Instructions were drawn up, there was a Clause Tack'd at the End of 'em, which gave the Army Leave to come off when they would . . . It was the Tacking of this unobserved Clause at last, that Confounded all, and brought on a Story, which all the Letters from *New-England* we have yet seen, say, *They Blush to Write it.*

The blushing pamphleteers wrote it nonetheless, claiming that two thousand of New England's bravest were sent to Port Royal in 1707, only to be undone by duplicitous leaders. When March's officers showed up in Boston, "tho' they were Chidden by the Governour, in the Council Chamber, yet we understand, they were Hugged and Caress'd by him, below Stairs, to the great Scandal of the People." And the second attack, when Wainwright commanded, was another prearranged defeat: "After a little Skirmish on the opposite Shore, and some Follies not to be mention'd, away they came for *Boston.* . . . And so much for *Port Royal,* until the *dark designs* come into further light."[7]

This was strong stuff, but Dudley, thick-skinned and accustomed to such talk, mounted a winning defense. His London friends pitched in, and in 1708, the Privy Council dismissed the charges, calling them frivolous.[8] Once again he had handily survived Puritan vitriol, and he had not even left home to do it. Cotton Mather must have been enraged.

Vetch was a winner, too. If Dudley fell, he fell. But with Dudley firmly in power, Massachusetts would be friendly territory, and it would be even friendlier if Vetch should return with an army ready and able to put an end to the troublesome French on the colony's border. A new committee, the Board of Trade, had replaced King Charles's Lords of Trade as overseer of the colonies, and in July 1708, Vetch handed it a long memorandum with all the arguments for a conquest of New France and a thumping title: *Canada Survey'd, or the French Dominions upon the Continent of America briefly considered in their situation, strength, trade and number, more particularly how vastly prejudiciall they are to the British interest, and a method proposed of easily removing them.*[9]

In a supplement, Vetch suggested a way to deal with the French settlers who lived in the places the British troops would conquer.

"When it pleases God they shall be masters of it," he wrote, "it will be necessary to send all or att least by much the greater number of the inhabitants in their own small barks to Martinico [Martinique] . . . the greatest part of the inhabitants being removed from thence is absolutely necessary, as well for the security of our own people, in case of ane attempt from France to recover it, as to make the natives come over intirely to the interest and obedience of the Crown."[10]

Canada Survey'd . . . was persuasive, and Vetch found a powerful supporter in Francis Nicholson, the officer who had reconnoitered Port Royal for Sir Edmund Andros in 1687. Nicholson was now a colonel, and despite an extraordinarily abrasive personality, he had risen very high in colonial administration.[11] Under Andros and the Dominion of New England, he had been in command in New York when that colony had its own Glorious Revolution. He survived that debacle and was made lieutenant governor of Virginia, then lieutenant governor and governor of Maryland; from 1698 to 1705, he was governor of Virginia. A Tory, he had lost his place to a candidate of the Whigs and Marlborough, but he kept his interest and his influence, and when the Board of Trade asked his advice on Vetch's plan, he gave it his enthusiastic support. Seeing, too, that there might be something in it for him as well as Vetch, he jumped at the chance to join.

By March 1709, Vetch had the queen's order for an invasion, a commission as colonel, and a promise of the governorship of Canada.[12] The ambitious Scot had come a long way from Darien. He and Nicholson sailed to Boston, where with Dudley's help they set off an awesome burst of colonial energy.[13] From Maine to New Jersey, the drums beat. Men were enlisted; barracks were built; boats were launched. Nicholson took command of an army that was to march from Albany and invade from the west, forming a pincers with a seaborne attack up the St. Lawrence. Vetch would join the main force, which would sail as soon as the regulars arrived from Britain.

Gallingly, it all came to nothing. The promised British troops were sent instead to fight in Portugal. The queen's order, written on July 1, was not put aboard ship until August, and it did not reach Boston until October.[14] In the meantime, men had been encamped all summer, training to fight the French, and the cost was enormous. Might something be salvaged? The order permitted an attack on Port Royal, but it was late in the year for operations in the Bay of Fundy, and who could forget what had happened the last time colonials went on their own to test Subercase and his fortress? A conference of governors decided to give it up for 1709 and to send Nicholson to London to promote a new invasion the next year. If it made it easier, this one might be limited to Acadia.[15]

The queen's ministers said yes, and this time they came through. When Nicholson returned in July, he had four hundred royal marines and orders to use them against Port Royal.[16]

Fifteen hundred colonials were added, and six Royal Navy warships joined one from Massachusetts and some thirty transports to make up the fleet. Nicholson was commander-in-chief. Vetch was adjutant general, and the queen's new orders included this plum: "If it shall please God to give such success to this Enterprise as that Port royal shall be reduced to our obedience[,] It is our pleasure that Coll: Vetch have the command of it."[17]

They sailed at the end of September. The only setback came at Digby Gut, where twenty-six men drowned when a transport vessel slammed into the rocks. The rest made the Annapolis Basin safely. Seeing them, Subercase knew that his time was up. He had not enough men to mount the aggressive defense that had defeated March and Wainwright. The Acadians would not fight, and his regulars were nearly as bad. Nor, as it turned out, could he count on the enemy incompetence that had served him so well three years earlier. The royal marines were a different matter, and the men of New England had learned something about soldiering since the disasters of 1707. Under British officers, they had practiced hard for the aborted invasion of Canada. There would be no serious contest between the ragged French garrison and Nicholson's well-schooled, well-equipped invaders.

On Monday, October 6, 1710—a fine, clear day—they landed. When the sun rose the next morning, they began their march, the marines in the vanguard. Drums beating, flags snapping, bayonets flashing, the redcoats made a stirring sight. British victory was in the air.

The siege lasted six days. Honor required that Subercase not give up without a fight. On Wednesday, the weather changed. Dark clouds moved in and a chilly autumn rain began. It might have helped the French, under cover in their fort, but the British knew how to serve their cannon, rain or no. The battle became an artillery duel, and Subercase was the loser. The fleet's guns answered his, volley for volley, and the fort became a scene of misery and terror. The defenders broke under the shelling. Some deserted and others begged their commander to surrender.

An exchange of the formal letters of civilized war began on Friday, when Subercase sent officers with a drummer and a flag of truce to ask that Nicholson shelter the French ladies, who, he wrote, "did all along Flatter themselves that they could hear and bear the noise of your Bombs without fear, but they now find themselves a little mistaken."[18] Nicholson parried, complaining that the French drummer had improperly signaled the intention to parley. Very politely, he accused Subercase of sending spies to the British camp. Just as politely, Subercase complained of Nicholson's failure to write his letter in French.

As Friday ended, Nicholson agreed to take under his protection the ladies with young children and those who were pregnant, "for the Queen, my Royal Mistrese hath not sent me hither to make War with Women, especially in their condition."[19] On Saturday, while the guns still roared, he agreed to write in French if Subercase would put his own letters in English. The two commanders also continued to dispute their mutual observance of correct procedure, but it was all form. The substance was that the French were beaten. In a letter on Saturday, Subercase acquiesced: "I now write to you, to tell you Sir, that for to prevent the spilling of both English and French Blood, I am ready to hold up both hands for a Capitulation that will be honourable to both of us."[20] On Sunday, Nicholson sent a demand that his opponent "deliver up to me for the Queen of Great Britain, the Fort now in your Possession, as what of Right belongs to Her said Majesty: Together with all the Territories under you[r] command, by virtue of an undoubted right of Her Royal Predecessors."[21] Subercase would concede no such right, but he agreed to capitulate "in order to avoid any Effusion of Blood, and untill your pretented Right can be decided, which one day or other, no doubt will take place."[22]

Among the articles signed on Monday, October 13, 1710, were these:

1. That the Garrison shall march out with their Arms and Baggage, Drums beating, and Colours flying.
2. That there shall be a sufficient number of Ships and Provisions to Transport the said Garrison to Rochell or Rochford. . . .
5. That the Inhabitants within Cannon shot of the Fort of Port Royal, shall remain upon their Estates, with their Corn,

Cattle and Furniture, During two years, in case they are not Desirous to go before, they taking the Oaths of Allegiance and Fidelity to Her Sacred Majesty of Great Britain.[23]

Thus the French soldiers had the honors of war and ships to take them home. The people of Port Royal would not be prisoners, they would not lose their property, and they could stay or go as they chose. Nicholson declared that a cannon shot meant three miles. He counted within a three-mile radius 487 civilians who would have the benefit of article 5.

They were generous terms, but cheap if they bought all of Acadia, and Nicholson and Vetch had no doubt that they did. As soon as the capitulation was signed, they wrote the queen to advise that her "mighty empire in America" now included Acadia and Nova Scotia, "from the River of St. Croy to the Cape Gaspee . . . together with all Islands whatsoever within the said district."[24]

17 | REBELLION AND PARTITION

The Victors Hold On

1710–1713

AT SUNRISE ON THURSDAY, October 16, 1710, the banner of France was raised for the last time at Port Royal. Later that morning, Francis Nicholson's men fell into ranks to watch Daniel Subercase formally surrender. Then the French marched out and the British and Americans marched in—to hoist the Union Jack, drink to Queen Anne's health, and give the town the queen's name. From that day, it has been Annapolis Royal.

The French officials and the garrison and their families—258 people in all—boarded British ships and sailed home.[1] Nicholson sent candy for the women and children, spirits for the men, and two barrels of beer as a bon voyage gift for his gallant opponent. Subercase sent back his thanks for "all your own particular favours and Civility to me" and his hope "that you have given Col: Vetch, an order to be as just and as good as you have been, and that he do Justice to those French that remain behind, as has been done to those that now are going away."[2]

Nicholson himself sailed at the end of October, leaving Vetch in command of 200 royal marines and 250 New Englanders.[3] They were a big force, but not big enough for the job they had to do. By 1710, there were almost two thousand Acadians.[4] They were a well-settled, widely scattered, independent-minded, and surpassingly stubborn people. They had seen Britons come, and they had seen Britons go.

Vetch and the men who came after him might have tamed them nonetheless had more of the Britons been like Paul Mascarene, the young captain who received the coveted order to command the first guard.[5] He was French born, a Huguenot who had fled the land of his

birth and found a career in Queen Anne's army. During the siege of
Port Royal, he had ably led a company of New Hampshire grenadiers,
and the honor Nicholson gave him was prophetic. Mascarene was to
spend the rest of his life in America, to save Annapolis Royal for Britain in a dark hour, and to come to know the people of Acadia, even
to build something of a rapport with them. In that way, he was very
much an exception among the British, most of whom wanted nothing to do with the men and women they had conquered. Nicholson
had warned his men that the Acadians were all "rebells and would
certainly cut their throats if they went into their houses."[6]

The answer seemed to be expulsion. It was the fate Vetch had
urged for the French inhabitants of Canada, and it could easily have
happened in Acadia after Subercase's surrender. In the letter they sent
Queen Anne announcing their triumph, Nicholson and Vetch proposed "that in order to bring the native Indians entirely under your
Majesty's subjection as well as to convert them to the protestant religion it will be necessary to transport all the French from the country save such as shall come over to the Protestant religion."[7] Again
the next January, Vetch recommended expulsion. He would have sent
the Acadians to Newfoundland, or perhaps the Caribbean.[8]

But no one in London was willing to take responsibility, and
later, when it seemed they might leave of their own will, Vetch had
second thoughts.[9] Their departure would leave emptiness where now
there were men and women, farms and cattle. Without them, Britain's new province would be little more than trees. Someone had to
raise crops, tend livestock, chop wood. They might not be the most
trustworthy population, but they were better than no population
at all.

And so began a half century of chary coexistence. Like their grand-
parents during the 1650s and 1660s, the Acadians would cope by
interacting as little as possible with the Britons who came to govern
them. The British, too, would keep to themselves—in armed enclaves
where they could feel safe from the peaceable farmers who were the
queen's new subjects and, with much more cause, from the Indians,
who would not admit to being anyone's subjects.[10]

Through all the years of the French regime, the freedom-loving
Micmacs had gone their separate way, trying their best to maintain
their way of life in the face of alien intrusion. At the same time, they
had cooperated with the French, and never had they found any reason to oppose the light-handed government that ruled Acadia before

1710. Now things were different. Nicholson and Vetch brought a new version of European rule, and the Micmacs knew they had to fight it. They knew that Britons were not like Frenchmen, that Britons grabbed Indian land, that they had no respect for Indian customs and Indian rights. Too, there was the religion the Micmacs shared with the French. And, most important of all, was the success of the French and the failure of the British in the art of persuasion.

Since the days of Fléché, Biard, and Massé, Micmacs had been enthusiastic if perhaps not fully comprehending Catholics, and despite the British conquest, the French kept sending missionary priests. The Indians listened to the priests, and the priests taught resistance. French officers came too, and along with exhortations, they brought presents from the king—useful items like powder and shot, blankets and food—courtesies that were important in Indian diplomacy. Britons might have stepped in with gifts of their own, and they might have tried to show goodwill, but they turned out to be stingy, and nowhere were they noted for goodwill to native Americans.

The French treated the Micmacs as a sovereign nation, their allies in a common cause. Britons treated them the way they treated Indians everywhere. Their manner was contemptuous, their gestures of friendship patently insincere. The Micmacs were never strong enough to throw the British out, but they were determined enough—and, after a while, they were bitter enough—that whenever in later years Frenchmen marched to reconquer Acadia, Micmac warriors marched at their side.

The British began their rule by imposing a military government. Their laws were the decrees of a council of war, purporting to bind Indians and Acadians alike. One of the first laws prohibited trade with France or Canada and required that trade with anyone, even among themselves, take place at Annapolis Royal, where it could be watched.[11] It was typical of the unrealism of British administration, then and later. It could not be enforced, and the Acadians knew it. The Indians, if they paid attention at all, probably just laughed.

In the same decree, the Acadians were promised that "while they behave themselves civily and peaceably they shall meet with all the good treatment Imaginable."[12] That was not, however, what Nicholson and his council said in a letter to the governor of New France. The marquis de Vaudreuil was told that Acadians would suffer "Military Execution" if the French did not put a stop to the Indian raids that plagued the New England and New York frontiers.[13] It was a bluff, but the people must have learned of it, and it was no way to earn their favor.

The letter was taken to Quebec by Vetch's brother-in-law, John Livingston, and by Bernard-Anselme de Saint-Castin, heir of Jean-Vincent. After thirty years of adventure and exotic companions in the Maine woods, the old baron had finally gone home to die, his place left in the capable hands of the half-Abenaki son who was now the fourth baron Saint-Castin. Nicholson and Vetch should have packed him off to France with the rest of their prisoners. Instead, they let him be Livingston's guide and gave him a chance to plot with Vaudreuil, and he came back with a lieutenant's commission and orders to command a guerrilla war.[14] If Bernard-Anselme could keep the British harassed and the Acadians and Indians on France's side, Vaudreuil was ready to send troops to restore French rule.

At Annapolis Royal, Vetch played into their hands. Instead of letting the Acadians believe the proclamation that promised good treatment, he began his administration by trying to extort their money. Nicholson's ship was hardly out of sight when the French-speaking Captain Mascarene was sent to the Minas Basin to roust the inhabitants. A declaration of British sovereignty would have been reasonable enough, but Vetch was after "a good present . . . towards maintaining my Table."[15] British and French alike believed that the Acadians had wealth stashed away. Subercase had been ordered to find it. Vetch would have it. Mascarene was to assemble everyone and tell them that it was only Vetch's benevolence that kept the army from plunder and destruction. He was ordered to demand six thousand livres and a monthly payment of twenty pistoles. That would ensure the governor's restraint of the soldiers.

Mascarene dutifully made his speech, then approved the people's selection of deputies to discuss Vetch's demands. Thus he blessed a practice that would be followed whenever in the years ahead Acadians needed to negotiate with the British. In 1710, eight deputies were chosen, including, according to Mascarene's report, "Peter Melanzon" of Grand Pré and "Matt. Martin" from Cobequid.[16] Could those have been the founders? Probably. Acadians lived long lives.

On behalf of everyone, they pleaded poverty, and they argued Mascarene down from six thousand livres to three. But he failed to collect even that. Only a parcel of furs, some grain and dried beans, and a few of Subercase's tattered old bills of credit were forthcoming. The monthly pistoles were never paid at all.[17]

Vetch tried the same approach on the residents of Annapolis Royal, who responded by sending a letter to Vaudreuil asking him to help them escape "this unhappy country."[18] And indeed, as things turned out, it would have been better for everyone had they all gone to Canada in 1710. Vaudreuil could have arranged it. But whoever wrote the letter was putting words in Acadian mouths. They did not really mean it. The Fundy marshes were home, the home of their ancestors, and no one wanted to leave, Vetch or no Vetch.

Besides, they could hope for better things. When peace came, Acadia probably would be handed back to France. It had happened before—every time, in fact, that Britons had professed sovereignty—and most recently in 1697, when the Treaty of Ryswick ended King William's War. Or the British might be thrown out the way they had come in—by force. With the help of the soldiers Saint-Castin could summon from Canada, Acadians might even manage it themselves.

They could see that the prerogative Vetch was trying to exercise had nothing behind it. Few ships showed up. No more soldiers came. Acadians were not the only ones who could remember the past and expect a diplomatic restoration when the guns stopped firing, and no one in London was interested in spending money on a place that would soon be ceded away. Vetch said later that not only was he sent no arms or pay for his soldiers, he was bereft even of orders and instructions.[19] As far as the queen's ministers were concerned, Vetch and Nova Scotia did not exist.

To clothe and feed his men, he wrote bills on the royal treasury. That worked for a while—until Boston merchants began to suspect that the bills might not be honored. From then on, it was hand-to-mouth at Annapolis Royal, Vetch scraping by on his personal credit and the hopes of his suppliers for eventual payment, and the garrison ill-clothed, ill-fed, and sick of duty amid sullen foreigners who wished them gone and rejoiced in their misery.

Instead of cooperation, the British received foot-dragging and excuses. When timber was needed to rebuild drafty barracks and shore up crumbling parapets, it seemed, alas, that the creeks were too full of ice to float it, the oxen too weak to haul it.[20] The few Acadians who were willing to work for their new masters were snubbed by their neighbors and terrorized by the Indians. One of the priests, Father Gaulin, boasted that he had "induced the savages to . . . openly oppose themselves to the transport of wood, which the English governors obliged the inhabitants to furnish for re-establishing the fortifications."[21]

Young Saint-Castin likely was orchestrating it all. And who should appear at Annapolis Royal one wintry day but Madame Freneuse—come from the Saint John, so she said, in a canoe with her son and a lone Indian to find shelter among the kindhearted Britons. Mascarene was sure she was a spy, sent "to keep the French in a Ferment and make them backward in supplying the Garrison with any necessary's, and pry into and give an Accot of our Secrets."[22] Nevertheless, the beguiling widow was received hospitably, even given the liberty of the town.

The crisis came in June 1711. Woodcutters in the Annapolis Valley had been forced off the job by social pressure and Indian threats. Vetch sent a detachment upriver to get them back to work, but Micmac warriors waited at a tributary known afterward as Bloody Creek, and the soldiers rowed their boats into a deadly trap.[23] Eighteen were killed, and it was plain that Queen Anne's writ did not run far beyond the ramparts of her new fort.

Encouraged, a few of the more audacious Acadians joined a band of Micmacs in an ad hoc siege. Father Gaulin sailed to Newfoundland to obtain troops from Philippe de Pastour de Costabelle, the commander at Placentia, and Vaudreuil mustered the men he had promised to send from Canada. Disease, desertion, and Indian muskets at Bloody Creek had so weakened Vetch's garrison that they might not have been able to hold off a well-conducted attack, had it come, but support for the militants was never sent, and the siege sputtered out. Annapolis Royal was saved when Vaudreuil and Costabelle found themselves facing a vast new threat—a revival of the scheme Vetch had proposed in 1708 for a grand invasion of Canada.

In London, the government had changed. The Tories were in, the Whigs out. But the war went on, and the duke of Marlborough still had the army and the acclaim due a victorious commander-in-chief. The Tories needed a victory of their own to counter the luster the duke had earned on the Continent, and Canada was their chance. It could be taken, and Louis XIV driven closer to the peace table, if a powerful enough force was sent.

Back home, amid friendly Tory ministers, Francis Nicholson promoted the scheme as hard as he could. With his party in control, his time was ripe, and this time he saw himself strutting across a continental stage at the head of a military regime that would rule all the colonies, including Canada.[24] In June 1711, he sailed to Boston with the advance party and orders for the governors, who must have been awed when they heard the plan. The strike would be overpowering: some fifty ships and nearly ten thousand men.

Unfortunately, both for the prospect of Canada's becoming British in 1711 and for Nicholson's hopes of becoming an American Caesar, the Tories' choice of commanders was no match for the resources they committed. The admiral was Sir Hovenden Walker, an officer who, to put it charitably, was not very good at his job. The general was "Jack" Hill, brother of the queen's favorite Abigail Masham. Hill's military skills were at best untested, but as it turned out, he never had a chance to try them. Walker's incompetence did them all in.[25]

Vetch was recalled from Annapolis Royal to join the seaborne force, and just as in 1709, Nicholson would command a western army, its mission to invade from Lake Champlain and close on Quebec from upriver. The tactics were sound. The problem was in their execution. The fleet sailed from Boston at the end of July, bristling with armament but without pilots who knew the St. Lawrence. Walker sailed too close to the Isle aux Oeufs, which hugs the shore near the river's mouth. Even though there are almost seventy miles of open water there, the admiral managed to find the rocks. Ten ships went aground, and nearly a thousand sailors and soldiers drowned.

Enough were left, however, to give Walker the odds had he been willing to brave the river. Vetch urged him on. Phips, after all, had done it in 1690. Surely the Royal Navy could do the same. But the Isle aux Oeufs drained Walker of whatever starch he had brought to the grand invasion. Declaring it all too dangerous, he gathered his remaining ships and sailed home, a sorry performance from a senior officer of the world's greatest navy. When Nicholson heard the news at Lake Champlain, he tore off his wig and stamped on it, crying, "Roguery, treachery!"[26]

All that was accomplished was relief of the garrison Vetch had left behind. Reports of Walker's fleet compelled Vaudreuil and Costabelle to pull in their men, and Bernard-Anselme Saint-Castin's guerrilla war was over. Annapolis Royal was reinforced by troops detached from Hill's army, and by December, Vetch's deputy, Major Thomas Caulfeild, could report that he was strong enough to defend his post no matter what the French might try. The Acadians, he said, were quiet, reassured by a proclamation Hill had issued promising that they would be well treated, their property and their religion undisturbed.[27]

And for a time, they were indeed let alone. In Europe, the war was winding down. The Austrian Archduke Charles, the allies' candidate for king of Spain, had lost his shine when his brother Joseph I died and he became Emperor Charles VI. Britain and Holland thus found themselves fighting to merge the Spanish and Holy Roman empires, which was not what they had had in mind when they began the war. When he agreed to renounce the throne of France if he could keep that of Spain, Philip V became acceptable, even desirable. Britain's Tory government had already begun secret talks looking to a separate peace; Joseph's death brought the Dutch to the table. At the end of 1711, Marlborough was dismissed, and the next year a peace conference convened at Utrecht. It dragged on for fifteen months, then in April 1713 produced a series of agreements that are among history's most important—an amalgam of treaties among Britain, France, Spain, and Holland that form the Peace of Utrecht. The Treaty of Rastadt, concluded in 1714 between Spain and Austria, wrapped it up.[28]

The issues were complex, the bargaining tough. When it was over, Philip V had the throne of Spain. A Bourbon king still has it. Spain kept her overseas empire but lost Gibraltar to Britain and all of Belgium and most of Italy to Austria. Louis XIV gave the Dutch a string of border fortresses and made solemn promises that the crowns of France and Spain would remain forever separate. Britain got Hudson Bay, the *asiento,* and the pieces of Newfoundland and St. Christopher that had belonged to France before the war. She wound up, too, with the greater part of Acadia.

French diplomats had tried hard, but this time the British insisted on their prize, and the real key for the French was not so much rule over Acadia and the Acadians as it was access to the Gulf of St. Lawrence and the North Atlantic fishing banks. If the British wound up with both Newfoundland and Cape Breton Island, they would have the fishery to themselves. Too, they would be astride the Cabot Strait and thus able to shut down communication between France and Canada. The answer was to divide Acadia. Let Britain have the Nova Scotia Peninsula, but keep Cape Breton Island, fortify it, and make it a base for the fishery.

Article XII of the treaty between France and Britain required that the French king, known in the language of diplomacy as "the most Christian King," deliver to the British queen:

> solemn and authentick Letters, or Instruments, by virtue whereof it shall appear that the Island of *Saint Christophers* is to be possessed alone hereafter by *British* Subjects; likewise all *Nova Scotia* or *Accadie,* with its antient Boundaries; as also the City of *Port Royal,* now called *Annapolis Royal,* and all other things in those Parts, which depend on the said Lands and Islands; together with the Dominion, Propriety, and Possession of the said Islands, Lands, and Places: And all Right whatsoever, by Treaties, or by any other way obtained, which the most Christian King, the Crown of *France,* or any of the Subjects thereof, have hitherto had to the said Islands, Lands, and Places, and the Inhabitants of the same, are yielded and made over to the Queen of *Great Britain,* and to her Crown for ever.[29]

The next clause, article XIII, provided that Placentia would be abandoned and that Newfoundland would thereafter belong wholly to Britain, although Frenchmen would still be allowed to dry fish on its wild northern coast. By the same article, the British agreed that Cape Breton Island and the other islands in the Gulf of St. Lawrence might be retained by France, and that the French might fortify them.

Thus Acadia, or most of it, was British, but Acadia was described only by reference to ancient boundaries, and if the past was any guide, it was unlikely that Britain and France would ever agree on what they were. The Board of Trade had warned that vagueness would not do, that a definition was necessary, that Nova Scotia "does comprehend all that the French call Accadie, and is bounded by the River St. Croix on the west, by the sea on the south and east, and by [the St. Lawrence] on the north and ought to be so describ'd for avoiding future disputes."[30] The Tory negotiators, however, ignored the advice. It was a mistake that would dog the relations of Britain and France for half a century

18 | DILEMMAS

Acadians Make Hard Choices

1713–1717

THE PEACE OF UTRECHT WAS A TRIUMPH for Britain's Tories, but their moment was short. A year later, Queen Anne died, and with her successor's coronation came a Whig supremacy that would last nearly fifty years.

By the Act of Settlement in 1701, Parliament had provided that the line of succession after Anne and her heirs be through King James I's granddaughter Sophia, who was electress of Hanover. Anne outlived her children, a German dynasty thus replaced the House of Stuart, and in 1714 the throne was assumed by Sophia's dull son George, a prince who had little to recommend him except Protestantism. He was, though, awake enough to realize that his future lay with the Whigs, who rallied 'round him while the Tories—torn between loathing of Stuart Catholicism and reverence for Stuart divine right—dithered. Then, in 1715, Jacobites—so-called after the Latin *Jacobus* for James—raised the Stuart banner in a failed revolution in Scotland, and the Tory demise was assured. Few of them ever really supported the Jacobites, but there was enough Tory involvement to break the party, seemingly forever.

In France, the sun was setting. In the year of Britain's Jacobite Rebellion, death ended the incredible reign of Louis XIV. For the next eight years, government was led by the old king's nephew, the duc d'Orléans, regent for the child-king Louis XV. Peace and rebuilding, not the sword, became the policy of France, and Britain's Whigs, governing a nation nearly as exhausted, were happy to go along. A quarter century would pass before the great antagonists were again at each other's throats.

The pacific air did not reach across the sea. That it did not, that the Peace of Utrecht started a cold war in America, was the fault of diplomats who divided their sovereigns' possessions but neglected to fix the bounds. Perhaps they can be forgiven for ducking at Utrecht what would be the most explosive issue of all, the American West, the land beyond the Appalachians. Few in 1713 understood what was out there or could foresee how the spread of Britain's coastal colonies and the pull of the Ohio Valley would bring hot war later in the century. No such ignorance, however, excused cession by France and acceptance by Britain of an Acadia defined only by reference to ancient boundaries. The Board of Trade had warned against vagueness, and a century of experience—an even hundred years of conflict beginning with Argall's raids on Saint-Sauveur and Port Royal in 1613—should have made it plain that a definition was required. Yet none was given.

The French had nearly always defined Acadia to include the Nova Scotia Peninsula, Cape Breton Island, and the mainland above the Kennebec, but after Utrecht, it occurred to them that Acadia had never really been that big.[1] If the territory ceded to Britain included the mainland, Canada might indeed be cut off. Frenchmen might wake up one morning to find Britons on the south bank of the St. Lawrence.[2] Thus, mainland Acadia must still belong to France. All they had given up was the Nova Scotia Peninsula—or, better yet, just Port Royal and the peninsula's Atlantic coast.

There was no escaping, though, the fact that some part of Acadia, however defined, was now Britain's Nova Scotia, and French men, women, and children still lived there. What was to become of them?

They could take comfort from article XIV of the treaty, which provided that "in all the said Places and Colonies to be yielded and restored by the most Christian King . . . the Subjects of the said King may have Liberty to remove themselves within a Year to any other Place, as they shall think fit, together with all their moveable Effects." Article XIV also promised that "those who are willing to remain there, and be subject to the Kingdom of *Great Britain,* are to enjoy the free exercise of their Religion, according to the Usage of the Church of *Rome,* as far as the Laws of *Great Britain* do allow the same."[3]

That was fine, but what about their land? Was it forfeited to the conquerors? And there was a paradox in article XIV: The laws of Great Britain prohibited Roman Catholicism.

The language about religion, however, was neither intended nor read to incorporate Britain's anti-Catholic laws, which existed to quiet the rabidly intolerant and were largely unenforced. The British accepted article XIV as a guarantee of religious freedom, and they respected it. It was one of the few things on which they and the Acadians ever agreed. The land question, too, seemed at first to be resolved in the Acadians' favor. It was addressed in a letter to Francis Nicholson after the treaty was signed. To console him for hopes wrecked on the Isle aux Oeufs, the Tories had made him governor of Newfoundland and Nova Scotia, replacing Samuel Vetch, and when he sailed to America in the summer of 1713, he had this letter from the queen:

> Trusty and well beloved, we greet you well. Whereas our good brother, the most christian King, hath, at our desire, released from imprisonment on board his galleys, such of his subjects as were detained there on account of their professing the Protestant religion. We being willing to show by some mark of our favour towards his subjects how kind we take his compliance therein, have therefore thought fit hereby to signify our will and pleasure to you, that you permit such of them as have any lands or tenements in the places under our government in Accadie and Newfoundland, that have been or are to be yielded to us by virtue of the late treaty of peace, and are willing to continue our subjects, to retain and enjoy their said lands and tenements without any molestation, as fully and as freely as our other subjects do or may possess their lands or estates, or to sell the same, if they shall rather choose to remove elsewhere. And for so doing, this shall be your warrant, and so we bid you heartily farewell.[4]

Thus, by a humanitarian bargain, the Acadians could stay and keep their farms or sell them and leave, assuming they could find buyers. If they stayed, their lands were secure, and their deadline for deciding seemed to have been extended indefinitely.

Still, they were going to have to make a hard choice, and they could not put it off forever. They could stay and be British subjects, with whatever consequences that might bring, or they could give up the things they and their fathers and mothers had built and begin again in some other place. They had to decide what to do with their lives and their land, and their new masters were not at all helpful. The British wanted them gone, but at the same time they wanted them to stay. Even in 1755, when the final decision to expel them was taken by an officer on the spot, the official policy of Britain was pro-crastination, really no policy at all. Britons argued, pondered, and postponed—and they never decided.

French policy was more to the point. The Acadians must go to Cape Breton Island. It was given a new name, Isle Royale, and a governor of its own, Philippe Costabelle from Placentia, and in September 1713, some 150 settlers were relocated from French Newfoundland to the fine, deep bay called Havre à l'Anglois.[5] It, too, received a new name—Louisbourg—and everyone expected that the Acadians would join the men and women from Placentia to build a colony around it.

But the Acadians dug in their heels. The rocky slopes of Isle Royale were not made for their way of farming. Their loyalty to king and country might be undying, but upland agriculture was another matter. One of their priests wrote Costabelle:

> It would expose us manifestly (they say) to die of hunger, bur-thened as we are with large families, to quit the dwelling places and clearances from which we derive our usual sub-sistence, without any other resource, to take rough, new lands, from which the standing wood must be removed, with-out any advances or assistance. . . . We know, further, from the exact visit we have made, that there are no lands in the whole island of cape Breton which would be suitable for the mainte-nance of our families, since there are not meadows sufficient to nourish our cattle, from which we draw our principal sub-sistence.

The priest also spoke for the Micmacs, whom Costabelle wanted to bring to Isle Royale as well, but who, like the Acadians, were of no mind to leave the Nova Scotia Peninsula:

> The Indians say, that to shut them up in the island of cape Breton would be to damage their liberty, and that it would be a thing inconsistent with their natural freedom and the means of providing for their subsistence. That with regard to their attachment to the king and to the French, that is in-violable; and if the queen of England had the meadows of Acadie, by the cession made by his majesty of them, they, the Indians, had the woods, out of which no one could ever dis-lodge them.[6]

Costabelle was not convinced. He might have to get along without the Indians, but the Acadians were Frenchmen who would do as they were told. In the summer of 1714, he sent officers to rally them to France and her new colony. His men delivered pep talks at meetings in Annapolis Royal, Grand Pré, and Cobequid, and most of the heads of families swore allegiance and agreed to go.[7] But promise was one thing, performance another. In typical Acadian fashion, they said they would leave, then stayed where they were. The hard choice was made. There would be no starting over on Isle Royale.

And the British, for a while anyway, were content that they stay. The Board of Trade agreed with Vetch, who advised that to let them go would reduce Acadia "to its primitive state" and make of Isle Royale "the most powerful colony, the French have in America."[8] The board decided that for the time being, they should be encouraged to stay, their fidelity guaranteed by oaths of allegiance.[9]

Now they had another choice. Should they swear to obey a new king, and a Protestant king at that? They were reluctant, but had the British been firm, they probably would have put their names and marks to oaths, and they probably would have done it, in the end, without quibbles and conditions. Instead, the British fudged, the Acadians dodged, and for forty years there festered the question of whether they would take the same unqualified oaths that other British subjects subscribed as a matter of course.

Oaths had been taken in 1690 when Phips captured Port Royal. Probably without thinking much about it, Acadians swore then to bear true faith and allegiance to King William and Queen Mary. Their oaths did not keep them from making it clear throughout King William's War that they would not help the British fight Frenchmen or Indians. The same thing happened in 1710, when Vetch obtained oaths from the men who lived within cannonshot of the fort.[10] Again, probably not much thought was given it. The oathtakers of 1710, or some of them, were undoubtedly among the men who besieged Annapolis Royal the next year.

It was not until after the Peace of Utrecht and the decision of the Acadians to stay on their farms that the oaths became a critical issue. The British, as was their right, began earnestly to proffer them, and the French began to work just as hard to stifle them. Their instruments were the priests, who the British permitted to stay and serve their flocks. The French took advantage, using them as political agents. It was probably from the priests that Acadians first got the idea of refusing, and later the idea that they might make conditions, that they might swear fidelity, obedience, devotion, or whatever the British wanted, as long as it was understood that they would never have to fight Frenchmen.

Their cautious resolve first showed itself in the winter of 1714–15. It was necessary on the accession of a new monarch that subjects swear allegiance, but these particular subjects would not cooperate. Thomas Caulfeild, who had become lieutenant governor, had George I duly proclaimed king in the Acadian settlements, then sent officers around the province to see that the people did the right thing. They refused, and the baffled major, not knowing what to do, wrote home for instructions.[11]

No one in London knew either, and Francis Nicholson and Samuel Vetch, the men who might have straightened things out, were too busy calling each other names to lend a hand.

In 1712, before their fall, the Tories had given Nicholson not only the governorship of Nova Scotia and Newfoundland but also authority as a roving auditor in the northern colonies. When he arrived in Boston the next year, he set his sights on his erstwhile partner Vetch, who owed his office to the Whigs and whose reputation for probity was anyway not very high, and Nicholson found what he was looking for. In 1714, he sent home a report alleging that Vetch had "defrauded Her Majesty very considerably."[12]

Vetch fled to London, and as soon as the Whigs returned to power, he fired back. Earlier he had found it useful to praise Nicholson's "zeall to serve his Soveraigne and country . . . particularly these three years last past in which his vast fatigue and matchless generosity hath been verry conspicuous."[13] That was in 1711, but now that Nicholson was looking too closely at his accounts, the encomiums were forgotten and Vetch remembered a Jacobite who "not only reputed it a Crime to drink the Succession in the house of Hanover . . . but us'd to Swear in publick Company's that who Ever was not for Indefeasible Hereditary Right was Damnd Whigs and Enemy's to the Church and Crown." Raging on, he called his colleague "Intirely Illiterate . . . an Ignorant madman."[14]

Beyond the calumny, typical of the time, lay perhaps a whit of truth. Nicholson was a Tory who had risen to prominence under James II, and he may have had Jacobite leanings. Too, his irascibility was noted by everyone, and to some it may have seemed madness. But Nicholson was no revolutionary, and Vetch's words ill befit an officer who reached the rank of major general, helped found both Maryland's St. John's College and Virginia's William and Mary, and under Tory and Whig alike served as chief executive of five American colonies.[15]

Nicholson was an emotional man. Red-faced passion, table thumping, and shouting were his style. Vetch was another sort, effective in a far different way. He would never have torn off his wig and stamped on it. He was a man of business, a schemer, one of that breed of not very scrupulous adventurers who joined robust men of action like Nicholson to build the British empire. Together they took Acadia away from France. Together they must be reckoned the founders of Nova Scotia. Had they worked together afterward, they might have made something of the province they had won. Instead, they fought, and a chance was missed.

19 | FAILURE

Britons Miss Their Chance

1717–1720

FRANCIS NICHOLSON'S INVESTIGATION PETERED OUT and Samuel Vetch regained his job—Whig connections counted in Hanoverian Britain. But both Vetch and Nicholson had seen the last of Annapolis Royal. Vetch never went back, and he held office only until 1717. Nicholson closed out his career with an appointment as governor of South Carolina, where he served from 1720 to 1725.

After 1717, Nova Scotia's governor was Colonel Richard Philipps, a career soldier who had been an early adherent of William of Orange and was a proud veteran of the Battle of the Boyne and the campaigns of Marlborough.[1] His service had earned him a reward, and he got it. The companies stationed at Annapolis Royal and Placentia were merged into a new regiment under his command, and at the same time he was made governor of Nova Scotia and Newfoundland. Philipps gave up Newfoundland in 1727, but he kept Nova Scotia until 1749, when he was eighty-eight. He visited his province twice, once in 1720–22, again in 1729–31. The rest of his time was spent in London reading reports and skimming a nice living from funds appropriated for the king's garrison. During nearly all the thirty-two years that Philipps held office, the government of Nova Scotia was administered by junior officers.

The first of them was Captain John Doucett, who took Caulfeild's place in 1717. He arrived in November, ready to do something about the lax administration that had allowed the Acadians to avoid oaths of allegiance, and straightaway he gave the residents of Annapolis Royal a paper to sign or mark in which they would "most solemnly swear before God to own [King George I] as our Sovereign

King and to obey him as his true and Lawfull subjects."[2] He was handed this in return, probably from the pen of one of the priests:

> For the present, we can only answer, that we shall be ready to carry into effect the demand proposed to us, as soon as his Majesty shall have done us the favor of providing some means of sheltering us from the savage tribes, who are always ready to do all kinds of mischief.
>
> Unless we are protected from these savages, we cannot take the oath demanded of us without exposing ourselves to have our throats cut in our houses at any time, which they have already threatened to do.
>
> In case other means cannot be found, we are ready to take an oath, that we will take up arms neither against his Britannic Majesty, nor against France, nor against any of their subjects or allies.[3]

It was a portentous answer. Hiding behind a spurious Indian threat was the notion that would guide Acadian policy until 1755—the notion that Acadians had a niche of their own, that in all the world they were a unique people, the "neutral French."[4] Here, too, was plain defiance, and Doucett let them get away with it. Their resolve—tentative, probably even fearful at the start—was met by dark looks, reports home, and nothing more.

In London, a thick file was building: letters bewailing the intransigence of the Acadians and the impotence of the king's officers to do anything about it. The missives were read with concern, but no one could decide on anything except delay. The members of the Board of Trade were beginning to think that once the government of Nova Scotia was strong enough, the people should either take appropriate oaths or be expelled. Until then, however, and until British colonists were on hand to replace them, they "should not be treated in the manner they deserve for so undutiful behavior."[5]

Surely a regular civil administration would make things better. When Philipps arrived in Annapolis Royal in 1720, he had orders to organize a government modeled on Virginia's.[6] But Virginia was one thing, Nova Scotia quite another. Virginia had educated, English-speaking people raised in the traditions of the common law. It had institutions, among them a legislature. Nova Scotia had illiterate French-speakers and hostile Indians, and there was no chance that it would soon if ever have a legislature: The Acadians were Catholics, disqualified by law from electing or serving in one. Nor, for the same reason, could they fill the offices a royal governor might normally hand out. To run his government, Philipps would have to rely on his powers as military commander and on a council appointed from among his officers and the few literate Protestants he could find at Annapolis Royal.[7]

The matter of the oaths was worrisome. Philipps was told to invite the Acadians "in the most friendly manner" to swear allegiance.[8] Anyone who refused was to be prohibited from fishing. It was a senseless sanction, as unenforceable as Vetch and Nicholson's regulation of trade in 1710, but it was all Philipps could do. He was not to expel recusants without further orders.

He published his friendly invitation, but no one took an oath. The Acadians trotted out the old excuse. The Indians' wrath, they said, would be terrible. And a new rationale appeared. To swear allegiance to King George would violate the pledges of loyalty to France they had given Costabelle's officers in 1714.[9] Never mind that in 1714 they had also promised to pack up children and livestock and move en masse to French territory. In reality, their loyalty was to themselves alone. If they could help it, no nation would have its way with them.

The Acadians offered a compromise, just as they had done when they defied Doucett three years earlier. They proposed again that they wrap themselves in a cloak of neutrality, agreeing to be good British subjects in every way but one. And, after thinking it over, Philipps decided that might not be such a bad way out. He convened the council, then concluded "that I have neither order, or sufficient power to drive these people out, nor prevent their doeing what damage they please to their houses and possessions." He sent the Acadian deputies home "with smooth words, and promise of enlargement of time," and he proposed in a letter to the Board of Trade "that if an Oath were formed for them to take whereby they should oblige themselves to take up arms against the Indians if required, to live quietly and peaceably in their houses, not to harbour, or give any manner of assistance to any of the King's Enemies, to acknowledge his Majesty's rights to these countrys, to pay obedience to his Goverment . . . how farr this may be thought sufficient to bind them."[10]

He had the same dread as Vetch about what might happen if he pushed the Acadians too far. Suddenly they might be gone, leaving abandoned fields and empty villages. Without someone to take their place, "smooth words, and promise of enlargement of time" would have to do—and such was British policy all through the third of a century that Philipps held office. Never did he or his officers achieve a rational relationship with the Acadians. It was the first time since they had taken New York from the Dutch in 1664 that Britons had tried to govern newly conquered Europeans, and they made a mess of it.

From the start, they failed to convince anyone that their presence was real. There were a few British soldiers at Annapolis Royal, and a few at Canso after 1720. The Union Jack flew at those places, nowhere else: not at Grand Pré, Pisiquid, Cobequid, or Beaubassin, where most of the people lived. The conquest of 1710 must have seemed to the Acadians a reprise of their experience with Phips in 1690, and some were still alive who remembered Sir Thomas Temple's absentee rule in the 1650s and 1660s. Foreigners came and rattled their sabers, nothing changed, and after a while they were gone.

If the Acadians had seen British settlers, they might have reacted differently, but none appeared. It was not until midcentury that the British made anything of Nova Scotia beyond a bare military outpost and a fishing station. The civil government fancied by the Board of Trade was impossible unless there was colonization, but despite recommendations that were made and schemes that were floated, nothing was done about colonization. The only English-speaking civilians the Acadians saw were a handful of military hangers-on at Annapolis Royal, gangs of seasonal fishermen at Canso, and the New England traders who came to buy and sell.

In London, there were flashes of interest, but no action. In January 1720, the celebrated South Sea Company proposed that it be given Nova Scotia so it might "people, cultivate, and improve the same."[11] A few months later, the South Sea Bubble burst, bringing on Britain's worst-ever financial panic and the elevation in government of the man who saved public credit, Sir Robert Walpole. There were also groups of discharged officers who petitioned for development rights, promising to bring families and build towns.[12] Vetch lent his name to one of the veterans' groups, but like the others, it got nowhere, its plans mired in red tape and delay.[13]

Then there was an energetic philanthropist named Thomas Coram, whose proposals were the most abiding and probably the most viable of all.[14] Beginning in August 1713, a few months after the Peace of Utrecht, he peppered the government with ideas for gathering disbanded war veterans and German and Swiss Protestants and sending them to Nova Scotia to build new farms and take up new lives. In 1717, he said he had more than a thousand families ready to sail and populate a colony he would call Georgia, after the king.[15] It was to be on land below the St. Croix, land claimed by Massachusetts, but Coram was flexible, and the site could have been worked out. Too, he was a man who could have brought it off. Later he would build London's Foundling Hospital, and he would be a trustee of the very successful colony that was begun on the Savannah River in 1733, the enduring Georgia. As late as 1737, he was still trying to settle men and women in Nova Scotia, blaming his frustration on the province's military government, "detestable to all thinking men."[16]

Coram's plans and the hopes of others foundered on barriers erected in Britain. First, there was simple inertia. Paper shuffling took time, and while the wheels of government ground, promoters lost interest. Then there was niggardliness. Developers wanted financial help: a year's pay for the war veterans, or transportation at the king's expense. Colonies, however, were supposed to be self-supporting. Money was not spent on them. Why make an exception for Nova Scotia? And if private funds were to be used, there were questions a prudent investor might ask, questions about ownership. Whose property was Nova Scotia anyway? Who had authority to make land grants? Not only the land below the St. Croix, but also the land above it—indeed, all the territory "commonly called Accadia or Nova Scotia"—had in 1691 been made part of Massachusetts. The Board of Trade reasoned that because it was held by France in 1691, Acadia had never really been added to Massachusetts, despite what the royal charter said.[17] That made sense, but would a court agree? Should grants come from London and Annapolis Royal or should they come from Boston?

Finally there was timber. To a nation setting forth on the road to naval and commercial dominance, it was vital that timber be preserved for masts and spars. Nova Scotia was covered with trees, and Philipps's instructions provided that no land could be granted until a survey was made and at least two hundred thousand acres reserved for the Royal Navy. The survey, however, was never done, and the restriction sat in the governor's book of instructions, unchanged until 1731.[18]

The barriers could have been overcome. Coram, for example, could have had official encouragement. He was the most likely promoter, and if he had received even a little government help, things might have turned out differently. His discharged soldiers and his

German and Swiss Protestants would have settled near the Acadian communities. In time, friendships might have been struck. Children would have grown up, courted, and perhaps married outside their nationalities and religions. Any mixing of populations—if not intermarriage, at least neighborliness—would have eased the isolation of the Acadians and might have led them to an accommodation with the Britons who were trying to govern them. It might thus have prevented the estrangement that plagued Britain's rule and produced the debacle of 1755.

20 | CHECKMATE

*Whigs Falter
And the French Rebuild*

1720–1722

BRITONS WHO KNEW MUCH ABOUT Nova Scotia in 1720 knew that they had accomplished nothing in ten years. No produce or profit was flowing to the mother country. No settlers had come. At Annapolis Royal, there were some two hundred soldiers and their officers.[1] Nothing else attested that Nova Scotia was British.

Hoping to prod the home government, Paul Mascarene prepared a long memorandum touting the province and its potential. Nova Scotia produced, he said, not only furs but also wheat, rye, barley, oats, and beans. Its codfish were inexhaustible, and it was rich in minerals and covered with valuable timber. It needed only Britons to come and tap its bounty. "It would be therefore necessary," he wrote, "for the interest of Great Britain, and in order to reap the benefit, which will accrue from the acquisition of this country, not to delay any longer the settling of it, but to go about it in good earnest."[2] It was good advice, although nearly thirty years would pass before it was taken.

In the same memorandum, Mascarene recommended that "the French Inhabitants . . . not be tolerated any longer in their non-allegiance, but . . . have the test put to them without granting them any further delay."[3] And Richard Philipps agreed that something had to be done. If not a promise of neutrality, then force the Acadians to submit or leave, and bring Britons to take their place. He sent Mascarene's report to London with a formal request by all his officers for troops "to curb the insolent temper of the present Inhabitants, if they are allowed to stay, or to oblige them to depart . . . and at the same time to protect those of his Majesty's subjects who will come to settle in their stead.”⁴ In his cover letter, he reported “no likelyhood of [Nova Scotia] being settled under the King's obedience upon the footing it is, and therefore it is necessary that the government at home exert itself a little, and be at some extraordinary expence, for this has been hitherto no more than a mock Government: its authority haveing never yet extended beyond Cannon reach of this fort.”⁵

The Board of Trade got the message. In a report to the king in 1721, it proposed a new start, noting that with only the garrison and a few British civilians at Annapolis Royal, “there is very little room for the exercise of Civil Government.” It recommended that four regiments be sent, and that the Acadians be replaced by British settlers, “for it is not to be expected, that they will ever become good subjects to Your Majesty, and there is all the reason in the world to apprehend, that, upon any rupture between the two Crowns, they may openly declare in favour of France.”⁶

This was the first firm recommendation the board had made on the fate of the Acadians, and it turned out to be the last. The reason it was not adopted was probably that it was part of a much broader analysis of colonial administration. The 1721 report was an important document, a tough assessment of everything Britain was doing wrong in North America. It dwelt on the French threat, and it recommended that settlement be pushed beyond the Alleghenies, that frontier forts be built, and that fundamental changes be made in the way the colonies were governed. If the board had had its way, the charters of the proprietary colonies would have been canceled, nonresident sinecures like Philipps's would have been abolished, and all the colonies would have been brought under one central government headed by a single executive. It was far-reaching, too far-reaching, and it was shelved, lost in the fog and sleaze of early Hanoverian politics.

The Whig government of Sir Robert Walpole—the government of Britain from 1721 to 1742—was built on patronage, graft, peace with France, and status quo. During the Walpole years, controversy was smothered; boats were not rocked. An activist policy in North America would offend the French. Besides, cushy colonial offices could be traded for electoral support at home. Why change a system that, whatever its effects across the Atlantic, preserved calm in Europe and gave the party chieftains a lode of favors to dispense? Management of the colonies stayed the same, and neither settlers nor regiments were sent to Nova Scotia. Indeed, nothing happened, and the Acadians were left to go their anomalous way.

That suited the Acadians, but inaction was no answer to a stagnant province or to the pressure building on the frontier. Britain and France might be temporary friends in Europe, but Frenchmen were pushing at the edges of empire in the New World. In Acadia, they were rebuilding, creating on empty Isle Royale something new and threatening.

By their victory in 1710, and by the bargaining at Utrecht, Britons had won most of what had been French Acadia, only to botch the chance to do something with it. The French made much better use of the parts they kept. The place we know today as Prince Edward Island, then Isle St. Jean, was still a wilderness in 1720. On Isle Royale, however, a brand new colony was growing, and a great fortress was rising. The fortress would have a reputation that considerably exceeded its might, but for a quarter century it would lurk in the North Atlantic fog, menacing the commerce and, some thought, even the survival of British North America. The colony that lived in its shadow would never equal New England. Indeed, it would never even feed itself. But it would far eclipse its nearest neighbor, Britain's lackluster Nova Scotia, and by its mere existence, the French community on Isle Royale—and the battlements that protected it—would checkmate British power in all the northeast.

The new colony had its start in 1713 with the arrival of the first exiles from Placentia. Philippe Costabelle came the next year with more of the remnants of French Newfoundland, and fortune seekers began to trickle in from France and Canada. The lure of America also brought back some of the officers and officials Nicholson and Vetch had deported from Port Royal in 1710. One of them was old Acadia's long-lived judge Mathieu de Goutin, ready to lend his talents to what turned out to be an astounding rebirth. In 1720, when construction of the fortress began, men and money began to arrive in Louisbourg in numbers that were, for the time and place, extraordinary.

Engineers and artisans were sent to build it, soldiers to man it, cannon to arm it. Nothing was spared to make it state-of-the-art. Defenses were plotted in the elegant geometric patterns pioneered by the great Sébastien Vauban, the engineer whose genius in the science of fortification and siege had won campaign after campaign for the armies of Louis XIV. Angled walls and projecting bastions closed off the peninsula that separates Louisbourg Harbor from nearby Gabarus Bay. Carefully planned fields of fire covered the swampy ground beyond the walls, and independent batteries—one on an island, one on the harbor's north shore—were designed to dominate any fleet that might try a run past the reefs at the harbor entrance. City blocks were laid out between walls and waterfront; sites were allotted to fishermen for their wharves and sheds; and, as the fortress grew, a colonial metropolis grew with it.

Visitors can see it today. Part of the town, complete with streets and buildings and eighteenth-century ambiance, and two of the bastions, with their big guns and the towering wall that connected them, are faithfully re-created at the Fortress of Louisbourg National Historic Park, a half-hour drive south of Sydney. It looks much like it did in the summer of 1744, when the building was done, the colony was thriving, and the fortress was nearing its first test in battle.

What tourists cannot see, and what the builders did not understand, are the inherent weaknesses that spelled Louisbourg's doom. Huge as it was, mighty as it seemed, the fort could not withstand a siege by determined infantrymen and artillerymen. Vauban's theories worked in Europe, where there was always a French army near enough to march to the relief of one of his forts and lift a siege before it had gone on too long. There was no such thing on Isle Royale, and since Louisbourg could be blockaded, there might be no way a friendly army could ever reach it. To make matters worse, there were unoccupied heights within easy range, and when the high ground was topped by an enemy's guns, Vauban's geometry was little use. Finally, there was sea sand in the mortar that held walls and bastions together. When the walls came under heavy fire, as they did in 1745, they crumbled.[7]

But if francs could create invincibility, they would be thrown at Louisbourg, and with construction and military buildup came economic boom. Homes, stores, taverns, warehouses, shops, a hospital, barracks, and guardhouses were built. Along with soldiers, sailors, and fishermen there were merchants, innkeepers, carpenters, masons, tailors, seamstresses, butchers, bakers, cobblers, coopers, smiths, laborers, clerks, servants, and prostitutes. All found work, and in the wake of lavish public spending, European civilization sprouted and flourished on Isle Royale. By 1726, only thirteen years after its founding, Louisbourg and its outports held more than three thousand people.[8]

21 | RALE'S WAR

Indians Have a Proxy

1722–1725

FRANCE WAS NOT YET READY TO FIGHT A WAR for North America, but there were other ways the British could be checked. In Acadia, the imprecision of the Treaty of Utrecht would support all the claims to territory that a fertile French imagination might conjure up.

The idea was to pen the British, to confine them at Annapolis Royal, and at all costs to keep them off the coast of eastern Maine and out of what is now New Brunswick. Ancient Acadia was the Nova Scotia Peninsula, nothing more, and in one particularly creative interpretation of history and geography, it was not even that. It was only Annapolis Royal itself and the area between the ocean and a line drawn the length of the peninsula from present-day Yarmouth to Canso.[1] Thus, the Acadians at Beaubassin and the Minas settlements were told that despite British pretensions, they really lived in French territory. The Indians of Maine and the Saint John Valley were told that New Englanders had no business anywhere east of the Kennebec, that France had ceded none of the mainland.

From Quebec, Vaudreuil warned British ships away from the Saint John, which was "still a part of the French dominion."[2] From Louisbourg, a new governor of Isle Royale, Joseph de Brouillan de St.-Ovide, declared that Canso and its fishery were still French, that the ancient boundary lay fifty miles down the peninsula. And St.-Ovide had another thesis, one nearly as inventive. By the French-language version of article XIII of the treaty, France had kept the islands *"dans l'embouchure et dans le Golphe de St Laurent."*[3] The Strait of Canso, he said, is a mouth of the gulf, and the Canso islands are in the Strait of Canso.[4]

The French claims were loud, but nothing was done to enforce them. Instead, Acadia's Indians carried a French proxy. In Maine, it was the Abenakis' last chance to save their land.

Settlers from Massachusetts and New Hampshire had been crossing the Kennebec since 1713, when the Indians had made peace. Left by the Treaty of Utrecht to fight alone, the sagamores who showed up at Portsmouth, New Hampshire, that summer had agreed that they were "the lawfull subjects of our Sovereign Lady, Queen Anne," and they had seemingly given carte blanche to settlement anywhere the New Englanders made a claim.[5] That, at least, was what New Englanders thought, what the English-language text of the Treaty of Portsmouth seemed to say. But the Abenakis had other ideas, and when their land was taken, they reacted as they always had. Barns were burned. Wandering cattle were killed. Whatever the French king had given away at Utrecht, he had not given away fields and forests that belonged to the Indians.

Indian treaties—like the deeds to land that Indians signed from time to time—were written in English to mean what Englishmen wanted them to mean. Even if the treaties were faithfully translated, which was not always the case, they said things that meant little to people who lived by hunting and gathering, moving from place to place and never settling on land in a way that made it theirs to cede by treaty or sell by deed. Land was owned by the spirits. Men and women used it, and they might let others share the use. Those were the treaties and deeds the New Englanders considered so important. The Abenakis were not sanctioning forts and fences to keep them away.[6]

New Englanders reasoned differently. They relied on those same nomadic Indian ways to justify what otherwise would have seemed naked aggression. John Winthrop had rationalized it in the previous century, and the wisdom of the founder could hardly be faulted:

This savage people ruleth over many lands without title or property; for they inclose no ground, neither have they cattell to maintayne it, but remove their dwellings as they have occasion, or as they can prevail against their neighbors. And why may not christians have liberty to go and dwell amongst them in their waste lands and woods (leaving them such places as they have manured for their corne) as lawfully as Abraham did among the Sodomites?[7]

Thus, by New England lights, the land the Indians considered their own was actually empty. The treaties and deeds only recognized the obvious.

In August 1717, a new royal governor, Samuel Shute, tried to straighten out the muddle of settlers' claims and Indian rights. He went to Arrowsick (now Arrowsic) Island at the mouth of the Kennebec to meet the Abenaki sagamores. In pompous splendor under a big tent, attended by members of his council and notables of Massachusetts and New Hampshire, he delivered a patronizing speech, reminding everyone that Indian and Briton alike were dutiful subjects of "Great, Good and Wise . . . King George . . . and they must by no means hearken to any contrary Insinuations, that they will always find themselves safest under the government of *Great Britain.*"[8] Just one big, happy family! He promised friendship and fair dealing, and to make it all even more wonderful, he told the Indians that as a mark of the king's special favor, they were to have a Protestant minister, and bibles all their own.

That must have raised eyebrows among men who thought themselves sovereign and were, as well, duly baptized Catholics. And the Indians probably found particularly galling Shute's telling them that settlement on their land was for their own good, that "they will find the benefit of them in having Trade brought so near them, besides the advantage of the Neighborhood and Conversation of the English."[9] The trade was all right. The neighbors they could get along without.

Indian negotiators liked to avoid controversy, to talk around hard subjects, to parley by making long, dignified orations. Disputation was not appreciated; interruption was unheard of. But Shute was an impatient man. Like Winthrop, he believed that British rights to Indian land were divinely ordained, and when the Indians gave their response, there were matters he could not let pass. The Abenakis' orator, Wiwurna, had little chance to speak without Shute's breaking in to proclaim the authority of the king and the property rights of New Englanders. Here is how it went, according to a British transcript:

> *Wiwurna.* We have had the same Discourse from other Governours, as from your Excellency: and we have said the same, to them; Other Governours have said to us that we are under no other Government but our own.
>
> *Governor.* How is that?
>
> *Wiwurna.* We Pray leave to Speak out. Your Excellency was

pleased to say that we must be Obedient to KING GEORGE, which we shall if we like the Offers made us.

Governor. They must be Obedient to KING GEORGE, and all just Offers and Usage shall be given them.

Wiwurna. We will be very Obedient to the KING, if we are not Molested in the Improvement of our Lands.

Governor. They shall not be Interrupted in the Improvement of their Lands; and the English must not be Molested by them in theirs.

Wiwurna. We are pleased with the liberty your Excellency gives us, of making Mention of any wrong we have suffered.

Governor. They must Desist from any Pretensions to Lands which the English own.

Wiwurna. We Pray leave to go on in order with our Answer.

When Wiwurna held up an olive branch, suggesting that the Indians might "Imbrace them in our Bosoms that come to Settle on our Lands," Shute interrupted again. "They must not call it their Land," he said, "for the English have bought it of them and their Ancestors."[10]

This was getting nowhere, so Wiwurna took an unaccustomed, direct approach. "We Desire there may be no further Settlements made," he said. "We shan't be able to hold them all in our Bosoms, and to take care to shelter them, if it be like to be bad Weather, and Mischief be Threatned." Furthermore, he and his friends would not be needing those Protestant bibles. "We desire to be Excused on that Point. GOD has given us Teaching already, and if we should go from that, we should displease GOD."[11]

Later in the day, Wiwurna drew the line: "As for the West side of the *Kennebeck River* I have nothing to say, but am sure nothing has been Sold on the East side."[12] Then he and the others walked out, deliberately leaving behind a British flag Shute had given them. In the evening, they sent back a letter from their missionary, Father Sébastien Rale, pledging that France would help them defend themselves.

This was tough talk, but there was a peace party in the Abenaki camp, Indians who worried about what might be coming. They must have prevailed at the council fire that night, because they showed up in the morning with apologies for Wiwurna's rudeness and a plea for another meeting. And could they please have the British flag?

The next day, the Abenakis affixed their marks to a new treaty

Shute wrote for them ratifying the Treaty of Portsmouth and disowning "rash and inconsiderate Persons amongst us [who] have molested some of our good fellow Subjects the English in the Possession of their Lands, and otherwise ill-Treated them." They promised, too, "that our English Friends shall Possess, Enjoy and Improve all the Lands which they have formerly Possessed, and all which they have obtained a Right and Title unto: Hoping it will prove of mutual and reciprocal Benefit and Advantage to them and us, that they Cohabit with us."[13]

The Abenaki peacemakers were right to be worried. France was not going to deliver the direct help that Wiwurna and his friends expected. Frenchmen were walking a line that kept them close to but never part of the Abenakis' fight. Vaudreuil had orders "to prevent the English settling on those lands . . . either by means of the Indians or in any other way that would not, however, bring about any cause of rupture with England."[14] Thus, France would wage covert war, proxy war. No Frenchmen would fight it, but the Indians would be armed and supplied by the French. France also furnished the Abenakis' goad and spokesman, the Jesuit Father Rale.

He had come to Acadia in 1694 and built a mission at Norridgewock, far up the Kennebec. He was New England's particular *bête noire,* but he was not merely the political agitator New Englanders thought him. His concern was for the Indians and their land, not the territorial ambitions of his native country.[15] In fact, however, his goals and those of France were the same: to stop the British at the Kennebec.

In February 1720, Rale stirred the wrath of Boston by repudiating Shute's Treaty of Arrowsick. By his *ipse dixit,* the treaty was no more. "A Missionary," he wrote, "is not a Cipher like a Minister. The Indians hold no council but they call me to it and when they have deliberated ask my thoughts. If I approve, I say that's well, If not, I say so and give my reasons, for we must give them reasons." The British "have not one interpreter that can Explain faithfully in the Indian Language; they speak nothing but Gibberish." The treaty is "null, If I don't approve it, though the Indians have consented, for I bring them so many reasons against it that they absolutely condemn what they have done." New Englanders who did not abandon the east side of the Kennebec would be "driven away by the Indians, for assuredly, there shall not one remain there."[16]

In the summer of 1721, there were more pronouncements that

the New Englanders did not want to hear. An eloquent letter to the "Great Captain of the English," probably written by Rale, recalled that the British had agreed at Utrecht to live in peace with the tribes that were friends of France, then asked,

> Is it living peacefully with me to take my land away from me against my will? My land which I received from God alone, my land of which no king nor foreign power has been allowed or is allowed to dispose against my will. . . .
>
> Consider, great captain, that I have often told thee to withdraw from my land and that I am telling thee so again for the last time. My land is not thine either by right of conquest, or by grant or by purchase. . . .
>
> When didst thou drive me away from it? And did I not drive thee away from it every time we waged war together. . . .
>
> It is not thine by grant. The king of France, sayest thou, gave thee it. But could he give thee it? Am I his subject?
>
> The savages, sayest thou, gave thee it. Could a few savages whom thou caughtest by surprise by getting them drunk give thee it to the detriment of their entire nation which, far from ratifying that grant, which would be necessary to give thee any right, declares it invalid and illusory?
>
> Some of us had lent thee a few places but know now that the entire nation revokes those loans because thou misusedst them. When did they allow thee to build forts and advance as much as thou doest along their River?
>
> It is not thine by right of purchase. And thou art telling me something which my grand-fathers and fathers never told me. . . . I have the right to take back a property which should never have been taken to my detriment and which I reconquered so many times.

Again the line was drawn at the Kennebec, and New Englanders were warned again of what would happen to those who crossed it:

> These are the words of the entire Abenaquis nation . . . summoning thee to withdraw from the land of the Abenaquis which thou unjustly wantest to usurp and which has for boundaries the Kenibege River. . . .
>
> If a few individual savages, addicted to drinking, tell thee thou mayest dwell where thou dwellest formerly, Know that

the entire nation disapproves of that permission and that
I will go and burn down those dwellings after plundering
them.[17]

It was one threat too many, and Shute sent raiders to Norridgewock to silence the Jesuit. Warned in time, he escaped, but his papers
were taken, and among them were letters proving what had been suspected all along: that France was the arsenal of Indian resistance.[18] In
the summer of 1722, when Abenakis retaliated by attacking settlements lower down the Kennebec, Shute declared war, proclaiming
"the . . . Eastern Indians, with their confederates, to be Rebels, Traitors and Enemies to His Majesty King George, His Crown and Dig-
nity, and that they be henceforth proceeded against as such."[19]

The war in Nova Scotia began and ended that same summer. Just
as they did in Maine, Indians carried the burden for France. And just
as in Maine, they lost.

Canso was the catalyst. New Englanders had begun fishing there
after the Peace of Utrecht. Frenchmen were there too, working from
their side of the strait and sometimes from the Canso islands themselves, and there were fish enough for everyone. A visitor in 1718
reported everything "peaceable and quiet, the French and English
fishing with all friendship and love, and the Indians thô numerous
very ready to do all friendly offices."[20] But the men who held the
purse strings in Boston wanted it all for themselves, and a frigate was
sent to Louisbourg with a demand that the French abandon their
Canso bases. When St.-Ovide said no, the Royal Navy captain sailed
to the fishing stations and seized the French ships and all the French
property.[21]

Afterward, the French fishermen drifted back, but the raid was remembered, and in 1720, while the French looked on, a band of Micmacs fell on the New Englanders, killing two and plundering the
rest.[22] Governor Philipps was sure that St.-Ovide had put the Indians
up to it, but he held his fire. He did, however, send troops to build a
fort and stop another attack.

The attack came in July 1722, while Philipps was still personally
in command in Nova Scotia, and he found himself "drawn into an Indian War, not withstanding all my endeavours to avoid it."[23] He was
with his Canso detachment when word came that Micmacs were
harassing traders in the Bay of Fundy. Then they hit the coves and
harbors on the Atlantic near Canso, taking eighteen ships, and Phil-

ipps struck back. He convinced the fishermen to fight, and with them and his own soldiers, he chased the marauders and retook every one of the captured ships. At the same time, his deputy, John Doucett, thwarted a Micmac siege of Annapolis Royal by making hostages of a group of unwary Indian women and children. The little rebellion was quickly nipped.[24]

In Maine, the Abenakis held out for two more years, but in the end they were even more badly beaten. After his declaration of war, Shute had gone off to Britain, leaving the fighting to be managed by Lieutenant Governor William Dummer. The war sometimes has his name, Dummer's War, and sometimes it is called Rale's War, after the man New Englanders thought its protagonist.

In it the Abenakis learned a painful lesson. With France on the sidelines, they were no match for Massachusetts. Rale's War was not like the Abenaki wars at the turn of the century, when New Englanders strained to defend their frontiers and were preoccupied with the French. Now, with no French soldiers to worry about, the colonials took the offensive and went deep into the woods, running down and slaughtering Indian men, women, and children in their villages.

The deathblow came in a massacre at Norridgewock on a summer afternoon in 1724. Militiamen had quietly made their way up the Kennebec, and the Indians had no warning. They were in their huts when the New Englanders rushed out of the forest. A few warriors tried to resist, but after a volley or two, they broke and ran for the river, where women and children were already struggling to get away. Most of the people were shot, and most of the others drowned in the river. Rale was in his cabin when a lieutenant broke down the door and fired a ball through his head. His scalp was carried in triumph to Boston.[25]

Peace was made the next year, although the French tried their best to stop it. In an extraordinary meeting in Montreal, Vaudreuil wore the cloak of the conciliator and, thus disguised, did everything he could to keep the fighting going. Dummer had sent commissioners to protest the French infusion of arms for the Indians' war. Vaudreuil told them "that he had never supplied them any, and that the annual presents to the Abenakis and all other Indians, our allies, to whom the King is graciously pleased to grant yearly some token of his benevolence, could not be looked upon in that light." Indeed, added Vaudreuil, so eager was he for peace between his friends the Indians and his friends the British that he had summoned Indian delegates to meet Dummer's emissaries and settle their differences. He was careful, though, to closet himself with the Indians beforehand to make sure they would insist on British withdrawal from their land, and "being persuaded that nothing was more opposed to his Majesty's interests than peace between the Abenakis and the English . . . [he] also privately warned the English of the difficulties they might experience on the part of the Abenakis in concluding a peace."[26] His duplicity was appreciated in Paris, where his report got this endorsement: "It appears proper to approve what M. de Vaudreuil has done; it is of indispensable necessity to prevent the English becoming masters of the Abenakis country . . . nothing better can be done than to foment this war."[27]

But the war was over. In December 1725, the Abenakis of Maine, the Micmacs of Nova Scotia, and the Maliseets of the Saint John Valley sent delegates to Boston to approve a treaty in which they agreed to submit to British law, to live forever in peace with Britons in New England and Nova Scotia, and to allow them "all and singular their Rights of land and former Settlements, Properties and Possessions within the Eastern parts of the said Province of the *Massachusetts Bay* . . . without any Molestation or Claims by us or any other Indians."[28]

For Britain, for New England, and for Nova Scotia, the Treaty of Boston was very good news. The king of France found it "an unexpected inconvenience."[29]

22 | "FRENCH NEUTRALS"

Acadians Win a Promise

1725–1730

THE END OF RALE'S WAR brought another time of peace and another chance for the British to work things out with the Acadians. It would not, however, be done easily. Acadians found little in British authority to fear or respect, and small reason to turn their backs on the French flag.

It was not just language and religion that tied them to France. French officials were gone, but French power and French civilization were close at hand—even closer than they had been in the previous century, when Acadia had been French but the mother country had paid it no attention, and distant and inaccessible Quebec had been the closest hub of Gallic life and influence. By the mid-1720s, Louisbourg was booming. Anyone who made the short voyage from the Acadian heartland could return to tell of the great fortress at Louisbourg and the shops and taverns that filled the town, and wonder aloud at the visible wealth and sophistication of a real French city. Visitors could compare Louisbourg and its display of might and prosperity with Annapolis Royal and its crumbling earthworks, where British officers pretended to govern a colony that had no colonists, a backwater as neglected by the British king as old French Acadia had been neglected by the Sun King. Nova Scotia was a dismal failure, Isle Royale was a brilliant success, and Acadians could not help but notice.

As Isle Royale developed, so too, at last, did Isle St. Jean, closer still to the Acadians.[1] Micmacs had camped there, probably for centuries. Jacques Cartier had toured its coast, Champlain had put it on one of his charts, and Nicholas Denys had included it in his huge St.

Lawrence seigneurie—but nothing much had happened on Isle St. Jean, at least as far as recorded history knows, until 1720, when colonists were sent from France to begin a settlement at what is now Prince Edward Island's provincial capital of Charlottetown. After a few years, they drifted away, but in 1726, Joseph St.-Ovide sent soldiers from Isle Royale, hoping that a show of the flag would entice Acadians to cross Northumberland Strait and try farming—and some did. A few years later, a promoter brought new settlers from France, and suddenly Isle St. Jean had a population. A census in 1730 found 325 permanent inhabitants. By 1735, there would be 432, including 216 from France, 198 from Nova Scotia, 15 from Canada, and a lonesome and remarkable threesome who said they came from Spain.[2]

Thus, to go with the French colony blossoming on Isle Royale, there were French settlers and French authority on close-by Isle St. Jean. Given that only at Annapolis Royal and Canso was there a British presence of any kind in Nova Scotia—and it a presence that inspired no one's awe—the people of Grand Pré, Pisiquid, Cobequid, and Beaubassin, the bulk of the Acadian population, could be confident that little had really changed.

Most important was the fact that with the development of Isle Royale came a new market, a French market, for Acadian grain and livestock. France's big new colony lived on fishing, ocean trade, and the military. It had no agricultural base. Had Acadians emigrated, they might have built a farming community, but they preferred the marshes and the easy lifestyle of home. No farmers came, and the fishermen, artisans, laborers, soldiers, and sailors of Isle Royale needed bread and meat. They could not feed themselves, so Acadians fed them. The farms of the Minas Basin and the Isthmus of Chignecto became Isle Royale's granary.

As early as 1720, Paul Mascarene had reported a flow of trade by which the Acadians "have a continual intercourse with Cape Breton, carrying most of their Furs that way, and supplying it with provisions, of grain, cattle etc. and bringing for returns linens and other goods, to the prejudice of the British trade and manufactories."[3] And as the population of Isle Royale grew, so did the trade and the French influence that came with it. In 1743, Nova Scotia's collector of customs would complain that "thrô the Gut of Canso the French have for many years traded unmolested with His Majesty's subjects of Nova Scotia in French bottoms. . . . they have not only introduced amongst them large Quantities of various sorts of French goods, but also have with great Art and subtility endeavoured to alienate them from His Majesty's Allegiance, and to draw them over to the subjection of his most Christian Majesty's Governors in this Neighborhood."[4]

Before the British conquest, New Englanders had been the Acadians' trading partners, their only customers and suppliers. French merchants had ignored them. Now the goods of France came in exchange for Acadian produce, money flowed from France through Isle Royale into Acadian pockets, and francs became the basis of exchange.[5] Under Britain's Navigation Acts, the trade was illegal, but the British were as powerless to stop it as they were to impose oaths of allegiance.

All through the first half of the eighteenth century, the government of Nova Scotia was a weak, garrison government produced by ministerial indifference. It was a product of Britain's policy of inertia, a policy that matured when management of the colonies came into the hands of Thomas Pelham-Holles, duke of Newcastle. First an ally, later an enemy of Sir Robert Walpole, Newcastle was a fussy, prissy aristocrat, a sure target for the caricaturists of his day, but at the same time he was a coldly calculating and very successful politician. Like Walpole, he was a master of compromise and patronage. From 1724 to 1748, nearly a quarter century, he held the office of secretary of state for the southern department, in charge of diplomatic relations with southern Europe and, more or less incidentally, in charge of the colonies.[6] His administration was negligent and corrupt, and for most of the American colonies, it was supremely beneficial. They were the colonies with something to build on, the colonies that wanted and needed no help from Britain. Strengthened by the mother country's neglect, they became independent and self-reliant. In 1776, they made a revolution.

Nova Scotia was different. Nova Scotia needed attention and got none. During the Walpole–Newcastle years, its administration and the relations between its government and its people sank into blurry disarray.

The governor, Colonel Philipps, had returned to Britain in 1722. He had shown his skill by quelling the Micmacs' rebellion, but his "smooth words, and promise of enlargement of time" in 1720 had postponed hard decisions, and his superiors in London had done nothing to bring about colonization or strengthen a government that was incapable of governing. In 1725, a new lieutenant governor was appointed, but nothing changed. He was Lieutenant Colonel Lawrence Armstrong, a conscientious officer who tried his best but was nervous and morose—not the man to sort out Nova Scotia.[7] He held office until 1739, when his own paranoia and the impossibility of his job overcame his will to live. Armstrong died just before Christmas that year, a victim of his own sword and his own hand.

In 1726, Armstrong had made a try at solving the problem of the oaths. On a Sunday afternoon in October, he summoned the deputies from Annapolis Royal. Their neighbors came along, probably to make sure that their representatives did not cave in. Armstrong had drafted an appropriate oath, and he had someone read it aloud. The response was what Philipps had heard in 1720, what Doucett had been told in 1717. The Acadians would sign only if language were added exempting them from bearing arms.

Armstrong insisted that was unnecessary. Under the laws of Great Britain, Catholics could not serve in the army anyway. But the deputies were firm, and finally it was Armstrong who capitulated. According to the minutes of the council, he "granted the same to be writ upon the margin of the French translation in order to get them over by Degrees." And thus reassured in writing, on the only copy that mattered to them, the men of Annapolis Royal signed an oath in which they promised: "by the Great name of the everliving God that from hence forward we will be faithfull and true Subjects to his Sovereign Majesty George of Great Britain France and Ireland . . . [and] we do therefore promise with all submission and obedience to behave ourselves as Subjects of so good and great a King and Crown of Great Britain which we swear ever to be faithfull to."[8]

The next spring, Armstrong sent officers to the Minas Basin and the Isthmus of Chignecto to administer the same oath. No doubt they would have made the same concession, but they never had the chance. The Minas and Chignecto communities were close to Isle Royale and Isle St. Jean. The people felt more the influence of French than British authority, and they would take no oath "but to their Notre Bon Roy de France, as they express it."[9] For their insolence, the governing council prohibited trade with them.[10] How the council thought it could stop trade with them is, of course, another matter.

In September came news of the death of King George I and the accession of his son, George II. Poor Armstrong had to try again, and it all went even more wrong. The people at Annapolis Royal decided that if they could have one condition, they could have more. Their deputies presented a list of demands, which incensed Armstrong. No writing in the margin this time. Instead, he ordered two of the deputies to be thrown in jail as ringleaders in the Acadians' "contempt and disrespect to His Majesty's Government and authority."[11] But his tantrum changed no minds, and the result of all the arguing and bad feeling was that no oaths were taken at Annapolis Royal.

Oaths were, however, taken at the other Acadian settlements—but only because the officer Armstrong sent granted the people every concession they could think up. Worse, he put it all in writing. In return for pledges of allegiance, Ensign Robert Wroth signed guarantees in the name of the king that Acadians were exempt from bearing arms against anyone, that they were free to leave Nova Scotia whenever they wanted, that their oaths would be canceled if they should leave, and that they were free to practice their religion and enjoy the ministrations of the French priests if they stayed.[12] As a practical matter, none of it went much beyond what Armstrong had already promised and what had been conceded at Utrecht and in Queen Anne's letter to Francis Nicholson in 1713. No doubt Wroth knew that and thought he was doing the right thing, but in a package, in writing, in the king's name, and signed by a mere ensign, his concessions were too much. At Annapolis Royal, the council ruled them "unwarrantable and dishonorable to His Majesty's Government and Authority, and consequently null and void." And, that said, like magic the problem vanished. The council lifted its embargo and declared that the settlers of Minas and Chignecto, "having signed and proclaimed His Majesty and thereby acknowledged his title and authority to and over this Province, shall have the liberties and privileges of English subjects."[13]

It was all absurd, and it was all duly reported, with the result that Governor Philipps, nearly seventy now, had to leave what must have been a comfortable chair in his London club and sail once again to Nova Scotia. By November 1729, he was at Annapolis Royal, and soon afterward everything was resolved—or so it seemed. In January 1730, he sent Newcastle copies of unqualified oaths signed by every man in the community. By the following September, he had extracted the same from the other settlements, and he could congratulate himself and the duke on "the entire submission of all those so long obstinate people, and His Majesty on the acquisition of so many subjects." He had done it, he said, without "threats or compulsion, nor have I prostituted the King's Honor in making a scandalous capitulation in his name and contrary to His Majesty's express orders as has been done by one Ensign Wroth of my Regiment." Even the Micmacs had "made their own submission to the English government in their manner, and with dancing and Hizzas parted with great satisfaction."[14]

In the case of the Indians, Philipps was surely overstating, but, exaggeration aside, he had indeed obtained oaths from the Acadians, and on paper they were unqualified. He had gone in person to each of the settlements. No malleable ensign was given the job. He had the prestige of rank, and he was wise enough to placate the Acadians in matters he could control. Colonel Armstrong had banished Father Breslay, the priest who served Annapolis Royal, for acting as a judge in disputes among his parishioners.[15] Breslay reported that there was a more mundane reason for the ouster: He had refused to lend Armstrong money.[16] No matter. Philipps suavely reunited pastor and flock, and the goodwill he created contributed no little to his success.

Yet how, really, did he do it? Philipps was authoritative and smooth, but it was not just firmness and tact that made the Acadians see the light. In fact, he did it by making the same concession Armstrong had written in the margin at Annapolis Royal in 1726. The Acadians' concern was neutrality, and Philipps promised it. He was clever enough, though, to do it without leaving a paper trail, and his reports home indicated nothing about the bargain he had made.[17]

In a contemporaneous affidavit, the priests at the Minas settlements explained how the people came to swear allegiance to the British king:

> We, Charles de la Goudalie, priest missionary of the parish of [Minas] and Noel Alexandre De Noinville . . . Missionary and Parish Priest of the Assumption and of the Holy Family of [Pisiquid], certify to whom this may concern, that His Excellency Richard Phillips etc., etc., has promised to the inhabitants of [Minas] and other rivers dependent thereon, that he exempts them from bearing arms and fighting in wars against the French and the Indians, and that the said inhabitants have only accepted allegiance and promised never to take up arms in the event of a war against the Kingdom of England and its Government.[18]

Later, the British themselves confirmed the arrangement. In a report written in 1745, the council at Annapolis Royal recalled the oath-taking this way:

In the year 1730 when General Philipps returned to his government he again in the mildest Forms requir'd them to repair
their past misbehaviour by voluntarily Swearing Allegiance
(without Stipulation) to their Lawfull Sovereign His Majesty
King George the Second, and those of Annapolis Royal at first
comply'd, but on the Governours making the same demand
on the other more numerous Settlements, they at first absolutely refus'd; but on expostulation they at last Swore Allegiance after having extorted the same Assurance from under
the Generals Hand that they should not be oblig'd to bear
arms, and the Inhabitants of Annapolis have since lookd upon
themselves to be included in the Same Conditions.[19]

It was the compromise Philipps himself had recommended ten
years earlier, and it nicely resolved a nasty problem. It was a solution
of the sort Newcastle himself might have approved, and perhaps the
duke did approve it, with a wink or a nod before Philipps sailed in
1729. The files now contained this, with the signatures or marks of
most of the men of Annapolis Royal:

> *Je Promets et Jure Sincèrement en Foi de Chrêtien que Je serai en-
> tièrement Fidèle, et Obeirai Vraiment Sa Majesté Le Roy George le
> Second, qui je reconnais pour Le Souverain Seigneur de L'Acadie ou
> Nouvelle Ecosse. Ainsi Dieu me Soit en Aide.[20]*

> (I promise and swear sincerely as a Christian that I will be en-
> tirely faithful, and truly obey His Majesty King George II,
> who I acknowledge as Supreme Lord of Acadia or Nova Sco-
> tia. So help me God.)

The oaths from the other settlements were slightly but immaterially
different.[21] Most important, almost everyone had signed them, and
no qualification, no promise of neutrality, was anywhere in the files.

The Board of Trade quibbled with the wording. For reasons a
schoolmaster might appreciate, having to do with dative and ac-
cusative cases of the French words *fidèle* and *obeirai,* the board wanted
Philipps to go back and do it again. The Acadians had sworn to be
faithful, but to whom? Grammatically, as Philipps had constructed
the oath, *fidèle* had no object. There was always the fear that a Jesuit
might find the flaw and thus deprive King George of his Nova Sco-
tian subjects.[22]

Philipps argued back that the conjunction *et* took care of the problem, "according as I have learned grammar," and he pointed out "that the Jesuits would as easily explain away the strongest oaths that could possibly be framed." He was, in any case, "much indisposed and fatigued with voyaging from almost one end of the Province to t'other."[23] The Board of Trade would have to take it or leave it, and the board took it. The Acadians had what they wanted and the British could pretend that they did, too. An accommodation was made. A promise was won. Questions of oaths, loyalty, neutrality, all now would lie dormant, as would Nova Scotia itself, until the war of the superpowers turned hot again.

23 | ISOLATION

Nova Scotia Stays a Backwater

1730–1732

AFTER THE OATHTAKING, the promise of neutrality, and the official deception of 1730, Richard Philipps made his weary way home to Britain, turning over to Lawrence Armstrong the task of presiding over Nova Scotia and the king's troublesome Acadian subjects. They were, he told the duke of Newcastle, "a formidable body and like Noah's progeny spreading themselves over the face of the Province."[1] Armstrong called them "a very ungovernable people and growing very numberous."[2]

There were between four and five thousand Acadians in 1730, and they were indeed still multiplying fast. Their number had more than doubled since 1710; it would double again in another twenty years.[3] Abundant marshland, theirs for the taking, gave young Acadians incentive and opportunity to marry and start families while years of fertility lay ahead. Parish registers show that women began having children in their early twenties and continued until their forties. The 295 couples who were married at Annapolis Royal between 1702 and 1730 had, on the average, 6.75 children.[4]

And the children grew up and grew old. Acadians were not maimed and killed in wars like those that ravaged Europe, and famines and epidemics—the other regular killers of Europeans—were nearly unknown. Nor were Acadians ground down to early deaths by hard work. The Acadian lifestyle fostered longevity.

It was, though, a lifestyle that depended not only on fertile marshland but also on the world's disinterest, and there were evils in the isolation that Acadians cherished, evils that had worsened with the end of immigration after 1710.

The community was inbred. A few women found husbands among lonely British soldiers, but that option was not available to most or wanted by many. In each of the Acadian settlements, a young person had to look hard to find a wife or husband who was not a second or third cousin. By midcentury, nearly half the marriages at Annapolis Royal needed a priest's dispensation for consanguinity.[5] And with no more immigration, Acadians became, if possible, even more parochial than they had been in the days of the French regime. Before 1710, there had been newcomers, some with educations gained in France or Canada. Now the only new faces the people saw belonged to Britons and New Englanders, and occasionally to a new priest from Quebec or Louisbourg. Almost everyone avoided the English-speakers, and in any case, most Acadians did not know and would not learn their language. What little exposure they had to learning, and what news they had of the outside world, came from the French priests and from voyages some of them made to Louisbourg. Everything the priests taught, and everything travelers heard at Louisbourg, was tailored to the aspirations of France.

Acadians needed to adapt. Nova Scotia belonged to King George, and although the British were ineffective and unimpressive rulers, they were not going to go away. The accommodation the people had made with Philipps would not serve them long. They could not forever be "French neutrals" on British soil. There had been a fundamental change, and they would not accept it.

Some of them lived at or near Annapolis Royal, where they could see British guns and hear the English language, but most were far from British influence and authority. The settlements at the Minas Basin held about half the population. The Isthmus of Chignecto, even farther from Annapolis Royal and the Union Jack, was home to another fourth.[6] Via Baie Verte, only a few miles across the isthmus from Beaubassin, it was easy for the Chignecto settlers to trade with Isle Royale and thus reinforce their ties with France, and the people of the Minas communities also had ready access to Isle Royale—by trail through the woods from Cobequid to Baie Verte, or via even closer Tatamagouche Bay. Through those harbors Acadians sent the cattle, sheep, and grain that helped keep Louisbourg alive. Through them came back the goods, money, and influence that kept the Acadians French.

The goings and comings at Baie Verte and Tatamagouche were a constant irritation, a reminder of Britain's failure to exploit the land

Nicholson and Vetch had won in 1710. The only bright spot that a Briton might have found after twenty years of proprietorship was the Canso fishery, which by 1730 had become a big and profitable business.

Good-quality fish, nicely salted and dried, were shipped from Canso to southern Europe, where they sold for high prices. The poorer, less tasty product went to the southern colonies as food for slaves. Ships crossed and recrossed the ocean, bringing salt and supplies and carrying away cured fish. They were called sack ships, from the French word *sec,* for the dry wine they brought back to the mother country from Spain, the Canary Islands, and the Mediterranean on the last leg of their trade route. They were sent by businessmen from England's West Country, and much of the capital that supported Canso came from Britain, but for the most part the fishery was New England's. Yankee fishermen came in the spring and stayed into the fall, sailing in and out as long as the fish ran. During the 1730 season, some 130 vessels worked the banks. With an average five-man crew, that meant 650 New Englanders at Canso. Each winter, a few stayed behind to look after sheds and gear that would be reused the next spring, and with the little garrison Philipps had stationed there after the Indian uprising in 1720, they constituted a year-round population. But there was nothing permanent about it, nothing that might nudge Nova Scotia along the road to self-sufficiency. Beyond codfish, the only commodity that produced revenue at Canso was liquor. The fishery supported eleven taverns.[7]

Everyone knew the solution to Nova Scotia's problems, but just as in the years after the Treaty of Utrecht, all the hopes and plans for British settlement collapsed. Nova Scotia stayed a backwater, an undeveloped outpost populated by a handful of soldiers, gangs of seasonal fishermen, bands of hostile Indians, and what seemed to the British a swarm of peculiar foreigners who called themselves neutrals.

When he returned to London in 1722, Philipps had explained how the timber set-aside regulation delayed land grants. It was not a barrier that was difficult to understand or hard to remove, but things moved slowly in the government of Walpole and Newcastle. Nine years passed before the governor's instructions were changed, and then only to provide that as soon as any land was surveyed and reserved for the Royal Navy, an equal amount might be allotted to settlers.[8] Still there was no survey, and even had the surveyor done his job, few settlers would have come. The more serious obstacle was the lure of the other colonies. Poor but ambitious young Britons could indenture themselves and thus pay their own way to fast-developing places like Virginia, Maryland, and Pennsylvania, where land was cheap and labor dear. They could dream that one day they would be landowners, free of their indentures and themselves members of the employer class. The conditions that made indenture possible and emigration enticing—an opening frontier and entrepreneurs scrambling for labor—did not exist in Nova Scotia. If men and women were to seek their fortunes in Nova Scotia, the king would have to pay their way.

It would have helped, too, if the surveyor, one David Dunbar, had run his lines and drawn his plats. But Dunbar had ambitions beyond counting trees in Nova Scotia, and he convinced the Board of Trade to let him chase them.[9] He had joined Thomas Coram to promote a colony on the Maine coast, and by 1729 he was at Pemaquid—with a handful of followers and the board's backing as governor of a new province with the name Coram had proposed twenty years earlier. He rebuilt the fort the French and Indians had destroyed in 1696, and New England's "Georgia" was begun. A visitor in 1731 found streets laid out, houses under construction, and a hundred settlers.[10]

Then, however, the Board of Trade had second thoughts. The community at Pemaquid should not be the start of something new. Rather, it might be a way to revive Nova Scotia. Dunbar was told that treating it as a separate province and naming it Georgia would not do, that "because it is a part of, and under the government of Nova Scotia, and being call'd a Province, it may be thought distinct, and not under any Government; My Lords therefore think it shou'd be named George County, in Nova Scotia."[11] That meant that Philipps, not Dunbar, was governor. And there was worse to come. Dunbar's settlement was a challenge to the New Englanders who held the old claims to eastern Maine. They took their case to court in London and won an opinion holding that Massachusetts had never forfeited the territory between the Kennebec and the St. Croix, that the French capture of Pemaquid in 1696 had only suspended the rights of the former owners, and that all was restored by Nicholson's victory at Port Royal in 1710.[12] Thus, Dunbar and the Board of Trade were both wrong. The land below the St. Croix was not Georgia, nor was it George County, Nova Scotia. It was part of Massachusetts, where it would stay until 1820, when the Missouri Compromise made Maine one of the United States. Dunbar was a trespasser, and in 1732 the Privy Council ordered him out.[13] There would be a Georgia, but it would not be on the coast of Maine.

More promising for Nova Scotia was Coram's idea of bringing Protestant settlers from the Continent, and in 1729 the Board of Trade hired a recruiter to find them in the Rhine Valley. It turned out, however, that the Rhinelanders felt the same as prospective emigrants from Britain. If they were to go, someone else would have to buy the tickets.[14] The idea would be revived twenty years later, but only after the home government finally realized that it had to spend money to make something of Nova Scotia.

Another proposal came from Boston's Huguenot church, where someone thought of peopling Nova Scotia with refugees from persecution in France.[15] They could speak the language of the Acadians, and they were certifiably Protestant. A scheme was devised to finance them by paper bills secured on land the government would grant, but it died in an eighteenth-century Catch-22. Until Nova Scotia had a legislative assembly, bills could not be issued on land security; Nova Scotia could not have a legislative assembly until there were Protestant settlers.

A particularly magnificent project was touted by a promoter from Maine named Samuel Waldo, who in 1730 bought the rights of the aging John Nelson.[16] By that late date, Nelson must have realized that his claim to Acadia was not very good. It was said that he let it go for £100. But Waldo pushed it in London, promising to bring thousands of Protestants from Germany and Switzerland and to settle them on twenty million acres. It was grandiose, too grandiose, and no one took it seriously. Waldo's £100 bought him nothing more than a souvenir.

In 1732, Lawrence Armstrong sent Paul Mascarene to induce New Englanders to come and settle—and if anyone could do it, it was Mascarene. He had married a Bostonian and he had influential friends in New England, including Jonathan Belcher, who became governor of Massachusetts in 1730. Indeed, Belcher had such high regard for Mascarene that in 1732 he wrote Newcastle to propose that "worthy, ingenious gentleman" as his lieutenant governor.[17] The post went to another, but Mascarene kept the regard of New Englanders. Everyone liked him, and if his character and career are any indication, he must have tried hard to enlist the settlers who would make Nova

Scotia a success. But he found not a one.[18] Belcher thought it was military rule that kept freethinking Yankees away. "God deliver me and mine," he said, "from the government of soldiers."[19]

And perhaps he was right. Years later, when civil government and a legislature were finally established in Nova Scotia, New Englanders showed up in droves.

24 | FRUSTRATION

Britons Govern
Ungovernable People

1732–1739

IF GOVERNMENT IS TO FUNCTION, one of its pillars needs to be a tax base, but Nova Scotia had almost none. In 1731, Lawrence Armstrong complained that "there is not an inhabitant that pays a farthing rent towards defraying of such necessary charges that attends all governments."[1] That same year, the Board of Trade was told that "the whole Revenue of this Government in its present Situation, doth not amount to about Thirty Pounds Sterling, which arises from a Quintal of Cod fish or the Value thereof paid yearly by every Proprietor of a Fishing Room at Canso."[2]

There was little else to tax. Smugglers pay no customs, and most of Nova Scotia's trade was smuggling. New settlers might have become taxable landowners, but there were no new settlers. Land taxes might have been levied on the Acadians, but no one knew who owned the Acadians' land. They claimed it on the basis of the vague seigneurial grants of the French regime, and some still paid feudal dues to heirs of Charles La Tour, Charles d'Aulnay, Emmanuel Le Borgne, and Michel La Vallière. There were many heirs, many claims, many would-be seigneurs, and much confusion. "These Seignoirs," Armstrong complained, "pretend a right to the greatest part, if not the whole Province."[3]

In 1733, a member of the native aristocracy sailed to London to try to persuade British officialdom that she held all the old rights. Amazingly, she succeeded. She was Agathe de Saint-Etienne de La Tour, a granddaughter of Charles La Tour and Jeanne Motin, the widow of one British lieutenant and now the wife of another. She had conveniently enrolled herself in the Church of England, and with documents adroitly gathered at Annapolis Royal, she was able to convince the Board of Trade that she was "sole Lady of the Manour Lands and Premises of all the Inhabited Part of [Nova Scotia] . . . and greatly beloved by the Inhabitants her Tenants."[4] The board concluded that her fief was worth £2,000, and that with the payment of that amount, all the seigneurial rights would lodge with King George II.

Whereupon Mrs. Campbell—for that was then her name—took the money and retired to live in Ireland.[5] Her grandfather, who had tried a similar scam on Oliver Cromwell in 1656, would have been proud.

Her tenants may have loved her, but they had not paid her much in the way of rent, and the British fared no better at collecting the taxes they thought their due once Mrs. Campbell was bought out. As late as 1745, it was reported that the "Inhabitants pay no Taxes towards the Support of His Majesties Government, only a Small Quit Rent for their Lands in Fowles and Wheat amounting in the whole to about 15 £ Sterling."[6] Not much return on an investment of £2,000. The Acadians paid little or nothing, in effect daring anyone to throw them out. In the end, of course, someone did.

British power showed itself in 1755 in the cruelty of the expulsion, but it was almost invisible in the early years. In 1732, Armstrong tried to have a barracks built at Grand Pré, only to have Indians chase his men back to Annapolis Royal. One of the officers argued with them. Nova Scotia belongs to King George, he insisted. Surely the king's men should be allowed to build wherever they want. "One of them answered that he would not suffer it . . . for that King George had conquered Annapolis, but not Menis [Minas]; and in a most insolent manner, order[ed] Mr. Cottnam and me to be gone, for that we had no business there."[7]

An attempt to develop natural resources met the same fate. It was a grant to a Boston group to mine coal near the Isthmus of Chignecto. The miners were thrown out by Indians who claimed "rent due to them for the land and liberty of digging."[8] There was nothing Armstrong could do about it. He did not have muscle enough to coerce either the Indians or the Acadians.

His administration rested on the instructions Philipps had brought in 1720 and on a scheme of government borrowed from the model colony Virginia, but because the people were Catholic, there was no legislature, and because there was no legislature, no laws could be enacted. He and the council had to rule by proclamation. By analogy to the governor and council of Virginia, they in effect became a court to hear and decide disputes, and they assumed the power to punish noncapital crimes.[9] Luckily, during the first thirty-eight years of British rule, only one capital crime was committed. When the council wrote home asking what to do, there was no response.[10]

The council members wanted to be fair. In disputes between Acadians, they did the best they could, even trying to apply French law. And they tried to give the people a share in government. They recognized Acadians' deputies and appointed notaries—literate Acadians who could prepare legal documents and perhaps even collect taxes in the distant settlements. Had the Board of Trade not refused to allow it because of religious disqualification, Armstrong would have appointed Acadian justices of the peace as well.[11]

Good intentions and a measure of goodwill were not, however, good enough. Armstrong could not really govern. He could only grit his teeth. In 1732, he reported that "the French continue as disobedient to the Government as ever, both in respect of their own private affairs [and] as to what concerns the public, for they despise all orders . . . and obstruct everything proposed for his Majesty's service."[12] In a letter to Newcastle in 1735, he called the Acadians "a very rebellious crew," and the Indians "poor ignorant wretches . . . so guided and led by the French, that they will not scruple to do any base action at their desire."[13]

It all must have been terribly frustrating, and after fourteen years, Armstrong chose his grisly way out. His officers called it lunacy.[14]

For leadership, the Acadians looked to the deputies they themselves elected. It was a democratic system, with its genesis in the scheme Paul Mascarene had blessed in 1710 when he tried to extort money for Vetch. Afterward it was regularized, and deputies were chosen every October in each of the Acadian communities. They published decrees, made representations to the government, kept order in the villages, and settled disputes.[15] To the extent that Acadians accepted any government at all, the deputies governed.

So too, in their own way, did the priests, and this rubbed raw nerves at Annapolis Royal. One of the reasons the Church of Rome was so feared by Britons was the penchant of popes, bishops, and priests to intrude in civil affairs. The Acadians' priests were not trying to run a government, but, just as they had under the French regime, they sometimes exercised authority that transcended the spiritual. Of course, it was natural that people should come to them when an educated hand was needed to write a response to a British demand or when an argument threatened the peace of a community. The British resented them anyway as agents of the pope, and they resented even more their seeming to usurp the functions of the king's officers. Armstrong justified his banishment of Father Breslay in 1729 by blaming the priest's "notorious insolence . . . assuming to himself the authority of a Judge in Civil affairs and Employing his Spiritual Censures to force [the people] to a submission."[16]

The priests did indeed sometimes step across the line, yet they were accepted. Even the man who had made so much trouble in 1711—"that old mischievous incendiary Gaulin," as Armstrong called him—kept his post.[17] The British felt they had no choice. At Utrecht they had promised to tolerate the Acadians' religion, and they kept their promise.

From the first, however, they found it impossible to be tolerant of the Acadians themselves. Armstrong called them "perfidious, headstrong, obstinate and as conceited a crew as any in the world."[18] Philipps thought them "a pest, and incumbrance . . . being a proud, lazy, obstinate and untractable people, unskillful in the methods of Agriculture, nor will be led or drove into a better way of thinking, and (and what is still worse) greatly disaffected to the Government. They raise (tis true) both Corn and Cattle on Marsh lands, that wants no clearing, but they have not in almost a century, cleared the quantity of 300 acres of Woodland."[19] Even Mascarene, who understood Acadians best, disdained their way of life. He found them "very little industrious, their lands not improved as might be expected, they living in a manner from hand to mouth, and provided they have a good field of Cabbages and Bread enough for their families with what fodder is sufficient for their cattle they seldom look for much further improvement."[20] Another officer wrote that they "raise their Provision with the least Labour of any People upon Earth."[21]

National and religious prejudice perhaps, but those judgments are a remarkable echo of the views of the men who had tried to govern Acadia and understand Acadians before the British came. They could have been copied from old French files, from the reports of Villebon, Brouillan, and Subercase. The Acadian lifestyle was unique, and to Frenchman and Briton alike, it was incomprehensible.

Acadians *were* different. They were peasants, but they neither lived nor acted the part. They had learned how to get by without the dawn-to-dark toil that was the God-given lot of common people the world over, and circumstances had let them build their society in an undergoverned, neglected corner of the world, where they were never burdened by taxes, never subject to the heavy hand of a seigneur, never liable to forced labor or military service. The British paid them for the work they did and for whatever food and firewood they delivered. Their religion was secured by the Treaty of Utrecht, their land by Queen Anne's letter to Francis Nicholson, their neutrality by the promises of British governors—and, except for religion, land, and neutrality, and big families, there was very little that Acadians thought important.

A New Englander visiting Beaubassin in the 1730s described life as he found it:

> They have but one Room in their Houses besides a Cockloft, Cellar, and Sometimes a Closet. Their Bedrooms are made something after the Manner of a Sailor's Cabbin, but boarded all round about the bigness of the Bed, except one little hole on the Foreside, just big enough to crawl into, before which is a Curtain drawn and as a Step to get into it, there stands a Chest. They have not above 2 or 3 chairs in a house, and those Wooden ones, bottom and all. I saw but 2 Muggs among all the French and the lip of one of them was broken down above 2 inches. When they treat you with strong drink they bring it in a large Bason and give you a Porringer to dip it with. . . . The Women's Cloaths are good enough but they look as if they were pitched on with pitchforks, and very often the Stockings are down about their heels."[22]

Not fancy, but it was everything they needed, and everything they wanted.

They could have had more, purchased with the surplus from their farms. They took some goods in trade. Tools, cloth, molasses, rum, and maybe a little brandy came in exchange for grain and livestock. Hard money, though, was squirreled away, just in case. The governor and intendant of New France, writing in 1745, thought the people had an inkling that some day they would need it:

> The Acadians, have not extended their plantations since they have come under English dominion; their houses are wretched wooden boxes, without conveniences, and without ornaments, and scarcely containing the most necessary furniture;

but they are extremely covetous of specie. Since the settlement of Ile Royale they have drawn from Louisbourg, by means of their trade in cattle, and all the other provisions, almost all the specie the King annually sent out; it never makes its appearance again, they are particularly careful to conceal it. What object can they have, except to secure for themselves a resource for an evil day?[23]

25 | LOUISBOURG

France's New Colony Thrives

1739–1744

WHILE THE ACADIANS WERE GOING THEIR OWN bucolic way in Nova Scotia, other French-speaking men and women were living dramatically different lives on nearby Isle Royale. The city that lived in the shadow of the fortress of Louisbourg was remarkable for its sophistication, its commerce, and its military display. It was remarkable, too, for the shortness of its life, but while Louisbourg lived, it glittered. Its golden years show what might have been, what the French might have made of Port Royal had their ambition in the early days matched the money and energy they were willing to spend in the decades after the Peace of Utrecht.

When a new governor, Isaac-Louis de Forant, arrived in 1739, he found a boomtown. The Fleur-de-Lis atop the clock tower overlooked a crowded harbor, lively streets, block after block of substantial buildings, and a society that was a clone of the *ancien régime.* Men of wealth and position gambled and intrigued. Their wives and daughters gossiped and flirted. The aristocratic and would-be aristocratic strutted and postured like their counterparts at Versailles, while artisans, petty tradesmen, laborers, and servants knew and kept their places in a community as ordered as Paris.[1] Louisbourg's merchants fattened on commerce that outstripped all the ports of North America save Boston, New York, and Philadelphia.[2] Its soldiers gloried in lofty battlements, glowering cannon, and a fearsome reputation. Theirs was a stronghold that everyone believed impregnable.

In 1739, the town held more than two thousand civilians and soldiers. The lesser settlements up and down the coast had another twenty-five hundred, and there were perhaps as many as six hundred

French immigrants and Acadian farmers on Isle St. Jean.[3] In twenty-five years, the population of France's remarkable new colony and its poorer dependency had grown from zero to more than five thousand—nearly three-fourths as many as the total European population of Nova Scotia after a century and a half of settlement.

Some of them depended for their livelihoods on the military and the money that was lavished on the fortress. Others lived lives tied to the ocean—lives made possible by the almighty codfish and by the fact that in the age of sail, Louisbourg was perfectly sited to be the pivot of French trade in the Atlantic.

In the bargaining at Utrecht, France had surrendered Placentia, the base of her fishery. Isle Royale was the replacement, and the establishments of the fishing proprietors, the *habitants-pêcheurs,* lined coves and bays from Ingonish in the north to Isle Madame and the Strait of Canso in the south. Each was a center of commerce and life, including a dwelling for the owner and his family, cabins for fishermen and laborers, storehouses, a wharf, a garden, a shed for livestock, perhaps a chicken house. The fishermen sailed in little vessels called shallops, hardly more than masted rowboats. Three men, fishing with handlines, were the crew. In later years, the *habitants-pêcheurs* tried using schooners, making longer voyages to the banks like the New Englanders at Canso, but the shallop and the fish that swam close inshore were always the mainstay of Isle Royale's fishery.[4]

The other leg of the economic base was ocean commerce. The French king's American domain now included not only Isle Royale and Isle St. Jean and the original New France stretching along the St. Lawrence, but also Louisiana and the Mississippi Valley, the Caribbean islands of Martinique, Guadeloupe, Marie-Galante, and St. Barthélemy, the part of Hispaniola that is now Haiti, a piece of St. Martin, and a steamy South American foothold in what is now called French Guiana. The products of his New World empire were furs from the continent's woods and streams, fish from the North Atlantic and the Gulf of St. Lawrence, and sugar and molasses from the West Indies. At Louisbourg, the trading routes met. Ships riding the Gulf Stream and the westerlies to Europe from the Gulf of Mexico and the Caribbean sailed northeast to make their crossing at the latitude of Cape Breton. Ships from Quebec leaving the Gulf of St. Lawrence via Cabot Strait had to pass close by Louisbourg. And fish were already there, dried and stacked in sheds and warehouses, waiting to be carried east to markets in Europe and the Mediterranean and south to the slave colonies. Louisbourg was an entrepôt, a trans-shipment center and a hub for ships trading among the mother country, the Caribbean, the Gulf of Mexico, and Canada.

It was all within the tidy system French mercantilists had foreseen when the colony was planned, but markets follow their own laws, and Louisbourg had not been in existence long before New England's hustling businessmen added another corner to its trade. Mercantile laws or no mercantile laws, ships from New England brought manufactured goods and building materials and, most important, grain and livestock, then sailed home with sugar, molasses, brandy, wine, coffee, French linen, and whatever other forbidden but profitable goods might be bought or bartered on the busy quay of America's newest port. In 1740, some 164 ships were counted, most of them at Louisbourg. Thirty-nine had sailed from New England, seventy-three from France, nineteen from Canada, twenty-two from the Caribbean, and eleven from Nova Scotia.[5]

The New England trade was actually greater than anyone cared to acknowledge in a count of ships. Some of it took place at Canso, where Frenchmen and Americans could discreetly meet and exchange cargoes without anyone's noticing. Or captains would clear New England ports with papers showing freight for British Newfoundland, then deliver their goods to Louisbourg.[6] It was lucrative, so no one in Boston worried much about its illegality under both British and French laws. The trade was a lifeline for Isle Royale, where scarcity was a disturbing part of life, and French officials usually looked the other way, particularly if they were offered a cut of the profit. Sometimes, when shortages threatened, French mercantile rules were waived entirely.[7]

The French could have made Isle Royale self-sufficient. They could have farmed it. Most of the workingmen, however, were fishermen with no penchant for agriculture. Others were soldiers and artisans who sought quicker rewards than those at the point of a plow. The fishermen clung to the coast and the smell of the sea. The others stayed close to Louisbourg, where everyone could enjoy the sky-high wages of a labor-short economy. Few of Isle Royale's settlers ever saw the island's interior, where they might have planted crops. They thought that no place on their island had the soil or climate to support agriculture, and that ended the matter.[8]

Too, they were French and set in their ways, especially when it came to what they ate. The wheat they preferred for breadmaking would not grow during Isle Royale's cool, foggy summers.[9] They might have planted hardier grains, such as oats and barley, had they thought of it. They might have planted potatoes, but eighteenth-century Frenchmen disdained potatoes.[10] There were always dried codfish, but how many dried codfish can you eat?

The Acadians sent grain and livestock to Isle Royale, but never enough. Ships brought food from France, but still there was not enough. Their holds were more often filled with salt and other supplies for the fishery, or luxury goods that could be sold or traded at Louisbourg for resale in New England, Canada, or the Caribbean. The gap might have been filled from Isle St. Jean, but that island's agriculture had developed too slowly to keep up with the exploding population of Isle Royale. The fields that lined the St. Lawrence were another source of supply, but ships could not leave Quebec until the river thawed in the spring, and even then, better and less expensive supplies were usually available from New England. Because of New England's competition, flour was sometimes cheaper on the quay at Louisbourg than it was in the markets of Quebec itself. It was, in fact, from New England—and to a lesser degree from Nova Scotia—that Louisbourg was fed during all the years of its glory.[11]

It was a feast-or-famine town. Sometimes there was plenty for everyone. Sometimes bread was rationed and men who came to find work were sent home.[12] With its dependence on outside sources, Louisbourg was not nearly as impregnable as everyone thought. Despite its ramparts and its cannon, it was ripe for a fall.

It did, though, have an aura of strength and permanence. From far at sea, sailors could pick out the graceful spire of the hospital, then the tall chimneys of the citadel, the huge and handsome building that was the symbol of the power of King Louis XV. Within its massive stone walls, the governor had his residence, soldiers and junior officers their quarters, priests their chapel, and the colony its prison. There, too, was the inner redoubt, the haven of last resort should a siege turn out badly. Not many structures in colonial America were the equal of Louisbourg's citadel.

It sat athwart the gorge of the King's Bastion, the keystone of the defense plan. To complete Vauban's geometry, there were also a Dauphin Bastion, a Queen's Bastion, and a Princess Bastion—all packed with big guns and connected by the great wall that ran a half mile between the inner harbor and the sea. Thirty feet high, it blocked the approach an attacker would surely take—unless he was foolhardy enough to brave the Island Battery at the harbor's mouth and the Grand Battery on the north shore.

Between the citadel and the harbor lay the town, its streets laid out north-south, east-west, in city planners' neat squares. The poorer buildings had walls made of wooden poles chinked with mortar and topped by a plank roof. The better structures were timber-framed on stone foundations, with masonry or wooden walls and dormer windows poking through steep-pitched, shingled roofs. One of the grandest, fronting the harbor, was the home of the colony's second-ranking official, the *commissaire-ordonnateur.* Another fine structure, two blocks away, belonged to the engineer. Their offices gave them ample power to look out for themselves, and the *ordonnateur* and engineer had residences superior even to that of the commander-in-chief. When the new governor Isaac Forant arrived in 1739, he found his rooms uncomfortable and leaky and asked permission from Versailles to take the cozier house of the engineer.[13] Turned down, he stayed in the drafty citadel, caught pneumonia, and died within a year.

No doubt Forant also coveted the stately quarters of the *ordonnateur,* but he had brought with him a new man for that office, a wily civil servant named François Bigot, whom no one, not even a governor, wanted to cross. In 1739, Bigot settled at the house on the quay and began a remarkably successful—if notably corrupt—career as a colonial administrator. It would take him in time to Quebec and the intendancy of New France, and in the end to the Bastille and enduring fame for grand-scale thievery.

Louisbourg was Bigot's first major post, and it must have seemed a particularly fine one. With the governor who succeeded Forant—a one-legged navy veteran named Jean-Baptiste-Louis Le Prévost Duquesnel—he presided over a colony that was, for its elite anyway, a promised land. Within the town's fine residences, the well-to-do enjoyed lives of grandeur. Some families had slaves brought from the West Indies. Others had their fires tended and their chamber pots emptied by sons or daughters of the poor, or bourgeoisie fallen on hard times. Dressmakers, a wigmaker, even a dancing master found plenty to do in Louisbourg. Busy clerks scribbled away at the records so dear to French businessmen and officials. An efficient judicial system maintained order, the souls of rich and poor alike were tended by Recollet friars, and there were Brothers of Charity to operate the hospital and Sisters of the Congregation to run a school.[14]

Drink was a curse at Isle Royale, where winters seemed interminable. If bread was sometimes scarce, wine and brandy were always available. Too, Louisbourg had its share of crime. Its soldiers were more often called upon to guard property from thieves than to protect territory from the king's enemies. Indeed, during its first three decades, Louisbourg knew no enemies, and the garrison moldered in a peacetime environment and a society that honored its officer class but despised the men in the ranks.

They were not even regulars. Most were Swiss mercenaries, many of them Protestants. Others were Frenchmen specially recruited for service on Isle Royale. Their rations were slim, their quarters wretched, and in 1744 their discontent overcame them. It was after war had been declared, and operations had already begun against British Nova Scotia, but even the spur of battle could not keep them in submission. Fed up with their duty, their lives, and Louisbourg, they did something almost unthinkable for eighteenth-century soldiers. On a cold December morning just after Christmas, they formed in ranks before the citadel and demanded proper rations, more firewood, and better clothing.[15] Frantic officers promised changed conditions and got them back to their barracks, but it was not a happy portent for the test that was coming.

Deteriorated morale was not the soldiers' only failing. They were part of Louisbourg's labor pool, and most of the hours they should have used for drill were spent sawing wood and pounding nails.[16] In truth, they were uniformed carpenters and laborers, hardly the awesome professional army everyone thought them, and their officers were not much better. With no battle experience—not even an Indian threat to keep them on their toes—they were as ill-prepared as their men.

There was, though, nothing wrong with the officers' way of life. They were Louisbourg's hereditary aristocracy, the colony's upper crust. In France, they would have been expected to live off ancestral estates or whatever they could skim from soldiers' pay and allotments. In America, no stigma attached to commerce, and from the early days, they had jumped in. Some were *habitants-pêcheurs,* others busied themselves in trade. Once sent to the colony, almost no one left. Descendants of six of the eight officers who had taken formal possession of Isle Royale for France in 1713 were among the defenders of Louisbourg in 1745.[17]

Leading the dynasties were the Du Ponts, a family whose roots lay in old French Acadia. The patriarchs were brothers, Louis Du Pont Duchambon and François Du Pont Duvivier.[18] As young officers, they had been posted to Port Royal, where each had found a well-connected wife. Duchambon's was a granddaughter of Philippe Mius d'Entrement. Duvivier's was a d'Entrement on her father's side and, on her mother's side, yet another granddaughter of Charles La Tour and Jeanne Motin. Nicholson and Vetch had banished the Du Pont brothers after the siege of Port Royal in 1710. Then, with other refugees, they had come back to build the new colony on Isle Royale.

Duchambon rose through the ranks to become second-in-command. His brother died, leaving a son, also named François Du Pont Duvivier, who took the commercial route to prominence, becoming one of Louisbourg's wealthiest traders. He was, though, still a soldier, expected to take up arms when the colony was threatened—and in 1744, his time came.

26 | KING GEORGE'S WAR

Acadians Are Tested

1744

BY 1744, THE LONG PEACE, the achievement of Sir Robert Walpole, was undone. In 1742, his support in Parliament had disappeared and Walpole retired to the House of Lords. His place at the head of government was taken in tandem by the duke of Newcastle and his brother, Henry Pelham, and soon after the rise of the Pelhams came another war with France.

The clouds had begun to gather in 1739, when Britain and Spain began the oddly named War of Jenkins' Ear. Along with the *asiento,* the Peace of Utrecht had given Britons limited trading rights on the Spanish Main. British sailors pushed past the limits, the Spanish pushed back, and a smuggler named Robert Jenkins lost his ear in one of the clashes. When Jenkins appeared in Parliament and waved the shriveled ear, carefully preserved in a bottle, Britain's hawks were inflamed beyond any reason the dovish Walpole could summon. The naval war they started with Spain presaged the much greater conflict that began in 1744, the War of the Austrian Succession.

It was sparked by the death of that same Charles VI whose ambition for the throne of Spain had brought on the last big war. He had emerged from the settlement at Utrecht without Spain but with Austria and Hungary and the still imposing if somewhat tattered title of Holy Roman Emperor, and he wanted more than anything else that his daughter, Maria Theresa, inherit all his realm. Before his death, he worked hard for the agreement of the powers, but there were other claimants and a skein of national ambitions, and the deal came unglued. Spain set out to dislodge Maria Theresa's hold on Italy; Prussia's new King Frederick II invaded her province of Silesia; and

France, seeing a chance to finish off the Hapsburg dynasty for good, invaded Austria itself. Britain, fearing the alliance of France and Spain, and worried about what Frederick might have in mind for the royal family's beloved homeland of Hanover, sided with Maria Theresa. So did the Dutch, and an argument over a princess's inheritance became a world war. It would go on until 1748 and end in a truce disguised as a peace, just as the Treaty of Ryswick had ended the War of the League of Augsburg a half century earlier. The only real change accomplished by the fighting was the rise of Prussia and Frederick the Great.

In America it was called King George's War. It was fought in the Caribbean and in Acadia, where the treasured neutrality of the Acadians had its severest test.

Word that war was declared reached Louisbourg on May 3, 1744.[1] Resolving to strike first, Governor Duquesnel organized an attack on Canso. To command it, he named Duvivier, the merchant-soldier. He knew little about war, but few at Louisbourg knew more, and the Canso campaign turned out to require not much in the way of skill. Surprise was complete, resistance only a few pops from the guns of a sloop anchored offshore, and Duvivier's first military adventure was a big success.

It had, however, unfortunate consequences for the French. The British garrison and the New England fishermen who were caught in port were taken to Louisbourg, where they had to be fed. Supplies were short, so Duquesnel exacted a promise that the soldiers would not take up arms for a year and then exchanged everyone for a handful of Frenchmen held in Boston.[2] Before they left, Britons and New Englanders had a good look at the fortress and learned about the shortages that plagued the French colony and the discontent of the men who defended it. It occurred to some of them that Louisbourg might not be so unassailable after all.

One particularly discerning prisoner was Lieutenant John Bradstreet, an officer whose posting to Canso and interest in trade had already taken him more than once to the countinghouses and taverns of Louisbourg. He knew his captors, he spoke their language, and he could judge their weaknesses. Indeed, he was himself half French. Like Duvivier, he was another of the remarkable progeny of Charles La Tour and Jeanne Motin, a son of Agathe de La Tour and her first British lieutenant. Christened Jean-Baptiste, he had anglicized as fast as he could. As John Bradstreet, he had followed his father into

George II's army, where the chance to spy on Louisbourg in 1744 launched a brilliant career. Before this great-grandson of the Acadian warlord was laid to rest thirty years later in New York's Trinity churchyard, he had become a major general.[3]

Naturally enough, Bradstreet had little to say about his ancestry as he began his extraordinary rise in the British army, but his distant cousin Duvivier, campaigning under a different flag, found his own ancestry useful. After his success at Canso, he was chosen to head another invasion, this one aimed at Annapolis Royal. As he led his men down the Nova Scotia Peninsula, he could wear the cloak of Acadian liberator, scion of the great La Tour, come finally to free his people from the British yoke. That it did not work out the way he planned was the result of French mistakes, dogged Britons, and the determined neutrality of the men and women Duvivier planned to liberate.[4]

He landed in August at Baie Verte, confident that he could convince or coerce Acadians to his banner. At Beaubassin and Grand Pré, he made his demands, declaring that anyone who did not cooperate would be "punished as rebellious subjects, and delivered into the hands of the savages as enemies of the state."[5] That was not the way to Acadian hearts, and the people responded by becoming even balkier than usual. A few joined the French. Most just kept their heads down, guarding their neutrality and giving Duvivier no help at all.

He had more success with the Indians. When he marched from Grand Pré, he was accompanied by several hundred Micmacs and Maliseets, persuaded that the time had come to drive the hated British into the sea. Duquesnel had promised warships to blockade Annapolis Royal and lend firepower for a siege, and Duvivier knew that he faced a broken-down fort and a puny garrison. Even without the Acadians, Annapolis Royal would be taken. Then, he assumed, the people would come to their senses.

But when he made his camp, he saw no French ships—they had never left Louisbourg. Too, he discovered that he faced an opponent who would not be bullied.

After Lawrence Armstrong's suicide, Paul Mascarene had taken command. In March 1740, the council made him its president; later, he was sent official appointments as lieutenant governor and lieutenant colonel of Philipps's regiment. As the war began, he was as close as anyone could come, while Philipps lived, to being Nova Scotia's commander-in-chief.[6] Even so, he did not command very much.

Years of neglect had left crumbling battlements and misfiring guns, and with the Canso garrison lost to the enemy, only about a hundred men were fit for duty. But Mascarene would do his best.

The first crisis came even before Duvivier landed at Baie Verte. In July, three hundred Indians appeared, brandishing weapons and demanding surrender. At their head was an extraordinary priest, Jean-Louis Le Loutre, a missionary who, when the war began, had traded his cassock for a musket and found his niche.[7] All through the next decade, the warrior-abbé would be an unyielding thorn in the British side. Later they would put a price on his head.

Le Loutre should have waited for Duvivier. If he had, and if the warships Duquesnel had promised to send from Louisbourg had arrived, Mascarene's defense probably would have collapsed. Instead, Le Loutre arrived too soon, the warships never arrived at all, and Mascarene became the hero of 1744. A message of defiance during the July attack shows the state of mind that saved Annapolis Royal for Britain. On July 14, Mascarene sent this to Le Loutre and his Indians:

Gentlemen. The first shot you heard fired from the Fort was according to our custom when we think we have enemies. Afterwards your people killed two of our soldiers who were in the gardens without arms. I am resolved to defend this Fort until the last drop of my blood against all the enemies of the king of Great Britain, my master, whereupon you can take your course.[8]

When reinforcements arrived from Boston, the Indians gave up, and Le Loutre had no choice but to watch them disperse.

Mascarene was just as resolute when Duvivier showed up two months later. Finding no ships, the Frenchman tried to parley the fort into submission. He proposed a truce until the navy came. Then the defenders would know they had no chance and could surrender with honor. Some of the British officers wanted to agree. Mascarene talked them out of it, then found out that his men, few and ragged, were ready for a fight. When they heard that negotiations had ended, "they express'd their assent by three chearfull Huzzas to my great satisfaction."[9]

Duvivier mounted a formal siege, but he had too little artillery, his French soldiers were too few, and his Indian allies were no help. It was not their way of fighting. The techniques of siege were for Europeans, not Indians. After three weeks of desultory fire, the French

side had advanced not at all and the French warships were still miss-
ing. When Mascarene was reinforced again, Duvivier's men grew
even more discouraged, and they abandoned Annapolis Royal for
good when an officer named de Gannes arrived from Louisbourg with
definite word that the French ships would not be coming. They
would be used instead to protect Isle Royale's shipping, threatened
now by New England privateers cruising off Cape Breton. Duvivier
returned to Louisbourg, then sailed to France to plan a new and bigger Nova Scotia campaign for the next year. de Gannes took command and set out to find winter quarters.

"[To] the timely Succours receiv'd from the Governor of Massachusetts," Mascarene said, "and our French Inhabitants refusing to
take up arms against us, we owe our preservation."[10] He might, in
fairness, also have thanked the French planners.

Mascarene did what he could to identify the few Acadians who
had gone over to Duvivier, but for the most part he accepted the explanation that what little had been given the French in the way of
supplies and labor was coerced, and he accepted as well the Acadians'
argument that their obligations as subjects of the British king required nothing more than that they sit on their hands when an enemy invaded. In November, he sent a letter to Beaubassin, warning
the people against helping the French but giving them implicit permission to stay out of the war. "If in taking this oath of allegiance,"
he said, "the government was kind enough to say to you, that it
would not compel you to take up arms, it was out of pure deference,
and more than had been stipulated for you. In consequence of your
oath you owe every obedience and every assistance to the King your
Sovereign; and you ought to take it as a great favour that he does not
compel you to take up arms."[11] Thus Acadian neutrality, tested now
in war, was once again officially blessed.

Even when the Acadians were confronted by soldiers marching
under the old flag, neutrality remained their credo. When de Gannes
appeared at Grand Pré in October, the deputies begged him to go
away. "We live," they said, "under a mild and tranquil government,
and we have all good reason to be faithful to it. We hope therefore,
that you will have the goodness not to separate us from it; and that
you will grant us the favour not to plunge us into utter misery."[12]
Whereupon de Gannes, unwilling to endure a winter of Acadian ran-
cor, withdrew to Louisbourg with all his men.

Neutrality, it seemed, was a viable policy. Too, Acadians could tell that someone, for a change, was paying attention to British Nova Scotia. In each of the sieges in 1744, Mascarene had help when he needed it, help that discouraged the French and Indians and opened the eyes of the Acadians. It was of no consequence to them that it came not from London, where apathy still ruled, but from Boston and a powerful governor who, almost alone among British officials, believed that Nova Scotia was important.

The governor was William Shirley.[13] He had come to Massachusetts in 1731, an ambitious barrister and protégé of Newcastle, sent by his patron to find the fame and fortune that probably would elude him in a London overrun by lawyers. At first Jonathan Belcher's ally, he later turned on his friend and procured the governorship for himself. Shirley held it from 1741 to 1757, sixteen tumultuous years, and more than anyone else, British or French, he held in his hands through all those years the future of Nova Scotia.

Indeed, he had a fixation on Nova Scotia, calling it "the key of all the Eastern Colonies upon the Northern Continent on this side of Newfoundland."[14] Time and again he stressed its importance and predicted disaster should the French win it back—and eventually his voice was heard. No one before Shirley had been able to interest the home government in colonizing or even taking particular notice of the place Nicholson and Vetch had won in 1710. His arguments would finally overcome thirty-five years of indifference.

In the summer of 1744, Shirley's task was to convince the General Court to defend Annapolis Royal, and he obtained the members' approval of the reinforcements that helped save Mascarene. The thrifty Yankees insisted that he look to London for financing, and he prevailed even in that. In September, a royal order was issued, promising to pay for everything.[15]

Then, the following year, Shirley met and won the greatest test of his powers of leadership and organization, embarking New England on an adventure that would astound Europe and America alike.

27 | INCREDIBLE VICTORY

New Englanders Do the Impossible

1744–1745

By 1744, THE FRENCH COLONY ON ISLE ROYALE was more than an annoyance. Men who made their livings from the fishery feared the *habitants-pêcheurs,* and the trade of Boston and other New England ports was plainly at risk as long as French men-of-war sailed in and out of their Cape Breton refuge. The loss of Canso and two attempted assaults on Annapolis Royal in the opening months of the war showed, too, that with the French so near, the border of Massachusetts itself might be vulnerable.

Everyone in Boston, though, including Governor Shirley, thought the conquest of Louisbourg too much for New England to undertake. It was a job for professionals. Untrained colonials would be no match for French regulars and Vauban's deadly fields of fire. In the War of Jenkins' Ear, New England had lent its young men to a disastrous expedition against a similar stronghold, Spanish Cartagena on the coast of present-day Colombia. Most of them never came back, and Cartagena was remembered in their hometowns.

But minds began to change late in 1744, when the prisoners from Canso returned to report that the French at Louisbourg were short of supplies and riven by discontent. If New England struck quickly, before ships and soldiers came from France, the fortress would fall. John Bradstreet had a plan—and a voice to go with it. An even louder proponent was William Vaughan, a clamorous merchant and would-be soldier from Maine's Damariscotta River. He had traded at Louisbourg and claimed to know how the fortress could be taken, and, with Bradstreet and a few others, he convinced Shirley. In January 1745, the governor summoned the General Court, swore its members to secrecy, and proposed an invasion.[1]

They turned him down. It was too risky. Let the British do it! But Shirley's enthusiasm was growing, and it was contagious. He lobbied the legislators harder. Vaughan scurried around the colony drumming up support, and petitions were presented from Boston, Salem, and Marblehead—from shipowners and fishermen who had most to lose from the French threat to ocean commerce and most to gain from elimination of French competition. A committee reconsidered, met with some of the released prisoners, and reported favorably. Three weeks after their first refusal, the members of the General Court debated for a day and a night and then, by a margin of one vote, authorized Shirley to raise three thousand men to send against Louisbourg.[2]

Now the doubts of the prudent were forgotten, and war fever raged. Shirley threw all his prodigious energy into recruiting and equipping an army. He obtained pledges of men and ships from the other New England colonies, he alerted the duke of Newcastle and the lords of the Admiralty in London, and he wrote urgently to Commodore Peter Warren, the Royal Navy's commander in the West Indies, seeking warships to help blockade the French. He created a navy of his own out of sloops and schooners and Massachusetts's own newly commissioned twenty-gun frigate. Finally, he affixed his name to a naively detailed plan for a night landing and precisely timed assaults—all to be launched just before dawn, while the French slept.[3]

Shirley was a strategist, not a tactician. His scheme made no allowance for drifting ice, fog, surf, lost soldiers, and boggy ground between landing place and fortress—to say nothing of wakeful Frenchmen. Fortunately, however, the general he chose was a realist who would go his own way. He was William Pepperrell, another Maine merchant, the popular squire of Kittery, at the mouth of the Piscataqua. Except as colonel of the militia, jovially commanding friends and neighbors on drill days, Pepperrell had no military experience. He was, though, shrewd and practical, and he was so well liked that he was the best choice Shirley could have made to lead the spirited amateurs who set out early in April 1745 to batter down the walls of Louisbourg.

Other high-ranking positions went to men Shirley wanted to favor. One of the brigadiers was Samuel Waldo—he who had claimed John Nelson's inheritance of Nova Scotia in 1730. The irrepressible William Vaughan was made a member of Pepperrell's council. John Bradstreet, a professional, would be lieutenant colonel of one of the

Massachusetts regiments. The parole he and the other Canso prisoners had given the previous year was simply ignored. To be commodore of the provincial navy, Shirley named Captain Edward Tyng, sailor son of the ill-fated governor the Puritans had sent to Port Royal after Phips's conquest in 1690.

Recruiting was helped by promises of plunder in the mansions and storehouses of the French and by the religious passion that had always set New Englander against Frenchman. Louisbourg was not just a nest of privateers and a mine of booty. It was a den of popery. The touring evangelist George Whitefield composed a motto: *Nil desperandum Christo duce*—Never despair when Christ leads—and an expedition that was meant to stop a threat to profitable trade and build a monopoly of dried codfish became a latter-day Crusade. Pepperrell's chaplain, seventy-year-old Samuel Moody, armed himself with an ax, the better to smash the idols he knew he would find behind the walls.

Letters poured in with advice for Pepperrell, pleas for commissions, and prayers for success. "O," pined one writer, "that I could be with you and dear Mr. Moodey in that single church to destroy the images their sett up, and the true Gospel of our Lord and Saviour Jesus Christ their preached."[4] From a church in Marblehead came a plan for the army's encampment, advice for conduct of the siege, and assurance that "the cause is God's so far as we can well say any cause of this nature can be; for all that is dear to us in our country, our flourishing, yea, our very subsistence in it, yea, our religion, all lyes at stake."[5] On the military side at least, Pepperrell's Marblehead correspondent knew what he was talking about. He was that same Reverend John Barnard whose wig was shot off in Wainwright's retreat from Port Royal in 1707.

Benjamin Franklin, in Philadelphia with his tongue in his cheek, calculated that forty-five million prayers were offered. So much supplication, he told his brother in Boston, "set against the prayers of a few priests in the garrison, to the Virgin Mary, give a vast balance in your favor. If you do not succeed, I fear I shall have but an indifferent opinion of Presbyterian prayers in such cases, as long as I live. Indeed, in attacking strong towns I should have more dependence on *works,* than on *faith.*"[6]

Neither works nor faith, however, nor even the lure of loot and glory, were likely to take Pepperrell's army over the walls if the French were resupplied and reinforced. Ships to blockade Louisbourg were indispensable, and it seemed for a time that, except for Tyng's ragtag squadron, there would be none. Commodore Warren, on station in Antigua, badly wanted to join. He was an ambitious officer with an American wife, a countryseat on Manhattan Island, and an itch to be governor of New York.[7] He saw in the invasion of Isle Royale a chance for Anglo-American cooperation in a glorious cause—and, not so incidentally, a chance to boost his own career—but he had orders that did not permit him to leave the Caribbean. Regretfully, he declined Shirley's plea.

Then new orders arrived. Warren was to "attack and distress the Enemy in their Settlements, and annoy their Fishery and Commerce."[8] That was all he needed to race north with his flagship and two other big ships of the line. Two more would join them off Cape Breton Island to complete the blockade that sealed Louisbourg's fate.

The besiegers were 4,250 strong. Massachusetts enlistments had swelled to about 3,300, and there were 500 men from Connecticut and 450 from New Hampshire. They sailed in some ninety fishing boats and other odd transports—the landlubbers quaking from seasickness but bursting with excitement—to reach their rendezvous at Canso in mid-April. Easterly winds had piled drifting ice in Gabarus Bay, where Shirley and Pepperrell had planned their landing, and there could be no invasion until it cleared. Pepperrell used the delay to give his men the rudiments of drill and a little familiarity with the ordnance they had brought. It included a supply of specially cast forty-two-pound cannonballs, but no forty-two-pound cannon. The New Englanders knew the French had the heavy guns. Providence, they expected, would deliver them.

By May 10, 1775, the ice was gone and the fleet set sail from Canso. Toward evening, the ships were becalmed, and it was not until the next morning that they made good the sixty miles to Louisbourg. That took care of the nighttime surprise Shirley had planned, but when the towers of the town came in view at dawn on May 11, the men could take heart in a glistening spring morning, a portent of New England luck. During the seven-week siege that followed, they had to contend with fog and sometimes a chilly wind, but there were only four days of rain to bedevil them. Here was the divine intervention they expected. Even more telling was the fact that in the days to come, unruly and unskilled fishermen and farmboys showed uncommon tenacity and bravery.

To fight them, there were 560 French and Swiss soldiers and 900 militiamen drawn from Louisbourg and the fishing stations around it. At their head was François Duvivier's uncle, Louis Duchambon, who had taken command in October 1744 on the untimely death of Duquesnel. A peacetime soldier who had not heard the sound of a gun fired in anger since the surrender of Port Royal in 1710, Duchambon was ill-prepared for the job, and he had as little faith in his troops as they probably had in him. After the 1744 Christmas mutiny, he and François Bigot had recommended that the entire garrison be replaced.[9]

But when the test came, rebellious soldiers joined soft civilians to fight with courage and dash. It was not a lack of valor that lost Louisbourg for France. Despite their discontent, and despite the fate that might await them at home because of their mutiny, very few soldiers deserted. There were blunders on the French side; New Englanders were determined and lucky; British sailors knew their business; and walls, bastions, and fields of fire were not as well built and cleverly designed as everyone thought. Those were the determinants of New England's stunning victory.

Duchambon knew that trouble might be coming, but not until the last moment did he realize that he faced an invasion. He had sent Duvivier to France to find ships and men for a new campaign against Annapolis Royal, which would remove the pressure. The worst that might happen, he thought, was an attempted blockade and perhaps a try at forcing the harbor. Warships would surely come from France to lift a blockade, and with the Island Battery and the Grand Battery armed and ready, he was confident that he could fight off an attack by sea.

The New Englanders, however, were about to attack from the land. And Duvivier's mission had failed. Ships would be sent to Louisbourg, but no soldiers to campaign in Nova Scotia. The frigate *Renommée* had sailed with dispatches telling Duchambon the decision, but she was held up by contrary winds. When she finally arrived at the end of April, drifting ice kept her at sea. Then, in a running fight, Tyng's squadron drove off the frigate, and Duchambon never received the word. He was still looking ahead to a Nova Scotia campaign, and trusting to his harbor batteries, even as Pepperrell's men were about to land at his back.

Duchambon had seen Tyng's ships on the horizon, but he thought they were French, waiting for the ice to clear so they could enter the harbor with reinforcements. On May 7, however, a Basque vessel slipped through the blockade with the news that they were American. Still, it was a naval problem. The ships from France would deal with it. Then, on the morning of May 11, when men on the parapets saw masts and sails crowding Gabarus Bay, Duchambon finally understood what was happening.

He ordered a sortie. Pepperrell sent boats and men to make a feint on the north shore, while oarsmen pulled the main force to a cove two miles away. The French followed the fake, and by the time they had raced back along the beach, enough New Englanders were ashore to win a firefight. It left six Frenchmen dead, six wounded, one captured, and the others fleeing for the fortress. Afterward, it was only the surf that held up the invaders.

During the next few days, they manhandled munitions and supplies ashore and set up a camp. The biggest problem was the heavy cannon. Between Gabarus Bay and Louisbourg are two miles of swamp, and it seemed impossible that the guns could be moved close enough. But with men pulling and pushing through the mud, and an ingenious use of sleds hammered together to support the gun carriages, they managed it. Four days after they landed, they had the citadel under fire. In the following weeks, they pushed cannon and mortars closer and closer, planting batteries on undefended high ground west of the fortress, then relentlessly pounding the King's Bastion, the Dauphin Bastion, and the town's west gate.

Their big break came two days after the landing. Keen to make his mark, Vaughan led a raid around the harbor, burning storehouses and doing what damage he could across from the town. He was making his way back when he passed through the woods behind the Grand Battery and saw no flag flying. Could it have been abandoned? His men crept through the gate and found no Frenchmen, whereupon Vaughan sent a runner to tell Pepperrell "that with the grace of God and the courage of about thirteen men I entred this place about nine a clock and am waiting here for reinforcement and flag."[10]

The Grand Battery had not been given up lightly. It was a key to the French scheme of defense, a self-contained fortress with walls and towers and twenty-eight of the forty-two-pounders the New Englanders were looking for. It was, however, planned for use against a navy. Most of its guns were fixed in positions to fire at the harbor, and although it was not untenable in the event of attack from the land, its defense in the face of infantry would require more men than Duchambon could spare. He and his officers had made what seemed a wise decision to abandon it, pull back the men who held it, and rely on the Island Battery to drive off enemy ships. The flaw in their plan was that the Grand Battery could fire not only on the harbor but also across it onto the town; its defenders, in a hurry to leave, neither removed nor properly spiked the guns.

Vaughan's summons was answered by Bradstreet, accompanied by men to hold the place won so fortunately and bloodlessly. Gunsmiths were sent to drill out the metal rods that Duchambon's gunners had not very carefully hammered into the touchholes of the big guns, and within a day they were firing. Pepperrell's cannon were blasting away from the south and Warren's squadron and Tyng's ships were cruising off the coast. Louisbourg was in a vise.

On May 18, Pepperrell sent a messenger with a summons to surrender. Duchambon's answer was a courteous refusal, so Pepperrell and his council decided on an assault. The fortress would be taken by storm on the night of May 20. But if the officers had been impressed with their cheap victory at the Grand Battery, the soldiers, looking up at thirty-foot walls and booming French cannon, were not so sure. It was a democratic army, and as the day went on and orders circulated from company to company, the men put it plainly. They were not about to rush those walls. Their leaders thought again and decided that if the troops felt that way, they would call off the whole thing. Warren, who had come ashore to survey the situation, was appalled. Matters were not resolved that way in the Royal Navy.

Warren's ships had firepower that could make a big difference, but only if they could enter the harbor. Somehow, the Island Battery had to be silenced—a tough assignment for anyone, let alone Pepperrell's untrained provincials. The battery sat squarely in the harbor entrance, the rocks around it pounded by the surf. There were only two landing places, and behind the parapets were two hundred Frenchmen and thirty-six cannon. Pepperrell had plenty of men who were willing to dare it, but try after aborted try attested to the disorder and confusion that ruled his army—as well as the fact that his men's élan was too often fueled by rum. One attack was canceled when boats failed to appear in time to carry the troops, another when boats and men were lost in fog. Still another had to be called off because the men were "noisy and in liquor."[11]

Finally, on the night of June 6, four hundred men were ferried across the harbor to launch a surprise attack. The first few boats scraped ashore without alerting the French, but surprise was lost when an overenthusiastic and probably overindulgent militiaman bellowed out three cheers, sending the defenders to their guns. After a two-hour fight, the New Englanders withdrew in disorder. Nearly two hundred had been killed, wounded, or captured, and all thoughts of storming the Island Battery were forgotten.

Now Pepperrell had to be concerned about a siege bogged down and an army on the verge of disintegration. Despite the blessing of good weather, the sick list grew longer and longer. No one in those days knew much about camps and sanitation, and dysentery swept the ranks. Too, men were being maimed and killed not only by the French but also by their own cannon. In the finest American tradition, if one measure of powder was good, two were better. Overloaded by overeager hands, the guns sometimes exploded in the gunners' faces. The men were brave enough, but they were woefully inexpert. Besides, they were on a lark, cut loose from wives and families and the restraints of home, and their officers were not the disciplinarians needed to keep them in line. Liquor was deemed indispensable by men and officers alike. Pepperrell's council ordered a rum ration to ward off the fog and chill, and more was easily found. Samuel Waldo, who had taken command of the Grand Battery, had to ask Pepperrell to send "good gunners that have a disposition to be sober in the daytime."[12]

Nor were matters very rosy on Duchambon's side of the walls. Food and powder were running out, and the guns were taking a toll on the fortress and the morale of its defenders. To escape the shells, women and children were sequestered day and night in casements covered with timbers. Soldiers and militiamen fought sleeplessness to keep the guns firing. By night, they carried timber and stone and labored with hands and shovels to shore up crumbling walls and gates. They could not keep it up forever. Unless relief came soon, Louisbourg would fall.

For a while, relief was teasingly close. In January 1745, a lieutenant named Marin had set out with six hundred soldiers and Indians overland from Quebec to join the campaign Duchambon had planned in Nova Scotia. In April, with his eyes still firmly glued on that project, and with no idea that Louisbourg was about to be besieged, Duchambon sent them orders to march on Annapolis Royal, and it was not until May 16, much too late, that he hurried off a messenger to bring them back. Had they reached Louisbourg in time, Marin and his men might have fallen on Pepperrell's rear. As it turned out, they pulled back from Annapolis Royal before they had accomplished anything beyond the capture of two schooners bringing supplies to Paul Mascarene, and they never reached Louisbourg at all. They made a try, only to be stopped in a brisk skirmish at Tatamagouche Bay by men and ships from Tyng's squadron.[13]

Even more devastating was the blunder of the captain of the sixty-four-gun *Vigilant,* which had sailed from France next after the frigate *Renommée* and was laden with men, food, and munitions. Screened by fog, the *Vigilant* penetrated the blockade, and by May 30, she was just outside the harbor. Her captain had only to conn his ship to the Island Battery and safety under its guns, but he could not resist a prize. When a smaller British ship came into view, he turned away to charge after it. The Briton led him over the horizon to Warren's squadron and into a battle the foolish Frenchman lost. Soon British officers were toasting each other with wine the *Vigilant* had carried, and New Englanders were consuming the stores and firing the ordnance that might have saved Louisbourg.

The final blow came when Pepperrell's officers found a way to quiet the Island Battery. On the opposite shore, along the northern arm of the harbor entrance, was more unoccupied high ground. Conveniently, the French had even dumped a few old cannon in the water below it. The guns were dried out, more cannon and mortars were hauled to the site, and a new battery was mounted. By June 21, it was firing from the heights, and the French gunners were driven away within a few days.

With the Island Battery out of action, an assault could be made by land and sea. Warren's ships would force the now-defenseless harbor and pour broadsides into the town. From the land, Pepperrell's men would scale the walls and charge through the gaps their guns had blasted, and this time there would be no holding back. Everyone could taste victory and plunder. Warren wrote Pepperrell to suggest that they "soon . . . keep a good house together, and give the ladys of Lewisbourg a gallant ball."[14]

The attack was planned for the first fair wind that would bring the ships in range, but late Saturday afternoon, June 26, before anyone had to pick up a musket and steel himself for hand-to-hand combat, an officer appeared at the west gate with a truce flag and a note from Duchambon. Two days later, Pepperrell and Warren accepted his surrender.

28 | ANXIETIES

An Army Chafes, Britons Talk of Expulsion, and Campaigns Collapse

1745–1747

BONFIRES BLAZED IN BOSTON, and New York and Philadelphia also celebrated, for New England's triumph was a boost to the budding pride and confidence of all Americans. An army of amateurs had beaten the cream of the Old World. They had outfought the soldiers of Louis XV. They had mastered a Vauban fortress. There was professional help at sea—particularly the defeat of the *Vigilant* by Warren and his sailors—but the men who conquered Louisbourg were civilians, hometown boys from Massachusetts, Maine, New Hampshire, and Connecticut.

William Pepperrell was made a baronet, the first American ever so honored. Peter Warren received his admiral's flag, and both Pepperrell and William Shirley became colonels of the regular army, with lucrative commissions to raise regiments. For the men who had done the fighting, however, there was no reward beyond glory. Instead of being allowed to pillage the homes and businesses of the French, they had been ordered to guard them. It was not what they had been led to expect when they enlisted, and they did not like it at all.

Then misery compounded their anger. The fine weather they had enjoyed nearly every day of the siege turned nasty. The heroes of Louisbourg found themselves doing hated garrison duty under a chill Cape Breton rain in a town knocked apart and grown pestilential after seven weeks of bombardment—and sickness did what French guns could not. Before the next spring, nearly nine hundred men would die, proof of the sad truth that in eighteenth-century warfare, the casualties of camp and garrison were almost always far greater than those of the battlefield.[1] In the campaign itself, only about 130 lives had been lost.[2]

There was no lack of booty for the British. Within a month, three fat prizes were in port—ships of the French East India Company homeward bound with goods and treasure, lured to Louisbourg by French colors left flying for just that purpose. All the prize money went to Warren and his crews, none to the New Englanders. Too, word began to go around that Britons were taking credit for the victory. In Boston, there was talk that the keys to the city were in Warren's hands, not Pepperrell's, that the surrender had been to British, not American arms. Letters to sons, husbands, and brothers fed the jealousy and discontent of the men on the spot. Sick of it all, they yearned for home, but until troops could be sent from Europe, they had to stay.

At the commanders' level, Anglo-American relations were not so strained. Pepperrell, a model of friendliness and tact in nearly everything he did, kept a rapport with the British throughout the campaign, and Warren—who, as the siege dragged on, had given way to flashes of impatience with New England's clumsy warriors—could not help but admire the affable citizen-general from Maine. Together they prodded unhappy men to rebuild shattered defenses, anticipating the counterattack the French would surely launch. In August 1775, Shirley paid a triumphal visit to Isle Royale. In elegant style, he held a review. More important, he promised higher pay and convinced the men to try a little longer to act the part of soldiers.[3]

Warren, who was named governor, had much to worry him. The condition of the town was deplorable; the morale of the troops was awful. His first concern, however, was to get rid of the French. He thought Britons would never be safe while Frenchmen remained on Isle Royale—or, for that matter, while there were Frenchmen anywhere in Acadia. His answer was to deport them all.

Louisbourg's elite went off immediately, glad to escape to France with their fortunes and their finery. The working men and women wanted to stay, but Warren was "determined by no means to let them remain here longer than until vessels can be procured to transport them."[4] He wanted everyone gone from Isle Royale and Isle St. Jean, and he felt the same about the Acadians in Nova Scotia. He told the duke of Newcastle that he had decided to deport the Isle St. Jean settlers in the spring, because "we see the ill consequences in Nova Scotia that attend keeping any of them in our territories. Indeed it would be a good thing if those now at Annapolis could be removed."[5] In a particularly portentous message, he suggested that the Acadians be scattered among the other British colonies, where they would be forever removed from the pernicious influence of the French.[6]

Warren was convinced that French Acadia must be emptied, and on Isle Royale he had his way. When the French regained their colony after peace was made, they found only ninety-four of the settlers who were there before the siege.[7] The farmers of Isle St. Jean, however, had a reprieve. In June 1746, Warren gave up his governorship to Commodore Charles Knowles, who, like Warren, wanted to deport everyone, and who took a particularly dim view of the Acadians, offering to travel to Nova Scotia and expel them himself.[8] But Knowles could not bring himself to worry much about the "poor miserable inoffensive People" on Isle St. Jean.[9] They were not, he thought, worth the expense of shipping them away. Pepperrell's men had paid a visit and burned their settlements. Perhaps they would starve. Surely they were no threat. He made them send hostages to Louisbourg, then let them alone.[10]

And, as always, British officials were simply unable to decide about the Acadians. Shirley at first made the same prejudgment as Warren and Knowles: The Acadians must go. Despite their demonstrated neutrality in 1744, they were, he said, "all Frenchmen and Roman Catholicks, and who ought to be look'd upon (be their pretensions what they will) as ready in their Hearts to join with the Enemy, whenever a French Force sufficient in their Imagination to subdue it shall appear in their Country."[11] In May 1745, when he learned of Lieutenant Marin's march on Annapolis Royal, he assumed that the people had risen up against Paul Mascarene, and he wrote to Pepperrell with a vindictiveness as unbecoming as it was unjustified. "It grieves me much," he wrote, "that I have not it in my power to send a party of 500 men forthwith to Menis [Minas], and burn Grand Pré, their chief town, and open all their sluices, and lay their country waste."[12]

But Shirley was not really a town burner and a dike breaker, nor was he, like Warren and Knowles, bent on wholesale expulsion. The solution he proposed in 1746, after he had cooled off, was not so draconian.[13] He would round up and deport those Acadians who had actively supported the French. The others would be let alone if they took oaths of allegiance. He did not say what sort of oaths, or what he would do if they refused. Blockhouses would be built to keep the adults in line, and schools to teach children to speak English. The troublemaking French priests would be replaced by Protestant ministers. In a generation, the Acadians would be good subjects.

When Knowles sent home his proposal that everyone be deported, Shirley was quick to disagree. It would, he said, be an expensive operation, and a hard one. Nova Scotia would be weakened, Canada strengthened. And for what seems to have been the first and last time in Britain's official deliberations on the fate of the Acadians, someone raised the question of fairness. "After their having remain'd so long in the Country upon the foot of British Subjects under the Sanction of the Treaty of Utrecht," Shirley wrote, "to drive 'em all off their Settlements without farther Inquiry seems to be liable to many Objections. Among others it may be doubted whether under the Circumstance of these Inhabitants it would clearly appear to be a just Usage of 'em." Their notion of neutrality might be wrong, but it had been implicitly accepted by the British, and it was based on what appeared to have been authentic acts of British governors. Allowances ought to be made, Shirley thought, for a people "continually plac'd between two fires."[14]

The man on the spot felt the same, although he was neither so firm nor so articulate. Years earlier, Mascarene had favored a forcible solution, urging that the Acadians "not be tolerated any longer in their non-allegiance."[15] That was in 1720, when there were fewer Acadians, when the question of the oaths had not yet been compromised, and when there was reason to expect that Britain's government would send colonists. Mascarene had aged with his troubled province, and in 1745 he waffled. Expulsion was an extreme solution. Who would replace the Acadians? What if they resisted? What if they took up their muskets and went to war? It would be a happy thing if Nova Scotia were filled with sturdy, English-speaking yeomen, faithful to their king and ready to spring to arms to resist an invader, but Mascarene himself had tried and failed to recruit settlers of that kind. He had to be thankful for what he had, and what he had were "French neutrals." They came with the territory. Given time and goodwill, they perhaps could be brought around, although he had his doubts. "Nor can it be expected," he said, "that if they are suffered to remain in this province, that notwithstanding the mildest treatment, they will make good subjects for some generations."[16]

At Annapolis Royal, the members of the council were in no mood to wait. In 1744, Jean-Louis Le Loutre and François Duvivier had attacked the British fort, and no one had given a warning. When Marin and his men marched down the peninsula the next year, the same thing happened. Very few Acadians had joined the invaders, but neither had many of them troubled to help the British. After two summers of watching them mind their own business and look the other way, Mascarene's officers were more than usually fed up. In November 1745, they adopted a formal report that detailed the help a few Acadians had given Duvivier and Marin, then faulted them all for not actively taking the British side. "Upon the whole," they said, "it is most humbly submitted whether the said French Inhabitants may not be transported out of the Province of NOVA SCOTIA and be re-plac'd by good Protestant subjects."[17]

Mascarene bowed to the council and signed his name, even though in his heart he thought deportation unfair and unwise. Later, he called his officers prejudiced, refusing to understand the Acadians' language, their religion, and their ways, "ever talking of outing them, transplanting or destroying them, without considering the circumstances this province has lately been, and still is, in, and the fatal consequences that might have ensued from any violent measures."[18] But prejudiced or not, the council's report added pages to the file and weight to the view that wholesale expulsion was the only solution, that the Acadians were dangerous revolutionaries who might at any time go over to the enemy en masse.

Some of them had indeed helped the French, but the uprising the British feared and the French expected never happened. When, in 1746, a force from Canada threatened yet another siege of Annapolis Royal, the Acadians sat on their hands, just as they had in 1744 and 1745. After the threat was gone that year, Mascarene reported that the inhabitants had done nothing that "can justly be taken amiss in this last affair, except their not giving us intelligence of their own accord."[19]

Each time they had a chance to side with France, they declined. Instead of rising up, they laid low. It was the bargain they had made with Philipps, it served them well, and they kept it.

In the fall of 1746, the Acadians were told that the bargain was still valid. A letter came from Shirley with a message for them. It threatened punishment for anyone who supported the French but included these soothing words:

Having been informed that the French Inhabitants of Nova Scotia entertain some Jealousy of a Design in the English Gov-

ernment to remove them with their Families from their Settlements, and to transport them to France or elsewhere; I desire . . . that you would be pleas'd to signify to 'em, that it is
probable if his Majesty had declar'd such Intention I might
have heard of the same, but that I am perfectly unacquainted
with any such Design, and am perswaded there is no just
Ground for this Jealousy; And be pleas'd to assure 'em that I
shall use my best Endeavours by a proper Representation of
their Case to be laid before his Majesty, to obtain the Con-
tinuance of his Royal Favour and Protection to such of them,
as shall behave dutifully and peaceably, and refuse to hold any
Correspondence with his Enemies; and I doubt not but that
all such of 'em will be protected by his Majesty in the Possession of their Estates and Settlements in Nova Scotia.[20]

Thus, they had only to be peaceable and keep out of the way and all
would be well. Since "it confirms what has been so frequently told
them," the council had Shirley's letter read aloud, and copies were
sent around the province.[21] That was the council that only a year
earlier had recommended that everyone be deported.

Shirley's message came at a time when there was good reason to
confer an official blessing on Acadian neutrality. Big operations were
underway, both British and French. When he sent his letter, Shirley
was expecting an army from home that would invade and crush New
France. At the same time, French regulars were on Nova Scotia's Atlantic coast, and Canadians were menacing Annapolis Royal. The
war, it seemed, was about to become very hot.

The French campaign of 1746 was born in shock waves from the
loss of Louisbourg. After they learned what had happened on Isle
Royale, the marquis de Beauharnois, then governor of New France,
and Gilles Hocquart, the intendant, sent a plea for an expedition to
win back Louisbourg and Nova Scotia. The preservation of Canada,
they said, depended on it. They would send troops, and this time the
Acadians would join the fight. Assuredly, "all, with the exception
of a very small portion, are desirous of returning under the French
dominion."[22]

Even if the desire was there, though, would the people act on it?
In truth, the Acadians were as much an enigma in Quebec as they
were in London and Boston. Beauharnois and Hocquart could not
know whose side they would take, or whether they would take any

side. The home government, they said, must pay for supplies Lieutenant Marin had requisitioned in 1745, "otherwise, future difficulties must be expected which would cause the Acadians to look upon us as real enemies."[23]

Not so with the Indians, who could be trusted to stay in the French camp. After Louisbourg fell, Jean-Louis Le Loutre had fled a British summons and made his way to Quebec with five of the Micmacs' sagamores, "to inquire their Father's orders."[24] They were promised arms and ammunition and sent back to fight the British. Le Loutre returned with them, carrying secret signals to coordinate their raids with the men who would be sent from Quebec and the armada that would come from the mother country.

And an armada was indeed coming. At Versailles, a decision had been made to commit men and ships enough to drive the British out of Acadia for good. When six hundred Canadians under Jean-Baptiste-Nicholas-Roch de Ramezay landed at Baie Verte in July 1746, they knew that five battalions—3,150 soldiers—from the king's European army were on their way. The fleet bringing them included sixty-five ships, nearly half the French navy, and the commander, the duc d'Anville, had orders for a campaign even more ambitious than Beauharnois and Hocquart had proposed. He was to retake Louisbourg, then Annapolis Royal, and then lay waste the coast of New England.[25]

It came to nothing. Like the British Admiral Walker in 1711, d'Anville was beaten before a shot was fired.[26] North Atlantic gales scattered his ships. Some were lost; some turned tail; some fled to quiet waters in the Caribbean. Worse, an epidemic struck, and by the time the fleet's battered remnants gathered near the end of September at Chebucto Bay (today's Halifax), more than two thousand men were dead or dying. Among them was the duke himself, who expired a few days after his flagship made its lonely landfall. More ships straggled in, but it was obvious that even if not wholly ruined, the expedition was far too crippled to permit an invasion of Isle Royale.

There was a lesser but still attractive target, and one of the survivors—a newly named governor of New France, the marquis de La Jonquière—rallied officers and men for an attack on Annapolis Royal, where Ramezay and his men were already encamped. Enough ships and soldiers were left from d'Anville's force to ensure a successful siege, and, after a month of refitting, La Jonquière led them out of Chebucto Bay, toward the Bay of Fundy and the Annapolis Basin.

Fate, however, had decreed that nothing about the 1746 French campaign would go right. When another violent storm mauled his ships at Cape Sable, La Jonquière decided that enough was enough. Ramezay withdrew to Grand Pré, and when he found that he would have no support from its uncooperative inhabitants, he went on to winter quarters at Beaubassin. Le Loutre made his own retreat, all the way to France in one of La Jonquière's ships.[27]

La Jonquière and Le Loutre set out again for the New World in May 1747, but four days out of La Rochelle, in the Bay of Biscay off Spain's Cape Ortegal, their fleet met a squadron commanded by Peter Warren and Britain's senior admiral, Lord George Anson, and the British won the fight. La Jonquière was taken prisoner, and Le Loutre fared only a little better. He adopted an assumed name, and his captors, not realizing whom they had bagged, let him go. He sailed again in a merchant ship, only to be captured again, recognized, and locked up until the war was over.[28]

The Battle of Cape Ortegal was the end of French hopes to recoup the loss of Louisbourg, and by the time La Jonquière's ambitions were vanishing in gunsmoke in the Bay of Biscay, the British had already written finis to their own grand design. Like the French, theirs was a major commitment, but its genesis was in political necessity, not imperial ambition. It was a grudging effort, readily abandoned.

In Europe, Britons were having very little success fighting the War of the Austrian Succession. There was no Marlborough to roll up French armies, and the government of Newcastle and Henry Pelham had been rocked by a second Jacobite Rebellion, this one sparked by the glamorous young son of James Edward Stuart. Preoccupied with Bonnie Prince Charlie at home and French military might on the Continent, the Pelhams wanted no adventures in America. Louisbourg, however, had given London's fire-breathing imperialists a rallying cry, and the Canada Expedition of 1746 was the price the duke and his brother had to pay for the support of the hawks and thus a few more years in office.[29] They agreed to send five thousand men, and the usual pincers strategy was planned—upriver from the Gulf of St. Lawrence, downriver from Montreal. Men from New England would join the regulars at Louisbourg to mount the seaborne attack. Men from New York, New Jersey, Pennsylvania, Maryland, and Virginia would march to Lake Champlain and on to the St. Lawrence.[30]

In America, the militia drilled, but onshore winds kept the British transports in port all through spring and summer, and doubts gnawed. The campaign was postponed, and by the end of 1746, the idea of sending five thousand soldiers across the ocean had lost all appeal.

Still, with d'Anville defeated by storms and disease and La Jonquière by Anson's and Warren's guns, Britons on Isle Royale and the Nova Scotia Peninsula could breathe easily. At Louisbourg, regulars had arrived to relieve William Pepperrell's unhappy farmboys; at Annapolis Royal, Paul Mascarene's garrison had been strengthened and the fort repaired. There would be no invasion of Canada, but there was room for aggressive action in Nova Scotia—or at least a maneuver that would give bellicose Frenchmen and fence-straddling Acadians something to think about.

In December, a big detachment—470 men from Massachusetts—was sent to Grand Pré to counter Ramezay and the troops he commanded at Beaubassin.[31] Their commander was a Louisbourg veteran, Colonel Arthur Noble. He was to show the flag for the first time in a substantial way in the largest of the Acadian communities.

His men brought ready-cut timber to build a blockhouse, but Noble decided it could wait until spring. He quartered them in the Acadians' dwellings, scattering them around the village and trusting snow and cold to keep the French away. At the head of the Bay of Fundy, however, were Canadians who had grown up with snow and cold, and when Ramezay learned that Noble and his men were at Grand Pré, he decided to drive them out. Having injured a leg on the march from Annapolis Royal, Ramezay entrusted the mission to one of his officers, Nicholas-Antoine Coulon de Villiers. Second in command was Louis La Corne. At the end of January, they set out with three hundred soldiers on a winter march by way of Tatamagouche Bay and Cobequid, to arrive at Grand Pré at three in the morning on February 11, 1747. In a snowstorm, in the dark of night, they stormed the village.

Noble had posted guards, but the alarm came too late. As the battle began, the Massachusetts commander was killed. His men nevertheless staged a gallant fight, one that raged through dawn and into the morning hours. When Coulon was wounded, La Corne took his place. The French captured all the houses but one, which Noble's men turned into a stronghold and defended with their cannon. By midday, some seventy New Englanders were dead and sixty were prisoners. French losses were smaller, but La Corne's men were exhausted from marching and fighting in deep snow, and both sides accepted a truce. Frenchmen and Americans built fires and slept, and then negotiated the terms the next day. They were generous, requiring only that the New Englanders withdraw to Annapolis Royal and promise that during the following six months they would not take up arms at the Minas Basin or on the Isthmus of Chignecto. Toasts were drunk and compliments were exchanged. It was civilized if bloody warfare in the snow.

Except for François Duvivier's cheap win at Canso at the beginning, the Battle of Grand Pré was France's only substantial victory in King George's War. It gave luster to Canadian arms, and it compounded Acadian confusion. Britons had seemed to be winning. Now who could tell? Otherwise it accomplished nothing at all. Coulon and La Corne abandoned the village shortly after they had taken it, and Ramezay withdrew from Beaubassin after he learned of La Jonquière's defeat at Cape Ortegal. The Nova Scotia Peninsula, Isle Royale, and Isle St. Jean were all firmly in British hands. It was left to France's diplomats to win back at the peace table what territory they could find.

29 | HALIFAX

*Britons Build
And Acadians Persevere*

1747–1750

NEGOTIATIONS TO END THE War of the Austrian Succession began in earnest in 1747. Louisbourg was the only significant card Britain's diplomats held, and in the end they traded it away to get the French out of the Austrian Netherlands.[1] Preliminary Articles of Peace were agreed in April 1748; the final treaty was signed at Aix-la-Chapelle in October.[2] It confirmed Frederick the Great's theft of Silesia but otherwise upheld Maria Theresa's Austrian inheritance, and, in the time-honored European way out of war, it provided for mutual restoration of everyone's other conquests. Thus the French regained Isle Royale and Isle St. Jean, but in every other part of America, the pretensions of the great powers were left as tangled as ever, their claims as discordant as they had been since the Peace of Utrecht sowed its confusion in 1713.

The French would use the years before the next war to rearm and rebuild Louisbourg and to put teeth in their claim to mainland Acadia. Britons, at the same time, would finally and emphatically discard their policy of neglect.

In a complex shift of power in London, the duke of Newcastle had given up his place as secretary of state to the duke of Bedford, leader of the hawks who had pushed the Canada Expedition in 1746. Bedford named to the presidency of the Board of Trade the earl of Halifax—an even more ardent imperialist than his patron—and suddenly North America's forgotten corner became important. Hearkening to Shirley's pleas, Bedford and Halifax resolved to make Nova Scotia a fourteenth American colony, a counterpoise to French Canada and Isle Royale. To make up for the abandonment of Louisbourg, which

had seemed to Americans a wicked betrayal, British America would
have a Louisbourg of its own. It would be at Chebucto Bay, where the
duc d'Anville and so many of his men lay buried. It would have Halifax's name, the army would fortify it, and the Board of Trade would
see that men and women came to people it. It was a new beginning,
and Bedford and Halifax had no reluctance about the funds that were
required. Nor were they afraid of the conflict with France that a
metamorphosed Nova Scotia would surely inflame—a conflict that
had indeed rekindled almost as soon as the Treaty of Aix-la-Chapelle
was signed.

In Quebec, waiting for the unlucky marquis de La Jonquière, was
the acting governor, Roland-Michel Barrin, marquis de La Galissonière. At the beginning of 1749, he sent a formal protest over attempts Paul Mascarene had made to have the Indians in the Saint
John Valley acknowledge the British king. All the mainland, he insisted, was French. At the same time, he challenged Mascarene's assertions of authority at the Isthmus of Chignecto, and even at the
Minas settlements.[3]

Mascarene responded by rejecting any French claim on the loyalty
of the Indians and any French right to the Saint John, the isthmus, or
any part of the Nova Scotia Peninsula. He would enforce his king's
prerogative throughout his province, and he had no doubt that the
Saint John, Chignecto, and the Minas Basin were parts of it.[4] He sent
a copy of La Galissonière's letter to William Shirley, who fired off a
blast of his own. The Saint John, he proclaimed, was "within the
heart of Nova Scotia."[5]

To face them down, La Galissonière sent soldiers to Saint John
Harbor, and when La Jonquière finally reached Quebec late in 1749,
he ordered Louis La Corne, victor of Grand Pré, to lead a detachment
to Chignecto to occupy a ridge called Beauséjour, just across the Missaguash River from Beaubassin. The Nova Scotia Peninsula, perhaps,
was lost; the mainland would be held. The line was drawn at the
Missaguash, a sluggish little creek suddenly prominent in the affairs
of great nations.

The French gained strength when their flag was raised again on
Isle Royale. In July 1749, Colonel Peregrine Hopson, the last British
commander, surrendered Louisbourg, and soon the fortress town was
its old self. François Bigot stopped off en route to new duties in Quebec to organize a government. Officers and officials reappeared from

the exile to which Peter Warren had sent them in 1745, and, just as in the old days, the French government sent soldiers and sailors and lots of money. Bastions were rebuilt, the fishery was revived, and commerce resumed as though there had been no war and there were no palpable threat of another. By 1752, the reborn Isle Royale would have a population of more than four thousand.[6]

Halifax, capital of Britain's new Nova Scotia, had its start at the same time, and the Board of Trade moved with a fast and lavish hand. Everything that should have been done to promote colonization in the earlier years was done, it seemed, overnight during the first few months of 1749. In March, an advertisement ran in the *London Gazette*: Officers and men discharged from the army and navy were invited to come and settle, and bring their families.[7] The government would pay their way, and everyone would be fed at public expense for a year. A civil government would be organized. Arms, tools, and building materials would be handed out. Land was free, and there would be no taxes for ten years. Anyone, veteran or not, could come and share the largesse. The ships would sail in April.

The destination might be wild and unknown, but the terms were exceptional. Emigrants flocked to sign up, eager to dip hands in what has been called "the greatest public porkbarrel yet opened in British North America."[8] The doddering Colonel Richard Philipps, nearly ninety now, was eased from the office he had held and the perks he had enjoyed since 1717 and replaced by one of Bedford's men, Colonel Edward Cornwallis. On July 1, 1749, Cornwallis's flagship splashed her anchor in Chebucto Bay. She was followed by thirteen more ships, carrying 2,576 people. Mascarene was summoned from Annapolis Royal, and on July 25, aboard the transport *Beaufort,* the reins were passed.[9]

The era of tattered uniforms and makeshift government was over. Mascarene, the faithful old Huguenot who had held Britain's shabbiest province together through so many years of neglect, could go off to honorable retirement. In due course, he sailed to Boston to live out his life amid doting children and grandchildren. After a half century of exceptional service to an adopted crown, one of the few real heroes of Acadia's disorderly history quietly faded away.

Cornwallis admired Mascarene's staying power, but the prim and proper colonel was horrified at what he found in the government he had taken over, in the regiment that was his to command, and in the men and women he was expected to bring to obedience. In September, he wrote Bedford to tell him how badly Nova Scotia had been administered:

> My Lord, these Companies are as prepared for service as a Regiment raised yesterday. The whole management of this Province both with regard to the Inhabitants and these Companies has been such that tis scandalous the Crown should be so served. It has been called an English Province these thirty-four years and I don't believe that the King had one true subject without the Fort of Annapolis. I cannot trace the least glimpse of an English government. I cannot help saying that General Phillips deserved the highest punishment for what he did here—his allowing a reserve to the Oath of Allegiance[,] his receiving money for public works without disbursing one penny[,] particularly for Canso . . . his never allowing the Regiment half their clothing, I am told not one of them ever had a knapsack or Haversack.[10]

Cornwallis also complained about the settlers who had come with him. There were, he said, no more than three hundred men who were willing to work. The rest were sick or unfit, or idlers lured by the promise of free food.[11]

He was determined, however, that Nova Scotia be made over, and, except for rebellious Indians and the everlasting problem of mulish Acadians and their conditional oaths of allegiance, he succeeded. The regulars who had been stationed at Louisbourg were redeployed to Halifax, and more and better settlers were coming. Some were expatriate Britons evacuated with the Louisbourg garrison. Many were New Englanders, lured finally to Nova Scotia by new opportunities for trade and the promise of civil government. Before summer ended, streets were laid out, lots were surveyed, wharves and buildings were begun, and a palisade was built to hold off the Indians. A militia was recruited, the first land grants were awarded, and a system of justice was organized. In September 1749, a grand jury was summoned, and one Abram Goodside was indicted for assault with a knife. He was tried, convicted, and hanged—the first civilian execution by operation of law in the history of Nova Scotia.[12]

Over the next two years, the population of Halifax grew to more than five thousand.[13] It declined thereafter, as lazier settlers soured on pioneer life and others, fearful of Indian raids, sought shelter in

New England. There was, too, a big group that never fit in with the English-speakers and left after a few years to start a separate community. They were German-speaking Protestants from the Rhine Valley, immigrants of the sort the Board of Trade had wanted to recruit in 1729. It was thought that they would scatter around the province, perhaps intermixing in the Acadian settlements. Unfortunately, they never left the Atlantic coast. They were an unhappy and expensive ethnic enclave, stranded in Halifax until 1753, when they moved, nearly two thousand strong, to a settlement marked out for them at the locale the Acadians and Indians called Mirligueche.[14] Lunenburg, the pretty seaport town they built there, still has traces of its Teutonic origin.

It was Indian hostility that kept the Rhinelanders and Cornwallis's British and American settlers from expanding farther. The building, the bustle, and the colonists swarming around Halifax provoked the Micmacs to renew the war they had fought in fits and starts since 1710. The men who arrived with Cornwallis were not just soldiers and traders. They were land-grabbing civilians, the kind who had taken away the Abenakis' hunting grounds in Maine, and the community they built at Halifax obviously would be something far different from the feeble presence the British had maintained at Annapolis Royal. Indian land and Indian freedom were now truly at risk, and the Indians had to protect themselves. Just as in Rale's War, they fought France's fight, and just as in Rale's War, they had France's secret backing.[15] Arms were sent from Louisbourg and Quebec, and the abbé Le Loutre came back to exhort and lead them—and to give Britons a target for their rage. Cornwallis offered £100 in reward money for the priest he learned to hate, the missionary he called "a-good-for-nothing Scoundrel as ever lived."[16]

As always, the Indians were overmatched. Counting men, women, and children, the Micmacs' numbers had dropped to about two thousand.[17] They had to be satisfied with hit-and-run raids and ambushes laid for luckless stragglers. Their forays served the French by confining Cornwallis's jittery colonists to the coast, but they won no lasting Indian objective. They were too few and too weak, the British too many and too strong. John Salusbury, a member of Cornwallis's council, summed it up in a letter to his wife. "These cursed Indians plague Us," he wrote, "worked up and Assisted by the French to do it, but thank God they can not Hurt us much."[18]

Cornwallis also had to grapple with the Acadians. Their neutrality in King George's War proved that they would tolerate British rule, but it was grudging toleration—good as long as the British let them alone, doubtful if they were pushed too far. They would not be forced easily from the status they had come to believe immutable—the status that had grown from forty years of Acadian obstinacy and British ineptitude. They were the "French neutrals."

They had been given a second message of reassurance, this one a declaration by William Shirley near the end of 1747, promising:

> in His Majesty's name, that there is not the least foundation for any Apprehensions of his Majesty's intending to remove the said Inhabitants of Nova Scotia from their Settlements and Habitations within his said Province; but that on the contrary, it is His Majesty's Resolution to protect and maintain all such of 'em as have adher'd to, and shall continue in their Duty and Allegiance to him, in the quiet and peaceable Possession of their respective Habitations and Settlements, and in the Enjoyment of all their Rights and Privileges as his Subjects.[19]

It was another welcome guarantee of land and homes, but the arrival of Cornwallis brought new fears. This governor wanted to assimilate them. His instructions required him to go seriously about the business of turning them into Britons. He was to build Protestant schools, encourage intermarriage with Protestant newcomers, and award tax-free grants of land to Acadians who saw the light. The old worship would not be barred, but Cornwallis was to publish a proclamation in 1749 threatening that both it and continued possession of Acadian land depended on renewed oaths of allegiance, and this time there was to be no nonsense about not bearing arms. Cornwallis told everyone right away that they must take the oaths "without any Conditional Clauses understood or any reservation whatever."[20]

The Acadians dreaded assimilation, and they were terrified at the thought of Protestantism, for it meant damnation. The talk about oaths, however, was nothing new. They had always insisted on conditions. They would insist now.

Cornwallis's proclamation gave them three months.[21] In response, deputies from all the Acadian settlements journeyed to Halifax to demand the old exemption.[22] Thereupon Cornwallis published another proclamation. The king, he said, "is not willing that any of his subjects . . . who possess habitations and lands in this province, shall be exempted from an entire allegiance or from the natural obligation to defend themselves, their habitations, their lands, and the government under which they enjoy so many advantages." They had until the middle of October to take unconditional oaths and thus continue "to enjoy their possessions."[23]

Their answer was the same. In a letter delivered to Cornwallis and the council in September—supposedly signed by a thousand men—the Acadians recalled the bargain they had made with Philipps in 1730 and Shirley's promises that they would be undisturbed on their lands and in their lives. They also brought out the red herring their fathers had handed John Doucett in 1717. To subscribe an unqualified oath, they said, would expose them to the Indians' "barbarous cruelty." They could not "take the oath which Your Excellency requires of us; but if Your Excellency will grant us our old oath which was given at Mines to Mr. Richard Philipps, with an exemption for ourselves and for our heirs from taking up arms, we will accept it." Otherwise, "we are resolved, every one of us, to leave the country."[24]

Nonplussed, Cornwallis watched his deadline pass, then wrote the Board of Trade to describe his frustration and his fears. The Acadians, he said, "behave strangely, insisting upon the reserve of not carrying Arms or not taking the Oaths, and leaving the Country; leaving the Country is bad, as it strengthens the Enemy. But my Lords in my poor opinion, better it should happen than yield to them[.] You have a secret, I fear an inveterate enemy preying upon your Bowels masked, but rotten at bottom, whom no leniency can please, nor anything but severity or greater power awe and bring them to their duty and allegiance."[25]

Yet Cornwallis, like every governor before him, could not bring himself to see them go. The next spring, some of them, frightened by the flow of Britons and Germans into the province, asked permission to leave. He told them to go home and sow their crops.[26] The thought of adding their numbers to the French on Isle Royale and Isle St. Jean was too much. His councilor Salusbury called "every proceeding . . . extremely critical[,] for the Inhabitants are on the balance now either to go or stay, and that is of great consequence to us, for if they go they will greatly reinforce the French, which is the great design of [Le] Loutre. If they stay, tho' they are not hearty in our interest, they are not actually against us—which they must be if they quit the Province[,] and truly they are a great body of people."[27]

The Board of Trade felt the same. Cornwallis was told "that any forcible measures which may induce [the Acadians] to leave their settlements ought for the present at least to be waved."[28]

Once again, Acadian perversity had won the day.

30 | COLD WAR

The Great Powers Maneuver
And a Governor Makes Up His Mind

1750–1754

THE COLD WAR THAT PRECEDED AND SPARKED the great Seven Years' War for empire in America had its beginning in Acadia, where Britain and France were still arguing over territory just as they had since 1613. When the new year arrived in 1750, French troops held the Saint John, more were on the Isthmus of Chignecto, and the British were about to make their move.

The marquis de La Jonquière had warned Edward Cornwallis in October 1749 that Louis La Corne and the men he commanded at Chignecto would "prevent the formation, by you, of any establishment until the true limits of Acadia and New France have been regulated by the two crowns."[1] In November, the British governor had sent back a declaration of his own. True enough, boundary negotiations were about to begin in Europe. "Does it follow from that," he asked, "that I am to send detachments through the whole of Canada, or you through Nova Scotia?" Until Britain and France could agree on some other definition, both Chignecto and the Saint John "are comprised in Nova Scotia."[2] When spring came, he sent regulars to occupy the isthmus.

Their commander was Major Charles Lawrence, a forty-one-year-old veteran of the war in Europe who had come to Halifax from Louisbourg.[3] He led his men overland to the Minas Basin, then by ship to the head of Chignecto Bay, landing on a rainy Sunday morning in May 1750 just west of the Missaguash River—right in the teeth of La Corne and his men encamped on Beauséjour Ridge. To the east, the British could see the Acadian village; even before they landed, they could see that it was in flames. When a white flag appeared, and a parley was held, they found out why. Until the boundary was settled, the French would concede the east bank of the Missaguash, but they would defend the west bank and the ground behind it, modern New Brunswick. To drive the people of Beaubassin over the line and into claimed French territory, the abbé Le Loutre and a band of Micmacs were burning it: homes, barns, church, and all.[4]

Lawrence had to decide among battle, stalemate, and retreat. The French were dug in, and their commander knew his trade. So did Lawrence, and a professional evaluation convinced him he could not take La Corne's position. He had an alternative: He could move his men across the river and occupy the burned Acadian settlement. Instead, he decided to retreat, because "to have Sat down on one side of the River and Leave the Enemy in possession of the other was a tacit acknowledgment of the Justice of his claim."[5]

More likely it was the cold rain that had been falling since the British landed, the ashes and desolation of Beaubassin, and the sight of a Micmac war party lining a nearby dike that sent Lawrence and his sodden soldiers to their ships and prudent withdrawal to the Minas Basin.[6] There they spent the summer—showing the flag, welcoming reinforcements, and building a blockhouse to daunt both Acadians and Indians. To honor Cornwallis, they called it Fort Edward, and there it stands today—a national historic site on a bluff overlooking the Avon River and the modern town of Windsor.

In September, Lawrence sailed back to Chignecto with a bigger force. This time he landed on the east bank of the Missaguash, ground not disputed by the French. His men nevertheless had to fight off a band of Indians—probably stiffened by covert Frenchmen sent by La Corne—but they managed their landing in good order. Within a few weeks, they had built a fort of timber and earth, which they named for Lawrence. From its rampart, they could watch La Corne's men building their own stronghold on the high ground across the river. Its works partly restored, the French Fort Beauséjour is today the centerpiece of a national park just off the Trans Canada Highway at the border of Nova Scotia and New Brunswick.

A few months later, a murder managed to inflame British passions. Captain How, a trader from Annapolis Royal, was shot from ambush outside Fort Lawrence. The British blamed the French. Cornwallis called it "an instance of treachery and barbarity not to be paralleled in history."[7] But, short of open war, there was no means of retaliation, or indeed any way the British could really be sure that

How's killer was not just an Indian with a grudge. Both sides settled down to wary watching, and for the next five years, the twin forts Lawrence and Beauséjour glowered at each other across the marshes, enforcers of an armed and uneasy truce.

For Britain and France, the time of truce was a time of negotiation, a time of hope that another world war somehow might be avoided. For the Acadians, it was a time of hardship and dilemma. The French wanted them to move, to expand the populations of Isle St. Jean and Isle Royale and create new settlements on the mainland. The British wanted them to stay and assimilate, to become good subjects and eventually good Protestants. Afraid for their religion, their property, and their way of life, the Acadians were in a bind.

Those on the Isthmus of Chignecto had little choice except to go along with the French. Beaubassin was destroyed, La Corne's troops were close by, and Le Loutre was preaching and pressing, invoking damnation and Indian threats to push men and women out of British territory. Acadians from the isthmus began to overrun the little settlements and the inadequate resources of Isle St. Jean. Because of their migration, the island's population in 1752 had grown to more than two thousand.[8] Others moved west to Shepody Bay and the valleys of the Petitcodiac and Memramcook Rivers in what is now New Brunswick—where there was little cleared land and little chance of rebuilding the old life.

They were sorrowful refugees, and La Jonquière made it worse by demanding oaths of allegiance and imposing a militia obligation on the men.[9] Those were the things they had tried so hard for so long to avoid at the hands of the British. Disillusioned, they wanted to go home, but at home were Britons who were finally serious about building a proper colony. Men and women who went back might be anglicized, mixed with Protestants. If not their own, their children's and their grandchildren's religion might be lost, and with it the chance for salvation. On the British side of the Missaguash lay false religion, an alien way of life, and officials who would no longer tolerate neutrality. On the French side were undiked marshes, uncleared land, and service in a Canadian militia.

Most of the Acadians—those in the Annapolis Valley and the Minas settlements—stayed home and hoped for the best, but time was running out for them as well as their friends and relatives at Chignecto. A few more years of cold war and feckless diplomacy lay ahead; then the determinative conflict would begin. Even before the

Seven Years' War was formally declared, they would all be unwitting victims of soldiers' nerves.

The diplomatic battling began in 1750. In the Preliminary Articles of Peace that ended the War of the Austrian Succession, Britain and France had agreed to appoint commissioners to decide the ownership of prizes taken at sea. Later, the prize commission was converted to a boundary commission and given the task of defining the two powers' American possessions. It met at Paris and stayed formally in session until 1755.[10] Its members never reached the biggest issue of all—the land beyond the Appalachians. They did, however, debate at length the status of St. Lucia, St. Vincent, Dominica, and Tobago—the so-called neutral islands in the Caribbean—and they devoted meeting after meeting and ream after ream of paper to the dilemma left from the 1713 Peace of Utrecht: What were the ancient boundaries of Acadia?

Because there was no willingness to compromise, the commission failed. Its members, two on each side, took extreme positions and stuck to them. Leading the charge for Britain was William Shirley—temporarily reassigned from his post in Boston and sent to Paris, expansionist brief in hand, demanding every bit of territory from New England to the St. Lawrence. Facing him was an old adversary, the marquis de La Galissonière—just as insistent that the mainland was French. The other commissioners were William Mildmay for Britain and Etiènne de Silhouette for France. Had either of these two been disposed to compromise, he would have found little room for it with Shirley and La Galissonière calling the tunes.

When he was named to the commission, La Galissonière prepared a blueprint for French strategy. The British must, he said, be kept far from Canada and Louisbourg, and at all costs they must be denied the Saint John, which during the cold months was the mother country's only means of communication with Quebec. Britain must have none of the mainland east of the Kennebec, and on the Nova Scotia Peninsula she should be limited, if possible, to Annapolis Royal and the Atlantic coast.[11]

It became the official French position, supported by carefully winnowed historical references and argument that Acadia had always been a very small place that never included any part of the mainland. This was nothing new. It was essentially the argument the French had been putting forward ever since Utrecht. Indeed, it was the argument Sir Thomas Temple had tried in 1668 when the Treaty of

Breda required cession of his British Acadia to France. Temple's protestations, the French commissioners discovered, had not been so frivolous after all.[12]

Legally and historically, the British had the better of it. Shirley
and the Board of Trade's lawyers marshaled a century of evidence, beginning with King Louis XIV's 1647 decree making Charles d'Aulnay
seigneur of an Acadia that extended from the mouth of the St. Lawrence to "the Virginias." They cited Joseph Villebon's note in 1698
claiming the Kennebec as the border, and they dredged from the files
a paper Daniel Subercase had given Francis Nicholson in 1710, in
which he described himself as governor of all the mainland between
the Kennebec and the St. Lawrence Rivers. Most tellingly, they
pointed out that in 1668, the courts of Britain and France had actually agreed—as shown in the French ambassador's insertion in King
Charles's orders to Temple—that Acadia included not only Port
Royal, Cape Sable, and La Have on the Nova Scotia Peninsula, but
also the Saint John and Fort Pentagoet and thus mainland North
America as far west as Penobscot Bay.[13]

An impartial arbiter might have split the difference. Recalling
that the original grant from King Henry IV to de Monts in 1603—the
earliest definition of Acadia in any official paper—ran only a little farther north than the head of the Bay of Fundy, a judge could reasonably have decided that the Acadia that France surrendered to Britain
at Utrecht included all the Nova Scotia Peninsula, the Isthmus of
Chignecto, and the mainland west and south to New England, leaving the territory above Chignecto to the French.

But there was no judge. The commissioners exchanged elaborate
arguments and exhaustive memorials. They enjoyed themselves in
Paris, and they defined no boundaries. Shirley, a widower, fell in love
with his landlord's daughter and married her, a remarkable blunder
for a man so politically astute.[14] Along with his intransigence, which
embarrassed the ministry, his *mésalliance* probably contributed to the
loss of favor that brought his recall from the negotiations in 1752. It
did not, however, prevent his return the next year to Boston, without his Parisienne, to take a leading role in the war that would be the
ultimate arbiter of the commissioners' disputes.

There was much more at stake in America than Acadia and the
neutral islands. It was in the valley of the Ohio River that the flames
would actually ignite, that the first shots would be fired in the fusillade that dragged the Old World into war over the New.

The French had claimed the Ohio country since the explorations of René-Robert Cavelier de La Salle in the seventeenth century, but they had never occupied it, and traders from Virginia, Pennsylvania, and the Carolinas were crossing the mountains. In 1748, Pennsylvanians had concluded an Indian treaty that stripped France of the tribes she thought were her Ohio allies, and a Virginia land company was talking about settlement. The French, needing to respond, sent an expedition to rally the Indians and show the flag. In the summer of 1749, Captain Pierre-Joseph Céloron de Blainville made his way down the Allegheny and the Ohio as far as modern Cincinnati, ordering out the traders, nailing the French coat of arms on trees, and burying lead plates proclaiming French sovereignty.

Unimpressed, the traders stayed put. Nor did Céloron's proclamations stop the probing of Virginia's land agents, but the British had to pay more attention after a 1752 raid by French-led Indians on the chief trading house of the Pennsylvanians and Virginians, a village called Pickawillany (today's Piqua, Ohio). The village's Indian leader, a fast friend of Britain, was boiled and eaten.

Next a new governor of Canada, Marquis Duquesne, sent an army to occupy the upper tributaries of the Ohio, and British nerves pulled tighter. In August 1753, the earl of Holderness, who had replaced the duke of Bedford as secretary of state, sent letters to each colonial governor directing that

> in the case the subjects of any Foreign Prince or State, should presume to make any incroachment on the limits of His Majesty's dominions, or to erect any Forts on His Majesty's Land, or comit any other act of hostility, you are immediately, to represent the injustice of such proceeding, and to require them forthwith to desist from any such unlawful undertaking; but if notwithstanding your requisition, they should still persist, you are then to draw forth the armed Force of the Province, and to use your best endeavours, to repel force by force.[15]

Here was license to begin a war, and Virginia's acting governor, Robert Dinwiddie, was spoiling for it. He selected a promising officer of the militia, a twenty-one-year-old surveyor named George Washington, and sent him on a wintertime journey nearly to Lake Erie to demand that the French withdraw. At Fort Le Boeuf (now Waterford, Pennsylvania), Washington handed Dinwiddie's letter to the French commander. It was just before Christmas, and food, wine, and conviviality were laid on, but Washington's diplomacy got nowhere. He carried back to Williamsburg a polite but contemptuous response: "As to the summons you sent me to retire," the Frenchman said, "I do not think myself obliged to obey it."[16]

Dinwiddie had given his warning. Now he would "repell force by force." He sent militiamen to fortify the forks of the Ohio, where the Allegheny and Monongahela flow together and the skyscrapers of Pittsburgh rise today. Unwisely, he sent too few. In April 1754, six hundred Frenchmen appeared and, in a bloodless confrontation, ousted the Virginians. Then they built France's own Fort Duquesne.

Other colonials accompanied Washington on the upper Potomac River. Their commander, not yet the soldier who would win a revolution and shake the world, had only a small force, and he knew a big French army awaited at the forks. Nevertheless, he blundered on.

First there was a skirmish. Washington's men surprised and killed ten Frenchmen, including Ensign Joseph Coulon de Villiers de Jumonville, younger brother of Nicholas-Antoine Coulon de Villiers, who had led the French on their march to Grand Pré in 1747. Washington said it was self-defense. Enraged Frenchmen called it murder, and they had their revenge when another of the Coulon brothers, Louis Coulon de Villiers, caught up with Washington at a place called Great Meadows, near today's Uniontown, Pennsylvania. The Virginians had been reinforced, but they were no match for Coulon and the men who marched with him from Fort Duquesne. On July 3, 1754, there was an all-day battle. At nightfall, Washington surrendered, and the next day he began a sad march back across the mountains. Virginia was beaten, France had the Ohio, and the Seven Years' War was inevitable.

In Europe, there were new efforts to save the peace. The boundary commission was a failure, so it was time for conventional diplomacy.[17] Each side professed peaceful intentions and taxed the other with warlike acts in America. To the British, the French forts in Pennsylvania were usurpations. So was Fort Beauséjour at the Isthmus of Chignecto. To the French, Washington's march to Great Meadows was an armed invasion. When the French complained about the killing of Jumonville in Pennsylvania, the British recalled the death of Captain How in Nova Scotia.

Compromises were proposed. A neutral zone might separate the Ohio and the mountains; another might buffer the south bank of the St. Lawrence. But the differences were too deep, and the offers passed in the night. As negotiations neared their end, the French finally threw in their weakest card. They would recognize Britain's right to all the Nova Scotia Peninsula, provided that France could keep the Isthmus of Chignecto and the mainland above Penobscot Bay and that the Acadians still on the peninsula would have three years to pick up their possessions and go. In response, Britain's negotiators insisted on the isthmus and at least the mainland shore of the Bay of Fundy, and they objected to the very idea of losing the Acadians—which would, they said in a note to the French ambassador, "be depriving Great Britain of a very considerable Number of useful Subjects."[18]

Perhaps that was how they felt in London, but in Halifax, on the eve of war, there was a governor who would not be at all distressed to see the last of the Acadians. Government was in the hands of a man to whom it was intolerable that men and women should profess neutrality. The Board of Trade might not be able to make a decision. Charles Lawrence had no such problem.

Cornwallis had gone home in 1752, his place taken first by Colonel Peregrine Hopson, the former commander at Louisbourg, an easygoing officer who had seen how ineffective Cornwallis's proclamations had been and wanted no more trouble about Acadians' oathtaking. Better, he advised the Board of Trade, to have "silence on this head till a more convenient opportunity."[19] And the board, as usual, agreed that temporization was best. "The bringing the French Inhabitants to take the oaths," it replied, "is certainly a very desirable thing, and the sooner they are brought to it the better; but it would be highly imprudent to disgust them by forcing it upon them at an improper time, and when they are quiet and at peace."[20]

Bad health sent Hopson home in 1753, and Lawrence took his place. It was Lawrence who ordered the expulsion of the Acadians. It is Lawrence who has been damned for it ever since. It was indeed a cruel act, but it was not the act of a cruel man. It was the act of a soldier who saw matters in a simple, straightforward, soldier's way.[21] Men and women were either loyal or they were disloyal. The Acadians sought a middle ground. To Lawrence there was no such thing, and even had he been willing to accept the idea of their neutrality, he would not have trusted them to stay neutral. He had read the 1745 report of the council at Annapolis Royal—the report that even the conciliatory Paul Mascarene had signed. He knew the recommendations of Peter Warren and Charles Knowles. He felt as Cornwallis did, that the Acadians would always be "an inveterate enemy preying upon your Bowels . . . whom no leniency can please."[22] He was responsible for defending Nova Scotia, a big war was coming, and at his back were ten thousand subversives. The Acadians would have to change their ways. They would have to declare unconditional loyalty or depart.

The Board of Trade was on the fence, just where it had always been. In March 1754, it sent Lawrence this unhelpful advice:

> The more We consider this Point the more nice and difficult it appears to us; for, as on the one hand great Caution ought to be used to avoid giving any Alarm, and creating such a Diffidence in their Minds as might induce them to quit the Province, and by their Numbers add Strength to the French Settlements, so as on the other hand We should be equally cautious of creating an improper and false Confidence in them, that by a Perseverance in refusing to take the Oath of Allegiance, they may gradually work out in their own way a Right to their Lands, and to the Benefit and Protection of the Law, which they are not entitled to but on that condition.[23]

Lawrence wrote back to state exactly how he felt. The Acadians had for years been guilty of "obstinacy, treachery, partiality to their own Countrymen, and . . . ingratitude for the favor, indulgence and protection they have at all times so undeservedly received from His Majesty's Government." He was, he said, "very far from attempting such a step without your Lordships approbation, yet I cannot help being of opinion that it would be much better, if they refuse the Oaths, that they were away."[24]

The board responded by fussing again about land ownership. Had the Acadians, by refusing the oaths, forfeited their titles? The board would not take such a decision upon itself, but Nova Scotia had a chief justice—Jonathan Belcher Jr., son of the former Massachusetts governor. Lawrence could consult him.[25]

Lawrence had in mind a remedy grimmer than forfeiture of titles. The next summer, when the time was ripe, he would solicit and gain Belcher's support for banishing the Acadians forever. For a little while longer, however, he would bide his time and watch the effects of governance already becoming harsher than anything the people had ever known.

When, in September 1753, a group that had fled Chignecto sought permission to return home, its members were told that they must first take unqualified oaths.[26] They were to "have no other assurances given them of not bearing arms except a verbal intimation that we have no such design at present as arming them, and that the nature of our constitution makes it both unsafe and unprecedented to trust our cause in the Hands of people of their persuasion."[27] That was the dodge Lawrence Armstrong had tried in 1726, and even for the wretched Chignecto refugees, it was not good enough. They wanted it in writing that they "should remain neuter, and be exempt from taking up arms against any person whatsoever," but Lawrence would have none of it, and the council "resolved that nothing further could be done."[28]

In September 1754, Lawrence prohibited anyone from taking grain out of the province.[29] He claimed this was to ensure supplies for Halifax, but the Acadians knew that the real purpose was to stifle their contacts with the French. At the same time, British troops patrolling the Minas communities were told to forget the old policy of restraint. When the farmers who lived near Pisiquid balked at cutting wood for Fort Edward, the commander, Captain Alexander Murray, ordered their priest arrested and hauled off to Halifax. In the spring, to enforce the grain embargo, Murray ordered the people to turn in their boats and canoes. In June 1755, after military operations had begun at Chignecto, he ordered them to give up their arms.[30] Times had changed.

31 | BEAUSÉJOUR

France Loses a Fort

1754–1755

WHILE CHARLES LAWRENCE WAS TIGHTENING his grip on the Acadians, he was working on a military solution to his other big problem—the French soldiers who held the mouth of the Saint John and the Isthmus of Chignecto. Fort Beauséjour was their stronghold. If it could be conquered, British sovereignty would be upheld and Nova Scotia made whole. The time had come to break the truce established at the Missaguash.

He proposed a joint campaign with Massachusetts, and he found warm support in Boston. William Shirley was back, energetic as ever, and ready as ever to bash the French. In the summer of 1754, he organized a foray to the head of the Kennebec to intimidate Indians and throw out encroaching Frenchmen. Even though no Frenchmen were found, or even many Indians, everyone came home covered with glory. Massachusetts's right to the land was proclaimed vigorously, and Shirley, who had gone along, was again the man of the hour.[1] His standing was such that he would have no difficulty enlisting men for almost any armed venture, and no sooner had he returned from the Kennebec than he had the home government's blessing for Lawrence's project to dislodge the French at Fort Beauséjour.

In London, hawks were winning the arguments. The duke of Newcastle, who on the death of Henry Pelham had become sole head of government, still hoped for an accommodation, a diplomatic solution that would not plunge Europe into war. He was not, however, ready to hand British America to France, and he and his ministers decided it was time to start taking chances.[2] In the face of limited pressure, the French might back down. An attack on Fort Beauséjour would be a discrete use of force at a single point, an exercise that would teach the French a lesson. In July 1754, a new secretary of state, Sir Thomas Robinson, wrote Lawrence and Shirley approving the plan.[3] In December, one of Lawrence's officers, Robert Moncton, sailed to Boston to organize the campaign. Shirley furnished the men, and they were ready to sail by spring.

They would, as it turned out, be part of an undertaking that was anything but limited, and hardly discrete. When they boarded ships in Boston in May 1755, Shirley's recruits formed one arm of a multi-pronged, all-out offensive, an enormous roll of the dice that would turn the war for America from cold to hot.

In September 1754, news of Washington's defeat at Great Meadows had reached London, where it shook the remnants of caution loose from Newcastle's government. Early the next year, Major General Edward Braddock arrived in Virginia with two regiments, plans for recruiting more men in the colonies, and a design to lay French pretensions finally and firmly in the dust. Braddock's orders called for a campaign in the Ohio Valley and attacks on French forts built on the Niagara River and at Crown Point on Lake Champlain. The attack on Fort Beauséjour was to proceed as well. If it could not be mounted with forces from New England and Nova Scotia, Braddock was to do it himself.[4]

In April 1755, in Alexandria, Braddock convened a conference with Shirley and Dinwiddie and the governors of Maryland, Pennsylvania, and New York. The governors were told that the general and his regulars would march immediately on Fort Duquesne. Shirley, who was named second in command in America, would lead colonial troops against Fort Niagara. New York's Colonel William Johnson would command the assault on Crown Point. The Beauséjour campaign was already organized and ready to go. An urgent message was sent to Lawrence telling him to get it underway.

It was a gamble, but Shirley was sure it would work—sure that when men were marching and guns firing, the French would back down. "According to this plan," he wrote, "the French will be attack'd almost at the same time in all their incroachments in North America; and if it should be successfully executed in every part, it seems highly probable that all points in dispute there with them may be adjusted this year, and in case of a sudden rupture between the two Crowns the way pav'd for the reduction of Canada, whenever it shall be His Majesty's pleasure to order it."[5]

The plan, however, went awry. The French did not back down. Instead, they fought.

Braddock's preparations were known at Versailles, and a highly regarded general, baron de Dieskau, was ordered to New France with three thousand soldiers. On May 3, 1755, he and his army sailed from Brest, unknowingly headed for a British trap across the ocean. Admiral Edward Boscawen had weighed anchor a week earlier with eleven ships of the line and two frigates and had raced to Cabot Strait ahead of the French. His orders were to stop Dieskau and turn him around, but to do it in American waters. The British thus hoped the fighting might be contained, that the war they were starting might be a small blaze in America, not a conflagration in Europe.

In June, the fleets brushed and battled, and all but two of the French ships escaped in fog, high seas, and massive confusion. Boscawen had failed; New France was reinforced.

The next month, Braddock met his death and his regulars met crushing defeat on the Monongahela River, just a few miles short of Fort Duquesne. Shirley's campaign, begun that same month, bogged down at Lake Ontario. Johnson won a victory of sorts over Dieskau in the Battle of Lake George, but it was a hollow triumph, one the New Yorker could not follow up. As the summer of 1755 ended, the French still held Crown Point and Fort Niagara, and they were still firmly in control of the Ohio River Valley. It was only in Nova Scotia that the British found something to cheer about in the undeclared war of 1755.

The Beauséjour campaign had needed nothing from Braddock beyond his blessing. With money supplied by Lawrence, and popular support left over from his gambol on the Kennebec, Shirley had enlisted two thousand volunteers. They rendezvoused at Annapolis Royal with 250 of Lawrence's regulars, and on June 2, they landed at Chignecto.[6] Moncton was in command. Serving under him was a veteran of the Cartagena and Kennebec campaigns, a popular Massachusetts colonel named John Winslow.

The men they faced were well entrenched but poorly led. Their commander was Louis Du Pont Duchambon de Vergor, son of the man who had lost Louisbourg to William Pepperrell and Peter Warren in 1745.[7] He was a particular friend of the larcenous François Bigot, whose advice when he received the appointment had been to "profit by your place, my dear Vergor; clip and cut—you are free to do what you please—so that you can come soon to join me in France and buy an estate near me."[8] Whether or not he shared the intendant's bent, it seems clear that Vergor was not much of a soldier. Four years after he surrendered Fort Beauséjour to Moncton, he commanded the detachment whose surprise and dispersal on the cliffs that edge the Plains of Abraham handed James Wolfe his epic victory and gave Canada finally to Britain.

Vergor was not the man to meet the test, and his officers were not much better. One witness wrote that when French resistance ended, most of them were too busy helping themselves to the king's stores to attend to the formalities. "We had," he said, "considerable difficulty in making them cease pillaging in order to have them sign the articles of capitulation."[9]

Had Vergor held out longer, the outcome might have been different. Fort Beauséjour was formidable. It was a classic fortress—a pentagon with earth, masonry, and timber walls—that dominated the Missaguash and the surrounding marshes. It was defended by 150 regular soldiers and 14 officers, with 21 cannon, a mortar, and ample stores. There were also three hundred Acadians, who had reluctantly agreed to take up arms when Vergor issued written orders threatening death should they refuse. With them and the regulars there were men enough, and there were arms, powder, and supplies enough, to permit a steadfast defense. Too, Moncton's men never surrounded the French. They never cut their lifeline to the mainland and their communications with Quebec and Louisbourg.

Quebec, however, was too far away to send reinforcements before Vergor gave up, and with Boscawen's squadron cruising offshore, a nervous commander at Louisbourg would spare none. The defenders were on their own, and, to make matters worse, they harbored a traitor—Thomas Pichon, a commissary officer who helped with correspondence, performed administrative jobs, and knew all the secrets. Since his posting, he had kept the British supplied with information, spying for cash and a promise that "I should acquire a position of pleasant ease and should lack nothing for my satisfaction"[10]

On June 4, 1755, Moncton and his men marched up the Missaguash and crossed to the west bank, above the fort. They had to fight a few Acadians and Indians whom Vergor sent to hold them off, but the skirmishers fled when light artillery fired on them. The British and Americans camped, then spent ten days building a road and a bridge and bringing up their big guns. By June 14, they had mortars in position, and there was heavy firing for the next two days. On the morning of June 16, a shell broke through a casement, killing two French officers and a British prisoner. Word had come two days earlier that there would be no reinforcement from Louisbourg, and, learning the news—probably from Pichon—the Acadians had begun to mutiny. When the casement blew, up Vergor's demoralization was complete, and a white flag appeared.

Under the terms agreed upon by the two commanders, the French soldiers and their officers withdrew to Louisbourg and promised not to take up arms for six months. The Acadians, who were said to have acted under compulsion, were pardoned. On the afternoon of June 16, the Union Jack was raised and Fort Beauséjour received a new name—Fort Cumberland, for King George's second son, the duke of Cumberland. On June 18, Winslow took possession of Fort Gaspereau, a little post at Baie Verte. At the end of the month, the Royal Navy drove off the men who held the mouth of the Saint John, and Nova Scotia was rid of the French.

32 | EXPULSION

A People Lose Their Homeland

1755

THE BEAUSÉJOUR CAMPAIGN WAS A HUGE SUCCESS, and a cheap one. Robert Moncton's British-American force lost only twenty men killed and twenty wounded.[1] The French threat, for a time anyway, was ended, and Charles Lawrence was free to solve the problem of the Acadians.

He had no authority for what he was about to do—and he had told the Board of Trade that he would not do it without authority—but he was not going to put up with them any longer. Buoyed by a major victory—one for which he could claim much of the credit—he was ready to force the question of the oaths and drive into exile anyone who would not submit.

In June 1755, just before Louis Vergor surrendered Fort Beauséjour, the Acadian deputies from the Minas settlements had submitted a petition complaining about Alexander Murray's confiscation of the residents' boats and his order that they turn in their arms. Living in a watery wilderness, those were items they could hardly do without. Yet if the deputies' plea was reasonable, its reception at Halifax was not. Lawrence used it as an excuse to summon them to a meeting of the council, where he intended to force them, as individuals, to swear unqualified oaths of allegiance, then and there.

They arrived on July 3, ready to explain why they needed boats and guns, only to hear a tongue-lashing and a litany of Acadian faults and misdeeds throughout forty years of British rule. They were called disloyal and impertinent, undutiful and ungrateful, indolent and idle, insincere and contemptuous. They had helped the king's enemies in the last war. Now they wanted boats so they could help them again.

And as Catholics they had no right to guns in the first place. When they proclaimed their loyalty, they were told to prove it by swearing the same oath of allegiance as other British subjects, and they were to do it right away, on the spot.[2]

They were stunned. Not since Samuel Vetch had a governor treated Acadians so badly. Caulfeild, Doucett, Philipps, Mascarene, Cornwallis, Hopson, even Armstrong—all had made at least a show of reasoning with them. All had seemed to respect their neutrality, to accept their special status. This man would not.

The deputies pleaded for time to go home and consult their neighbors, but Lawrence was unyielding. They were given just that night to make up their minds, and when they came back the next morning with the same answer, the council formally ruled that they be deported.[3]

Hearing that, the deputies panicked. They offered to take the oath without qualification, but Lawrence announced that there would be no second chance. Having once refused, they were "popish Recusants; Therefore they would not now be indulged with such Permission, And they were thereupon ordered into confinement."[4]

By making an example of them, Lawrence sought to jar the rest, to break the Acadians' confidence that if they stood firm, all would be well. He ordered new deputies chosen to replace the men he had locked up, and he ordered that they and the deputies from Annapolis Royal bring in the final answer. In a letter to the Board of Trade—a letter delivered long after the fact—he explained what he was doing:

> As the French Inhabitants of this Province have never yet, at any time, taken the oath of allegiance to His Majesty, unqualified, I thought it my duty to avail myself of the present occasion, to propose it to them; and, as the deputies of the different districts in Mines Basin, were attending in Town upon a very insolent Memorial . . . I was determined to begin with them. . . . The oath was proposed to them; they endeavoured, as much as possible, to evade it, and at last desired to return home and consult the rest of the Inhabitants, that they might either accept or refuse the Oath in a body; but they were informed that we expected every man upon this occasion to answer for himself. . . . The next morning, they appeared and refused to take the oath without the old reserve of not being obliged to bear arms, upon which they were acquainted, that as they refused to become English subjects, we could no

longer look upon them in that light; that we should send them to France by the first opportunity, and till then, they were ordered to be kept prisoners at George's Island, where they were immediately conducted. They have since earnestly desired to be admitted to take the oath, but have not been admitted, nor will any answer be given them until we see how the rest of the Inhabitants are disposed.

I have ordered new Deputies to be elected, and sent hither immediately, and am determined to bring the Inhabitants to a compliance, or rid the province of such perfidious subjects.[5]

Probably he still thought he would have his way, that if he applied enough pressure, the body of the people would cave in. If they did not, he would take upon himself and the council the responsibility for the ultimate solution—the step the Board of Trade could never bring itself to approve.

Chief Justice Belcher prepared a written opinion. Short on legal reasoning but long on rhetoric, and filled with phrases like "Rebels to His Majesty. . . . Perfidy and Treacheries. . . . Acts of Hostility. . . . inveterate enmity. . . . insolence and Hostilities," it held that deportation was justified by military necessity—or, as the learned justice put it, the *"Lex temporis."*[6] And Edward Boscawen's flagship was in Halifax. At Lawrence's request, the admiral and another senior officer, Admiral Savage Mostyn, attended a meeting of the council and "gave it as their Opinion, That it was now the properest Time to oblige the said Inhabitants to Take the Oath of Allegiance to His Majesty, or to quit the Country."[7]

Belcher's, though, was legal advice, and Boscawen and Mostyn's was military. Neither judge nor admirals had political authority, and the men who did would not have permitted the course Lawrence and the council chose to follow.

After the surrender of Fort Beauséjour, Lawrence had reported to the Board of Trade that some of the Acadians had helped the French defense and that he had "given [Moncton] orders to drive them out of the Country."[8] In a response that came too late to change events, Sir Thomas Robinson protested that the articles of capitulation called for a pardon. "It cannot," he said, "be too much recommended to you, to use the greatest Caution and Prudence in your conduct towards these Neutrals, and to assure such of them, as may be trusted, especially upon their taking the Oaths to His Majesty . . . That they may remain in the quiet Possession of Their Settlements, under proper regulations."[9] To make his point, Robinson sent along the text of the note British diplomats had just handed the French in which they objected even to the thought of Acadians leaving Nova Scotia.

The next year, when it was a fait accompli, the Board of Trade approved what Lawrence had done. "As you represent it to have been indispensably necessary for the Security and Protection of the Province," the board wrote, "we doubt not but that your Conduct herein will meet with His Majesty's Approbation."[10] Thus the policy of equivocation ended, but only after the question was moot. Had electronic communication existed in the eighteenth century, the expulsion of the Acadians would not have occurred.

Nor would it have occurred had the Acadians heeded unmistakable signals that the years of toleration were over. Even the deputies imprisoned on George's Island would have been released and left to live their lives if the Acadians had agreed to unqualified oaths of allegiance. But they would not. They must have argued long and prayed hard. Surely there were many who would have submitted. In the end, however, a rule of unity prevailed, and the Acadian response was unanimous. On Friday, July 25, and again on the following Monday, deputies from Annapolis Royal and new deputies from the Minas settlements arrived in Halifax with memorials and all the old arguments. On behalf of everyone, they refused the oath unless it were qualified by exemption from bearing arms.[11] It remained only for Lawrence and the council to decide how to deport them and where to send them.

In his letter to the Board of Trade, Lawrence had talked of exile to France. In the meantime, someone remembered the suggestion Peter Warren had made in 1745. If the Acadians were scattered among the different British colonies up and down the coast of North America, the king would not lose his subjects, the French would not be strengthened, and the unity of the Acadians would be broken forever. In the end, that was the plan adopted by Lawrence and the council, with Boscawen and Mostyn attending and agreeing, at a session held on July 28, 1755. The other councilmen—the men who took upon themselves the decision to exile a people—were the secretary of the province, William Cotterell; a New England merchant named Benjamin Green; Chief Justice Jonathan Belcher Jr.; a British settler named John Collier; and John Rous, a ship captain.[12]

Money was available, ships could be hired in Boston, and there were New Englanders still on hand from the Beauséjour campaign to do the dirty work. Lawrence laid it on in a torrent of paper. Orders were sent to Moncton at Fort Cumberland; to Captain John Handfield, the commander at Annapolis Royal; to Alexander Murray at Pisiquid; and to John Winslow, who with four companies of Americans would be in charge of depopulating and destroying Grand Pré and the farms around it.[13] The commanders were to use whatever stratagems they could devise to lure the men into confinement. When the ships came, and the men were aboard, the women and children would surely follow. The people's land, their livestock, and the grain they had harvested and stored for the winter was to be forfeited to the Crown. To discourage escape, homes and barns were to be burned. Not only would the land be emptied; it would be laid waste.

Passenger numbers and destinations were prescribed, and letters were prepared for the governors of the other colonies. Since the measures he was taking were necessary for the security of Nova Scotia, Lawrence was sure they would "receive the inhabitants I now send and dispose of them in such manner as may best answer our design in preventing their reunion." Dispersed, they would be no threat, and as "most of them are healthy, strong people . . . they may become profitable and it is possible, in time, faithful subjects."[14]

A note of urgency was added when word arrived of the Battle of the Monongahela and its terrible outcome. On August 8, Lawrence wrote Moncton to be on his guard, "and use your utmost endeavours to prevent, as much as possible, this bad news reaching the ears of the French inhabitants."[15] He hoped the roundup had begun, and indeed it had. Moncton's troops were ranging the countryside, taking prisoners and burning everything in sight. By August 11, they had already imprisoned 250 Acadians at Fort Cumberland.[16]

The operation at Chignecto did not, however, go smoothly. The French commander who had been forced from the Saint John showed up with his soldiers to help the Acadians fight back, and a guerrilla war began in the countryside behind the isthmus. On September 2, one of Moncton's detachments was surprised near the Petitcodiac River in the act of torching one of the refugee Acadians' little churches. Twenty-three soldiers were killed and seven were wounded —almost as many casualties as Moncton's whole army suffered in the siege of Fort Beauséjour. On October 1, eighty-six prisoners at Fort Lawrence escaped through a tunnel under the wall.[17]

Captain Handfield had nearly as much trouble at Annapolis

Royal, although he faced no armed opposition and lost no men. The people of the Annapolis Valley had the closest ties to the British. Some had friends and kinsmen among those who would deport them, and Handfield's was not the ruthless sweep Lawrence wanted. He apparently even spared some on purpose. A British officer visiting Annapolis Royal two years after the expulsion reported being entertained by a grande dame "of Romish Persuasion," an Acadian survivor.[18] She was Marie-Madeline Maisonnat, daughter of a privateer captain from the days of Villebon. She was also Handfield's mother-in-law.[19]

The roundup and embarkation were most efficient at the Minas settlements, where Winslow at Grand Pré and Murray at Pisiquid were in command. Since the greater numbers lived near Grand Pré, it fell to the American to be chief executioner.

Winslow was from Marshfield, near Plymouth, a great-grandson of one of the Pilgrim fathers and a well-respected soldier—stern when duty required, humane when duty allowed. Winslow did not like what he had to do at Grand Pré that summer and fall. His journal reveals a conscientious if not very well-lettered officer, one who would obey his orders, who shared Lawrence's fear of a populace whose sympathies lay with the enemy, but who knew that in ridding Nova Scotia of the Acadians he was ruining the lives of mostly innocent men, women, and children.[20] "Altho it is a Disagreeable Part of Duty wee are Put Upon," he wrote Lawrence, "I am Sensible it is a Necessary one, And Shall Endeavor Strictly to Obey your Excellency's Orders [and] Do Everything in me to Remove the Neighbors About me to a Better Country."[21]

He set up camp in the churchyard, and on September 2, he posted a summons requiring men and teenage boys to appear and hear the king's orders. Unsuspecting, they came. As they gathered, more than four hundred strong, they watched the soldiers close in. Then they heard Winslow deliver the awful verdict:

Your Lands and Tennements, Cattle of all [kinds] and Live Stock of all Sortes are Forfitted to the Crown with all your other Effects Saving your Money and Household Goods and you your selves to be removed from this . . . Province.

That it is Preremtorily his Majesty's orders That the whole French Inhabitants of these Districts, be removed, and I am Throh his Majesty's Goodness Directed to allow you Liberty to Carry of your money and Household Goods as Many as you Can without Discomemoading [discommoding] the Vessels you Go in. I shall do Everything in my Power that all Those Goods be Secured to you and that you are Not Molested in Carrying of them of and also that whole Familys Shall go in the Same Vessel, and make this remove which I am Sensable must give you a great Deal of Trouble as Easy as his Majesty's Service will admit and hope that in what Ever part of the world you may Fall you may be Faithful Subjects, a Peasable and happy People.

I Must also inform you That it is his Majesty's Pleasure that you remain in Security under the Inspection and Direction of the Troops that I have the Honr. to Command.[22]

"Things," Winslow wrote later that day, "are Now Very heavy on my harte and hands."[23]

The people were frightened, bewildered, disbelieving. Winslow set a few men free to tell wives and children their fate, and there could be little doubt now that it was no bluff, that the British finally were serious. Still, they could not take it in. Winslow said later that they refused to accept what he told the men at the church. "They did not then Nor to this Day do Imagine that they are Actually to be removed." He could not, he said, "Perswade the People I was in Earnest."[24]

Yet there were some who knew, some who might have the will to resist. Winslow had to wait for provisions and more transports before he could ship the people away, but he detected a restiveness among his prisoners and decided to begin embarking them, to put those he thought might be the most troublesome on board the ships he already had. On September 10, he made the men gather in the churchyard, then ordered the youngest marched off. When they balked, he had his soldiers fix bayonets. He counted off twenty-four, the first to go, and gave one a shove. "He obeyed and the rest followed, thoh Slowly, and went of Praying, Singing and Crying being Met by the women and Children all the way (which is 1½ mile) with Great Lamentations upon their Knees, praying etc." Before the day was over, "the Ice being Broke," 230 young men were embarked. Thus, Winslow wrote, "Ended this Troublesome Jobb, which was Scheen of Sorrow."[25]

The job was just begun. It was not until the next month that enough ships were on hand to permit the loading of families. On October 8, the first of the women and children "went of Very Solentarily and unwillingly, the women in Great Distress Carrying off Their Children In their arms. Others Carrying their Decript Parents in their Carts and all their Goods Moving in great Confussion and appeard a Sceen of woe and Distress."[26] On October 13, Winslow issued sailing orders, and a few days later, nine transports weighed anchor in the Minas Basin with fifteen hundred Acadians bound for the Delaware and the Chesapeake—names most of them had never even heard. Some six hundred more would follow.

Winslow sent ships to take eleven hundred people Murray had rounded up at Pisiquid, and he sent troops to help Handfield scour the Annapolis Valley and embark sixteen hundred more at Annapolis Royal. He learned from Moncton that eleven hundred had been shipped from Chignecto. Meticulously, sadly, he recorded the buildings his men burned at Grand Pré and the farms nearby: 255 houses, 276 barns, 155 outhouses, 11 mills, and a church.[27] By December, the destruction was complete and the people were gone.

In all, nearly six thousand men, women, and children were torn from the homes they cherished and sent to exile in Massachusetts, Connecticut, New York, Pennsylvania, Maryland, Virginia, South Carolina, and Georgia. They were not by any means the whole of the population. When 1755 began, there had been between 11,000 and 12,500 Acadians living on the peninsula and on the Isthmus of Chignecto.[28] Some made their way out before the deportation started. Some escaped while it was going on. Perhaps two thousand—including nearly all the population of Cobequid—crossed Northumberland Strait to swell Acadian numbers on Isle St. Jean.[29] Others fled up the mainland coast to virgin land on what is now sometimes called the Acadian Peninsula of northeastern New Brunswick. Some made their way to Isle Royale, some to Quebec. Some vanished into the forests near home. A few, like Marie-Madeline Maisonnat, were allowed to stay.

But even for those who escaped the soldiers, Lawrence's scheme to empty the land and his policy of scorched earth worked with terrible effect. When the burning was over, there were no homes, no farms, no churches, no settlements. There was no Acadia.

33 | DIASPORA

Acadians Find New Lives

FOR YEARS THE EXILES WANDERED. Separated from friends, sometimes from families, scattered up and down the coast from Massachusetts to Georgia, thrown on the mercy of French-fearing, Catholic-hating strangers, they were unharbored and unwelcome misfits. No one knew they were coming. Charles Lawrence's letters to the governors arrived with the ships. And no one was glad when they did come. On the western frontier, the French and their Indian allies were winning the war; here were more Frenchmen, more enemies, right on American doorsteps.

Virginians would not have them. By the early months of 1756, more than a thousand Acadians were in the colony, and the House of Burgesses demanded that Robert Dinwiddie get rid of them. Ship them to Britain! Britons had caused the problem; let Britons solve it! Their passage would cost £5,000, but to Virginia's burgesses, it was worth it. Before the summer was over, the hapless foreigners were gone, launched on the second leg of an odyssey that would take them to virtual imprisonment in British ports for the duration of the war, then to France. The wandering would not end until 1785, when their survivors and descendants recrossed the ocean to join other Acadian refugees in Louisiana.[1]

In Georgia and South Carolina, the démarche was more devious. The Acadians who appeared on the docks of Savannah and Charleston came from Chignecto, and they included a number of the hard core—the men Robert Moncton had rounded up after the surrender of Fort Beauséjour. They were the Acadians who had fought back. Some had been among Beauséjour's defenders; others had joined the guerrilla war. Neutrals no longer, their minds were set on escape and renewal of the fight for homes and farms, and governors and legislators found it expedient to look the other way while they secured boats to try the long voyage home. In South Carolina, the legislature even raised money to speed them on their way. A few made it. Others were stopped when they reached Massachusetts, where the authorities took a sterner view.[2]

Those who stayed behind in the southern colonies had trouble adapting. Schemes to put them to work were failures, and they had to be fed and housed at public expense. Many died, victims of a hot climate, an unfamiliar diet, disease, and despair. After a few years, the survivors simply disappeared, gone to French islands in the Caribbean and to the Mississippi.[3]

Efforts to assimilate Acadians in the other colonies failed as well. In Maryland, Pennsylvania, New York, Connecticut, and Massachusetts, laws were passed parceling them out to local communities.[4] No one wanted them all in one place, where they might launch a rebellion. The thinking went that in isolated rural townships they might find work and justify Lawrence's hope that they would be "profitable and . . . in time, faithful subjects." In most cases, however, they wound up on the public dole, and in one way or another, most of them found their way back to the port cities. Friends and relatives might be there, and it was by sea that they might, perhaps, go home again.

In a few places, they found champions, humanitarians who tried to help them.[5] Thomas Hutchinson, who would himself be driven into exile in 1774 as the loyalist governor of Massachusetts, was one. And Philadelphia's Quakers did what they could, assisting Pennsylvania's allotted refugees with petitions for redress and raising money to provide clothing and shelter. Other Americans, too, realized that these were an unfortunate people, set adrift through no fault of their own. Witness the *Maryland Gazette,* reporting the arrival of the Acadians at Annapolis in the fall of 1755:

Sunday last (Nov 30) arrived here the last of the vessels from Nova Scotia with French neutrals for this place, which makes four within this fortnight who have brought upwards of 900 of them. As the poor people have been deprived of their settlements within Nova Scotia, and sent here for some political reason bare and destitute, Christian charity, nay common humanity, calls on every one according to their ability to lend their assistance and help to these objects of compassion.[6]

But in most of the places they were sent, and in the demeanor of most of their unwilling hosts, Acadians found fear and aversion— attitudes that their foreign ways, their strange language, and their hated religion did nothing to dispel. When, in 1763, the Peace of Paris ended the Seven Years' War, Americans were as relieved to see them go as their unfortunate visitors were happy to leave.

The roundup and deportation went on throughout the war. Those who had escaped to the Nova Scotia forests found they could not survive on their own. Most were captured in British raids or forced into surrender by cold and hunger. The biggest refugee group, those who had fled to Isle St. Jean, were shipped to France in 1758. That was the year the tide of war turned, the year when, for the second time, the fortress of Louisbourg was taken by siege. The next year, General James Wolfe's army conquered Quebec.

When the war finally ended, Acadians were scattered throughout the American colonies, as well as in Canada and Europe. Loss of life from shipwreck and sickness had been brutal, but Acadian fecundity was still at work, and after eight years, their numbers were nearly what they had been in 1755. What had been a near-nation, however, was now nothing more than a splay of lonely groups, dispersed, according to one recent estimate, as follows:

Massachusetts	1,050
Connecticut	650
New York	250
Maryland	810
Pennsylvania	400
South Carolina	300
Georgia	200
Nova Scotia	1,250
Saint John Valley	100
Louisiana	300
Britain	850
France	3,500
Quebec	2,000
Isle St. Jean	300
Chaleur Bay	700
TOTAL	12,660[7]

And the diaspora was only beginning.

Those who made their way back to old Acadia found strangers on their land. Immigration from New England had begun in earnest in 1760, when Lawrence finally gave in to pressure from the Board of Trade and permitted a legislative assembly. By 1763, Nova Scotia was filled with English-speakers, and there was little room left for Acadians. Some were given unoccupied land at St. Mary's Bay, where Samuel de Champlain had scouted sites for de Monts in 1604. Today their settlement is "the French shore," midway between Yarmouth and Digby. Others settled just across the Isthmus of Chignecto, on Shepody Bay and in the valleys of the Petitcodiac and Memramcook Rivers, where the first of the Chignecto refugees had sought shelter in the early 1750s.

For the most part, though, the returning exiles had to build their new lives far from the Fundy tides, moving on to mix with the French-Canadians on the St. Lawrence, or joining other Acadians who had already settled below Chaleur Bay. One group moved into the lower Saint John Valley, only to be forced upriver to the Madawaska region, where an Acadian community now straddles the Maine-New Brunswick border. The contribution of those Madawaska Acadians to the history and culture of the United States was recognized by Congress in the Maine Acadian Culture Preservation Act of 1990.[8] When the act is implemented, one or more Acadian cultural centers will be built in Maine, joining Canadian centers at St. Joseph de Memramcook near Moncton, New Brunswick, at the Université de Moncton, and at Caraquet, New Brunswick, on the Acadian Peninsula.

Not all of the exiles headed north. Some chose a different path, traveling by land and sea to join compatriots in the lower Mississippi Valley. As part of the bargaining that led to the Peace of Paris, France had ceded its western territory to Spain, but even if it was no longer French, Louisiana was still French-speaking and Catholic, and there was empty land where a new Acadia could be built. After 1763, Acadians made their way there from all the colonies and from their island refuges in the Caribbean, and in time a new, Cajun culture was born.[9] Twenty-two of present-day Louisiana's sixty-four civil parishes, or counties, now bear the state legislature's official designation as "Acadiana."

Louisiana's Cajuns also trace their ancestry to the Acadians whose exile took them to Europe. Indeed, it was those Acadians whose migrations were the longest of all. The group shipped out of Virginia in

1756 spent seven years in Britain. Then, when peace came, the government of France arranged their repatriation to what was naively thought to be the home they pined for, France itself, where they were to join the others Lawrence had expelled during the war and make up a sturdy new peasantry.

It did not work out that way. Acadians would be no one's peasants. True to their natures, they would not do what they were told. After a century and a half, they were their own people, and they would not meld into the docile masses. French society was not ready for people so far from the norm—people who were indifferent to authority, who ignored taxes, who refused to fight wars. It was as though the Acadians had dropped from another planet. In 1785, after twenty-two years of frustration, the ministers of King Louis XVI gave up and let them go off to Louisiana.[10]

King Charles III of Spain paid their way. His new province needed people, even if they were, to be sure, very difficult people.

ACKNOWLEDGMENTS

Among those whose help with illustrative material is greatly appreciated are: Professor Alaric Faulkner, Department of Anthropology, University of Maine at Orono; André Guindon, Canadian Heritage, Parks Canada, Hull, Quebec; and Wayne P. Kerr, Canadian Heritage, Parks Canada, Halifax, Nova Scotia. Valuable advice about sources of photographs and illustrations was provided by Professor Phyllis LeBlanc, Director of the Centre d'études acadiennes and Professor of History at the University of Moncton; and Lisa Ornstein, Director of the Acadian Archives / Archives acadiennes, University of Maine at Fort Kent. Allan Doyle, at the Nova Scotia Visitor Information Centre, provided a wealth of background material.

I also wish to thank Karin Womer, Kathleen Brandes, and Alice Devine, whose editing improved and enhanced the text. Don Cyr, Director of the Lille-sur-St-Jean Cultural Association, provided photographs that were helpful to artist Chris Van Dusen as he developed the cover illustration.

NOTES

The following abbreviations are used in the notes:

C.H.R.	*Canadian Historical Review*
C.S.P.,C.S.	Great Britain, Public Record Office, *Calendar of State Papers, Colonial Series,* 44 vols. (London, 1880; reprint, Liechtenstein: Kraus Reprint, 1964)
D.C.B.	*Dictionary of Canadian Biography.* Ed. George W. Brown, et al. (Toronto: University of Toronto Press, 1966)
M.H.S.	Massachusetts Historical Society
ME.H.S.	Maine Historical Society
N.Y.C.D.	*Documents Relative to the Colonial History of the State of New York, Procured in Holland, England and France by John Romeyn Brodhead, Esq. Agent,* 15 vols. (Albany, 1853–87; reprint, New York: AMS Press, 1969)
N.S.H.S.	Nova Scotia Historical Society
P.D.N.S.	*Acadia and Nova Scotia: Documents Relating to the Acadian French and the First British Colonization of the Province 1714–1758.* Ed. Thomas B. Akins (Halifax, 1869; reprint, Cottonport, LA: Polyanthos, 1972)
W.M.Q.	*William and Mary Quarterly*

Preface

1. Edmund Burke, quoted in Charles C. Smith, "The War on the Seaboard: The Struggle in Acadia and Cape Breton," in *Narrative and Critical History of America,* ed. Justin Winsor, 8 vols. (Boston, 1884–89; reprint, New York: A.M.S. Press, 1967), 5:457.

Chapter 1–Indians and Fishermen

1. K.G. Davies, *The North Atlantic World in the Seventeenth Century* (Minneapolis: University of Minnesota Press, 1974), 11–16; Harold A. Innis, *The Cod Fisheries: The History of an International Economy,* rev. ed. (Toronto: University of Toronto Press, 1954), 11–51.

2. H.P. Biggar, *The Early Trading Companies of New France: A Contribution*

to the History of Commerce and Discovery in North America (Toronto, 1901; reprint, Clifton, NJ: Augustus M. Kelley, 1972), 24.

3. Marc Lescarbot, *Nova Francia: A Description of Acadia, 1606,* trans. P. Erondelle (London, 1609; New York: Harper & Brothers, 1928), 137.

4. David B. Quinn, *North America from Earliest Discovery to First Settlements: The Norse Voyages to 1612* (New York: Harper & Row, 1977), 349.

5. The First Relation of Jaques Carthier of S. Malo, 1534, *Early English and French Voyages, Chiefly from Hakluyt, 1534–1608,* ed. Henry S. Burrage (1906; reprint, New York: Barnes & Noble, 1967), 19.

6. Neal Salisbury, *Manitou and Providence: Indians, Europeans, and the Making of New England, 1500–1643* (New York: Oxford University Press, 1982), 22–24; Philip K. Bock, "Micmac," Vincent O. Erickson, "Maliseet-Passamaquoddy," and Dean R. Snow, "Eastern Abenaki," in Bruce G. Trigger, vol. ed., *Handbook of North American Indians,* vol. 15, *Northeast* (Washington, D.C.: Smithsonian Institution, 1978), 117, 125–26, 137–38.

7. Salisbury, *Manitou and Providence,* 57–58; Virginia P. Miller, "Aboriginal Micmac Population: A Review of the Evidence," *Ethnohistory* 23 (1976): 117–27; Francis Jennings, *The Invasion of America: Indians, Colonialism, and the Cant of Conquest* (Chapel Hill: Univ. of North Carolina Press, 1975), 15–31.

8. On the life and culture of northeastern Indians before contact with Europeans, and on the effects of contact, see: James L. Axtell, *The Invasion Within: The Contest of Cultures in Colonial North America* (New York: Oxford University Press, 1985); Kenneth M. Morrison, *The Embattled Northeast: The Elusive Ideal of Alliance in Abenaki–Euramerican Relations* (Berkeley: University of California Press, 1984), 12–71, 99–101; Salisbury, *Manitou and Providence;* John G. Reid, *Acadia, Maine, and New Scotland: Marginal Colonies in the Seventeenth Century* (Toronto: University of Toronto Press, 1981), 58–79; T.J. Brasser, "Early Indian-European Contacts," in Trigger, *Handbook,* 82–88; Jennings, *Invasion of America;* Calvin Martin, "The European Impact on the Culture of a Northeastern Algonquian Tribe: An Ecological Interpretation," *W.M.Q.,* 3d ser., 31 (1974): 3–26.

9. Differences between British and French attitudes toward native Americans are discussed in: Axtell, *Invasion Within,* 247–54; Morrison, *Embattled Northeast,* 8–9, 42–60, 102–32; Reid, *Acadia, Maine, and New Scotland,* 62–79; Davies, *North Atlantic World,* 284–85; Gary B. Nash, *Red, White, and Black: The Peoples of Early America* (Englewood Cliffs, NJ: Prentice-Hall, 1974), 88–120.

Chapter 2–St. Croix

1. George MacBeath, "Pierre Du Gua de Monts," *D.C.B.,* 1:291–95.

2. Lescarbot, *Nova Francia,* 1–6.

3. Samuel Eliot Morison, *The European Discovery of America: The Northern Voyages, A.D. 500–1600* (New York: Oxford University Press, 1971), 295–99; Ernest H. Wilkins, "Arcadia in America," American Philosophical Society, *Proceedings* 101 (1957): 4–30.

4. Andrew Hill Clark, *Acadia: The Geography of Early Nova Scotia to 1760* (Madison: University of Wisconsin Press, 1968), 71n.

5. Lescarbot, *Nova Francia,* 1.

6. Francis Parkman, *France and England in North America* (Boston, 1865–92; 2 vols., New York: Library of America, 1983), 1:184.

7. Sigmund Diamond, "An Experiment in 'Feudalism': French Canada in the Seventeenth Century," in *Essays on American Colonial History,* ed. Paul Goodman, 2d ed. (New York: Holt, Rinehart and Winston, 1972), 49–66.

8. Charter of Acadia, 18 Dec. 1603, W. Keith Kavenagh, ed., *Foundations of Colonial America: A Documentary History,* 3 vols. (New York, 1974; reprint, New York: Chelsea House, 1983), 1:19–20.

9. Biggar, *Early Trading Companies of New France,* 51–52.

10. Huia Ryder, "Jean de Biencourt de Poutrincourt et de Saint-Just," *D.C.B.,* 1:96–99.

11. Marc Lescarbot, Last Relation of what Took Place in the Voyage Made by Sieur de Poutrincourt to New France Twenty Months Ago, *The Jesuit Relations and Allied Documents: Travels and Explorations of the Jesuit Missionaries in New France 1610–1791,* ed. Reuben Gold Thwaites, 73 vols. (Cleveland: Burrows Brothers, 1896–1901), 2:125.

12. Lescarbot, *Nova Francia,* 14; Elizabeth Jones, *Gentlemen and Jesuits: Quests for Glory and Adventure in the Early Days of New France* (Toronto: University of Toronto Press, 1986), 7, 125–28.

13. Samuel Eliot Morison, *Samuel de Champlain: Father of New France* (Boston: Little, Brown, 1972); Morris Bishop, *Champlain: The Life of Fortitude* (New York, 1948; reprint, New York: Octagon Books, 1979).

14. Samuel de Champlain, *Voyages of Samuel de Champlain, 1604– 1618,* ed. W.L. Grant (New York: Charles Scribner's Sons, 1907), 36–37.

15. Biggar, *Early Trading Companies of New France,* 48. In describing the voyages of 1604 and events in Acadia that year and during the winter of 1604–5, I have relied on Champlain, *Voyages,* 19–56, and Lescarbot, *Nova Francia,* 7–47.

16. Champlain, *Voyages,* 40.

17. Ibid., 52.

18. Ibid., 34.

19. Lescarbot, *Nova Francia,* 13.

20. Ibid.

21. Champlain, *Voyages,* 42.

22. Morison, *Samuel de Champlain,* 36, 45.

23. Quinn, *North America,* 182.

Chapter 3–Port Royal

1. Except as otherwise noted, this account of French explorations of the New England coast in 1605 and 1606, of Poutrincourt's expedition of 1606,

and of events at Port Royal in 1606 and 1607 is based on Champlain, *Voyages*, 56–114, and Lescarbot, *Nova Francia*, 48–135.

2. Champlain, *Voyages*, 72.

3. Quinn, *North America*, 400.

4. Champlain's plan of the habitation is in *The Works of Samuel de Champlain*, ed. H.P. Biggar, 6 vols. (Toronto: Champlain Society, 1922–36), 1:373.

5. Champlain, *Voyages*, 79.

6. Ibid., 79–80.

7. Ibid., 85.

8. Ibid., 84.

9. Huia Ryder, "Charles de Biencourt de Saint-Just," *D.C.B.*, 1:99–102.

10. Lescarbot, *Nova Francia*, 62.

11. Lescarbot's *Nova Francia*, which was translated and published in London in 1609, is a part of his comprehensive *History of New France*, first published in Paris that same year and republished in second and third editions in 1611 and 1617. On Lescarbot's life and writings, see H.P. Biggar, "The French Hakluyt: Marc Lescarbot of Vervins," *American Historical Review* 6 (1900–1901): 671–92.

12. Lescarbot, *Nova Francia*, 64.

13. Ibid., 90.

14. Ibid., 111.

15. Ibid., 52, 103.

16. Marc Lescarbot, *The Theatre of Neptune in New France: Presented upon the Waves of Port Royal the Fourteenth Day of November, Sixteen Hundred and Six, on the Return of the Sieur de Poutrincourt from the Armouchiquois Country*, trans. Harriette Taber Richardson (Boston: Houghton Mifflin, 1927).

17. Lescarbot, *Nova Francia*, 121.

18. Ibid., 117.

19. Ibid., 130.

20. Alvin H. Morrison, "Membertou's Raid on the Chouacoet 'Almouchiquois'—The Micmac Sack of Saco in 1607," in *Papers of the Sixth Algonquian Conference*, ed. William Cowan (Ottawa: National Museums of Canada, 1975), 141–55.

Chapter 4–Britons and Jesuits

1. First Charter of Virginia, 10 Apr. 1606, Kavenagh, *Foundations of Colonial America*, 3:1698.

2. Lescarbot, *Nova Francia*, 142–44.

3. Ibid., 142.

4. Pierre Biard, Relation of New France, of its Lands, Nature of the Country and of Its Inhabitants. Also, of the Voyage of the Jesuit Fathers to said Country, and of their Work there up to the Time of their Capture by the English, *Jesuit Relations*, 3:163.

5. Ibid., 165.

6. Marc Lescarbot, *The History of New France,* trans. W.L. Grant, 3 vols. (Toronto: Champlain Society, 1907–14; reprint, New York: Greenwood Press, 1968), 3:35.

7. George MacBeath, "Claude de Saint-Etienne de La Tour," and "Charles de Saint-Etienne de La Tour," *D.C.B.,* 1:596–98, 592–96.

8. Lescarbot, *History of New France,* 37–39.

9. Lescarbot, Last Relation, *Jesuit Relations,* 2:155.

10. Lescarbot, *History of New France,* 3:47.

11. Ryder, "Charles de Biencourt de Saint-Just," *D.C.B.,* 1:99.

12. Parkman, *France and England in North America,* 1:211–14.

13. Lescarbot, *History of New France,* 3:48; Biard, Relation of New France, *Jesuit Relations,* 3:171–73.

14. Lescarbot, *History of New France,* 3:49–51.

15. Ibid., 52.

Chapter 5–Saint-Sauveur

1. Lescarbot, *History of New France,* 3:53.

2. Biard, Relation of New France, *Jesuit Relations,* 3:75.

3. Ibid., 197.

4. Ibid., 203–5.

5. Ibid., 235.

6. Ibid., 235–45; Lescarbot, *History of New France,* 3:57–59.

7. Lescarbot, *History of New France,* 3:60.

8. Poutrincourt to Lescarbot, 15 May 1613, Lescarbot, *History of New France,* 3:61–62.

9. Jones, *Gentlemen and Jesuits,* 217–18, 221–22.

10. Except as otherwise noted, this account of the Jesuit settlement and its demise is based on Biard, Relation of New France, *Jesuit Relations,* 3:261–4:75.

11. Biard, Relation of New France, *Jesuit Relations,* 3:271.

12. Quinn, *North America,* 412n; Parkman, *France and England in North America,* 1:226n.

13. "A Brief Relation of the Discovery of New England," M.H.S. *Collections,* 2d ser., 9 (1832): 5; W. Austin Squires, "Sir Samuel Argall," *D.C.B.,* 1:67.

14. Max Savelle, *The Origins of American Diplomacy: The International History of Angloamerica, 1492–1763* (New York: Macmillan, 1967), 199–201.

15. Biard, Relation of New France, *Jesuit Relations,* 3:279.

16. Ibid., 281.

17. Biard to Father Claude Aquaviva, 26 May 1614, *Jesuit Relations,* 3:11.

18. Biard, Relation of New France, *Jesuit Relations,* 4:45.

19. Complaint of Poutrincourt, 18 July 1614, Lescarbot, *History of New France,* 3:68–71.

20. Squires, "Sir Samuel Argall," *D.C.B.,* 1:67. The chart is in Alexander Brown, ed., *The Genesis of the United States,* 2 vols. (Boston: Houghton Mifflin, 1891), 1:457.

21. George Folsom, "Expedition of Captain Samuel Argall, Afterwards Governor of Virginia, Knight &c., to the French Settlements in Acadia and to Manhattan Island AD 1613," New York Historical Society, *Collections,* 2d ser., 1 (1841): 331–42.

22. H. de Montmorency, Admiral of France, to King James, 28 Oct. 1613, M.H.S. *Proceedings,* 2d ser., 1 (1884–85): 188.

23. Reply to the Complaints Presented to the King by the Sieur de Bisseaux, 1614, M.H.S. *Proceedings,* 2d ser., 1 (1884–85): 192.

24. H.P. Biggar, "The Death of Poutrincourt," *C.H.R.,* 1 (1920): 195–201.

Chapter 6–Nova Scotiae in America

1. Nicholas Denys, *The Description and Natural History of the Coasts of North America (Acadia),* trans. and ed. William F. Ganong (Toronto: The Champlain Society, 1908; reprint, 2 vols. in 1, New York: Greenwood Press, 1968), 97–98; Alaric Faulkner and Gretchen Fearon Faulkner, *The French at Pentagoet, 1635–1674: An Archaeological Portrait of the Acadian Frontier* (Augusta: Maine Historic Preservation Commission, 1987), 14.

2. Biencourt to the authorities in Paris, 1 Sept. 1618, *Collection de Manuscrits Contenant Lettres, Mémoires, et Autres Documents Historiques Relatifs à la Nouvelle-France,* 4 vols. (Quebec: Imprimerie A. Coté, 1883), 1:57–59.

3. Except as otherwise noted, in describing Sir William Alexander and his New Scotland, and the Knight Baronets of Nova Scotia, I have relied on: N.E.S. Griffiths and John G. Reid, "New Evidence on New Scotland, 1629," *W.M.Q.,* 3d ser., 49 (1992): 492–508; D.C. Harvey, "Sir William Alexander," *D.C.B.,* 1:50–54; D.C. Harvey, "Sir William Alexander and Nova Scotia," *N.S.H.S., Collections* 30 (1954): 1–26; Thomas H. McGrail, *Sir William Alexander First Earl of Stirling: A Biographical Study* (Edinburgh: Oliver & Boyd, 1940); George Pratt Insh, "Sir William Alexander's Colony at Port Royal," *The Dalhousie Review* 9 (1929–30): 439–47; J.E.A. Macleod, "Lord Ochiltree's Colony," *The Dalhousie Review* 4 (1924): 308–16; Edmund M. Slafter, *Sir William Alexander and American Colonization. . . .* (Boston, 1873; reprint, New York: Burt Franklin, 1972).

4. Sir William Alexander, *An Encouragement to Colonies,* London, 1624, in Slafter, *Sir William Alexander,* 196.

5. David Laing, ed., *Royal Letters, Charters, and Tracts, Relating to the Colonization of New Scotland, and the Institution of the Order of Knight Baronets of Nova Scotia, 1621–1638* (Edinburgh: Bannatyne Club Publications, 1867), Charters, 5.

6. Alexander, *An Encouragement to Colonies,* in Slafter, *Sir William Alexander,* 180–84.

7. Letter from the king, 17 Oct. 1629, Charles Rogers, ed., *The Earl of Stirling's Register of Royal Letters Relative to the Affairs of Scotland and Nova Scotia from 1615 to 1635,* 2 vols. (Edinburgh, 1885), 1:386.

8. Harvey, "Sir William Alexander and Nova Scotia," 10.

9. John S. Moir, "Sir David Kirke," *D.C.B.,* 1:404–7; Henry Kirke, *The First English Conquest of Canada,* 2d ed. (London, 1908).

10. Gustave Lanctot, *A History of Canada,* trans. Josephine Hambleton and Margaret M. Cameron, 3 vols. (Cambridge: Harvard University Press, 1963–65), 1:129–33; Biggar, *Early Trading Companies of New France,* 136.

11. Kirke to Champlain, 18 July 1628, Champlain, *Works,* 5:279–82.

12. Kirke, *The First English Conquest,* 77.

13. Griffiths and Reid, "New Evidence," 496–97.

14. Narrative of the Voyage Undertaken by Captain Daniel from Dieppe to New France in 1629, Richard Brown, *A History of the Island of Cape Breton: With Some Account of the Discovery and Settlement of Canada, Nova Scotia, and Newfoundland* (London, 1869; reprint, Belleville, Ont.: Mika Publishing, 1979), 76.

15. The Barbarous and Perfidious Cariage off the Frenche Towards the Lord Wchiltrie in the Ile off Cap Britaine Proved in the Court off Admiralty off Deepe, Brown, *History of the Island of Cape Breton,* 79–82.

16. Canada Archives, *Report of the Archives Branch for the Year 1912,* App. D, 23–24.

17. Beamish Murdoch, *A History of Nova Scotia, or Acadie,* 3 vols. (Halifax: James Barnes, 1865), 1:75.

18. Champlain, *Works,* 6:173.

19. Denys, *Description and Natural History,* 134.

20. Ibid., 135. In his *History of Canada,* Lanctot takes the view that Charles La Tour had joined the Charlesfort agreement in 1629 and that Denys's story of a battle at Cape Sable in 1630 is "pure fable." Lanctot, *History of Canada,* 1:145.

21. Denys, *Description and Natural History,* 137.

Chapter 7–Acadians and Puritans

1. *European Treaties Bearing on the History of the United States and Its Dependencies,* ed. Frances Gardiner Davenport and Charles Oscar Paullin, 4 vols. (Washington, 1917–37; reprint, Gloucester, MA: Peter Smith, 1967), 1:300–304.

2. Chateauneuf to Bouthillier, 20 Feb. 1630, Canada Archives, *Report of the Archives Branch for the Year 1912,* App. D, 36–37.

3. King to the inhabitants of Port Royal, 11 July 1631, Canada Archives, *Report of the Archives Branch for the Year 1912,* App. D, 49.

4. King to the baronets, 15 Aug. 1632, Rogers, ed. *The Earl of Stirling's Register,* 2:619.

5. *European Treaties,* 1:315–23.

6. In describing Razilly's settlement at La Have, I have relied on: Denys, *Description and Natural History,* 142–50; Joan E. Dawson, "Fort Sainte-Marie-de-Grâce, La Have, Nova Scotia: 350 Years of History," *Nova Scotia Historical Review* 2, no. 2 (1982): 52–56; George MacBeath, "Isaac de Razilly," *D.C.B.,* 1:567–69.

7. René Baudry, "Charles de Menou d'Aulnay," *D.C.B.,* 1:502–6.

8. George MacBeath, "Nicholas Denys," *D.C.B.,* 1:256–59.

9. Portland to Richelieu, 6 Dec. 1633, Canada Archives, *Report of the Archives Branch for the Year 1912,* App. D, 53; Lanctot, *History of Canada,* 1:275–76.

10. Lanctot, *History of Canada,* 1:276.

11. The background and organization of the Massachusetts Bay Company are described in: Charles M. Andrews, *The Colonial Period of American History,* 4 vols. (New Haven, CT: Yale University Press, 1934–38), 1:344–74; Samuel Eliot Morison, *Builders of the Bay Colony* (Boston, 1930; reprint, Boston: Northeastern University Press, 1981), 21–79; Herbert L. Osgood, *The American Colonies in the Seventeenth Century,* 3 vols. (New York, 1904; reprint, Gloucester, MA: Peter Smith, 1957), 1:98–166.

12. Winthrop to his wife, 15 May 1629, *Winthrop Papers,* ed. Allyn B. Forbes, 5 vols. (Boston: M.H.S., 1929–47), 2:91.

13. "A Model of Christian Charity," 1630, *Winthrop Papers,* 2:295.

14. Dean R. Snow and Kim M. Lanphear, "European Contact and Indian Depopulation in the Northeast: The Timing of the First Epidemics," *Ethnohistory,* 35 (1988): 15–33; Salisbury, *Manitou and Providence,* 101–6, 190–92.

15. U.S. Department of Commerce, Bureau of the Census, *Historical Statistics of the United States, Colonial Times to 1970,* Bicentennial Edition, Part 2 (Washington: Government Printing Office, 1975), 1168.

16. Muriel K. Roy, "Settlement and Population Growth in Acadia," in Jean Daigle, ed., *The Acadians of the Maritimes: Thematic Studies* (Moncton, N.B.: Centre d'études acadiennes, 1982), 133; Clark, *Acadia,* 100–101.

17. John Winthrop, *Winthrop's Journal, "History of New England" 1630–1649,* ed. James Kendall Hosmer, 2 vols. (New York, 1908; reprint, New York: Barnes & Noble, 1953), 1:97–98.

18. William Bradford, *Of Plymouth Plantation, 1620–1647,* ed. Samuel Eliot Morison (New York: Alfred A. Knopf, 1966), 246.

19. *Winthrop's Journal,* 1:113, 146.

20. Bradford, *Of Plymouth Plantation,* 275–76; *Winthrop's Journal,* 1:157.

21. *Winthrop's Journal,* 1:158–59; Bradford, *Of Plymouth Plantation,* 276–78.

22. Archange Godbout, "The Passenger List of the Ship *Saint-Jehan* and the Acadian Origins," *French Canadian and Acadian Genealogical Review* 1 (1968): 55–73; George MacBeath, "Jeanne Motin (Mottin)," *D.C.B.,* 1:514.

23. Godbout, "Passenger List of the *Saint-Jehan*," 70–71.

24. Léonie Comeau Poirier, *My Acadian Heritage* (Hantsport, N.S.: Lancelot Press, 1985).

Chapter 8–Warlords

1. Denys, *Description and Natural History*, 150–52; Bernard Pothier, "Nicholas Denys: The Chronology and Historiography of an Acadian Hero," *Acadiensis* 1, no. 1 (Autumn 1971): 54–70.

2. King to d'Aulnay, 10 Feb. 1638, *N.Y.C.D.*, 9:4–5.

3. M.A. MacDonald, *Fortune and La Tour: The Civil War in Acadia* (Toronto: Methuen, 1983), 186.

4. Ibid., 24–29, 53–54.

5. Ibid., 84–86.

6. Ibid., 87–88.

7. *Winthrop's Journal*, 2:43.

8. Baudry, "Charles de Menou d'Aulnay," *D.C.B.*, 1:504; MacDonald, *Fortune and La Tour*, 92–93.

9. MacDonald, *Fortune and La Tour*, 92, 96.

10. *Winthrop's Journal*, 2:85.

11. Ibid., 106–7; Davies, *North Atlantic World*, 239; MacDonald, *Fortune and La Tour*, 98–101.

12. Except as otherwise noted, this account of La Tour's visit to Boston in 1643 and of the deliberations of the Puritans is based on *Winthrop's Journal*, 2:105–16, 127–31.

13. Endecott to Winthrop, 19 June 1643, *Winthrop Papers*, 4:394.

14. Morison, *Builders of the Bay Colony*, 235–36.

15. Richard Saltonstall and others to the governor, deputy governor, assistants, and elders, 14 July 1643, *Winthrop Papers*, 4:398–401.

16. Winthrop to Saltonstall and others, July 1643, *Winthrop Papers*, 4:405, 410.

17. Suffolk County, Massachusetts, Registry of Deeds, *Suffolk Deeds*, ed. William D. Trask et al., 14 vols. (Boston: Rockwell and Churchill, 1880–1906), 1:7.

18. This account of the expedition of 1643 and the battle at the Allain River is drawn from a report by the Capuchins, 20 Oct. 1643, *Collection de Manuscrits*, 1:117–18, and *Winthrop's Journal*, 2:130, 136–37.

19. *Winthrop's Journal*, 2:136.

20. Ronald Dennis Cohen, "New England and New France, 1632 1651: External Relations and Internal Disagreements among the Puritans," Essex Institute, *Historical Collections* 108 (1972): 261–62.

21. MacDonald, *Fortune and La Tour*, 125–27.

22. Ibid., 127–29.

23. Ibid., 129–31; *Winthrop's Journal,* 2:194, 197.

24. Petition of John Bayley and Isaac Barkeley, 1644, M.H.S., *Collections,* 3d ser., 7 (1838): 98–99.

25. *Winthrop's Journal,* 2:181.

26. Governor and council to d'Aulnay, M.H.S., *Collections,* 3d ser., 7 (1838): 100–101.

27. *Winthrop's Journal,* 2:197.

28. *Collection of Original Papers Relative to the History of the Colony of Massachusetts Bay,* ed. Thomas Hutchinson (Boston, 1769; reprint under title *The Hutchinson Papers,* Boston, 1865; reprint, 2 vols., New York: Burt Franklin, 1967), 1:164–65.

29. *Winthrop's Journal,* 2:202.

30. Gilbert O. Bent, "The Procès-Verbal of Andrew Certain," *Acadiensis* 5 (1905): 40.

31. Denys, *Description and Natural History,* 114–16.

32. Bent, "Procès-Verbal," 44.

33. *Winthrop's Journal,* 2:226, 247.

34. Denys, *Description and Natural History,* 116.

35. Bent, "Procès-Verbal," 45.

Chapter 9–Progress and Chaos

1. *Winthrop's Journal,* 2:255.

2. Ibid., 247.

3. Ibid., 275.

4. D'Aulnay to the governor, 31 Mar. 1645, M.H.S., *Collections,* 3d ser., 7 (1838): 102–3.

5. M.H.S., *Collections,* 3d ser., 7 (1838): 109.

6. *Records of the Governor and Company of the Massachusetts Bay in New England,* ed. Nathaniel B. Shurtleff, 5 vols. (Boston, 1853–54; reprint, New York: A.M.S. Press, 1968), 2:158.

7. *Winthrop's Journal,* 2:270.

8. Ibid., 285.

9. Commission, Feb. 1647, M.H.S., *Collections,* 3d ser., 7 (1838): 110–11.

10. *Winthrop's Journal,* 2:326.

11. Pothier, "Nicholas Denys," 58.

12. Roy, "Settlement and Population Growth in Acadia," 133; Clark, *Acadia,* 100–102.

13. Denys, *Description and Natural History,* 124.

14. Alexander J. Savoie, "Education in Acadia: 1604 to 1970," in Daigle, *The Acadians of the Maritimes,* 385–86.

15. Samuel P. Arseneault, "Geography and the Acadians," in Daigle, *The Acadians of the Maritimes,* 96–98; Clark, *Acadia,* 24–31.

16. *Maritime Dykelands: The 350 Year Struggle* (Nova Scotia Department of Agriculture and Marketing, 1987), 8.

17. Pothier, "Nicholas Denys," 59; Lanctot, *History of Canada,* 1:295–96.

18. Patent, 25 Feb. 1651, Murdoch, *History of Nova Scotia,* 1:119.

19. Lanctot, *History of Canada,* 1:296.

20. Ibid., 296–97; Murdoch, *History of Nova Scotia,* 1:119.

21. Murdoch, *History of Nova Scotia,* 1:120–23; MacBeath, "Jeanne Motin," *D.C.B.,* 1:514.

22. Denys, *Description and Natural History,* 100.

23. Pothier, "Nicholas Denys," 60.

24. Patent, 30 Jan. 1654, Brown, *History of the Island of Cape Breton,* 92–96.

25. Denys, *Description and Natural History,* 100.

Chapter 10–New England Ascendant

1. William I. Roberts 3d, "Robert Sedgwick," *D.C.B.,* 1:604–5; Henry Dwight Sedgwick, "Robert Sedgwick," Colonial Society of Massachusetts, *Publications* 3 (1895): 155–73.

2. Leverett to the protector, 4 July 1654, Thomas Birch, *A Collection of the State Papers of John Thurloe, Esq.; Secretary, First, to the Council of State, And afterwards to the Two Protectors, Oliver and Richard Cromwell,* 7 vols. (London: Thomas Woodward and Charles Davis, 1742), 2:426.

3. Sedgwick to the protector, 1 July 1654, Birch, *State Papers,* 2:419.

4. Thomas Hutchinson, *The History of the Colony and Province of Massachusetts Bay,* ed. Lawrence Shaw Mayo, 3 vols. (Cambridge, MA, 1936; reprint, New York: Kraus Reprint, 1970), 1:156.

5. Leverett to the protector, 4 July 1654, Birch, *State Papers,* 2:426.

6. Leverett to the protector, 5 Sept. 1654, Birch, *State Papers,* 2:584; Denys, *Description and Natural History,* 100–101.

7. Denys, *Description and Natural History,* 101; Murdoch, *History of Nova Scotia,* 1:127.

8. Capitulation of Port Royal, Murdoch, *History of Nova Scotia,* 1:131–32.

9. George A. Rawlyk, *Nova Scotia's Massachusetts: A Study of Massachusetts–Nova Scotia Relations, 1630 to 1784* (Montreal: McGill–Queen's University Press, 1973), 24.

10. Instructions to Captain John Leverett, 23 Nov. 1655, *Hutchinson Papers,* 1:305–7.

11. Philip A. Knachel, *England and the Fronde: The Impact of the English Civil War and Revolution on France* (Ithaca, NY: Cornell University Press, 1967), 271.

12. *European Treaties,* 2:46.

13. Patent, 9 Aug. 1656, Murdoch, *History of Nova Scotia,* 1:138.

14. Reid, *Acadia, Maine, and New Scotland,* 137.

15. MacBeath, "Charles de Saint-Etienne de La Tour", *D.C.B.,* 1:595.

16. Temple to Thos. Povey, 1660, *C.S.P.,C.S.,* 1:496; Arthur Howland Buffinton, "Sir Thomas Temple in Boston: A Case of Benevolent Assimilation," Colonial Society of Massachusetts, *Publications,* 27 (1932): 310.

17. Denys, *Description and Natural History,* 105; Pothier, "Nicholas Denys," 60–62.

18. William F. Ganong, Introduction, in Denys, *Description and Natural History,* 25.

19. Denys, *Description and Natural History,* 102, 102n.

20. Temple to Lord Arlington, 2 Mar. 1669, *C.S.P.,C.S.,* 7:8–9; Buffinton, "Sir Thomas Temple," 313.

21. Buffinton, "Sir Thomas Temple," 313.

22. *European Treaties,* 2:119–31.

23. Ibid., 139.

24. Memorial of the English Commissaries, 11 Jan. 1751, *All the Memorials of the Courts of Great Britain and France Since the Peace of Aix La Chapelle, Relative to the Limits of the Territories of Both Crowns in North America and the Right to the Neutral Islands in the West Indies* (The Hague, 1756), 14.

25. Ibid., 15.

26. King to Temple, 6 Aug. 1669, *C.S.P.,C.S.,* 7:36.

27. *European Treaties,* 2:183–86.

Chapter 11–Confusion Renewed

1. Clark, *Acadia,* 121–24.

2. Ibid., 113–21.

3. Villebon to Count Pontchartrain, 27 Oct. 1699, John Clarence Webster, *Acadia at the End of the Seventeenth Century: Letters, Journals, and Memoirs of Joseph Robineau de Villebon, Commandant in Acadia, 1690–1700, and Other Contemporary Documents* (Saint John, N.B., 1934; reprint, New Brunswick Museum, 1979), 124; Clément Cormier, "Alexandre Le Borgne de Belle-Isle," *D.C.B.,* 1:436.

4. Account of the Voyage of Monsieur de Meulles to Acadie, Oct. 11, 1685–July 6, 1686, William Inglis Morse, *Acadiensa Nova, 1598–1779,* 2 vols. (London: Bernard Quaritch, 1935), 1:91–124.

5. This account of the Dutch conquest and its aftermath is drawn from: John Clarence Webster, "Cornelis Steenwyck: Dutch Governor of Acadie" (paper presented at the annual meeting of the Canadian Historical Association, Ottawa, May 22–23, 1929); Gilbert O. Bent, "The Dutch Conquest of Acadia," *Acadiensis* 5 (1905): 278–86; Charles Wesley Tuttle, *Capt. Francis Champernowne, The Dutch Conquest of Acadie, And Other Historical Papers,* ed. Albert Harrison Hoyt (Boston: John Wilson and Son, 1889), 127–59, 360–77.

6. Henri Brunet to the intendant, 5 Feb. 1675, Louis-André Vigneras, "Letters of an Acadian Trader, 1674–1676," *New England Quarterly* 13 (1940): 109.

7. Appointment of Cornelis Steenwyck, Amsterdam, 27 Oct. 1676, Webster, "Cornelis Steenwyck," 9.

8. *Major Peace Treaties of Modern History 1648–1967,* ed. Fred L. Israel, 4 vols. (New York: Chelsea House, 1967), 1:129–34.

9. Denys, *Description and Natural History,* 399–452.

10. Ibid., 444–45.

11. Wilcomb E. Washburn, "Seventeenth-Century Indian Wars," in Trigger, *Handbook,* 94.

12. Ibid., 93.

13. Osgood, *American Colonies in the Seventeenth Century,* 1:574.

Chapter 12–Before the Storm

1. J.-Roger Comeau, "Michel Leneuf de La Vallière de Beaubassin," *D.C.B.,* 2:409–11.

2. Clark, *Acadia,* 130–31; Gisa Hynes, "Some Aspects of the Demography of Port Royal, 1650–1755," *Acadiensis* 3, no. 1 (1973): 4–8.

3. Clément Cormier, "Jacques Bourgeois," *D.C.B.,* 2:94.

4. Clark, *Acadia,* 141–44; Will R. Bird, *A Century at Chignecto: The Key to Old Acadia* (Toronto: Ryerson Press, 1928), 5–9.

5. Clark, *Acadia,* 148.

6. Bona Arsenault, *History of the Acadians* (Ottawa: Editions Leméac, 1978), 44.

7. Clark, *Acadia,* 148–51; Hynes, "Demography of Port Royal," 5.

8. Robert Conkling, "Legitimacy and Conversion in Social Change: The Case of the French Missionaries and the Northeastern Algonkian," *Ethnohistory* 21 (1974): 1–24.

9. Paul Chassé, "The D'Abbadie de Saint-Castins and the Abenakis of Maine in the Seventeenth Century," *Proceedings of the Tenth Meeting of the French Colonial Historical Society, April 12–14, 1984* (Lanham, MD: University Press of America, 1985), 59–73; Gorham Munson, "St. Castin: A Legend Revised," *The Dalhousie Review* 45 (1965–66): 338–60; Georges Cerbelaud Salagnac, "Jean-Vincent d'Abbadie de Saint-Castin," *D.C.B.,* 2:4–7.

10. Faulkner and Faulkner, *The French at Pentagoet,* 2, 38.

11. "The Baron of St. Castine," *The Works of Henry Wadsworth Longfellow,* 14 vols. (Boston: Houghton Mifflin, 1886), 4:182.

12. "Mogg Megone," *The Complete Poetical Works of Whittier* (Boston: Houghton Mifflin, 1894), 505.

13. Baron de Lahontan, *New Voyages to North America,* ed. Reuben Gold Thwaites, 2 vols. (Chicago, 1905; reprint, New York: Burt Franklin, 1970), 1:329.

14. Richard R. Johnson, *John Nelson, Merchant Adventurer: A Life between Empires* (New York: Oxford University Press, 1991); Donald F. Chard, "John Nelson," *D.C.B.,* 2:493–94.

15. Petition of John Nelson, 12 Apr. 1697, *C.S.P.,C.S.,* 15:443.

16. Hutchinson, *History of the Colony and Province of Massachusetts Bay,* 1:321n.

17. Arthur Howland Buffinton, "John Nelson's Voyage to Quebec in 1682: A Chapter in the Fisheries Controversy," Colonial Society of Massachusetts, *Publications* 26 (1927): 427–37.

18. De la Barre to La Vallière, 4 Oct. 1683, *C.S.P.,C.S.,* 11:688.

19. *Records of the Governor and Company of the Massachusetts Bay,* 5:373–74.

20. Petition of Vaughan and others, 5 Dec. 1684, *C.S.P.,C.S.,* 11:743.

21. "The Company of Acadia," in Webster, *Acadia at the End of the Seventeenth Century,* 206–8.

22. W.J. Eccles, "François-Marie Perrot," *D.C.B.,* 1:540–42.

23. *European Treaties,* 2:322.

24. Savelle, *Origins of American Diplomacy,* 108.

Chapter 13 – King William's War

1. Morrison, *Embattled Northeast,* 113–15; Washburn, "Seventeenth-Century Indian Wars," 94–95.

2. Declaration of the Gentlemen, Merchants, and Inhabitants of Boston, and the Country Adjacent, 18 Apr. 1689, Peter Force, ed., *Tracts and Other Papers Relating Principally to the Origin, Settlement, and Progress of the Colonies in North America, from the Discovery of the Country to the Year 1776,* 4 vols. (1836; reprint, Gloucester, MA.: Peter Smith, 1963), 4, no. 10:10–11.

3. David S. Lovejoy, *The Glorious Revolution in America* (Middletown, CT: Wesleyan University Press, 1987), 240–45; Hutchinson, *History of the Colony and Province of Massachusetts Bay,* 1:319n.

4. Except as otherwise noted, this account of the 1690 invasion of Acadia and the occupation of Port Royal is based on "Journal of the Expedition under Sir William Phips against Port Royal, 1690," Canada Archives, *Report of the Archives Branch for the Year 1912 ,* App. E, 54–66, and Villebon to the Marquis de Chevry, 1690, Webster, *Acadia at the End of the Seventeenth Century,* 22–31.

5. C.P. Stacey, "Sir William Phips," *D.C.B.,* 1:544–46.

6. M. Gargas, Account of My Conduct During My Stay in Acadia, Morse, *Acadiensa Nova,* 1:144–55.

7. Lahontan, *New Voyages,* 1:330.

8. Nicholson to Secretary Blathwayt, 5 Sept. 1687, Bruce T. McCully, "The New England–Acadia Fishery Dispute and the Nicholson Mission of August, 1687," Essex Institute, *Historical Collections* 96 (1960): 288.

9. Murdoch, *History of Nova Scotia,* 1:185.

10. "Journal of the Expedition under Sir William Phips," 56.

11. Ibid., 62.

12. Ibid., 56, 60.

13. Villebon to Pontchartrain, 1692, Webster, *Acadia at the End of the Seventeenth Century,* 41.

14. Charter of the Massachusetts Bay, 7 Oct. 1691, Kavenagh, *Foundations of Colonial America,* 1:209.

15. Johnson, *John Nelson,* 69, 78; Webster, *Acadia at the End of the Seventeenth Century,* 2, 10, 200.

16. Villebon to Pontchartrain, 1692, Webster, *Acadia at the End of the Seventeenth Century,* 40–41.

17. Account of a Journey Made by M. de Villieu, Webster, *Acadia at the End of the Seventeenth Century,* 57–66.

18. Villebon, Events in Acadia since the Departure of the English from the Saint John River, October, 1696, Webster, *Acadia at the End of the Seventeenth Century,* 94–95.

19. Benjamin Church, *The History of the Eastern Expeditions of 1689, 1690, 1692, 1696, and 1704 Against the Indians and French,* ed. Henry Martyn Dexter (Boston: J.K. Wiggins and Wm. Parsons Lunt, 1867), 114.

20. Ibid., 121–25.

21. Villebon, Account of the Siege of Fort Natchouak by the English of Boston, and of their Retreat, 22 Oct. 1696, Webster, *Acadia at the End of the Seventeenth Century,* 89–94.

Chapter 14–Respite

1. *Major Peace Treaties,* 1:147.

2. Webster, *Acadia at the End of the Seventeenth Century,* 116–17.

3. Petition, 19 Nov. 1698, *The Acts and Resolves, Public and Private, of the Province of the Massachusetts Bay; to which Are Prefixed the Charters of the Province, with Historical and Explanatory Notes and an Appendix,* 21 vols. (Boston: State Printers, 1869–1922), 7:194–95.

4. For contemporary descriptions of Acadia and the Acadian lifestyle at the turn of the century, see: Villebon, Memoir on the Present Condition of Port Royal—Its Situation and the Reasons for Fortifying It, 27 Oct. 1699, Webster, *Acadia at the End of the Seventeenth Century,* 128–31; Sieur de Dièreville, *Relation of the Voyage to Port Royal in Acadia or New France,* trans. Mrs. J. Clarence Webster, ed. John Clarence Webster (Toronto: The Champlain Society, 1933; reprint, New York: Greenwood Press, 1968), 82–126; Sieur de La Mothe Cadillac, "The Cadillac Memoir of 1692," trans. W.F. Ganong, New Brunswick Historical Society, *Collections,* 13 (1930): 76–97.

5. Gargas, "Account of My Conduct," Morse, *Acadiensa Nova,* 1:178.

6. Villebon, Memoir on the Settlements and Harbors from Minas at the Head of the Bay of Fundy to Cape Breton, 27 Oct. 1699, Webster, *Acadia at the End of the Seventeenth Century,* 132.

7. Villebon, Memoir on the Coast Fisheries of Acadia and the Method of Conducting Them, 27 Oct. 1699, Webster, *Acadia at the End of the Seventeenth Century,* 138.

8. Daniel d'Auger de Subercase, quoted in Murdoch, *History of Nova Scotia,* 1:308.

9. Dièreville, *Relation of the Voyage to Port Royal,* 90–93.

10. Naomi E.S. Griffiths, *The Contexts of Acadian History, 1686–1784* (Montreal: McGill–Queen's University Press, 1992), 57.

11. Clark, *Acadia,* 129; Roy, "Settlement and Population Growth in Acadia," 134.

12. Clément Cormier, "Philippe Mius d'Entrement," *D.C.B.* 1:510; Rev. Clarence Joseph d'Entrement, *A Brief History of Pubnico,* 2d ed. (West Pubnico, N.S., 1984).

13. Quoted in Murdoch, *History of Nova Scotia,* 1:248

14. Bernard Pothier, "Mathieu de Goutin," *D.C.B.,* 2:257–58; Webster, *Acadia at the End of the Seventeenth Century,* 174–76.

15. Villebon to Pontchartrain, 1692, 1693, Webster, *Acadia at the End of the Seventeenth Century,* 35, 45.

16. Delabatt to Villermont, 20 Nov. 1703, Morse, *Acadiensa Nova,* 2:11.

17. Dièreville, *Relation of the Voyage to Port Royal,* 91.

18. Ibid., 96.

19. Ibid., 100.

20. Lahontan, *New Voyages,* 1:326.

21. Villebon to Pontchartrain, 1693, Webster, *Acadia at the End of the Seventeenth Century,* 46.

22. Villebon to Pontchartrain, 1692, Webster, *Acadia at the End of the Seventeenth Century,* 41.

Chapter 15–Queen Anne's War

1. Everett Kimball, *The Public Life of Joseph Dudley: A Study of the Colonial Policy of the Stuarts in New England, 1660–1715* (New York: Longmans, Green, 1911).

2. Parkman, *France and England in North America,* 2:373–98.

3. Hutchinson, *History of the Colony and Province of Massachusetts Bay,* 2:107; Church, *History of the Eastern Expeditions,* 160.

4. Church, *History of the Eastern Expeditions,* 144.

5. Ibid., 139–41.

6. Mather to Dudley, 20 Jan. 1707, Hutchinson, *History of the Colony and Province of Massachusetts Bay,* 2:109n.

7. G.M. Waller, *Samuel Vetch: Colonial Enterpriser* (Chapel Hill: University of North Carolina Press, 1960).

8. John Prebble, *The Darien Disaster: A Scots Colony in the New World, 1698–1700* (New York: Holt, Rinehart and Winston, 1968).

9. Letter from Brouillan, 8 Aug. 1701, *C.S.P.,C.S.,* 19:470.

10. Arthur H. Buffinton, "Governor Dudley and the Proposed Treaty of Neutrality, 1705," Colonial Society of Massachusetts, *Publications,* 26 (1927): 225–26.

11. Dudley to Vaudreuil, 4 July 1705, and Vaudreuil to Dudley, 2 June 1706, *Collection de Manuscrits,* 2:435–38, 451–52; Case of Samuel Vetch, 1707, *C.S.P.,C.S.,* 23:379–82.

12. Proposed treaty between Canada and New England, Oct. 1705, *Acts and Resolves of Massachusetts,* 8:541–43.

13. *Acts and Resolves of Massachusetts,* 6:62.

14. John (Jonathan) Winthrop to Fitz-John Winthrop, June 1706, M.H.S., *Collections,* 6th ser., 3 (1889): 335.

15. Opinion of the Attorney General, 28 Mar. 1707, *C.S.P.,C.S.,* 23:410.

16. Mather to Dudley, 20 Jan. 1707, Hutchinson, *History of the Colony and Province of Massachusetts Bay,* 2:121n.

17. Dudley to Fitz-John Winthrop, 31 Mar. 1707, M.H.S., *Collections,* 6th ser., 3 (1889): 375.

18. This description of the campaigns of 1707 is drawn from: John Barnard, "Autobiography of the Rev. John Barnard," M.H.S., *Collections,* 3d. ser., 5 (1836): 189–96; *Acts and Resolves of Massachusetts,* 8:668–96, 715–18, 722–51; Dièreville, *Relation of the Voyage to Port Royal,* Appendix, "The Publisher to the Reader," 209–15; Hutchinson, *History of the Colony and Province of Massachusetts Bay,* 2:122–27; Herbert L. Osgood, *The American Colonies in the Eighteenth Century,* 4 vols. (New York, 1924; reprint, Gloucester, MA: Peter Smith, 1958), 1:425–28; Murdoch, *History of Nova Scotia,* 1:286–95.

19. René Baudry, "Daniel d'Auger de Subercase," *D.C.B.,* 2:35–39.

20. John (Jonathan) Winthrop to Fitz-John Winthrop, July 1707, M.H.S., *Collections,* 6th. ser., 3 (1889): 387–89.

21. "Autobiography of the Rev. John Barnard," 196.

22. Wainwright to the commissioners, 14 Aug. 1707, Hutchinson, *History of the Colony and Province of Massachusetts Bay,* 2:127.

23. "Autobiography of the Rev. John Barnard," 195.

Chapter 16—Takeover

1. Letter, 30 June 1707, *Documents Relating to Currency, Exchange and Finance in Nova Scotia, with Prefatory Documents, 1675–1758,* ed. Adam Shortt, V.K. Johnston, and Gustave Lanctot (Ottawa: J.O. Patenaude, Acting King's Printer, 1933), 14–15.

2. Letter, 20 May 1710, *Documents Relating to Currency,* 16.

3. Murdoch, *History of Nova Scotia,* 1:304.

4. Webster, *Acadia at the End of the Seventeenth Century,* 172–73.

5. Parkman, *France and England in North America,* 2:414.

6. Brouillan to the minister, 21 Oct. 1702, Murdoch, *History of Nova Scotia,* 1:256.

7. "An ACCOUNT of the Shameful *Miscarriage* of the Late EXPEDI-
TION against PORT-ROYAL" (London, 1708), M.H.S., *Collections,* 5th ser.,
6 (1879): 126–29.

8. Kimball, *Joseph Dudley,* 189.

9. *C.S.P.,C.S.,* 24:41–51.

10. Ibid., 149.

11. Stephen S. Webb, "The Strange Career of Francis Nicholson," in
Colonial America: Essays in Politics and Social Development, ed. Stanley N.
Katz and John M. Murrin, 3d ed. (New York: Alfred A. Knopf, 1983).

12. Waller, *Samuel Vetch,* 119.

13. Osgood, *American Colonies in the Eighteenth Century,* 1:429–35.

14. Waller, *Samuel Vetch,* 155.

15. Letters from Dudley, Nicholson, Vetch, and Captain Moody, 24 and
25 Oct. 1709, *C.S.P.,C.S.,* 24:488–97.

16. This account of the expedition of 1710 and the siege and surrender
of Port Royal is based on: "Journal of Colonel Nicholson at the Capture of
Annapolis, 1710," N.S.H.S., *Report and Collections* 1 (1878): 59–104; sum-
maries of documents concerning the siege of Port Royal, *N.Y.C.D.,*
9:927–29; Osgood, *American Colonies in the Eighteenth Century,* 1:436–39;
Murdoch, *History of Nova Scotia,* 1:309–16.

17. "Journal of Colonel Nicholson," 62.

18. Ibid., 69–70.

19. Ibid., 72.

20. Ibid., 74.

21. Ibid., 79–80.

22. Ibid., 80.

23. Ibid., 82.

24. Nicholson and council to the queen, Oct. 1710, *C.S.P.,C.S.,* 25:245.

Chapter 17–Rebellion and Partition

1. "Journal of Colonel Nicholson," 88.

2. Ibid., 93.

3. Ibid., 86.

4. Clark, *Acadia,* 129–30.

5. Maxwell Sutherland, "Paul Mascarene," *D.C.B.,* 3:435–40; John Bartlet Brebner, "Paul Mascarene of Annapolis Royal," in G.A. Rawlyk, ed., *Historical Essays on the Atlantic Provinces* (Toronto: McClelland and Stewart,
1967), 17–32.

6. Letter from Thomas Caulfeild, 2 Nov. 1715, *Documents Relating to
Currency,* 96.

7. Nicholson and council to the queen, Oct. 1710, *C.S.P.,C.S.,* 25:246.

8. Vetch to the earl of Dartmouth, 22 Jan. 1711, *C.S.P.,C.S.,* 25:344.

9. Vetch to the Board of Trade, 24 Nov. 1714, *P.D.N.S.,* 5–7; Vetch to the Board of Trade, 21 Feb. 1715, *Documents Relating to Currency,* 97–99.

10. On the relations of Britain and France with the Micmacs, see: Olive Patricia Dickason, "Amerindians Between French and English in Nova Scotia, 1713–1763," *American Indian Culture and Research Journal* 10, no. 4 (1986): 31–56; L.F.S. Upton, *Micmacs and Colonists: Indian–White Relations in the Maritimes, 1713–1867* (Vancouver: University of British Columbia Press, 1979), 28–60; Ronald O. MacFarlane, "British Indian Policy in Nova Scotia to 1760," *C.H.R.,* 19 (1938): 154–67.

11. Decree, 12 Oct. 1710, "Journal of Colonel Nicholson," 95–96.

12. Ibid., 96.

13. Council to Vaudreuil, 11 Oct. 1710, "Journal of Colonel Nicholson," 98.

14. Vaudreuil to Ponchartrain, 25 Apr. 1711, *N.Y.C.D.,* 9:854.

15. Vetch to Mascarene, 1 Nov. 1710, Paul Mascarene, "A Narrative of Events at Annapolis from the Capture in Oct., 1710, till Sept., 1711," *N.S.H.S., Collections* 4 (1884): 86.

16. Mascarene, "Narrative of Events," 71–72.

17. Ibid., 71–73.

18. Murdoch, *History of Nova Scotia,* 1:321.

19. The Case of Coll. Vetch, late Governor of Annapolis Royal in Nova Scotia, Briefly stated, *Documents Relating to Currency,* 68–69.

20. Mascarene, "Narrative of Events," 77–78.

21. Letter from Gaulin, 5 Sept. 1711, Murdoch, *History of Nova Scotia,* 1:323.

22. Mascarene, "Narrative of Events," 78.

23. Letter from Vetch, 18 June 1711, *C.S.P.,C.S.,* 25:552–54.

24. Webb, "The Strange Career of Francis Nicholson," 338.

25. The story is told in Gerald S. Graham, *The Walker Expedition to Quebec, 1711* (Toronto: Champlain Society, 1953; reprint, New York: Greenwood Press, 1969).

26. *Peter Kalm's Travels in North America,* ed. Adolph B. Benson (New York: Dover Publications, 1987), 366.

27. Caulfeild to the earl of Dartmouth, 6 Dec. 1711, *C.S.P.,C.S.,* 26:173; Proclamation, July 1711, *C.S.P.,C.S.,* 26:66.

28. On the several treaties, see *European Treaties,* 3:133–255; Savelle, *Origins of American Diplomacy,* 122–56. The texts of the treaties between Great Britain and France, Great Britain and Spain, and Spain and Austria are in *Major Peace Treaties,* 1:177–260.

29. *Major Peace Treaties,* 1:209.

30. Board of Trade to Henry St. John, 5 Apr. 1712, *C.S.P.,C.S.,* 26:256–57.

Chapter 18–Dilemmas

1. Savelle, *Origins of American Diplomacy,* 240–42.
2. Memoir Respecting the Abanaquis of Acadia, *N.Y.C.D.,* 9:878–81.
3. *Major Peace Treaties,* 1:210.
4. Queen to Nicholson, 23 June 1713, *P.D.N.S.,* 15.
5. J.S. McLennan, *Louisbourg: From its Foundation to its Fall, 1713–1758* 3d ed. (Sydney, N.S.: Fortress Press, 1969), 11–12.
6. Father Felix Paim to Costabelle, 23 Sept. 1713, Murdoch, *History of Nova Scotia,* 1:336–37.
7. McLennan, *Louisbourg,* 15–18.
8. Vetch to the Board of Trade, 24 Nov. 1714, *P.D.N.S.,* 6.
9. Report on Nova Scotia, 17 Mar. 1715, *C.S.P.,C.S.,* 28:124–28.
10. Vetch to the earl of Dartmouth, 22 Jan. 1711, *C.S.P.,C.S.,* 25:343.
11. Caulfeild to the Secretary of State, 3 May 1715, *P.D.N.S.,* 7–8.
12. Nicholson to Bolingbroke, 23 Apr. 1714, *C.S.P.,C.S.,* 27:335.
13. Vetch to Dartmouth, 16 Nov. 1711, *C.S.P.,C.S.,* 26:151.
14. The Case of Coll. Vetch, late Governor of Annapolis Royal in Nova Scotia, Briefly stated, *Documents Relating to Currency,* 70.
15. Webb, "The Strange Career of Francis Nicholson"; Bruce T. McCully, "Francis Nicholson," *D.C.B.,* 2:496–98; "Francis Nicholson," *Dictionary of American Biography,* ed. Allen Johnson and Dumas Malone (New York: Charles Scribner's Sons, 1928–), 7:499–502.

Chapter 19–Failure

1. Maxwell Sutherland, "Richard Philipps," *D.C.B.,* 3:515–18.
2. *P.D.N.S.,* 14.
3. Ibid., 16.
4. Naomi E.S. Griffiths, "The Golden Age: Acadian Life, 1713–1748," *Histoire Sociale—Social History* 17 (1984): 21–34.
5. Board of Trade to the king, 30 May 1718, *C.S.P.,C.S.,* 30:259.
6. *Royal Instructions to British Colonial Governors, 1670–1776,* ed. Leonard Woods Labaree, 2 vols. (New York: Octagon Books, 1967), 1:85.
7. John Bartlet Brebner, *New England's Outpost: Acadia before the Conquest of Canada* (New York, 1927; reprint, Hamden, CT: Archon Books, 1965), 134–65.
8. *Royal Instructions,* 1:435.
9. Inhabitants of Minas to Philipps, May 1720, *P.D.N.S.,* 28–29.
10. Philipps to Secretary Craggs, 26 May 1720, *P.D.N.S.,* 33, 35.
11. South Sea Company Petition, 2 Jan. 1720, *C.S.P.,C.S.,* 32:229–30.
12. Winthrop Pickard Bell, *The "Foreign Protestants" and the Settlement of Nova Scotia: The History of a Piece of Arrested British Colonial Policy in the Eighteenth Century* (Toronto: University of Toronto Press, 1961), 19–21.

13. Memorial of Vetch and others, 12 Jan. 1721, *C.S.P.,C.S.,* 32:232; Waller, *Samuel Vetch,* 280.

14. "Thomas Coram," *Dictionary of National Biography,* ed. Sir Leslie Stephen and Sir Sidney Lee, 63 vols. (London, 1885–), 12:194–95.

15. *C.S.P.,C.S.,* 29:300, 308–9; Bell, *"Foreign Protestants,"* 30–34.

16. Letter from Coram, July 1737, "Letters of Thomas Coram," M.H.S., *Proceedings* 56 (1922–23): 37.

17. Representation of the Lords Commissioners for Trade and Plantations to the King upon the State of His Majesties Colonies and Plantations on the Continent of North America, 8 Sept. 1721, *N.Y.C.D.,* 5:596.

18. *Royal Instructions,* 2:599; Bell, *"Foreign Protestants,"* 43–51.

Chapter 20–Checkmate

1. Philipps to Lord Carteret, *P.D.N.S.,* 18.

2. Paul Mascarene, "Description of Nova Scotia," 1720, *P.D.N.S.,* 43.

3. Ibid.

4. Representation of the council, 27 Sept. 1720, *P.D.N.S.,* 56.

5. Philipps to Craggs, 26 Sept. 1720, *P.D.N.S.,* 51.

6. Representation of the Lords Commissioners for Trade and Plantations, 8 Sept. 1721, *N.Y.C.D.,* 5:592.

7. John Robert McNeil, *Atlantic Empires of France and Spain: Louisbourg and Havana, 1700–1763* (Chapel Hill: University of North Carolina Press, 1985), 94–96; Robert Emmet Wall Jr., "Louisbourg, 1745," *New England Quarterly* 37 (1964): 64–83.

8. Clark, *Acadia,* 276; McLennan, *Louisbourg,* 71.

Chapter 21–Rale's War

1. Memoir by M. Bobé Respecting the Boundaries, Mar. 1723, *N.Y.C.D.,* 9:913–17.

2. Vaudreuil to Doucett, 22 Sept. 1718, *C.S.P.,C.S.,* 30:405–6.

3. *European Treaties,* 3:213.

4. St.-Ovide to Doucett, 21 July 1718, *C.S.P.,C.S.,* 30:325–26; Savelle, *Origins of American Diplomacy,* 246.

5. Submission and Agreement of the Eastern Indians, Portsmouth, 13 July 1713, Frederick Kidder, "The Abenaki Indians; their Treaties of 1713 & 1717, and a Vocabulary: with a Historical Introduction," ME.H.S., *Collections,* 1st ser., 6 (1859): 251.

6. David L. Ghere, "Mistranslations and Misinformation: Diplomacy on the Maine Frontier, 1725 to 1755," *American Indian Culture and Research Journal* 8, no. 4 (1984): 3–26; Roger B. Ray, "Maine Indians' Concept of Land Tenure," ME.H.S., *Quarterly,* 13 (1973): 28–51.

7. John Winthrop, Generall considerations for the plantation in New England, *Winthrop Papers,* 2:120.

8. "Indian Treaties," ME.H.S., *Collections,* 1st ser., 3 (1853): 363.

9. Ibid., 364.

10. Ibid., 366–67.

11. Ibid., 367–68.

12. Ibid., 369.

13. Ibid., 374.

14. King to Vaudreuil and Begon, 23 May 1719, *N.Y.C.D.,* 9:892.

15. Kenneth M. Morrison, "Sebastien Racle and Norridgewock, 1724: The Eckstorm Conspiracy Thesis Reconsidered," ME.H.S., *Quarterly* 14 (1974): 76–97.

16. Rale to Captain Moody, 7 Feb. 1720, James Phinney Baxter, *The Pioneers of France in England, with Contemporary Letters and Documents,* (Albany, NY: Joel Munsell's Sons, 1894), 96, 99, 101.

17. Roger B. Ray, "Eastern Indians' Letter to the Governour," ME.H.S., *Quarterly* 13 (1974): 179–81.

18. Shute to the Board of Trade, 13 Mar. 1722, *C.S.P.,C.S.,* 33:27–30.

19. Declaration, 25 July 1722, Baxter, *Pioneers of France,* 314.

20. Letter from Nathaniel Shannon, 22 Oct. 1718, *C.S.P.,C.S.,* 30:403.

21. McLennan, *Louisbourg,* 62–63.

22. Memorial of John Henshaw, William Tayler, and Richard Picke, August 1720, *Documents Relating to Currency,* 133; McLennan, *Louisbourg,* 67–70.

23. Philipps to the Board of Trade, 19 Sept. 1722, *P.D.N.S.,* 61.

24. Ibid., 61–62.

25. Morrison, "Sebastien Racle and Norridgewock," 88–91; Baxter, *Pioneers of France,* 237–44; Hutchinson, *History of the Colony and Province of Massachusetts Bay,* 2:235–38.

26. Abstract of a Dispatch by Vaudreuil, 7 Aug. 1725, *N.Y.C.D.,* 9:947–49.

27. Ibid., 949.

28. Submission and Agreement of the Delegates of the Eastern Indians, Boston, 15 Dec. 1725, "Indian Treaties," 417.

29. King to Beauharnois and Dupoy, 14 May 1728, *N.Y.C.D.,* 9:1002.

Chapter 22–"French Neutrals"

1. On the early history and settlement of Isle St. Jean, see: Andrew Hill Clark, *Three Centuries and the Island: A Historical Geography of Settlement and Agriculture in Prince Edward Island, Canada* (Toronto: University of Toronto Press, 1959), 1–41; D.C. Harvey, *The French Régime in Prince Edward Island* (New Haven, CT: Yale University Press, 1926).

2. Clark, *Three Centuries and the Island,* 28–30.

3. Mascarene, "Description of Nova Scotia," *P.D.N.S.,* 47.

4. Letter from Hibbert Newton, 1 Sept. 1743, *Documents Relating to Currency,* 223–24.

5. *Documents Relating to Currency,* xxvi–xxviii.

6. On Newcastle's administration, see James A. Henretta, *"Salutary Neglect": Colonial Administration under the Duke of Newcastle* (Princeton, NJ: Princeton University Press, 1972).

7. Maxwell Sutherland, "Lawrence Armstrong," *D.C.B.,* 2:21–24.

8. Meeting of the council, 25 Sept. 1726, *P.D.N.S.,* 67; Cotterell to Hopson, 1 Oct. 1753, Placide Gaudet, "Acadian Genealogy and Notes," in *Report Concerning Canadian Archives for the Year 1905,* 3 vols. (Ottawa: E.S. Dawson, 1906), vol. 2, app. A, part III, 57.

9. Armstrong to the Secretary of State, 30 Apr. 1727, *P.D.N.S.,* 70.

10. Meeting of the council, 25 July 1727, *P.D.N.S.,* 74.

11. Meeting of the council, 16 Sept. 1727, *P.D.N.S.,* 77; Armstrong to the Secretary of State, 17 Nov. 1727, *P.D.N.S.,* 79–81.

12. Gaudet, "Acadian Genealogy and Notes," 299.

13. Meeting of the council, 13 Nov. 1727, *P.D.N.S.,* 78–79.

14. Philipps to Newcastle, 3 Jan. and 2 Sept. 1730, *P.D.N.S.,* 83–84, 86–87.

15. Armstrong to the Board of Trade, 23 June 1729, *P.D.N.S.,* 82–83.

16. Breslay to Philipps, 23 Dec. 1729, Gaudet, "Acadian Genealogy and Notes," 70.

17. Naomi E.S. Griffiths, *The Acadians: Creation of a People* (Toronto: McGraw-Hill Ryerson, 1973), 27; Lanctot, *A History of Canada,* 3:48; Brebner, *New England's Outpost,* 97.

18. Gaudet, "Acadian Genealogy and Notes," 24–25.

19. Representation of the State of His Majesties Province of Nova Scotia, 8 Nov. 1745, *Minutes of His Majesty's Council at Annapolis Royal, 1736–1749,* ed. Charles Bruce Fergusson (Halifax: Public Archives of Nova Scotia, 1967), 81.

20. *P.D.N.S.,* 84–85.

21. Oath of Allegiance Taken and Subscribed by the Acadians of Mines District, Cobequit, Piziquid and Beaubassin, Gaudet, "Acadian Genealogy and Notes," 77.

22. Secretary Popple to Philipps, 20 May 1730, *P.D.N.S.,* 84–85.

23. Philipps to the Board of Trade, 26 Nov. 1730, *P.D.N.S.,* 87–88.

Chapter 23 – Isolation

1. Philipps to Newcastle, 2 Sept. 1730, *P.D.N.S.,* 86

2. Armstrong to the Board of Trade, 5 Oct. 1731, *P.D.N.S.,* 92.

3. Clark, *Acadia,* 201.

4. Hynes, "Demography of Port Royal," 11.

5. Ibid., 7–8.

6. Clark, *Acadia,* 207–11.

7. Thomas Waterhouse, Scheme of the Fishery at Canso in Nova Scotia for the Year 1730, *Documents Relating to Currency,* 177–80.

8. *Royal Instructions,* 2:599–600.

9. Board of Trade to the Privy Council, 14 May 1729, *C.S.P.,C.S.,* 36:371–73.

10. Robert Hale, "Journal of a Voyage to Nova Scotia Made in 1731 by Robert Hale of Beverly," Essex Institute, *Historical Collections* 42 (1906): 220–21.

11. Popple to Dunbar, 7 May 1730, *C.S.P.,C.S.,* 37:101.

12. *Acts of the Privy Council of England, Colonial Series,* vol. 3, 1720–45, ed. W.L. Grant and James Monro (London, 1910; reprint, Liechtenstein: Kraus Reprint, 1966), 275–83.

13. Ibid., 283.

14. Board of Trade to the Privy Council, 14 May 1729, *C.S.P.,C.S.,* 36:371–73; Bell, *"Foreign Protestants,"* 34–40.

15. Board of Trade to Philipps, 20 May 1730, *Documents Relating to Currency,* 176; Bell, *"Foreign Protestants,"* 41–43.

16. Letter from Dunbar, 4 June 1731, *Documents Relating to Currency,* 182–83; Bell, *"Foreign Protestants,"* 59–63.

17. Belcher to Newcastle, 6 Mar. 1732, "The Belcher Papers," M.H.S., *Collections,* 6th ser., 6 (1893): 104.

18. Bell, *"Foreign Protestants,"* 52.

19. Belcher to Coram, 6 Oct. 1733, "Belcher Papers," 392.

Chapter 24 – Frustration

1. Armstrong to the Board of Trade, 5 Oct. 1731, *P.D.N.S.,* 91–92.

2. Account of the Situation, Commerce, etc. of the Province of Nova Scotia, 1731, *Documents Relating to Currency,* 181.

3. Armstrong to the Board of Trade, 5 Oct. 1731, *P.D.N.S.,* 91.

4. Board of Trade to the Privy Council, 23 Oct. 1733, *Documents Relating to Currency,* 193.

5. Clarence J. d'Entremont, "Agathe Saint-Etienne de La Tour," *D.C.B.,* 2:590–91.

6. Representation of the State of His Majesties Province of Nova Scotia, 8 Nov. 1745, *Minutes of His Majesty's Council at Annapolis Royal, 1736–1749,* 83.

7. Meeting of the council, 25 July 1732, *P.D.N.S.,* 97–98; Murdoch, *History of Nova Scotia,* 1:479–81.

8. Armstrong to Newcastle, 15 Nov. 1732, *P.D.N.S.,* 101.

9. Brebner, *New England's Outpost,* 134–42.

10. Mascarene to Shirley, 6 Apr. 1748, M.H.S., *Collections,* 1st ser., 6 (1799): 125.

11. Brebner, *New England's Outpost,* 147.

12. Armstrong to the Board of Trade, 15 Nov. 1732, *P.D.N.S.*, 99.

13. Armstrong to Newcastle, 8 Dec. 1735, *P.D.N.S.*, 102–3.

14. Sutherland, "Lawrence Armstrong," *D.C.B.*, 2:23.

15. Mascarene to Shirley, 6 Apr. 1748, M.H.S., *Collections*, 1st ser., 6 (1799): 124–25; Brebner, *New England's Outpost*, 149–50.

16. Armstrong to the Board of Trade, 23 June 1729, *P.D.N.S.*, 82.

17. Meeting of the council, 24 Oct. 1726, *P.D.N.S.*, 69; David Lee, "Antoine Gaulin," *D.C.B.*, 2:238.

18. Armstrong to the Board of Trade, 5 Oct. 1731, *C.S.P.,C.S.*, 38:286.

19. Philipps to the Board of Trade, 3 Aug. 1734, *P.D.N.S.*, 102.

20. Mascarene, "Description of Nova Scotia," *P.D.N.S.*, 42.

21. Charles Morris to Shirley, 1749, Canada Archives, *Report of the Archives Branch for the Year 1912*, App. H, 82.

22. Hale, "Journal of a Voyage to Nova Scotia," 233–34.

23. Beauharnois and Hocquart to Count de Maurepas, 12 Sept. 1745, *N.Y.C.D.*, 10:5.

Chapter 25 – Louisbourg

1. Kenneth Donovan, "Tattered Clothes and Powdered Wigs: Case Studies of the Poor and Well-To-Do in Eighteenth-Century Louisbourg," in Kenneth Donovan, ed., *Cape Breton at 200: Historical Essays in Honour of the Island's Bicentennial, 1785–1985* (Sydney, N.S.: University College of Cape Breton Press, 1985), 1–20.

2. McLennan, *Louisbourg*, 221–22.

3. McNeil, *Atlantic Empires of France and Spain*, 20–21; Clark, *Acadia*, 276; Harvey, *The French Régime in Prince Edward Island*, 243.

4. B.A. Balcom, *The Cod Fishery of Isle Royale, 1713–58* (National Historic Parks and Sites Branch, Parks Canada, Environment Canada, 1984), 24–25, 31–48; Clark, *Acadia*, 303–15; Harold A. Innis, "Cape Breton and the French Régime," Royal Society of Canada, *Transactions*, 3d ser., 29, Sec. 2 (1935): 51–62.

5. McLennan, *Louisbourg*, 222–23.

6. Letter from Hibbert Newton, 1 Sept. 1743, *Documents Relating to Currency*, 223–24.

7. McLennan, *Louisbourg*, 76.

8. Clark, *Acadia*, 297–303.

9. Ibid., 298.

10. Fernand Braudel, *Civilization and Capitalism, 15th–18th Century*, vol. 1, *The Structures of Everyday Life: The Limits of the Possible*, trans. Siân Reynolds (New York: Harper & Row, 1981), 169.

11. Clark, *Acadia*, 315–23; Andrew Hill Clark, "New England's Role in the Underdevelopment of Cape Breton Island during the French Régime, 1713–1758," *Canadian Geographer* 9 (1965): 1–12; Innis, "Cape Breton and the French Régime," 63–68.

12. Innis, "Cape Breton and the French Régime," 64.

13. Blaine Adams, "The Construction and Occupation of the Barracks of the King's Bastion at Louisbourg," in *Canadian Historic Sites: Occasional Papers in Archaeology and History,* no. 18 (National Historic Parks and Sites Branch, Parks Canada, Indian and Northern Affairs, 1978), 87.

14. McLennan, *Louisbourg,* 56–57, 88.

15. Ibid., 47, 91, 123–24.

16. Christopher Moore, *Louisbourg Portraits: Life in an Eighteenth-Century Garrison Town* (Toronto: Macmillan of Canada, 1982), 229.

17. McLennan, *Louisbourg,* 48.

18. T.A. Crowley and Bernard Pothier, "Louis Du Pont Duchambon" and "François Du Pont Duvivier," *D.C.B.,* 4:246–49, 251–55.

Chapter 26–King George's War

1. McLennan, *Louisbourg,* 109.

2. Ibid., 111–12.

3. William C. Godfrey, *Pursuit of Profit and Preferment in Colonial North America: John Bradstreet's Quest* (Waterloo, Ont.: Wilfrid Laurier University Press, 1982).

4. Except as otherwise noted, this account of Duvivier's Nova Scotia campaign and of events at Annapolis Royal during the summer of 1744 is based on: Mascarene to the Board of Trade, 20 and 25 Sept. 1744, *P.D.N.S.,* 131–34; Mascarene to Shirley and Mascarene to ——, Dec. 1744, *P.D.N.S.,* 140–50; Shirley to Newcastle and Shirley to the Board of Trade, 7 and 25 July and 10 Aug. 1744, *The Correspondence of William Shirley,* ed. Charles Henry Lincoln, 2 vols. (New York: Macmillan, 1912), 1:131–41; George M. Wrong, *Louisbourg in 1745: The Anonymous "Lettre d'un Habitant de Louisbourg" (Cape Breton), Containing a Narrative by an Eye-Witness of the Siege in 1745* (Toronto: University of Toronto Studies, 1897), 18–23; A.J.B. Johnston, *The Summer of 1744: A Portrait of Life in 18th-Century Louisbourg* (National Historic Parks and Sites Branch, Parks Canada, Environment Canada, 1983), 65–84; G.A. Rawlyk, *Yankees at Louisbourg* (Orono: University of Maine Press, 1967), 7–15; McLennan, *Louisbourg,* 113–16; Murdoch, *History of Nova Scotia,* 2:30–43.

5. Duvivier to the inhabitants of Minas, Pisiquid, River Canard, and Cobequid, 27 Aug. 1744, *P.D.N.S.,* 134.

6. Meeting of the council, 22 Mar. 1740, *Minutes of His Majesty's Council at Annapolis Royal, 1736–1749,* 25; Sutherland, "Paul Mascarene," *D.C.B.,* 3:437–38.

7. Gérard Finn, "Jean-Louis Le Loutre," *D.C.B.,* 4:453–58; Norman McLeod Rogers, "The Abbé Le Loutre," *C.H.R.,* 11 (1930): 105–28.

8. Murdoch, *History of Nova Scotia,* 2:30.

9. Mascarene to Shirley, Dec. 1744, *P.D.N.S.,* 145.

10. Mascarene to ——, Dec. 1744, *P.D.N.S.*, 148.

11. Mascarene to the Deputies of Chignecto, 16 Nov. 1744, *P.D.N.S.*, 139.

12. Deputies to De Gannes, 10 Oct. 1744, *P.D.N.S.*, 135.

13. John A. Schutz, *William Shirley: King's Governor of Massachusetts* (Chapel Hill: University of North Carolina Press, 1961).

14. Shirley to Sir Thomas Robinson, 24 Mar. 1755, *Shirley Correspondence*, 2:149.

15. *Shirley Correspondence*, 1:142–44.

Chapter 27—Incredible Victory

1. Shirley to the General Court, 9 Jan. 1745, *Shirley Correspondence*, 1:159–60.

2. Hutchinson, *History of the Colony and Province of Massachusetts Bay*, 2:311–13. Published reports by participants, collections of documents, and secondary descriptions of the Louisbourg campaign are abundant. I have relied primarily on: "The Pepperrell Papers," M.H.S., *Collections*, 6th ser., 10 (1899); *"Lettre d'un Habitant"*; Raymond F. Baker, "A Campaign of Amateurs: The Siege of Louisbourg, 1745," in *Canadian Historic Sites: Occasional Papers in Archaeology and History*, no. 18, 5–57; Wall, "Louisbourg, 1745"; Rawlyk, *Yankees at Louisbourg*; McLennan, *Louisbourg*, 128–80; Parkman, *France and England in North America*, 2:616–71.

3. Shirley to the Lords of the Admiralty, 29 Jan. 1744, *Shirley Correspondence*, 1:173–77.

4. John Gray to Pepperrell, 25 Feb. 1744, "Pepperrell Papers," 106.

5. Rev. John Barnard to Pepperrell, 11 Mar. 1744, "Pepperrell Papers," 116.

6. Quoted in Ronald W. Clark, *Benjamin Franklin: A Biography* (New York: Random House, 1983), 37.

7. "Sir Peter Warren," *Dictionary of National Biography*, 20:876–77.

8. Newcastle to Shirley, 3 Jan. 1744, *Shirley Correspondence*, 1:156.

9. Beauharnois to Count de Maurepas, 18 June 1745, *N.Y.C.D.*, 10:1–2.

10. Vaughan to Pepperrell, 2 May 1745, "Pepperrell Papers," 138.

11. Waldo to Pepperrell, 23 May 1745, "Pepperrell Papers," 214.

12. Waldo to Pepperrell, 13 May 1745, "Pepperrell Papers," 167.

13. William Pote Jr., *The Journal of Captain William Pote, Jr. During His Captivity in the French and Indian War from May, 1745, to August, 1747* (New York: Dodd, Mead, 1895), 40–45.

14. Warren to Pepperrell, 10 June 1745, "Pepperrell Papers," 268–69.

Chapter 28—Anxieties

1. McLennan, *Louisbourg*, 173.

2. Baker, "A Campaign of Amateurs," 37.

3. McLennan, *Louisbourg,* 169–70.

4. Warren to Corbett, 4 July 1745, *The Royal Navy and North America: The Warren Papers, 1736–1752,* ed. Julian Gwyn (London: Navy Records Society, 1973), 133.

5. Warren to Newcastle, 3 Oct. 1745, *Warren Papers,* 175.

6. Warren to Corbett, 3 Oct. 1745, *Warren Papers,* 169.

7. McLennan, *Louisbourg,* 188, 188n.

8. Knowles to Newcastle, 8 Nov. 1746, quoted in Murdoch, *History of Nova Scotia,* 2:99.

9. Knowles to Newcastle, 8 July 1746, Gaudet, "Acadian Genealogy and Notes," 45.

10. Harvey, *The French Régime in Prince Edward Island,* 110–11, 116–18.

11. Shirley to Newcastle, 14 Jan. 1745, *Shirley Correspondence,* 1:164.

12. Shirley to Pepperrell, 25 May 1745, *Shirley Correspondence,* 1:220.

13. Shirley to Newcastle, 15 Aug. 1746, *Shirley Correspondence,* 1:336–37.

14. Shirley to Newcastle, 21 Nov. 1746, quoted in Parkman, *France and England in North America,* 2:812–13.

15. Mascarene, "Description of Nova Scotia," *P.D.N.S.,* 43.

16. Mascarene to Warren, 11 Sept. 1745, *Warren Papers,* 162.

17. Representation of the State of His Majesties Province of Nova Scotia, 8 Nov. 1745, *Minutes of His Majesty's Council at Annapolis Royal, 1736–1749,* 84.

18. Mascarene to Shirley, 6 Apr. 1748, M.H.S., *Collections,* 1st ser., 6 (1799): 126.

19. Mascarene to Warren and Shirley, 26 Oct. 1746, *Warren Papers,* 365.

20. Shirley to Mascarene, 16 Sept. 1746, *Shirley Correspondence,* 1:354.

21. Meeting of the council, 26 Sept. 1746, *Minutes of His Majesty's Council at Annapolis Royal, 1736–1749,* 91.

22. Beauharnois and Hocquart to Maurepas, 12 Sept. 1745, *N.Y.C.D.,* 10:4.

23. Ibid., 16.

24. Ibid., 14.

25. Murdoch, *History of Nova Scotia,* 2:88–93.

26. Ibid., 93–94; Parkman, *France and England in North America,* 2:680–84.

27. Mascarene to Newcastle, 23 Jan. 1747, Gaudet, "Acadian Genealogy and Notes," 45–46; Rogers, "The Abbé Le Loutre," 115; Parkman, *France and England in North America,* 2:685–87.

28. Rogers, "The Abbé Le Loutre," 116; Murdoch, *History of Nova Scotia,* 2:110–11.

29. Arthur H. Buffinton, "The Canada Expedition of 1746: Its Relation to British Politics," *American Historical Review* 45 (1939–40): 572–80.

30. Parkman, *France and England in North America,* 2:676–77.

31. In describing Noble's occupation of Grand Pré and the Battle of Grand Pré, I have relied on: "Journal of Occurrences in Canada; 1746, 1747," *N.Y.C.D.*, 10:90–92; Parkman, *France and England in North America*, 2:696–708; Murdoch, *History of Nova Scotia*, 2:104–10, 114–15.

Chapter 29—Halifax

1. Jack M. Sosin, "Louisbourg and the Peace of Aix-la-Chapelle, 1748," *W.M.Q.*, 3d ser., 14 (1957): 516–35.

2. *Major Peace Treaties*, 1:269–304.

3. La Galissonière to Mascarene, 15 Jan. 1749, *N.Y.C.D.*, 6:478–79.

4. Mascarene to La Galissonière, 25 Apr. 1749, *N.Y.C.D.*, 6:479–81.

5. Shirley to the governor of Canada, 9 May 1749, *N.Y.C.D.*, 6:482.

6. Clark, *Acadia*, 276.

7. Advertisement, 7 Mar. 1749, *P.D.N.S.*, 495–97.

8. Clark, *Acadia*, 337.

9. T.B. Akins, "History of Halifax City," N.S.H.S., *Collections*, 8 (1892–94): 5–7, 9–10.

10. Cornwallis to the duke of Bedford, 11 Sept. 1749, *P.D.N.S.*, 586.

11. Akins, "History of Halifax City," 6–7n.

12. Ibid., 10–17.

13. Clark, *Acadia*, 351.

14. Ibid., 337–43; Bell, *"Foreign Protestants,"* 317–28.

15. Parkman, *France and England in North America*, 2:912–14.

16. Cornwallis to the Board of Trade, 17 Oct. 1749, *P.D.N.S.*, 591; Rogers, "The Abbé Le Loutre," 119.

17. Upton, *Micmacs and Colonists*, 33.

18. Salusbury to his wife, 17 July 1750, Ronald Rompkey, ed., *Expeditions of Honour: The Journal of John Salusbury in Halifax, Nova Scotia, 1749–53* (Newark, DE: University of Delaware Press, 1982), 142.

19. Declaration, 20 Oct. 1747, Gaudet, "Acadian Genealogy and Notes," 47–48.

20. Meeting of the council, 14 July 1749, *P.D.N.S.*, 167; *Royal Instructions*, 1:437–38, 498–99.

21. Declaration, 14 July 1749, *P.D.N.S.*, 165–66.

22. Meeting of the council, 31 July 1749, *P.D.N.S.*, 168–69.

23. Declaration, 1 Aug. 1749 (New Style), *P.D.N.S.*, 171.

24. Letter from the French inhabitants, Sept. 1749, *P.D.N.S.*, 173.

25. Cornwallis to the Board of Trade, 17 Oct. 1749, *P.D.N.S.*, 592.

26. Meeting of the council, 19 Apr. 1750, *P.D.N.S.*, 187.

27. Rompkey, ed., *Journal of John Salusbury*, 84.

28. Board of Trade to Cornwallis, 16 Feb. 1750, *P.D.N.S.*, 602.

Chapter 30–Cold War

1. La Jonquière to Cornwallis, 25 Oct. 1749, *P.D.N.S.,* 374.

2. Cornwallis to La Jonquière, 1 Nov. 1749, *P.D.N.S.,* 376.

3. Dominick Graham, "Charles Lawrence," *D.C.B.,* 3:361–66.

4. A Journal of the Proceedings of the Detachment under the Command of Major Lawrence, after Entering the Basin of Chignecto, Gaudet, "Acadian Genealogy and Notes," 320; Rompkey, ed., *Journal of John Salusbury,* 88–91.

5. Journal of Major Lawrence, Gaudet, "Acadian Genealogy and Notes," 322.

6. Rompkey, ed., *Journal of John Salusbury,* 192n.

7. Cornwallis to Bedford, 27 Nov. 1750, *P.D.N.S.,* 195.

8. Harvey, *The French Régime in Prince Edward Island,* 168.

9. J. Bartlet Brebner, "Canadian Policy towards the Acadians in 1751," *C.H.R.* 12 (1931): 284–87.

10. On the work of the commission, see: Savelle, *Origins of American Diplomacy,* 386–95; Lawrence Henry Gipson, *The British Empire before the American Revolution,* 15 vols. (New York: Alfred A. Knopf, 1936–70), 5:302–23.

11. Memoir by M. de La Galissonière, Dec. 1750, *N.Y.C.D.,* 10:220–32.

12. Memorial of the French Commissaries, 4 Oct. 1751, *Memorials of the Courts of Great Britain and France,* 45–192.

13. Memorial of the English Commissaries, 11 Jan. 1751, *Memorials of the Courts of Great Britain and France,* 10–44.

14. Schutz, *William Shirley,* 163–64.

15. Holderness to the governors in America, 28 Aug. 1753, *N.Y.C.D.,* 6:794.

16. St. Pierre to Dinwiddie, 15 Dec. 1753, *N.Y.C.D.,* 10:258.

17. Savelle, *Origins of American Diplomacy,* 395–419; Gipson, *The British Empire before the American Revolution,* 5:323–38.

18. Quoted in Robinson to Lawrence, 13 Aug. 1755, *P.D.N.S.,* 80; Savelle, *Origins of American Diplomacy,* 415–16.

19. Hopson to the Board of Trade, 10 Dec. 1752, Gaudet, "Acadian Genealogy and Notes," 55–56.

20. Board of Trade to Hopson, 28 Mar. 1753, Gaudet, "Acadian Genealogy and Notes," 56.

21. Brebner, *New England's Outpost,* 191–92.

22. Cornwallis to the Board of Trade, 17 Oct. 1749, *P.D.N.S.,* 592.

23. Board of Trade to Lawrence, 4 Mar. 1754, *P.D.N.S.,* 207.

24. Lawrence to the Board of Trade, 1 Aug. 1754, *P.D.N.S.,* 213.

25. Board of Trade to Lawrence, 29 Oct. 1754, *P.D.N.S.,* 235–37.

26. Meeting of the council, 27 Sept. 1753, *P.D.N.S.,* 203–5.

27. William Cotterell to Captain Scott, 12 Apr. 1754, *P.D.N.S.,* 209.

28. Meeting of the council, 21 June 1754, *P.D.N.S.,* 211.

29. Proclamation, 17 Sept. 1754, *P.D.N.S.,* 219–21.

30. Brebner, *New England's Outpost,* 211–13.

Chapter 31 – Beauséjour

1. Rawlyk, *Nova Scotia's Massachusetts,* 199–200; Schutz, *William Shirley,* 174–78.

2. T.R. Clayton, "The Duke of Newcastle, the Earl of Halifax, and the American Origins of the Seven Years War," *Historical Journal* 24 (1981): 571–603.

3. Robinson to Shirley and Lawrence, 5 July 1754, *P.D.N.S.,* 382–84.

4. Secret Instructions to General Braddock, 25 Nov. 1754, *N.Y.C.D.,* 6:920–22.

5. Shirley to Robinson, 20 June 1755, *N.Y.C.D.,* 6:954.

6. In describing the Beauséjour campaign, I have relied on: "Diary of John Thomas, Surgeon in Winslow's Expedition of 1755 against the Acadians," *New England Historical and Genealogical Register,* 33 (1879): 383–98; Journal of Louis de Courville, John Clarence Webster, ed., *Journals of Beauséjour: Diary of John Thomas [and] Journal of Louis de Courville* (Sackville, N.B.: Public Archives of Nova Scotia, 1937), 43–54; Journal of Thomas Pichon, John Clarence Webster, *Thomas Pichon "The Spy of Beauséjour": An Account of His Career in Europe and America, with Many Original Documents Translated by Alice Webster* (Sackville, N.B.: Public Archives of Nova Scotia, 1937), 100–107; Gipson, *The British Empire before the American Revolution,* 6:212–33; Parkman, *France and England in North America,* 2:1006–19.

7. Bernard Pothier, "Louis Du Pont Duchambon de Vergor," *D.C.B.,* 4:249–51.

8. Quoted in Parkman, *France and England in North America,* 2:1011.

9. Journal of Louis de Courville, Webster, *Journals of Beauséjour,* 50.

10. Pichon to Archibald Hinchelwood, 26 Sept. 1755, Webster, *Thomas Pichon,* 111.

Chapter 32 – Expulsion

1. Lawrence to the Board of Trade, 28 June 1755, *P.D.N.S.,* 408–9.

2. Meeting of the council, 3 July 1755, *P.D.N.S.,* 247–55.

3. Meeting of the council, 4 July 1755, *P.D.N.S.,* 255–56.

4. Ibid., 256.

5. Lawrence to the Board of Trade, 18 July 1755, *P.D.N.S.,* 259–60.

6. Opinion, 28 July 1755, Gaudet, "Acadian Genealogy and Notes," 63–65.

7. Meeting of the council, 15 July 1755, *P.D.N.S.,* 258.

8. Lawrence to the Board of Trade, 28 June 1755, *P.D.N.S.,* 409.

9. Robinson to Lawrence, 13 Aug. 1755, *P.D.N.S.,* 279.

10. Board of Trade to Lawrence, 25 Mar. 1756, *P.D.N.S.,* 298.

11. Meetings of the council, 25 and 28 July 1755, *P.D.N.S.,* 260–67.

12. Meeting of the council, 28 July 1755, *P.D.N.S.,* 263–67; Brebner, *New England's Outpost,* 222.

13. *P.D.N.S.,* 267–76.

14. Lawrence to the Governors on the Continent, 11 Aug. 1755, *P.D.N.S.,* 278.

15. Lawrence to Moncton, 8 Aug. 1755, *P.D.N.S.,* 269.

16. "Diary of John Thomas," 391–92.

17. Ibid., 392–93.

18. Captain John Knox, *An Historical Journal of the Campaigns in North America For the Years 1757, 1758, 1759, and 1760,* ed. Arthur G. Doughty (Toronto: Champlain Society, 1914; reprint, New York: Greenwood Press, 1968), 94.

19. Hector J. Hébert, "Marie-Madeline Maisonnat," *D.C.B.,* 3:421–22.

20. Winslow's journal, insofar as it relates to the expulsion of the Acadians, is in N.S.H.S., *Collections,* 3 (1882–83): 71–196. Extensive extracts are in Gaudet, "Acadian Genealogy and Notes," 9–37.

21. Winslow to Lawrence, 30 Aug. 1755, Gaudet, "Acadian Genealogy and Notes," 17.

22. Winslow's Journal, 5 Sept. 1755, Gaudet, "Acadian Genealogy and Notes," 20.

23. Winslow to Murray, 5 Sept. 1755, Gaudet, "Acadian Genealogy and Notes," 21.

24. Winslow to Lawrence, 17 Sept. 1755, and Winslow's Journal, 6 Oct. 1755, Gaudet, "Acadian Genealogy and Notes," 25, 29.

25. Winslow's Journal, 10 Sept. 1755, Gaudet, "Acadian Genealogy and Notes," 23.

26. Winslow's Journal, 8 Oct. 1755, Gaudet, "Acadian Genealogy and Notes," 29.

27. Extract from Winslow's Journal, Gaudet, "Acadian Genealogy and Notes," 36.

28. Clark, *Acadia,* 350.

29. Harvey, *The French Régime in Prince Edward Island,* 181.

Chapter 33–Diaspora

1. Naomi E.S. Griffiths, "Acadians in Exile: The Experiences of the Acadians in the British Seaports," *Acadiensis* 4, no. 1 (1974): 67–84; Gipson, *The British Empire before the American Revolution,* 6:299–304; Oscar William Winzerling, *Acadian Odyssey* (Baton Rouge: Louisiana State University Press, 1955).

2. Gipson, *The British Empire before the American Revolution,* 6:287–97.

3. E. Merton Coulter, "The Acadians in Georgia," *Georgia Historical Quarterly,* 47 (1963): 68–75; Marguerite B. Hamer, "The Fate of the Exiled

Acadians in South Carolina," *The Journal of Southern History,* 4 (1938): 199–208; Ruth Allison Hudnut and Hayes Baker-Carothers, "Acadian Transients in South Carolina," *American Historical Review,* 43 (1937–38): 500–513.

4. Gipson, *The British Empire before the American Revolution,* 6:307–8, 312–14, 320, 322–23, 327–28.

5. Richard G. Lowe, "Massachusetts and the Acadians," *W.M.Q.,* 3d ser., 25 (1968): 212–29; Gipson, *The British Empire before the American Revolution,* 6:305, 310–11, 325–26; Basil Sollers, "The Acadians (French Neutrals) Transported to Maryland," *Maryland Historical Magazine,* 3 (1908): 1–21.

6. Gaudet, "Acadian Genealogy and Notes," v.

7. *Historical Atlas of Canada,* ed. R. Cole Harris (Toronto: University of Toronto Press, 1987), vol. 1, plate 30.

8. Public Law 101-543, 101st Cong., 2d sess. (8 Nov. 1990).

9. Carl A. Brasseaux, *The Founding of New Acadia: The Beginnings of Acadian Life in Louisiana, 1765–1803* (Baton Rouge: Louisiana State University Press, 1987); William Faulkner Rushton, *The Cajuns: From Acadia to Louisiana* (New York: Farrar Straus Giroux, 1979).

10. Griffiths, *Contexts of Acadian History,* 121–25; Brasseaux, *Founding of New Acadia,* 55–74; Winzerling, *Acadian Odyssey,* 23–130.

BIBLIOGRAPHY

Acadia and Nova Scotia: Documents Relating to the Acadian French and the First British Colonization of the Province 1714–1758. Ed. Thomas B. Akins. Halifax, 1869. Reprint. Cottonport, LA: Polyanthos, 1972.

The Acts and Resolves, Public and Private, of the Province of the Massachusetts Bay; to which Are Prefixed the Charters of the Province, with Historical and Explanatory Notes and an Appendix. 21 vols. Boston: State Printers, 1869–1922.

Akins, T.B. "History of Halifax City." Nova Scotia Historical Society, *Collections* 8 (1892–94): 3–272.

Alexander, Sir William. *An Encouragement to Colonies.* London, 1624. In Edmund M. Slafter, *Sir William Alexander and American Colonization. . . .* Boston, 1873. Reprint. New York: Burt Franklin, 1972.

All the Memorials of the Courts of Great Britain and France Since the Peace of Aix La Chapelle, Relative to the Limits of the Territories of Both Crowns in North America and the Right to the Neutral Islands in the West Indies. The Hague, 1756.

Andrews, Charles M. *The Colonial Period of American History.* 4 vols. New Haven, CT: Yale University Press, 1934–38.

Arsenault, Bona. *History of the Acadians.* Ottawa: Editions Leméac, 1978.

Axtell, James L. *The Invasion Within: The Contest of Cultures in Colonial North America.* New York: Oxford University Press, 1985.

Bailey, Alfred G. *The Conflict of European and Eastern Algonkian Cultures, 1504–1700: A Study in Canadian Civilization.* 2d ed. Toronto: University of Toronto Press, 1969.

Baker, Raymond F. "A Campaign of Amateurs: The Siege of Louisbourg, 1745." In *Canadian Historic Sites: Occasional Papers in Archaeology and History,* no. 18. National Historic Parks and Sites Branch, Parks Canada, Indian and Northern Affairs, 1978.

Balcom, B.A. *The Cod Fishery of Isle Royale, 1713–58.* National Historic Parks and Sites Branch, Parks Canada, Environment Canada, 1984.

Barnard, John. "Autobiography of the Rev. John Barnard." Massachusetts Historical Society, *Collections,* 3d ser., 5 (1836): 177–242.

Baxter, James Phinney. *The Pioneers of France in New England, with Contemporary Letters and Documents.* Albany, NY: Joel Munsell's Sons, 1894.

Bell, Winthrop Pickard. *The "Foreign Protestants" and the Settlement of Nova Scotia: The History of a Piece of Arrested British Colonial Policy in the Eighteenth Century.* Toronto: University of Toronto Press, 1961.

Bent, Gilbert O. "The Procès-Verbal of Andrew Certain." *Acadiensis* 5 (1905): 37–46.

———. "The Dutch Conquest of Acadia." *Acadiensis* 5 (1905): 278–86.

Biggar, H.P. "The French Hakluyt, Marc Lescarbot of Vervins." *American Historical Review* 6 (1900–1901): 671–92.

———. *The Early Trading Companies of New France: A Contribution to the History of Commerce and Discovery in North America.* Toronto, 1901. Reprint. Clifton, NJ: Augustus M. Kelley, 1972.

Bird, Will R. *A Century at Chignecto: The Key to Old Acadia.* Toronto: Ryerson Press, 1928.

Bishop, Morris. *Champlain: The Life of Fortitude.* New York, 1948. Reprint. New York: Octagon Books, 1979.

Bradford, William. *Of Plymouth Plantation, 1620–1647.* Ed. Samuel Eliot Morison. New York: Alfred A. Knopf, 1966.

Brasseaux, Carl A. *The Founding of New Acadia: The Beginnings of Acadian Life in Louisiana, 1765–1803.* Baton Rouge: Louisiana State University Press, 1987.

Brault, Gerard J. *The French-Canadian Heritage in New England.* Hanover, NH: University Press of New England, 1986.

Brebner, John Bartlet. *New England's Outpost: Acadia before the Conquest of Canada.* New York, 1927. Reprint. Hamden, CT: Archon Books, 1965.

———. "Canadian Policy towards the Acadians in 1751." *Canadian Historical Review* 12 (1931): 284–87.

———. "Paul Mascarene of Annapolis Royal." In G.A. Rawlyk, ed. *Historical Essays on the Atlantic Provinces.* Toronto: McClelland and Stewart, 1967.

Brown, Richard. *A History of the Island of Cape Breton: With Some Account of the Discovery and Settlement of Canada, Nova Scotia, and Newfoundland.* London, 1869. Reprint. Belleville, Ont.: Mika Publishing, 1979.

Buffinton, Arthur Howland. "John Nelson's Voyage to Quebec in 1682: A Chapter in the Fisheries Controversy." Colonial Society of Massachusetts, *Publications* 26 (1927): 427–37.

———. "Governor Dudley and the Proposed Treaty of Neutrality, 1705." Colonial Society of Massachusetts, *Publications* 26 (1927): 221–29.

———. "Sir Thomas Temple in Boston, A Case of Benevolent Assimilation." Colonial Society of Massachusetts, *Publications* 27 (1932): 308–19.

———. "The Canada Expedition of 1746: Its Relation to British Politics." *American Historical Review* 45 (1939–40): 552–80.

Cadillac, Sieur de la Mothe. "The Cadillac Memoir of 1692." Trans. by W.F. Ganong. New Brunswick Historical Society, *Collections,* 13 (1930): 76–97.

Champlain, Samuel de. *Voyages of Samuel de Champlain, 1604–1618.* Ed. W.L. Grant. New York: Charles Scribner's Sons, 1907.

———. *The Works of Samuel de Champlain.* Ed. H.P. Biggar. 6 vols. Toronto: Champlain Society, 1922–36.

Chassé, Paul. "The D'Abbadie de Saint-Castins and the Abenakis of Maine in the Seventeenth Century." *Proceedings of the Tenth Meeting of the French Colonial Historical Society, April 12–14, 1984.* Lanham, MD: University Press of America, 1985.

Church, Benjamin. *The History of the Eastern Expeditions of 1689, 1690, 1692, 1696, and 1704 Against the Indians and French.* Ed. Henry Martyn Dexter. Boston: J.K. Wiggin and Wm. Parsons Lunt, 1867.

Clark, Andrew Hill. *Three Centuries and the Island: A Historical Geography of Settlement and Agriculture in Prince Edward Island, Canada.* Toronto: University of Toronto Press, 1959.

———. "New England's Role in the Underdevelopment of Cape Breton Island during the French Régime, 1713–1758." *Canadian Geographer* 9 (1965): 1–12.

———. *Acadia: The Geography of Early Nova Scotia to 1760.* Madison: University of Wisconsin Press, 1968.

Clayton, T.R. "The Duke of Newcastle, the Earl of Halifax, and the American Origins of the Seven Years War." *Historical Journal* 24 (1981): 571–603.

Cohen, Ronald Dennis. "New England and New France, 1632–1651: External Relations and Internal Disagreements among the Puritans." Essex Institute, *Historical Collections* 108 (1972): 252–71.

Collection de Manuscrits Contenant Lettres, Mémoires, et Autre Documents Historiques Relatifs à la Nouvelle-France. 4 vols. Quebec: Imprimerie A. Coté, 1883.

Collection of Original Papers Relative to the History of the Colony of Massachusetts Bay. Ed. Thomas Hutchinson. Boston, 1769. Reprint under title *The Hutchinson Papers.* Boston, 1865. Reprint. 2 vols. New York: Burt Franklin, 1967.

Conkling, Robert. "Legitimacy and Conversion in Social Change: The Case of the French Missionaries and the Northeastern Algonkian." *Ethnohistory* 21 (1974): 1–24.

Coram, Thomas. "Letters of Thomas Coram." Massachusetts Historical Society, *Proceedings* 56 (1922–23): 15–56.

Daigle, Jean., ed. *The Acadians of the Maritimes: Thematic Studies.* Moncton, N.B.: Centre d'études acadiennes, 1982.

Davies, K.G. *The North Atlantic World in the Seventeenth Century.* Minneapolis: University of Minnesota Press, 1974.

Dawson, Joan E. "Fort Sainte-Marie-de-Grâce, La Have, Nova Scotia: 350 Years of History." *Nova Scotia Historical Review* 2, no. 2 (1982): 52–64.

Denys, Nicholas. *The Description and Natural History of the Coasts of North America (Acadia).* Trans. and ed. William F. Ganong. 2 vols. Toronto: Champlain Society, 1908. Reprint. 2 vols. in 1. New York: Greenwood Press, 1968.

Diamond, Sigmund. "An Experiment in 'Feudalism': French Canada in the Seventeenth Century." In *Essays on American Colonial History.* Ed. Paul Goodman. 2d ed. New York: Holt, Rinehart and Winston, 1972.

Dickason, Olive Patricia. "Amerindians Between French and English in Nova Scotia, 1713–1763." *American Indian Culture and Research Journal* 10, no. 4 (1986): 31–56.

Dictionary of Canadian Biography. Ed. George W. Brown et al. Toronto: University of Toronto Press, 1966–.

Dièreville, Sieur de. *Relation of the Voyage to Port Royal in Acadia or New France.* Trans. Mrs. J. Clarence Webster. Ed. John Clarence Webster. Toronto: Champlain Society, 1933. Reprint. New York: Greenwood Press, 1968.

Documents Relating to Currency, Exchange and Finance in Nova Scotia, with Prefatory Documents, 1675–1758. Ed. Adam Shortt, V.K. Johnston, and Gustave Lanctot. Ottawa: J.O. Patenaude, Acting King's Printer, 1933.

"Documents Relating to Negotiations with England, 1629–1633, Copied in the Archives of the French Foreign Office." Canada Archives. *Report of the Archives Branch for the Year 1912.* App. D.

Documents Relative to the Colonial History of the State of New York, Procured in Holland, England and France by John Romeyn Brodhead, Esq. Agent. 15 vols. Albany, 1853–87. Reprint. New York: AMS Press, 1969.

Donovan, Kenneth. "Tattered Clothes and Powdered Wigs: Case Studies of the Poor and Well-To-Do in Eighteenth-Century Louisbourg." In Kenneth Donovan, ed. *Cape Breton at 200: Historical Essays in Honour of the Island's Bicentennial, 1785–1985.* Sydney, N.S.: University College of Cape Breton Press, 1985.

European Treaties Bearing on the History of the United States and Its Dependencies. Ed. Frances Gardiner Davenport and Charles Oscar Paullin. 4 vols. Washington, 1917–37. Reprint. Gloucester, MA: Peter Smith, 1967.

Faulkner, Alaric, and Gretchen Fearon Faulkner. *The French at Pentagoet, 1635–1674: An Archaeological Portrait of the Acadian Frontier.* Augusta: Maine Historic Preservation Commission, 1987.

Folsom, George. "Expedition of Captain Samuel Argall, Afterwards Governor of Virginia, Knight, &c., to the French Settlements in Acadia and to Manhattan Island AD 1613." New York Historical Society, *Collections,* 2d ser., 1 (1841): 331–42.

Gaudet, Placide. "Acadian Genealogy and Notes." In *Report Concerning Canadian Archives for the Year 1905.* 3 vols. Ottawa: E.S. Dawson, 1906. Vol. 2, App. A, Part III.

Ghere, David L. "Mistranslations and Misinformation: Diplomacy on the Maine Frontier, 1725 to 1755." *American Indian Culture and Research Journal* 8, no. 4 (1984): 3–26.

Gipson, Lawrence Henry. *The British Empire before the American Revolution.* 15 vols. New York: Alfred A. Knopf, 1936–70.

Godbout, Archange. "The Passenger List of the Ship *Saint-Jehan* and the Acadian Origins." *French Canadian and Acadian Genealogical Review* 1 (1968): 55–73.

Godfrey, William C. *Pursuit of Profit and Preferment in Colonial North America: John Bradstreet's Quest.* Waterloo, Ont.: Wilfrid Laurier University Press, 1982.

Graham, Dominick. "The Planning of the Beauséjour Operation and the Approaches to War in 1755." *New England Quarterly* 41 (1968): 551–66.

Graham, Gerald S. *The Walker Expedition to Quebec, 1711.* Toronto: Champlain Society, 1953. Reprint. New York: Greenwood Press, 1969.

Great Britain, Public Record Office. *Calendar of State Papers, Colonial Series.* 44 vols. London, 1880–. Reprint. Liechtenstein: Kraus Reprint, 1964.

Griffiths, Naomi E.S. *The Acadian Deportation: Deliberate Perfidy or Cruel Necessity?* Toronto: Copp Clark, 1969.

——. *The Acadians: Creation of a People.* Toronto: McGraw-Hill Ryerson, 1973.

——. "Acadians in Exile: The Experiences of the Acadians in the British Seaports." *Acadiensis* 4, no. 1 (1974): 67–84.

——. "The Golden Age: Acadian Life, 1713–1748." *Histoire Sociale Social History* 17 (1984): 21–34.

——. *The Contexts of Acadian History, 1686–1784* (Montreal: McGill–Queen's University Press, 1992).

Griffiths, N.E.S., and John G. Reid, "New Evidence on New Scotland, 1629." *William and Mary Quarterly,* 3d ser., 49 (1992): 492–508.

Hale, Robert. "Journal of a Voyage to Nova Scotia Made in 1731 by Robert Hale of Beverly." Essex Institute, *Historical Collections* 42 (1906): 217–44.

Harvey, D.C. *The French Régime in Prince Edward Island.* New Haven, CT: Yale University Press, 1926.

——. "Sir William Alexander and Nova Scotia." Nova Scotia Historical Society, *Collections* 30 (1954): 1–26.

Henretta, James A. *"Salutary Neglect": Colonial Administration under the Duke of Newcastle.* Princeton, NJ: Princeton University Press, 1972.

Hutchinson, Thomas. *The History of the Colony and Province of Massachusetts Bay.* Ed. Lawrence Shaw Mayo. 3 vols. Cambridge, MA, 1936. Reprint. New York: Kraus Reprint, 1970.

Hynes, Gisa. "Some Aspects of the Demography of Port Royal, 1650–1755." *Acadiensis* 3, no. 1 (1973): 3–17.

"Indian Treaties." Maine Historical Society, *Collections*, 1st ser., 3 (1853): 359–447.

Innis, Harold A. "Cape Breton and the French Régime." Royal Society of Canada, *Transactions*, 3d ser., 29, sec. 2 (1935): 51–87.

———. *The Cod Fisheries: The History of an International Economy*. Rev. ed. Toronto: University of Toronto Press, 1954.

Insh, George Pratt. "Sir William Alexander's Colony at Port Royal." *The Dalhousie Review* 9 (1929–30): 439–47.

Jennings, Francis. *The Invasion of America: Indians, Colonialism, and the Cant of Conquest*. Chapel Hill: University of North Carolina Press, 1975.

The Jesuit Relations and Allied Documents: Travels and Explorations of the Jesuit Missionaries in New France, 1610–1791. Ed. Reuben Gold Thwaites. 73 vols. Cleveland: Burrows Brothers, 1896–1901.

Johnson, Richard R. *John Nelson, Merchant Adventurer: A Life between Empires*. New York: Oxford University Press, 1991.

Johnston, A.J.B. *The Summer of 1744: A Portrait of Life in 18th-Century Louisbourg*. National Historic Parks and Sites Branch, Parks Canada, Environment Canada, 1983.

Jones, Elizabeth. *Gentlemen and Jesuits: Quests for Glory and Adventure in the Early Days of New France*. Toronto: University of Toronto Press, 1986.

"Journal of Colonel Nicholson at the Capture of Annapolis, 1710." Nova Scotia Historical Society, *Report and Collections* 1 (1878): 59–104.

"Journal of the Expedition under Sir William Phips against Port Royal, 1690." Canada Archives. *Report of the Archives Branch for the Year 1912*, App. E.

Kavenagh, W. Keith, ed. *Foundations of Colonial America: A Documentary History*. 3 vols. New York, 1974. Reprint. New York: Chelsea House, 1983.

Kidder, Frederick. "The Abenaki Indians; their Treaties of 1713 & 1717, and a Vocabulary: with a Historical Introduction." Maine Historical Society, *Collections*, 1st ser., 6 (1859): 250–63.

Kimball, Everett. *The Public Life of Joseph Dudley: A Study of the Colonial Policy of the Stuarts in New England, 1660–1715*. New York: Longmans, Green, 1911.

Kirke, Henry. *The First English Conquest of Canada*. 2d ed. London, 1908.

Lahontan, Baron de. *New Voyages to North America*. Ed. Reuben Gold Thwaites. 2 vols. Chicago, 1905. Reprint. New York: Burt Franklin, 1970.

Laing, David, ed. *Royal Letters, Charters, and Tracts, Relating to the Colonization of New Scotland, and the Institution of the Order of Knight Baronets of Nova Scotia, 1621–1638*. Edinburgh: Bannatyne Club Publications, 1867.

Lanctot, Gustave. *A History of Canada.* Trans. Josephine Hambleton and Margaret M. Cameron. Cambridge: Harvard University Press, 1963–65.

Lescarbot, Marc. *Nova Francia: A Description of Acadia, 1606.* Trans. P. Erondelle. London, 1609. New York: Harper & Brothers, 1928.

———. *The History of New France.* Trans. W.L. Grant. 3 vols. Toronto: Champlain Society, 1907–14. Reprint. New York: Greenwood Press, 1968.

Lovejoy, David S. *The Glorious Revolution in America.* Middletown, CT: Wesleyan University Press, 1987.

Lowe, Richard G. "Massachusetts and the Acadians." *William and Mary Quarterly*, 3d ser., 25 (1968): 212–29.

MacDonald, M.A. *Fortune and La Tour: The Civil War in Acadia.* Toronto: Methuen, 1983.

MacFarlane, Ronald O. "British Indian Policy in Nova Scotia to 1760." *Canadian Historical Review* 19 (1938): 154–67.

Macleod, J.E.A. "Lord Ochiltree's Colony." *The Dalhousie Review* 4 (1924): 308–16.

Major Peace Treaties of Modern History, 1648–1967. Ed. Fred L. Israel. 4 vols. New York: Chelsea House, 1967.

Maritime Dykelands: The 350 Year Struggle. Nova Scotia Department of Agriculture and Marketing, 1987.

Martin, Calvin. "The European Impact on the Culture of a Northeastern Algonquian Tribe: An Ecological Interpretation." *William and Mary Quarterly,* 3d ser., 31 (1974): 3–26.

Mascarene, Paul. "A Narrative of Events at Annapolis Royal from the Capture in Oct., 1710 till Sept., 1711." Nova Scotia Historical Society, *Collections* 4 (1884): 69–87.

McCully, Bruce T. "The New England–Acadia Fishery Dispute and the Nicholson Mission of August, 1687." Essex Institute, *Historical Collections* 96 (1960): 277–90.

McGrail, Thomas H. *Sir William Alexander, First Earl of Stirling: A Biographical Study.* Edinburgh: Oliver & Boyd, 1940.

McLennan, J.S. *Louisbourg from its Foundation to its Fall, 1713–1758.* 3d ed. Sydney, N.S.: Fortress Press, 1969.

McNeil, John Robert. *Atlantic Empires of France and Spain: Louisbourg and Havana, 1700–1763.* Chapel Hill: University of North Carolina Press, 1985.

Miller, Virginia. "Aboriginal Micmac Population: A Review of the Evidence." *Ethnohistory* 23 (1976): 117–27.

Minutes of His Majesty's Council at Annapolis Royal, 1736–1749. Ed. Charles Bruce Fergusson. Halifax: Public Archives of Nova Scotia, 1967.

Moore, Christopher. *Louisbourg Portraits: Life in an Eighteenth-Century Garrison Town.* Toronto: Macmillan of Canada, 1982.

Morison, Samuel Eliot. *Builders of the Bay Colony.* Boston, 1930. Reprint. Boston: Northeastern University Press, 1981.

———. *The European Discovery of America: The Northern Voyages, A.D. 500–1600.* New York: Oxford University Press, 1971.

———. *Samuel de Champlain: Father of New France.* Boston: Little, Brown, 1972.

Morrison, Alvin H. "Membertou's Raid on the Chouacoet 'Almouchiquois'—The Micmac Sack of Saco in 1607." In *Papers of the Sixth Algonquian Conference, 1974.* Ed. William Cowan. Ottawa: National Museums of Canada, 1975.

Morrison, Kenneth M. "Sebastien Racle and Norridgewock, 1724: The Eckstorm Conspiracy Thesis Reconsidered." *Maine Historical Society Quarterly* 14 (1974): 76–97.

———. *The Embattled Northeast: The Elusive Ideal of Alliance in Abenaki Euramerican Relations.* Berkeley: University of California Press, 1984.

Morse, William Inglis. *Acadiensa Nova, 1598–1779.* 2 vols. London: Bernard Quaritch, 1935.

Munson, Gorham. "St. Castin: A Legend Revised." *The Dalhousie Review* 45 (1965–66): 338–60.

Murdoch, Beamish. *A History of Nova Scotia, or Acadie.* 3 vols. Halifax: James Barnes, 1865.

Nash, Gary B. *Red, White, and Black: The Peoples of Early America.* Englewood Cliffs, NJ: Prentice-Hall, 1974.

Osgood, Herbert L. *The American Colonies in the Seventeenth Century.* 3 vols. New York, 1904. Reprint. Gloucester, MA: Peter Smith, 1957.

———. *The American Colonies in the Eighteenth Century.* 4 vols. New York, 1924. Reprint. Gloucester, MA: Peter Smith, 1958.

"Papers Relative to the Rival Chiefs D'Aulney and La Tour, Governors of Nova Scotia." Massachusetts Historical Society, *Collections,* 3d ser., 7 (1838): 90–121.

Parkman, Francis. *France and England in North America.* Boston, 1865–92. 2 vols. New York: Library of America, 1983.

Patterson, Rev. George. "Hon. Samuel Vetch, First English Governor of Nova Scotia." Nova Scotia Historical Society, *Collections* 4 (1884): 11–63.

———, ed. "Papers Connected with the Administration of Governor Vetch." Nova Scotia Historical Society, *Collections* 4 (1884): 64–112.

"The Pepperrell Papers." Massachusetts Historical Society, *Collections,* 6th ser., 10 (1899).

Pote, William Jr. *The Journal of Captain William Pote, Jr. During His Captivity in the French and Indian War from May, 1745, to August, 1747.* New York: Dodd, Mead, 1895.

Pothier, Bernard. "Nicholas Denys: The Chronology and Historiography of an Acadian Hero." *Acadiensis* 1, no. 1 (Autumn 1971): 54–70.

Quinn, David B. *North America from Earliest Discovery to First Settlements: The*

Norse Voyages to 1612. New York: Harper & Row, 1977.

Rawlyk, George A. *Yankees at Louisbourg.* Orono: University of Maine Press, 1967.

———. *Nova Scotia's Massachusetts: A Study of Massachusetts–Nova Scotia Relations, 1630 to 1784.* Montreal: McGill–Queen's University Press, 1973.

Ray, Roger B., "Maine Indians' Concept of Land Tenure." *Maine Historical Society Quarterly* 13 (1973): 28–51.

———. "Eastern Indians' Letter to the Governour." *Maine Historical Society Quarterly* 13 (1974): 178–84.

Records of the Governor and Company of the Massachusetts Bay in New England. Ed. Nathaniel B. Shurtleff. 5 vols. Boston, 1853–54. Reprint. New York: A.M.S. Press, 1968.

Reid, John G. *Acadia, Maine, and New Scotland: Marginal Colonies in the Seventeenth Century.* Toronto: University of Toronto Press, 1981.

Rogers, Charles, ed. *The Earl of Stirling's Register of Royal Letters Relative to the Affairs of Scotland and Nova Scotia from 1615 to 1635.* 2 vols. Edinburgh, 1885.

Rogers, Norman McLeod. "The Abbé Le Loutre." *Canadian Historical Review* 11 (1930): 105–28.

Rompkey, Ronald, ed. *Expeditions of Honour: The Journal of John Salusbury in Halifax, Nova Scotia, 1749–53.* Newark, DE: University of Delaware Press, 1982.

Royal Instructions to British Colonial Governors, 1670–1776. Ed. Leonard Woods Labaree. 2 vols. New York: Octagon Books, 1967.

Rushton, William Faulkner. *The Cajuns: From Acadia to Louisiana.* New York: Farrar Straus Giroux, 1979.

Salisbury, Neil. *Manitou and Providence: Indians, Europeans, and the Making of New England, 1500–1643.* New York: Oxford University Press, 1982.

Savelle, Max. *The Origins of American Diplomacy: The International History of Angloamerica, 1492–1763.* New York: Macmillan, 1967.

Schutz, John A. *William Shirley: King's Governor of Massachusetts.* Chapel Hill: University of North Carolina Press, 1961.

Sedgwick, Henry Dwight. "Robert Sedgwick." Colonial Society of Massachusetts, *Publications* 3 (1895): 155–73.

Shirley, William. *The Correspondence of William Shirley.* Ed. Charles Henry Lincoln. 2 vols. New York: Macmillan, 1912.

Slafter, Edmund M. *Sir William Alexander and American Colonization. . . .* Boston, 1873. Reprint. New York: Burt Franklin, 1972.

Smith, Charles C. "The War on the Seaboard: The Struggle in Acadia and Cape Breton." In *Narrative and Critical History of America.* Ed. Justin Winsor. 8 vols. Boston, 1884–89. Reprint. New York: A.M.S. Press, 1967. Vol. 5.

Snow, Dean R., and Kim M. Lanphear. "European Contact and Indian

Depopulation in the Northeast: The Timing of the First Epidemics." *Ethnohistory* 35 (1988): 15–33.

Sollers, Basil. "The Acadians (French Neutrals) Transported to Maryland." *Maryland Historical Magazine* 3 (1908): 1–21.

Sosin, Jack M. "Louisbourg and the Peace of Aix-la-Chapelle, 1748." *William and Mary Quarterly,* 3d ser., 14 (1957): 516–35.

Thomas, John. "Diary of John Thomas, Surgeon in Winslow's Expedition of 1755 against the Acadians." *New England Historical and Genealogical Register* 33 (1879): 383–98.

Trigger, Bruce G., vol. ed. *Handbook of North American Indians.* Vol. 15, *Northeast.* Washington: Smithsonian Institution, 1978.

Tuttle, Charles Wesley. *Capt. Francis Champernowne, The Dutch Conquest of Acadie, And Other Historical Papers.* Ed. Albert Harrison Hoyt. Boston: John Wilson and Son, 1889.

Upton, L.F.S. *Micmacs and Colonists: Indian–White Relations in the Maritimes, 1713–1867.* Vancouver: University of British Columbia Press, 1979.

Vigneras, Louis-André. "Letters of an Acadian Trader, 1674–1676." *New England Quarterly* 13 (1940): 98–110.

Wall, Robert Emmet Jr. "Louisbourg, 1745." *New England Quarterly* 37 (1964): 64–83.

———. *Massachusetts Bay: The Crucial Decade, 1640–1650.* New Haven, CT: Yale University Press, 1972.

Waller, G.M. *Samuel Vetch: Colonial Enterpriser.* Chapel Hill: University of North Carolina Press, 1960.

Warren, Sir Peter. *The Royal Navy and North America: The Warren Papers, 1736–1752.* Ed. Julian Gwyn. London: Navy Records Society, 1973.

Webb, Stephen S. "The Strange Career of Francis Nicholson." In *Colonial America: Essays in Politics and Social Development.* Ed. Stanley N. Katz and John M. Murrin. 3d ed. New York: Alfred A. Knopf, 1983.

Webster, John Clarence. "Cornelis Steenwyck: Dutch Governor of Acadie." Paper presented at the annual meeting of the Canadian Historical Association, Ottawa, May 22–23, 1929.

———. *Acadia at the End of the Seventeenth Century: Letters, Journals, and Memoirs of Joseph Robineau de Villebon, Commandant in Acadia, 1690– 1700, and Other Contemporary Documents.* Saint John, N.B., 1934. Reprint. New Brunswick Museum, 1979.

———. Thomas Pichon *"The Spy of Beauséjour": An Account of His Career in Europe and America, with Many Original Documents Translated by Alice Webster.* Sackville, N.B.: Public Archives of Nova Scotia, 1937.

———. ed. *Journals of Beauséjour: Diary of John Thomas [and] Journal of Louis de Courville.* Sackville, N.B.: Public Archives of Nova Scotia, 1937.

Wilkins, Ernest H. "Arcadia in America." American Philosophical Society, *Proceedings* 101 (1957): 4–30.

Winslow, John. "Journal of Colonel John Winslow of the Provincial Troops While Engaged in Removing the Acadian French Inhabitants from Grand Pré, and the Neighboring Settlements, in the Autumn of the Year 1755." Nova Scotia Historical Society, *Collections* 3 (1882–83): 71–196.

Winthrop, John. *Winthrop's Journal, "History of New England" 1630–1649.* Ed. James Kendall Hosmer. 2 vols. New York, 1908. Reprint. New York: Barnes & Noble, 1953.

Winthrop Papers. Ed. Allyn B. Forbes. 5 vols. Boston: Massachusetts Historical Society, 1929–1947.

Winzerling, Oscar William. *Acadian Odyssey.* Baton Rouge: Louisiana State University Press, 1955.

Wrong, George M. *Louisbourg in 1745: The Anonymous "Lettre d'un Habitant de Louisbourg" (Cape Breton) Containing a Narrative by an Eye-witness of the Siege in 1745.* Toronto: University of Toronto Studies, 1897.

INDEX

ABOUT THE AUTHOR

Educated at Amherst College and Harvard Law School, Charles Mahaffie Jr. was an attorney at the Antitrust Division of the Department of Justice, then a partner of Cleary Gottleib Steen & Hamilton in Washington, D. C. "I found the law entirely satisfying," he says. "But I hankered to try something different, and so, once the children were educated and the home paid for, I withdrew to apply myself to learning and writing history." His longtime interest in American colonial history led to a focus on the region once known as Acadia. "The story of Acadia furnished me a procession of colorful characters and the sort of accidents and event-shaping coincidences that make history an endless fascination."

The Mahaffies divide their time between Bethesda, Maryland, and Bethany Beach, Delaware.